THE TOURISM AND LEISURE INDUSTRY

SHAPING THE FUTURE

THE TOURISM AND LEISURE INDUSTRY

SHAPING THE FUTURE

Editors
Klaus Weiermair
Christine Mathies

ATLANTIC®
PUBLISHERS & DISTRIBUTORS

The Haworth Hospitality Press ®
New York • London • Oxford

ATLANTIC®

PUBLISHERS & DISTRIBUTORS
7/22, Ansari Road, Darya Ganj
New Delhi – 110 002
Tel: 2327 3880, 2327 5880, 2328 0451
Fax: 91-11-2328 5873
E-mail: info@atlanticbooks.com
Website: www.atlanticbooks.com

Published in India by
Atlantic Publishers and Distributors, New Delhi
in association with
The Haworth Hospitality Press®, an imprint of The Haworth Press, Inc.
10 Alice Street, Binghamton, New York 13904-1580

First published 2004 by The Haworth Hospitality Press®
First Indian Reprint 2005

ISBN 81-269-0499-2

Printed in India by
Nice Printing Press, Delhi

CONTENTS

About the Editors xiii

Contributors xv

Preface and Acknowledgments xxv

Introduction. After the Anthill Was Stomped: The Customization of Life and Leisure 1
Geoffrey Godbey

A Revolution in World Population and Living Arrangements 1
A Revolution in Work 6
A Revolution in the Bases of Modern Economies—Postcapitalist Economies of Knowledge and Experience 7
A Revolution of Networked Economies and Globalization 9
The Impact of Globalization 11
Multipolar and Multicivilizational Politics and Power 12
Revolutionary Changes in Environment 13
A Revolution in Urban Areas 15
A Revolution in the Mass Customization of Products and Services 15
Conclusion 16

SECTION I: CHANGES IN DEMOGRAPHICS, STAGES OF LIFE, AND LEISURE BEHAVIOR 19

Chapter 1. Leisure Futures: A Change in Demography? 21
David K. Foot

Introduction 21
Framework 22
Demographic Change 24
Data 26
Results 29
Conclusion 32

Chapter 2. Concerns and Considerations About the Future of Youth Leisure: An International Perspective 35

Linda L. Caldwell
Cheryl K. Baldwin

Introduction 35
Case Studies 38
Critical Questions and Issues for the Future of Youth Leisure 45
Time Use, Experience, and Human Development 46
Civic and Societal Benefits 48
Opportunities for Participation and Provision of Service 48
Conclusion 49

Chapter 3. A Leisure Lifestyle Study of Generation X in New Zealand 53

Sarah Todd
Rob Lawson
Juergen Gnoth

Introduction 53
Background 54
Methodology 56
Results 58
Discussion 63

SECTION II: THE GLOBALIZATION OF LEISURE OR REDISCOVERING SLOWNESS? 67

Chapter 4. Spacing and Timing in Leisure Activities 69

Gabriele Morello

Scenario 69
The Study of Leisure Activities 70
Space and Time 71
Spacing and Timing 73
Examples and Cases 75
Conclusion 79

Chapter 5. The Rediscovery of Slowness, or Leisure Time As One's Own and As Self-Aggrandizement? 83
Karlheinz Woehler

Introduction 83
The Formation of Personal Time 84
Leisure Time As an Institution 85
Vacation Time 88
Slowness During Vacation 90

Chapter 6. Can Slow Tourism Bring New Life to Alpine Regions? 93
Rafael Matos

Introduction 93
Slow Tourism: An Antidote to Speed and a Promising Niche 96
Slow Tourism and Its Principles 100
Conclusion 102

Chapter 7. Leisure Investments: Global Supply and Demand 105
John R. Kelly

Introduction 105
How, Then, Can We Even Begin to Look Ahead? 105
Megaperspectives 109
The Future 114
Alternatives 116

SECTION III: (INTER)CULTURAL LEISURE BEHAVIOR 121

Chapter 8. Intercultural Behavior: Glimpses of Leisure from an Asian Perspective 123
John Ap

Introduction 123
Collectivism and Face 125
Asian Hierarchy of Needs 127
The Concept and Meaning of Leisure: An Asian Perspective 129

Implications for Leisure Service Provision 131
Conclusion 133

Chapter 9. Cultural Tourism and the Leisure Paradigm: The Australian Experience **135**
Francis Lobo

Introduction 135
Understanding Leisure and Tourism 135
Leisure and Cultural Tourism 138
Leisure and the Arts 140
Australian Cultural Participation 141
Cultural Tourism 145
Conclusion 149

Chapter 10. A Comparison of Leisure Styles in Germany, France, Italy, Great Britain, Spain, and Portugal **151**
Joan Sureda
Josep-Francesc Valls

Introduction 151
Methodology 152
Lifestyles As a Criterion for Segmentation in the Leisure Age 153
Description of European Leisure Styles 155
Factors Impeding Homogenization of Results 164
Trends 167
Conclusion 169

SECTION IV: CHANGING PATTERNS IN LIFESTYLE AND IMPLICATIONS FOR LEISURE BEHAVIOR **171**

Chapter 11. The Hybrid Consumer of Leisure Squeezed Between Fun Maximization, Chill Out, and the Radical Search for Inner Values **173**
Andreas Reiter

Introduction 173
The Body As a Branding Tool 176

Chapter 12. Wellness: A New Perspective for Leisure Centers, Health Tourism, and Spas in Europe on the Global Health Market **181**
Wolfgang Nahrstedt

The European Health System Enters the Global Market 181
Health Care: Basic Innovation for the Next Millennium? 182
The WHO's New Definition of Health 183
The Wellness Concept 183
Differentiation of Wellness Facilities 188
Target Groups: From Young Females to Senior Citizens and Males 191
Spas: Between Leisure and Tourism 191
Wellness in the New Millennium: Recommendations 195

Chapter 13. Alpine Health Tourism: Future Prospects from a Medical Perspective **199**
Wolfgang Schobersberger
Sven Greie
Egon Humpeler

Introduction 199
A Magical Term: Wellness 199
Health and Wellness Tourism 200
AMAS 2000: An Example of Scientific Medically Oriented Holiday Research 202
Forecast 206

Chapter 14. Skiers, Ski Bums, Trust Fund Babies, Migrants, Techies, and Entrepreneurs: The Changing Face of the Colorado Ski Industry **209**
Richard R. Perdue

Introduction 209
Leisure-Lifestyle Segmentation 211
Study Methodology 213
Colorado Resort Community Lifestyles 213
Implications and Conclusion 222

Chapter 15. Theme Park Tourist Destinations: Creating an Experience Setting in Traditional Tourist Destinations with Staging Strategies of Theme Parks **227**
Roland Scheurer

Experiences: A New Product of a Future Experience Economy? 227
Experience Setting: The Future Concept for Traditional Tourist Destinations in the Experience Economy? 228
Experience Settings in Theme Parks 230
Conclusion 234

Chapter 16. The Future Role of Sporting Events: Evaluating the Impacts on Tourism **237**
Simon Hudson
Donald Getz
Graham Miller
Graham Brown

Introduction 237
The Study 238
Discussion 248
Limitations and Future Research 249

Chapter 17. Future Living Conditions and Mobility: Travel Behavior of Alpine Tourists **253**
Thomas Bieger
Christian Laesser

Leisure and Tourism Mobility: A Structural Concept 253
The Influence of Leisure Activities on Mobility 256
Leisure Trends and Mobility 262
Summary 264

Chapter 18. From "Predatory" to "Experience" Tourism: Estimating Tourist Fruition for a Greenway **271**
Maria Carla Furlan
Sabrina Meneghello
Valeria Minghetti

Introduction 271
The Greenway Concept: Mobility and Tourism 272

Greenways: Main Examples in Europe 273
The Lemene Greenway Project 275
Conclusion 281

SECTION V: INFORMATION TECHNOLOGIES IN LEISURE AND TOURISM 283

Chapter 19. Searching for Experience: Technology-Related Trends Shaping the Future of Tourism 285

Daniel R. Fesenmaier
Ulrike Gretzel

Introduction 285
Five Trends 286
Future Behaviors in Travel 296

Chapter 20. Italian Tourism on the Internet: New Business Models 301

Magda Antonioli Corigliano
Rodolfo Baggio

Tourism Online 301
Italian Tourism on the Web 306
Future Models of Being on the Web 311
Conclusion 314

Chapter 21. Electronic Travel Recommendation Agents and Tourist Choice 317

Gerald Häubl
Benedict G. C. Dellaert

Introduction 317
Theory 318
Research Method 319
Measures 320
Findings 321
Discussion and Conclusion 323

Chapter 22. The Assessment of Tourism and Leisure Trends by Means of Online Management Information Systems **325**

Karl Wöber

Introduction 325
Development of TourMIS 326
The Austrian Guest Survey in TourMIS 328
Analysis of User Behavior of TourMIS 332
Conclusion 334

Index **339**

ABOUT THE EDITORS

Klaus Weiermair, PhD, is the head of the Center of Tourism and Service Economics and the University of Innsbruck, Austria. He is a graduate of Vienna School of Economics and Business Administration where he received his masters and doctoral degrees. Dr. Weiermair's areas of interest include tourism management and entrepreneurship, labor economics, quality measurement and management, innovations, and product development in leisure and tourism. His publications can be found in well-known journals such as *Annals of Tourism Research,* the *Journal of Travel & Tourism Marketing,* and the *Journal of Management Studies.*

Christine Mathies, MAG, is Dr. Klaus Weiermair's assistant. She received her Master of International Business Administration degree from the University of Innsbruck, Austria. Her research focus is on e-tourism, especially customer data management and pricing decisions, event tourism, and health tourism. Ms. Mathies also works as a management consultant.

CONTRIBUTORS

Magda Antonioli Corigliano is a professor in economic theory and policy at the Bocconi University (Milan, Italy) and at the business school (Scuola di Direzione Aziendale) of the same university and is director of the master's degree in tourism and economics. She has carried out research and consulting activities in tourism and environmental economics and industrial economics for several national and international institutions. She has authored several studies on industrial economics, tourism, and environment economics.

John Ap is an associate professor in tourism management at The Hong Kong Polytechnic University. Prior to becoming an academic he worked for eleven years as a certified town planner in Australia where he specialized in open space, recreation, and tourism planning. Recent consultancy and related activities involve tourism and recreation planning studies, theme park studies, market research surveys, and service professionalism of tour guiding. Areas of Dr. Ap's expertise include impacts of tourism, social and cultural tourism, theme parks, consumer/tourist behavior, and tourism planning.

Rodolfo Baggio holds a degree in physics from the University of Milan. After performing research and teaching activities in astrophysics and radioastronomy, he has been involved with the computer industry for more than twenty years. He is presently a consultant and lecturer at the Bocconi University (Milan, Italy) where he teaches courses in computer science and coordinates the information and communication technologies area for the master in tourism and economics degree.

Cheryl K. Baldwin is an assistant professor of leisure studies at The Pennsylvania State University. Her research focuses on the motivation and developmental relevancy of adolescent free-time activities and the evaluation of community-based youth development programs.

Thomas Bieger is a professor of business administration with specialization in tourism and is head of the Institute for Public Services and Tourism at the University of St. Gallen, Switzerland. Apart from that he holds the following key positions: Secretary General of the AIEST (International Association of Scientific Experts in Tourism), responsible for the international CEMS (Community of European Management Schools) master's program at the University of St. Gallen, Associate Dean for International Exchanges and Dean of the Department of Business Administration of the University of St. Gallen, and member of the board of a number of companies in different branches of the service, tourism, and finance industry.

Graham Brown is a professor of tourism management at the University of South Australia and has been actively involved in education, training, and research for hospitality and tourism industries for over twenty years. Dr. Brown has published widely on the subjects of tourism planning and marketing and has served on a number of editorial boards and acted as the regional editor, Asia/Pacific, for the *International Journal of Contemporary Hospitality Management.* Current research interests include the planning of major events and the tourism marketing opportunities they present for host cities and market segment development associated with wine tourism and educational tourism.

Linda L. Caldwell is a professor of recreation and park management and Professor in Charge of Research for the School of Hotel, Restaurant, and Recreation Management at The Pennsylvania State University. Much of her research has centered around adolescents, leisure, and health; she is particularly interested in leisure education, prevention research, and the developmental affordances of leisure. Currently, she is the lead investigator on a National Institute on Drug Abuse (NIDA) funded substance-use prevention program that helps middle school youths learn to use their leisure time wisely. She also is involved with several international projects that focus on developing youth competencies and healthy lifestyles through leisure.

Benedict G. C. Dellaert is Professor and Meteor Research Chair at the Department of Marketing, Maastricht University, the Netherlands. He holds a master's degree in technology management and a PhD in technical sciences, both from Eindhoven University of Technology, the Netherlands. His research interests are in consumer decision making, consumer-producer interaction, and retailing and tourism. His work has appeared in journals such as the *Annals of Tourism Research, International Journal of Research in Marketing, Journal of Marketing Research,* and *Leisure Sciences.*

Daniel R. Fesenmaier is a professor in the Department of Leisure Studies and director of the National Laboratory for Tourism and *e*Commerce, University of Illinois. His main research and teaching interests focus on the use of information in travel decisions, the use of information technology for tourism marketing, and the development of knowledge-based systems for tourism marketing organizations.

David K. Foot, Professor of Economics at the University of Toronto, is co-author of the best-selling books *Boom Bust and Echo: How to Profit from the Coming Demographic Shift* and *Boom Bust and Echo: Profiting from the Demographic Shift in the 21st Century.* His interests lie in the interrelationships between economics and demographics and their implications for both private and public policies. Professor Foot is a two-time recipient of the University of Toronto undergraduate teaching award and a recipient of one of the nationwide 3M Awards for Teaching Excellence.

Maria Carla Furlan is a senior researcher at Centro Internazionale di Studi Sull' Economia Turistica (CISET) and in charge of CISET master's course. She specializes in human resource management, cultural tourism, destination management, communication, and marketing. She is a professor of tourism policies at the Department of Economics of Tourism of the Ca' Foscari University of Venice and has contributed several articles to books and journals on tourism in Italy.

Donald Getz is a professor of tourism and hospitality management at the University of Calgary. The author of three books, he conducts research, writes, and consults in the field of tourism and hospitality management and has developed an international reputation as a leading scholar and proponent of event management and event tourism. He co-founded and is editor in chief of *Festival Management and Event Tourism: An International Journal.*

Juergen Gnoth is a senior lecturer in the Department of Marketing at the University of Otago in New Zealand. His interests are in consumer behavior (particularly intention and satisfaction formation), ethics and social issues in marketing, tourism destination branding, and services network theory.

Geoffrey Godbey is a professor of leisure studies at The Pennsylvania State University. His academic interests include futures research, leisure in Asian countries, leisure and aging, and tourism. His leisure interests include playing conga drums, gardening, reading, squash, writing poetry, and talking to trees.

Sven Greie graduated from the University of Innsbruck in 2000 with a master of sports science degree. He teaches health and fitness professionals and is a research associate in the Institut Humpeler Schobersberger (IHS)-Research Institute of Leisure and Travel Medicine.

Ulrike Gretzel is a PhD student in the Institute of Communications Research at the University of Illinois and a research assistant at the National Laboratory for Tourism and *e*Commerce. Her research interests lie in the field of knowledge-based systems in tourism and the development and evaluation of humancentric design strategies for tourism Web sites.

Gerald Häubl is the Banister Professor of Electronic Commerce and an associate professor of marketing at the University of Alberta. He is the director of the Institute for Online Consumer Studies (www.iocs.org), is a research fellow of Pennsylvania State University's eBusiness Research Center, and was the recipient of the 2000 Petro-Canada Young Innovator Award. His primary areas of expertise are consumer decision making, preference construction, consumer behavior in personalized electronic environments, human-computer interaction, and bidding behavior in auctions.

Simon Hudson is an associate professor in the Tourism Management Group at the University of Calgary. Prior to working in academia, he spent several years working for U.K. tour operators, and he also ran his own successful business for eight years. Dr. Hudson specializes in the marketing of tourism. His research is focused on sports tourism, and he has published numerous articles and book chapters from his work on the ski industry. He is on the editorial board for the *Journal of Teaching in Travel and Tourism, International Journal of Tourism Research,* and the *Journal of Travel Research.*

Egon Humpeler is a professor of internal medicine, working in Bregenz, Austria. More than thirty years ago he began to initiate scientific projects on human adaptation to moderate altitudes. Humpeler was leader of the AMAS 2000 project (Austrian Moderate Altitude Study) and co-founder of the Austrian Society for Alpine and High Altitude Medicine. Together with Wolfgang Schobersberger he is founder of the IHS-Research Institute for Leisure and Travel Medicine and research manager of the Welltain leisure program.

John R. Kelly is Professor Emeritus at the University of Illinois at Urbana-Champaign. The author of twelve books, he has been a consultant for government agencies in the United States as well as several corporations in the United States and Japan. His focus on leisure as social interaction in common social environments has shifted to more economic issues, including investment and marketing directives in a global capitalist market economy. His PhD in sociology is from the University of Oregon, and he received master's degrees from Yale, Oregon, and Southern California. His own leisure includes tennis and flying his airplane.

Christian Laesser is a lecturer of business administration with specialization in the tourism and service industry, senior researcher, and deputy director of the Institute for Public Services and Tourism at the University of St. Gallen. Apart from that he holds a number of positions such as executive editor of the *Tourism Review,* secretary general of the Swiss Association for Transport Sciences, member of AIEST (International Association of Scientific Experts in Tourism), and member of the board of a number of companies in different branches of the service industry.

Rob Lawson is a professor of marketing at the University of Otago, Dunedin, New Zealand. His education and early career were based in the United Kingdom, including his PhD from The University of Sheffield. His main area of expertise is in consumer behavior, especially issues relating to values, lifestyles, and aspects of tourist behavior.

Francis Lobo is Senior Honorary Research Fellow in the School of Marketing Tourism and Leisure at Edith Cowan University in Western Australia. In a career spanning thirty years, Dr. Lobo has pioneered leisure and tourism courses at the university level in Australia. With schooling in India, teacher education in Uganda, an undergraduate degree from the United Kingdom, master's degrees from the United States and Australia, and a doctorate from the University of Western Australia, Dr. Lobo has been eminently qualified to lead numerous research projects in leisure and tourism studies.

Rafael Matos studied geography in Costa Rica and Switzerland, where he earned a PhD on the historical and economic geography of Tenerife, Canary Islands (1800-1914). After having worked as a researcher at the Universities of Geneva and Lausanne, as well as at the Ecole hôtelière de Lausanne, he is presently a research associate at the Research Group for Economy and Tourism, Haute Ecole Valaisanne (HEVs), Switzerland. Rafael has written some forty articles and is co-author of *Le tourisme à Genève: une géographie humaine* (Geneva, Metropolis, 2002).

Sabrina Meneghello is a junior researcher at CISET and specializes in cultural tourism, communication, and marketing. She is a coordinator and tutor of the CISET master's course in economics and management of tourism of the Ca' Foscari University of Venice.

Graham Miller is a lecturer in the School of Management at the University of Surrey, United Kingdom. Graham's main research interests are in the impacts of tourism and sustainability, which has increasingly led to an examination of corporate responsibility and business ethics in the tourism industry.

Valeria Minghetti is a senior researcher at CISET, the International Centre of Studies on the Tourist Economy of Ca' Foscari University, Venice, Italy. After specializing in tourism economics at the same university, she now coordinates various national and international projects for CISET. Her main fields of interest are tourism demand analysis and forecasting, tourism statistics, the economic impact of tourism at different territorial scales, tourism and transports, and tourism and information technology. She is a board member of IFITT, the International Federation for Information Technology and Travel and Tourism.

Gabriele Morello, Professor of Business Statistics at the University of Palermo and Professor Emeritus of Marketing at the Free University Amsterdam, is the founding director of Instituto Superiore per Imprenditori e Dirigenti di Azienda (ISIDA), the Italian Graduate School of Management Education in Palermo, Italy.

Wolfgang Nahrstedt has studied for more than forty years how megatrends such as leisure, tourism, and more recently wellness change the needs of people and the structures of society. He is Professor Emeritus of the University of Bielefeld, Germany, and an honorary chair of the Institute of Leisure Studies and Cultural Work (IFKA). See <www.ifka.de>.

Richard R. Perdue is a professor in the University of Colorado Leeds School of Business; a member of the International Academy for the Study of Tourism, the Travel and Tourism Research Association, and the International Association of Scientific Experts in Tourism (AIEST); editor of the *Journal of Travel Research;* and former editor of *Tourism Analysis.*

Andreas Reiter is a consumer trend expert. In 1996 he founded the consulting company ZTB Zukunftsbüro in Vienna, Austria, which helps clients develop strategic solutions for the future and innovative products.

Roland Scheurer, PhD, is a research associate at the Research Institute for Leisure and Tourism, University of Berne, Switzerland. His research interest is in experience economy and tourism.

Wolfgang Schobersberger is a specialist for anesthesia and intensive care medicine working at the University Hospital Innsbruck, Austria. He was the scientific coordinator of the AMAS 2000 project (Austrian Moderate Altitude Study) and co-founder of the Austrian Society for Alpine and High Altitude Medicine. Since 2000 he has worked together with Professor Egon Humpeler as manager of the IHS-Research Institute for Leisure and Travel Medicine. Since October 2003 he has also served as the head of a research group for Leisure, Travel, and Altitude Medicine at the University of Health Informatics and Technology Tyrol (UMIT). Schobersberger has published more than 150 articles in international journals and received several research awards.

Joan Sureda is a MBA graduate from ESADE and a visiting fellow on the postgraduate program in marketing research and system dynamics at the Sloan School of Management, Massachusetts. She was the chairperson of the Scientific Committee of the 22nd EMAC "European Marketing Academy" Conference (1993), is the director and a lecturer at the Department of Quantitative Methods Management, and is a lecturer in the Department of Marketing Management, ESADE.

Sarah Todd is in the Department of Marketing at the University of Otago (New Zealand). There she primarily teaches in the area of consumer behavior. Specific research interests include consumer lifestyles, values, tourism behavior, and children's consumption.

Josep-Francesc Valls is the director of the Centre for Tourism Management, Escuela Superior de Aministración y Dirección de Empresas-Centro de Dirección Turística (ESADE-CEDIT), a full professor at ESADE-Universitat Ramon Llull, and a lecturer at the Department of Marketing Management, ESADE. He is also the director of the Tourism Management-Executive program and the international master's in tourism and leisure at ESADE. He has published, among others, the following books: *La imagen de marca de los países* (McGraw-Hill, Madrid, 1992); *Las claves del mercado turístico* (Deusto, Barcelona, 1996); and *La gestión de las empresas de turismo y ocio* (Ediciones Columna, Barcelona, 1999). He has participated as co-author in the books *Donnar protagonisme a Catalunya, acció internacional i política de relacions exteriors catalana* (Editorial Pòrtic, 2003) and in the monograph on sustainable tourism in the publication *Adistancia* (Universidad Nacional de Educación a Distancia [UNED], 2003).

Karl Wöber is an associate professor at the Institute for Tourism and Leisure Studies, Vienna University of Economics and Business Administration. His main research activities are in the fields of marketing information and decision support systems in tourism and hospitality management. He is also a technical advisor to European Cities Tourism and the European Travel Commission in questions concerning the analysis and dissemination of market research information (see http://www.tourmis.info) and the development of a European City Tourism B2C Portal (see http://www.visiteuropeancities.info).

Wöber has written books on tourism and hospitality benchmarking, decision support systems, and city tourism management, as well as more than fifty articles, conference papers, and book contributions in these areas (see http://tourism.wu-wien.ac.at/cgi-bin/ift.pl?personal/woeber.html).

Karlheinz Woehler holds a chair in Empirical and Applied Tourism Sciences at the University of Lüeneburg, Germany. His numerous publications focus on various topics, such as tourism marketing, touristification of spaces, "eventification," and culturalization of tourism, as well as sustainable tourism. Mr. Woehler is editor in chief of *Tourismus Journal, Zeitschrift für tourismuswissenschaftliche Forschung und Praxis* [*Tourism Journal, Journal for Tourism Research*], as well as editor and co-editor of several book series and scientific journals.

Preface and Acknowledgments

Staging an international conference on the future of leisure had a number of both theoretical and practical antecedents. On the practical side is the perennial question as to what the future holds for leisure in general and tourism as one of the most prominent leisure industries in particular. Although the tourism industry steadily grew throughout the post-World War II era and was stable well into the 1980s and 1990s, the past five to ten years have shown a much more unstable environment for business growth.

It was no longer sensible to extrapolate leisure and tourism trends based on observable changing leisure time, income, and prices. These factors were no longer sufficient to have a firm grip on future developments. As "old tourism" slowly gave way to "new tourism," tourism and leisure practitioners suddenly realized the need for new concepts more in line with an environment characterized by globalization, rapid social value changes, a heightened technology race, and changing economic market conditions. At the beginning of the twenty-first century, a fair number of leisure and tourism industries were caught off guard by these environmental changes, some of which, such as demographics, could have easily been forecasted. Not surprisingly, a sudden demand for new research arose, which manifested itself through frequent calls from national and regional tourism organizations for a more thorough and relevant analysis of future tourism trends.

The need to reassess production and marketing practices in tourism was particularly acute among those subsectors and among those leisure and tourism enterprises that had continuously served conservative and loyal repeat customers with steady leisure preferences. The combined effects of the advent of the new tourism and leisure generation and heightened competition due to technical change and globalization put pressure on these sectors to explore new markets and new products. As a consequence, a number of tourism workshops/conferences and experts on both sides of the Atlantic have analyzed and reported on tourism trends. The advantage of past tourism-trend analyses carried out by tourism specialists lies in the great scope and technical detail that can be applied to the behavior of specific tourism markets and subsectors. As a drawback, such efforts may sometimes ignore the wide socioeconomic, political, and technological forces that ultimately drive tourism trends.

One of the prime objectives of the Leisure Futures: Shaping the Future of the Leisure and Tourism Industry conference was to draw conclusions and applications in the field of leisure and tourism from a wider observable and projectable set of societal forces of change. The conference attempted to cover major societal changes with a focus on future leisure applications ranging from changes in demographics (Section I), to changes in available leisure time and the antagonism of slowness and globalization (Section II), to cultural leisure behavior (Section III), to changing lifestyles and their manifestation in leisure and tourism products (Section IV), to the implication of information and communication technologies on future leisure and tourism behavior (Section V).

Some domains of expected changes in future leisure behavior received a proportionally wider coverage. This was particularly the case with demographic changes and the associated changing patterns of lifestyle (Sections I and IV), such as the phenomena of aging and the growth of health-related leisure and tourism markets. On the other hand, aspects such as the future interrelationship between leisure time, working time, education time, and household time could and should have received more attention. Because "Leisure Futures" is to develop into a biannual international conference, this and other relevant yet untapped topics might be covered at the next conference in 2004.

The editors would like to express their sincere thanks to all of the contributors and sponsors of the conference, particularly to ICRET (International Center for Research and Education in Tourism) and to the Austrian Ministry of Economic Affairs, Tourism Branch for the financial assistance with the book publication.

Introduction

After the Anthill Was Stomped: The Customization of Life and Leisure

Geoffrey Godbey

The future woke me with its silence.

W. S. Merwin

Every country, culture, and civilization has become like an anthill that has just been stomped by a large boot. The boot is massive change in every area of life. These changes cannot be imagined, let alone cataloged, and the algorithms of change in each area are out of sync with others. Changes in world population, immigration, technology, the bases of economies, work patterns, roles of women and men, environment, methods of war, definitions of literacy, use of time, and other changes are profound and continuing.

All of these interrelated changes, this chapter proposes, although apparently bringing about some level of sameness and harmonization of diversity, are actually creating more diversity and uncertainty in daily life and in leisure. Daily life is in the process of being customized for billions. As this happens, leisure behavior is being customized in terms of meaning, logistics, temporal aspects, benefits sought, and location.

A REVOLUTION IN WORLD POPULATION AND LIVING ARRANGEMENTS

All such change starts with population. The world's population is undergoing revolutionary growth in terms of number of people, massive immigration, rapid aging, rapidly increasing urbanization and population density, increasing disparity of wealth and life opportunities, the status of women, and the life course.

Explosive Population Growth

Although estimates vary, the United Nations (UN), World Bank, U.S. Census Bureau, and other demographic forecasters predict a world with from 8 to 8.5 billion people in 2025 (O'Neill and Balk, 2001). This unprecedented increase in the number of humans has profound consequences for every aspect of life, from food supply to leisure. It represents a plague for other animal and plant species.

Practically all of this increase will come from developing nations. Although in 1995 the portion of the world population living in industrial or developed nations compared to those in developing nations was less than one to two, in 2030 it will be about one to four (O'Meara, 1999). In 2030, it is projected that 59 percent of the world's population will live in Asia, 19 percent in Africa, 8 percent in Latin America, and only 14 percent in all industrialized countries combined (Lutz, 1994).

About half the population increase in developed countries is coming from international migration. Already, 15 percent of those residing in Canada and France were born in another country, as were one out of nine of those living in the United States. In Western Europe, migration accounted for more than 80 percent of the annual growth rate from 1990 to 1995. The United Nations projects that migration rates will increase substantially in order to replace the working-age population in countries with continuing low fertility rates. These immigrants are not becoming a melting culture pot but rather are customizing the culture to produce differing mosaics within each city, region, and country. What people think, eat, or do for fun will become more diverse—and so will when they do it.

Increasing Urbanization and Population Density

For the first time in history, over half of the world's population will be living in urban areas by 2010, and by 2030, the UN projects that 60 percent of the population will be urbanized (McGee, 2001). Within thirteen years there will be twenty-four megacities in the world with populations of over ten million. Increased urbanization will customize leisure behavior not only by social class, income, and ethnicity as it always has, but, due to the increasing cultural differences of urban residents and visitors, such differences will be magnified.

Higher population densities are associated with increased incidence of a variety of diseases, greater participation in welfare, higher rates of suicide, and numerous environmental impacts, from air pollution to airborne toxic chemical releases, related to increased industry and transportation infrastructures (Larsen, 1993). As higher densities occur, the sequencing of life's daily routines will need to be customized. Centralized periods of vacations, holidays, and other forms of mass leisure will be less likely to occur.

For instance, as the number of cars on the beltways around Washington, DC, or the new highways around Shanghai, China, increase, producing permanent gridlock, mass customization of travel patterns will occur. When people go to work (if they go at all), when they shop, vote, or visit the beach they will need to be spread out. Most models of mass transit will also require customization because increasingly no center of work exists for people to be transported to. Rush hour may take place across most of the hours of the day and night. Auto travel will be more highly guided, both by onboard technology, which directs the driver's travel in real time by voice command, and by software that provides non-real-time direction (Halal, Kull, and Leffman, 1997). "This technology will conserve fuel and save lives, but the pleasure of driving as you know it will be gone" (D'Agnese, 2000, p. 58). If driving becomes less pleasurable, it may mean fewer discretionary trips are taken.

Those who manage leisure and tourism services will do more to guide visitors to their sites, and such guidance will become customized for any inquiring visitor. Such customized guidance will be increasingly valuable to the potential visitor, as the logistics of visitation become more complex due to higher volumes of traffic, whether such traffic is automobiles, motor scooters, bicycles, or other people movers.

Mass leisure experience will become more likely to produce chaos. In the People's Republic of China, for instance, the establishment of three national holiday periods in May, October, and February has led to chaotic conditions for those who wish to travel for pleasure during these periods. Already talk is heard of customizing these "golden weeks" so the crush of humanity seeking leisure experience will be distributed across the year (E. Liu, personal communication, 2001).

Finally, "from Buenos Aires to Bangkok, dramatic population growth in the world's major cities—and the sprawl and pollution they bring—threatens natural recreation areas that lay beyond city limits" (Brown, Gardner, and Halwell, 1998, p. 46). Access to natural areas for recreation may become more limited or require more money and power to access them.

In sum, most forms of mass activity, including leisure, will be customized to the extent the population increases and becomes more dense and urban.

A Revolution in the Life Course and the Family

Modernity is reshaping the life course and family structure. Many developmental psychologists no longer speak of a life stage, since the comparatively common stages of life that individuals went through in an industrial economy no longer occur or do not occur at common ages. Modern nations are also "defamilied," with about one-fifth or more of households containing only one person and the average household containing fewer than three occupants. In the United States, almost half of the adult population is not married. Existing families are likely to be more diverse in form, often the result of divorce and remarriage, or may be gay or lesbian families, multiethnic or multiracial families, or a household of unrelated individuals. All of these trends encourage more customization of leisure behavior.

Rapid Aging of the World Population

People are also becoming more different because they are living longer. The average life expectancy in the world is now about sixty-five years and this average increases in modern nations to more than seventy-five years. Germany, together with other Western European nations, and Japan are the advance guard of the historic demographic changes accompanying the rise of technological societies. If the global economy continues to raise living standards, developing countries will most likely follow the European model to low fertility rates and large elderly populations. In 2025, those aged sixty and older will account for 25 percent of the U.S. population, compared to 31 percent in Western Europe.

Increasing Levels of Education

Higher levels of education, particularly for women, are occurring in many regions of the world. People with higher levels of education are more likely to become specialized in a given form of leisure behavior, moving from the general to the specific within the activity form and, often, from catharsis to pleasure to meaning in terms of benefits sought. Those with higher education are more likely to participate in most forms of outdoor recreation, sports, high culture, tourism, continuing education, reading, tourism, and volunteer activities.

More highly educated people will become more individually distinct in their participation in leisure activity, seeking more information and complexity in the experience. The increasingly diverse mix of education levels of people residing in close proximity will mean that providing mass leisure activities, such as local festivals, will need to be undertaken with multiple strategies.

Revolutionary Changes in the Roles of Women and Men

Roles of females (and, consequently, males) are in the middle or beginning of a revolution in every country in the world. One reason for this is simply massive declines in birthrates and increases in longevity. Women in eighteenth-century Europe, for example, gave birth to an average of eight children; today average birthrates are well below two children. While industrialism was built on specialization of work and other obligated activity, the postindustrial society is producing generalists, who undertake a broader range of activities and roles.

Because poverty and the second-class status of women are thought to be the key variables in the world's population explosion, limiting population increase will mean it is necessary for women to obtain more formal education (Ashford, 1995; Riley, 1997). A direct correlation exists between the years of formal education a woman attains and the number of children she has (Ashford, 1995; Riley, 1997).

In many countries, males are already beginning to emerge as the educationally disadvantaged group, as compared to females. In knowledge economies, this will change numerous forms of relationships.

The comparative power of women with high levels of education will increase, the wage gap will close or favor women, more joint career decisions will be made which consider women's job prospects first, and the centrality of women as decision makers will increase in regard to use of free time within families and couples. Such changes may mean that women's leisure patterns will diversify and their leisure desires will be addressed to a greater extent. When they are not, women will make increasing demands for differentiation of leisure sites and services to meet their interests and will exert more power in shaping them.

A REVOLUTION IN WORK

Changes in technology have revolutionized work in ways that are revolutionizing the rest of life, customizing every individual's life in the process. When the factory system standardized work in Europe and North America, which was done outside the home in big ugly buildings, public education followed suit. The factory approach to public education resulted in standardized buildings, curricula, textbooks, teacher qualifications, and notions of the truth.

Leisure became more standardized, too, from bowling alleys to shopping malls to TV shows, which were watched by over half the households in a country. The scientific management of factory work, including time and motion studies undertaken by Fredrick Taylor, carried over into leisure activities such as sports; coaches began to use the same time and motion analysis of athletes and specialization of tasks that Taylor used for workers (Kanigel, 1997). Standardized retirement assistance, social security, produced standardization of the age of retirement.

Work is going through a revolution, stomping the anthill and changing the rest of life. The notion that a job is a fixed bundle of tasks is disappearing (Bridges, 1994). Jobs are moving targets, demanding continuous learning and change on the part of the worker. More people work part-time, work at home, have no designated place to work, or combine work with college, raising children, or retirement. Workers who work during daylight hours on weekdays may become the minority.

The largest employer in the United States is Manpower Inc., a temporary-staffing firm, and one-fifth of Manpower's clients are highly skilled professionals in temporary positions. By some estimates, as much as one-half of the U.S. workforce will be contingent workers within the next five years (Sassen, 2002). Such changes affect even Japan, where the notion of lifetime employment has largely disappeared. "The geographic same-time-same-place workplace is being replaced by anytime-anywhere-workspaces" (Boyett, 1996, p. 89).

Work will intrude into every aspect of life including leisure, and leisure will intrude into work. "The barrier that since the 1800s has separated work and the rest of life is being shattered" (Boyett, 1996, p. 5). The home will often be where work is done, as it was prior to the Industrial Revolution. Leisure behavior will be customized to reflect such changes. Among some of the major impacts will be less distinction between weekday and weekend in terms of leisure activity. Already, the majority of hours of free time occur during weekdays in many modern nations, and this trend may intensify (Robinson and Godbey, 1999).

There is also less adherence to the daily industrial pattern of breakfast at home, travel to work, lunch at work, work all afternoon, travel home, dinner at home, evening at home on weekdays, and outside the home on weekends. The 24/7 economy has also produced 24/7 leisure activity.

As more workers telecommute or use satellite offices, cities no longer will be the center of commerce. Cities in developed nations will atrophy or re-create themselves as centers of leisure, culture, tourism, and entertainment. Simultaneously, cities in developing nations will become more critical, and the migration from rural to urban to suburban to small town will continue and intensify.

A REVOLUTION IN THE BASES OF MODERN ECONOMIES—POSTCAPITALIST ECONOMIES OF KNOWLEDGE AND EXPERIENCE

In most countries, and even within individual cities, a mosaic of economies exists alongside one another: from hunter-gatherer to agriculture to mercantilism and trade to industrialism to services to a knowledge and experience economy. Most modern economies are postcapitalist. That is, the ultimate basis of wealth is not capital, but rather knowledge and the application of knowledge to produce profit (Drucker, 1993).

Although part of the new economy may be described as a knowledge economy, another increasingly important part of the new economy is the offering of memorable experiences:

> When a person buys a service, he purchases a set of intangible activities carried out on his behalf. But when he buys an experience, he pays to spend time enjoying a series of memorable events that a company stages—as in a theatrical play—to engage him in a personal way. (Pine and Gilmore, 1999, p. 2)

Such experiences are as distinct from services as services are from products. The emergence of an experience economy may progress as follows.

In the emerging experience economy (see Table I.1), the experiential component of a product or service is increasingly the basis of profit. "Just as people have cut back on goods to spend more money on services, now they also scrutinize the time and money they spend on services to make way for the more memorable—and more highly valued—experiences" (Pine and Gilmore, 1999, p. 12).

Experiences are not synonymous with entertainment but rather with engaging the guest. Although many experiences are entertainment, experiences may also be educational, escapist, or aesthetic in nature.

As the experience economy grows, many managers of leisure and tourism sites will find that the issue will be less of managing people and natural resources than of managing "meaning." What does this site mean? What is worth doing, seeing, hearing, tasting, touching, smelling, feeling, and ultimately remembering? Those who seek to consume "experiences" in their leisure will exist side by side with those who seek to consume material goods. The desire for memorable experience will make diversity of environment and culture more valuable while simultaneously threatening it, as those seeking memorable experience want to swim with dolphins, visit the South Pole, or spend the night in a bamboo forest.

TABLE I.1. The Experience Economy

Economic offering	Commodities	Goods	Services	Experiences
Economy	Agrarian	Industrial	Service	Experience
Economic function	Extract	Make	Deliver	Stage
Nature of offering	Fungible	Tangible	Intangible	Memorable
Key attribute	Natural	Standardized	Customized	Personal
Method of supply	Stored in bulk	Inventoried	Delivered	Revealed
Seller	Trader	Manufacturer	Provider	Stager
Buyer	Market	User	Client	Guest
Factors of product	Characteristics	Features	Benefits	Sensations

Source: Adapted from Pine and Gilmore, 1999, p. 6.

A REVOLUTION OF NETWORKED ECONOMIES AND GLOBALIZATION

As every nation moves toward an economy that is networked by computers and globalized, the provision of leisure and tourism services will change how they operate in numerous ways, customizing services based on increasing levels of information about customers. The characteristics of a networked economy, as described by Kelly (1996, pp. 200-201), include numerous implications for the delivery of leisure and tourism services:

- *Distributed cores:* The boundaries of companies will blur to obscurity. Where the visitor base and organizational concerns of a country's national park system exist, for instance, will become more diverse and uncertain. It may have an increased virtual presence or staff involved in promotion in other parts of the world. The interests of the organization will transcend place.
- *Adaptive technologies:* If your organization is not operating in real time you are dead. A resort or theme park's information

base must change in real time. Attendance, environmental conditions, staff performance, visitor satisfaction, etc., will increasingly be monitored in real time and changes made almost instantly based on such assessment. Annual attendance reports and environmental reports may have less meaning due to constant monitoring.

- *Flex manufacturing:* Smaller numbers of items can be produced in smaller time periods with smaller equipment. For example, will customized audio tours be created and re-created in response to differing interests, lifestyles, and languages of specific groups of visitors—or each visitor?
- *Mass customization:* Individually customized products and services may be produced on a mass scale. All aspects of dealing with leisure service customers or tourists will be customized at a mass level. If you will be visiting a site with someone who has Alzheimer's disease, customized plans for your visit will be developed; if you do not speak the dominant language, do not eat meat, cannot walk, are a Civil War reenactor, or have five children with you, visitation will be increasingly customized to meet your needs and interests.
- *Industrial ecology:* Closed loop, no waste, zero-pollution manufacturing will expand. Major companies involved in leisure services will increasingly seek to function as zero-pollution organizations, showing environmental leadership in how they use fuel, consume electricity, and recycle waste.
- *Global accounting:* Even small businesses will become global in perspective. The revenue generation of many leisure service organizations will become increasingly international. Even local-level tourist promotion will take place in other countries.
- *Coevolved customers:* Customers will be trained and educated by the company, and then the company will be trained and educated by the customer. Leisure service organizations will increasingly seek to train visitors in terms of how they should visit sites. In turn, visitors will train staff in terms of what they seek and the meaning of visitation to them.
- *Knowledge-based, networked data:* Networked data make any job faster, better, and easier. The issue becomes not so much how to do a job but what job you do. The biggest issue for those in leisure services will be what task should be undertaken.

- *Free bandwidth:* You can send anyone anything at anytime. Selecting what not to connect to is the key. How to cut down communication will become a major issue. How to avoid communication will become increasingly critical.
- *Digital money:* Digital cash will replace batch-made paper money. All accounts will become real time. Leisure service organizations will increasingly operate in a cashless system, perhaps issuing their own currency for visitors.

In combination, then, a networked economy reshapes not only when leisure takes place but also how organizations that provide leisure and tourism services function to customize experience.

THE IMPACT OF GLOBALIZATION

Globalization of commerce has brought with it increasingly differentiated conditions both among countries and within countries. It is also an engine that drives immigration at a startling rate. The wealthiest fifth of the world's people now have 86 percent of the gross domestic product, and the bottom fifth have about 1 percent (UN Development Report, 1999, cited by Mitchell, 2002). As northern nations have increasingly pressured southern nations to open their economies to foreign trade and investment, about 20 percent of southern residents have increased their wealth but 80 percent have become poorer (Sassen, 2002). Overall, southern nations have become poorer.

This process also makes it certain that terrorism and low-intensity wars will become the ways of fighting for the "have-nots" against the "haves." The line between crime and war is disappearing, and, as that happens, low-intensity conflicts of attrition will largely replace wars fought from traditional strategies. According to military expert Martin Van Crevald (1991),

> the spread of sporadic small-scale war will cause regular armed forces themselves to change form, shrink in size, and wither away. As they do, much of the day-to-day burden of defending society against the threat of low-intensity conflict will be transferred to the booming security business. (p. 97)

Terrorism as a long-term condition of life will make leisure and especially tourism behavior more deliberate and more subject to sudden change. It may also mean that assurances of safety, predictability, and isolation from the increasing conflict between haves and have-nots will be more appealing.

Although globalization will bring sameness to some parts of life—"McDonaldization"—in many other ways it will further customize life. As federal governments seek to harmonize currencies, policies, and procedures, leisure behavior will become more diverse. Even the celebration of holidays will become customized as political or religious-based holidays become factionalized. Ramadan, Cinco de Mayo, or Chinese New Year celebrations may occur in San Diego, London, or Jakarta.

MULTIPOLAR AND MULTICIVILIZATIONAL POLITICS AND POWER

Globalization is taking place in a post-Cold War era in which "power is shifting from the long predominant West to non-Western civilizations" (Huntington, 1996, p. 29). Global politics have become multipolar and multicivilizational. Today, the most important countries in the world come from civilizations that are vastly different, and modernization of such countries does not mean that they will Westernize. Although during the past 400 years relations among civilizations "consisted of the subordination of other societies to Western civilization," this pattern has been broken.

> The West won the world not by the superiority of its ideas or values or religion (to which few members of other civilizations are converted), but rather by its superiority in applying organized violence. Westerners often forget this fact; non-Westerners do not. (Huntington, 1996, p. 51)

Although it is often assumed that English has become the international unifying language, the percentage of the world's people who speak English as a primary language is declining, constituting about 7.6 percent of the world's population. Indeed, all Western languages in combination are spoken by about only about one out of five people in the world.

In terms of religion, Christianity accounts for slightly less than 30 percent of the world's people. Islam, which accounts for a bit less than 20 percent of the world's population, will continue to increase in numbers since "Christianity spreads primarily by conversion, Islam by conversion and reproduction" (Huntington, 1996, p. 65). The ways in which various religions react to globalization will be diverse and unpredictable. In addition, the share of the world's population under the political control of various civilizations will shift so that the long dominant "West" will account for only about 10 percent of the world's citizens (see Table I.2).

All these trends mean that the power to shape leisure, popular culture, sport, tourism, hobbies, crafts, mass media, outdoor recreation, and a variety of other behavioral forms related to leisure will be diversified. Although global communication networks will show models of leisure from every country, culture, and civilization, it will be increasingly difficult to judge which ideas will succeed.

REVOLUTIONARY CHANGES IN ENVIRONMENT

Perhaps the most important revolution taking place is the transformation of the environment of the planet in ways that have no histori-

TABLE I.2. Shares of World Population Under the Political Control of Civilizations, 1900 and 2025

	1900	2025
Western	44.3	10.1
African	0.4	14.4
Sinitic	19.3	21.0
Hindu	0.3	16.9
Islamic	4.2	19.2
Japanese	3.5	1.5
Latin	3.2	9.2
Orthodox	8.5	4.9
Other	16.3	2.8

Source: Adapted from Huntington, 1996, p. 85.

cal precedent. Such change includes the mass extinction of animal life and plant life at a rate and magnitude unknown in human history. In addition, "we have driven atmospheric carbon dioxide to the highest levels in at least two hundred thousand years, unbalanced the nitrogen cycle, and contributed to a global warming that will ultimately be bad news everywhere" (Wilson, 2002, p. 23).

A combination of exponentially rising consumption and increasing population mean that "In short, earth has lost its ability to regenerate—unless global consumption is reduced, or global production is increased, or both" (Wilson, 2002, p. 27). Any birthrate above about 2.1 means that, eventually, the weight of humans will be more than the weight of the planet. It is therefore the developing nations who will, in many senses, control the world's future. The chances for human survival, even in the short run, are linked to the elimination of poverty and changes in the rights, education, and life opportunities of women in most nations.

Environmentally, we are entering an unprecedented era. The cost of natural disasters in 1998 alone, for instance, exceeded the cost for the entire previous decade. Although the causes remain disputed, the fact is that sea level rise in the twentieth century was double the rate of the nineteenth century. Although the rising water levels will have differential effects around the world, much of the shoreline of the world will be changed, sweeping many island nations under water in the process. Bangladesh, for example, may suffer a catastrophe.

There is complete certainty that stratospheric ozone depletion will increase the amount of harmful ultraviolet radiation reaching the earth's surface, and high certainty that global warming will increase average temperature and raise sea level. It is less certain, but still likely, that extreme weather and climate events (e.g., intense rain and snowstorms, floods, and droughts) will increase (Fisher et al., 2000).

Environmental change will customize leisure behavior everywhere. Many beaches will disappear, tourist seasons will change and customize, extreme weather events will cancel or interfere with more planned events, attitudes toward exposure to sunlight will become ambivalent, and environmental degradation will render some leisure environments uninhabitable or more highly regulated.

A REVOLUTION IN URBAN AREAS

Nucleated cities emerged in the nineteenth century where industrialization occurred. They had a well-defined commercial area, known as downtown, industry was lined up along the railroad tracks, and residential areas were arrayed around the edges and segregated along lines of income, ethnicity, and race (Lewis, 1995).

These cities were replaced by emerging galactic cities, as the automobile became the primary means of transport. Rather than thinking of this as urban sprawl, Lewis (1995) contends this is a new kind of city. The characteristics of the galactic city are (1) an internal transportation system made up of interstate and limited-access highways; (2) a considerable degree of internal commercial clustering, usually at the intersections of main arterial highways; (3) industrial clustering no longer based on manufacturing but more on technology, services, or clean industry; and (4) residential areas which are highly consumptive of space, with single houses with lawns and garages.

Galactic cities help ensure that travel by automobile dominates. Walking is often useless to get anywhere. Public transportation is sometimes ineffective because the city has no center.

Although not all the cities of the world are becoming galactic, many are. Such urban patterns ensure customization of daily life, transportation, work arrangement, and leisure. The automobile (along with motor scooters and other individual people movers) is the ultimate customizer of travel and, therefore, of daily life. It can carry one person on a customized travel pattern. Innovation in urban mass transportation will seek to mimic the automobile in terms of allowing the individual to undertake customized travel patterns.

A REVOLUTION IN THE MASS CUSTOMIZATION OF PRODUCTS AND SERVICES

In the twenty-first century, technological change is being organized around biological models, and biology operates on the principle that difference is better (Kelly, 1996). The revolution in how work is done is producing a revolution in what work provides: mass customized services based on greatly expanded information about the client or customer. Medicine, for instance, is beginning to be customized, taking the patient's medical history and physical condition into account (Anderson, 1997).

Some organizations are beginning to prepare for this mass customization. Other organizations and institutions, such as public schools, will follow. Not only will each public school customize pace, duration, and sequence of learning, but also each student will attend and learn in unique time patterns, based on their needs and those of their parent or parents. As public schools customize their schedules on an individual basis, the leisure and play of children and youth will follow more diverse patterns, often customized at the household level.

Although every living thing has its own unique sense of time, the ideal of the industrial society was to treat people *equally* and regiment them to common time patterns. The ideal will now become how to treat people *appropriately*—and that means to have sufficient information about them to recognize their unique needs with regard to time (Goldman, Nagel, and Preiss, 1995). Daily life will be reorganized with time patterns and schedules that vary for every single person. Treating people equally makes no sense in a decentralized society because we are not interchangeable parts. Treating people appropriately will make more sense, as we become even more diverse. The provision of leisure and tourism will be reshaped by this fundamental shift in human relations.

CONCLUSION

I come back to where I have never been.

W. S. Merwin

What can be concluded from the previous discussion? That reality is a moving target? That leisure and its use, which historically is defined and redefined by technological innovation and changes in the economy and in the processes of work, may undergo a series of continuing rapid transformations? Perhaps the most important transformation is that the customization of leisure experience will mirror the customization and diversification of work and daily life. For many, the seamless web of postmodern life will render distinctions between work and leisure almost meaningless. For others, often living in close proximity, culture, religion, and ethnicity will define leisure and its appropriate use. The customization of leisure will mirror the customization of reality.

The ants have run from their stomped hill—running in different directions at different speeds. Where they are going is not clear.

BIBLIOGRAPHY

Anderson, D., with an introduction by B. Joseph Pine II (1997). *Agile product development for mass customization, niche markets, jit, build-to-order, and flexible manufacturing.* New York: McGraw-Hill.

Ashford, L. (1995). New perspectives on population: Lessons from Cairo. *Population Bulletin,* 50(1).

Attali, J. (1991). *Millennium—Winners and losers in the new world order.* New York: Random House.

Ausubel, J. and A. Grubler (1994). Working less and living longer: Long-term trends in working time and time budgets. Working Paper 94-99. Laxenburg, Austria: International Institute for Applied Systems Analysis.

Boyett, J. (1996). *Beyond workplace 2000: Essential strategies for the new American corporation.* New York: Plume.

Bridges, W. (1994). *Jobshift—How to prosper in a workplace without jobs.* Reading, MA: Addison-Wesley.

Brown, L., G. Gardner, and B. Halwell (1998). Beyond Malthus: Sixteen dimensions of the population problem. Worldwatch Paper 143. Williamsport, PA: Worldwatch Institute.

D'Agnese, J. (2000). What you'll need to know in twenty years that you don't know. *Discover,* 21(10), 58-61.

Drucker, P. (1993). *Post-capitalist society.* New York: Harper Business.

Fisher, A., D. Abler, D. DeWalle, G. Knight, R. Najjar, C. Rogers, A. Rose, J. Shortle, and B. Yarnal (2000). *The Mid-Atlantic Regional Assessment of Climate Change Impacts: Overview report.* The U.S. Environmental Protection Agency and The Pennsylvania State University, Washington, DC, and University Park, PA.

Gilder, G. (1994). *Life after television: The coming transformation of media and American life.* New York: Norton.

Godbey, G. C. (1988). *The future of leisure services: Thriving on change.* State College, PA: Venture Publishing.

Godbey, G. (1998). *Leisure and leisure services in the 21st Century.* State College, PA: Venture Publishing.

Godbey, G., G. Dejong, V. Sasidharan, and C. Yarnal (2001). *The northeastern United States in the next two decades—Implications for the Northeast Region of the National Park Service.* Philadelphia, PA: NPS, Northeast Region.

Goldman, S., R. Nagel, and K. Preiss (1995). *Agile competitors and virtual organizations.* New York: Van Nostrand Reinhold.

Goodale, T. and G. Godbey (1989). *The evolution of leisure.* State College, PA: Venture Publishing.

Halal, M., B. Kull, and A. Leffman (1997). Emerging technologies: What's ahead for 2001-2030. *The Futurist,* 31, 20-28.

Huntington, S. (1996). *The clash of civilizations and the remaking of world order.* New York: Simon and Schuster.

Kanigel, R. (1997). *The one best way: Fredrick Winslow Taylor and the enigma of efficiency.* New York: Viking.

Kelly, K. (1996). *Out of control—The new biology of machines, social systems and the economic world.* Reading, MA: Addison-Wesley.

Kentworth, A. (1999). What trends tell. *Association Management,* 50(13), 30.

Kunreuther, H. and R. J. Roth Sr. (Eds.) (1998). *Paying the price: The status and role of insurance against natural disasters in the United States.* Washington, DC: Joseph Henry Press.

Kuntsler, J. (1993). *The geography of nowhere: The rise and fall of America's man-made landscape.* New York: Simon and Schuster.

Larsen, D. (1993). Density is destiny. *American Demographics,* 15 (January), 38-42.

Lemley, B. (2000). Twenty things that won't change in the next twenty years. *Discover,* 21(10), 92-96.

Lewis, P. (1995). The urban invasion of rural America: The emergence of the galactic city. In *The changing American countryside: Rural people and places,* Ed. E. Castle (pp. 61-85). Lawrence: University of Kansas Press.

Lutz, W. (1994). The future of world population. *Population Bulletin,* 49(1), 28.

McGee, T. (2001). Urbanization takes on new dimensions in Asia's population giants. *Population Today,* 29(7), 1-2.

Merwin, W. S. (1967). *The moving target.* New York: Antheneum.

Mitchell, L. (2002). American corporations; The new sovereigns. *The Chronicle Review,* January 18.

O'Meara, M. (1999). Reinventing cities for people and the planet. Worldwatch Paper 147. Williamsport, PA: Worldwatch Institute.

O'Neill, B. and D. Balk (2001). World population futures. *Population Bulletin,* 56(3).

Pine, B. and J. Gilmore (1999). *The experience economy.* Boston, MA: Harvard Business School Press.

Riley, N. (1997). Gender, power and population change. *Population Bulletin,* 52(1).

Robinson, J. and G. Godbey (1999). *Time for life—The surprising ways Americans use time,* Revised edition. University Park: Penn State Press.

Sassen, S. (2002). Globalization after September 11. *The Chronicle Review,* January 18.

Sommers, C. (2000). The war against boys. *The Atlantic Monthly* 285(5), 59-74.

Van Crevald, M. (1991). *The transformation of war.* New York: The Free Press.

Wilson, E. O. (2002). *The future of life.* New York: Alfred Knopf.

SECTION I:
CHANGES IN DEMOGRAPHICS, STAGES OF LIFE, AND LEISURE BEHAVIOR

Age has proven to be a valuable predictor of human behavior and economic demand. Far-reaching demographic changes such as the aging trend in industrialized countries and the dominance of the large baby-boomer generation, now aged between forty and fifty-eight, have strong and global effects on both leisure and tourism. More active leisure behavior, more frequent traveling, and the changing needs of the elderly stimulate the development of new products.

David Foot investigates the importance and needs of the aging population with regard to leisure behavior. Senior travelers have evolved into a fast-growing, promising market segment, and new leisure and tourism products, for example the hotels in Austria and Germany for those over age fifty, have been developed to accommodate their special needs.

The second study, conducted by Linda Caldwell and Cheryl Baldwin, shows how young people use their leisure time and the related experiences of that time use. Data from a diverse sample of five countries illustrate not only the international diversity of leisure, but also the main leisure activities of youth and their effect on personal development.

With a lifestyle study of the Generation X demographic in New Zealand, Sarah Todd, Rob Lawson, and Juergen Gnoth demarcate the leisure behavior of eighteen- to twenty-five-year-olds from other customer segments.

Chapter 1

Leisure Futures: A Change in Demography?

David K. Foot

INTRODUCTION

Population aging in the developed world presents challenges and opportunities for both business and government. Impacts of aging on public pensions and future health care costs in the Organisation for Economic Co-Operation and Development (OECD) and elsewhere have been carefully documented. The implications for future labor force and economic growth have also been studied. However, significantly less work has been devoted to other sectors of the economy, including the leisure and recreation sector.

This chapter outlines a methodology which combines leisure behavior with demographic information. Observed outcomes in any society reflect both changing behavior and changing demographics, including population aging. Most research in leisure and recreation studies focuses on explaining individual leisure participation using appropriate socioeconomic variables such as income, employment status, family composition, and, in certain cases, price. Most practitioners in leisure and recreation programs attempt to change individual participation for targeted groups or for a diverse population. In this approach, demographic information plays a minor role, and changes in observed outcomes are attributed to changes in individual behavior.

Age has been shown to be an important explanatory variable in individual participation. The finding of most research is that leisure participation for most activities, especially sporting activities, decreases with age. Population aging can, therefore, expect to have a significant impact on the future for leisure activities. It not only has a negative impact on the growth of these activities, but also affects their relative importance to society. This has important implications for facilities planning and other strategic decisions.

This chapter investigates these impacts using leisure data collected in association with a national health survey. This survey has the advantage that it also includes additional information on the frequency of leisure participation. Consequently, the sensitivity of the results to the inclusion or exclusion of the frequency of behavior at different ages can also be examined.

FRAMEWORK

To structure a study that combines behavioral and demographic information, consider the following simple equation:

$$N_j = \left(\frac{N}{P}\right)_j P \tag{1.1}$$

where N_j represents the number of people participating in activity j, and P represents the population size. In Equation 1.1 the ratio (N/P) represents the activity participation rate. This can be interpreted as the probability that any individual in the population participates in the activity in question. Therefore, this ratio captures individual and, by aggregation, group behavior in the activity within a given population.

The second variable in Equation 1.1 captures the demographic effect, represented by population size (P). In many applications P may be restricted to the non-child or adult population. Equation 1.1, therefore, simply separates the activity analysis into two determining components: the behavioral component, represented by the ratio N/P for that activity, and the demographic component represented by P.

Activity growth is, by definition, time dependent. Taking the time derivatives of Equation 1.1 results in the growth equation:

$$g(N_j) = g(N/P)_j + g(P) \tag{1.2}$$

where *g* denotes growth over time. Equation 1.2 shows that activity growth is the sum of participation rate growth (the behavioral component) and population growth (the demographic component). Note that these growth rates may be positive or negative and that the two components can have offsetting impacts. For example, if population growth is positive but aging results in a decreasing societal participation rate, then activity growth will not match population growth.

The impact of population aging can be explicitly incorporated into the analysis by dividing the population into an appropriate number of age groups. (Note that this analysis can be easily extended to include gender and other variables of interest.) Let there be i = 1, n such groups (so that $P = \sum_i P_i$), then Equation 1.1 can be rewritten as

$$\begin{aligned} N_j &= \sum_i N_{ij} \\ &= \sum_i \left(\frac{N}{P}\right)_{ij} P_i \\ &= \sum_i \left(\frac{N}{P}\right)_{ij} \left(\frac{P_i}{P}\right) P \end{aligned} \tag{1.3}$$

As before, the $(N/P)_{ij}$ ratios represent the behavioral component. These are the group-specific participation rates in the activity in question. Because the probability of activity participation can be expected to vary over an individual's life, the $(N/P)_{ij}$ will reflect life-course behavior in the observed population. The demographic component in Equation 1.3 is separated into two separate parts, the size of the population (P) and the age structure of the population (P_i/P). (Note that the P_i can also be made gender specific if warranted.)

Equation 1.3 can be rewritten to define the total participation rate of the activity in the population:

$$\frac{N_j}{P} = \sum_i \left(\frac{N}{P}\right)_{ij} \left(\frac{P_i}{P}\right) \tag{1.4}$$

which is a weighted sum of the group-specific activity rates where the weights are each age group's share in the total population. Equation

1.4 can be used to demonstrate the apparently contradictory conclusion that even if activity participation rates increase in all age groups, the total participation rate for the population can decline if lower-participation groups become a larger part of the population. This is a common characteristic of an aging population.

Although the growth equivalent of Equation 1.3 is no longer a simple expression, the effects of population aging can be captured through Equation 1.2 by assessing the impacts of population aging on the total participation rate. The following section outlines this procedure.

DEMOGRAPHIC CHANGE

For the purposes of this chapter, demographic change is defined as changes in the size and age structure of the population. (Changes in gender structure are easily accommodated in the analysis.) The impact of demographic change on the number of participants in any leisure activity over time *(t)* can be isolated by keeping participation behavior constant. In the context of Equation 1.3, this can be written as

$$N_{jt} = \sum_i \left(\frac{N}{P}\right)_{ij} \left(\frac{P_i}{P}\right)_t P_t \tag{1.5}$$

This assumption in no way implies that behavior will remain unchanged over time. Rather, it is akin to a controlled experiment in social science. The impact of one component, demographic change, is isolated by keeping the other component, behavioral change, unchanged.

It is important to reiterate that this approach still incorporates life-course participation behavior in its aging results. Perhaps this point is best illustrated by a simple numerical example. Table 1.1 represents a population divided into three (young, middle age, and senior) age groups. Activity participation is assumed to decline with age from 20 to 10 to 5 percent of the group population. Initially the three age groups are assumed to represent 35, 50, and 15 percent of the population, respectively. Application of Equation 1.4 shows that the participation rate for the total population is 12.75 percent.

TABLE 1.1. Population Aging and Total Activity Participation: An Example

	Young	Middle age	Seniors	Total participation (%)
Participation (%): $(N/P)_{ij}$	20	10	5	
Population share:				
$(P_i/P)_1$	0.35	0.50	0.15	12.75
$(P_i/P)_2$	0.30	0.50	0.20	12.00

Now assume that the population ages without any change in the group participation rates. Aging is reflected by 5 percent of the population moving from the young to the middle-age group and 5 percent moving from the middle-age to the senior group. The young group is a smaller share and the senior group is a larger share of the population, whereas the middle-age group share has not changed. Now application of Equation 1.4 yields a participation rate for the total population of only 12 percent, even though there has been no change in individual behavior. Aging alone has resulted in a decrease of 0.75 percentage points, or nearly 6 percent. (This number is the $g(N/P)_j$ that appears in Equation 1.2.) This means that population growth over the same period would have to equal 6 percent if there was to be no decline in activity numbers as a result of demographic change.

This analysis can be applied retrospectively using historically observed demographic data, or prospectively using population projections into the future. In the retrospective application, the counterfactual historical series generated by the calculation can be compared to actual data to see how much of the historical record can be accounted for by demographic change alone. By definition (see Equation 1.2), the remainder can be attributed to behavioral change. The following sections present an illustration of a prospective application using leisure participation data from a national health survey.

Note that in some applications N_j represents the amount of money spent on activity *j*. In this case, the $(N/P)_{ij}$ ratios represent average per capita expenditure in each age group for the activity in question. The impact of demographic change on activity expenditure can then be assessed using the same framework.

DATA

To illustrate how to measure the impact of a change in demography on leisure futures, data has been extracted from the 1998 U.S. National Health Institute Survey (Centers for Disease Control and Prevention [CDC], 1998). Respondents eighteen years and over were asked if they had participated in any of the twenty-one listed healthy leisure activities within the previous two weeks. Respondents who had participated in any of the listed leisure activities were then asked how often they participated in these activities over the previous two weeks. This measure of participation intensity provides an additional feature of activity participation that is seldom included in most leisure surveys.

Table 1.2 presents the activity participation results ranked from highest to lowest. Table 1.3 presents the associated frequency results using the same ranking as Table 1.2. The data are separated into ten-year age groups, with the exception of the youngest (eighteen to twenty-four) and the oldest (seventy-five-plus) age groups. The separation of the senior (sixty-five-plus) group into two groups is a beneficial feature of these data, especially when analyzing the impacts of population aging.

The most popular activity in the sample is walking for exercise. Participation in this activity peaks in the sixty-five to seventy-four age group at almost 55 percent. The second most popular activity is gardening or yard work which shows a similar age profile. Most activities, however, show maximum participation rates in the youngest age group. This occurs for fifteen of the twenty-one activities. For another two (bicycling and stair climbing) participation is equally high in more than one age group. Participation in cross-country skiing (the least popular on the list) peaks in the thirty-five to forty-four age group. Golf is a somewhat unusual activity which peaks in both younger (twenty-five to thirty-four) and older (sixty-five to seventy-four) age groups.

The frequency data (Table 1.3) present some further insights into leisure participation. These data are conditional on participation, so they must be interpreted with Table 1.2 in mind. Stretching is the most frequent activity, with those in the oldest age group participating in stretching activities every other day. Stair climbing now equals walking as the second most frequent activity for those that partici-

TABLE 1.2. Activity Participation in the Past Two Weeks, United States, 1998 (%)

Activity	Age Group							
	18-24	25-34	35-44	45-54	55-64	65-74	75+	Total
1. Walking for exercise	42.3	44.1	47.2	51.4	49.8	54.6	49.5	47.6
2. Gardening or yard work	14.4	25.8	34.3	37.7	38.2	41.5	32.0	31.2
3. Stretching exercises	36.3	33.0	31.7	29.8	25.9	23.9	21.5	30.4
4. Weight lifting	29.3	21.9	18.1	14.5	9.6	9.1	6.5	17.5
5. Bicycling	15.5	15.5	15.5	12.4	11.1	12.0	9.0	13.8
6. Jogging/running	24.1	16.4	12.6	9.2	3.9	2.1	1.4	12.0
7. Stair climbing	8.5	8.5	8.1	7.3	6.7	4.8	4.7	7.5
8. Aerobics	10.8	10.1	7.6	5.7	3.7	3.2	2.6	7.2
9. Playing basketball	17.7	9.1	7.2	3.0	1.4	0.3	0.1	6.8
10. Swimming	8.6	6.1	7.4	5.4	4.6	5.3	3.1	6.3
11. Playing golf	4.4	6.2	5.5	5.6	5.9	6.6	4.2	5.6
12. Bowling	7.5	3.8	3.5	2.4	2.1	3.0	1.6	3.6
13. Playing baseball/softball	6.2	5.2	4.0	1.8	0.6	0.2	0.0	3.3
14. Playing volleyball	5.3	2.9	1.9	0.9	0.3	0.0	0.0	2.0
15. Playing tennis	3.3	2.0	2.0	1.3	1.5	1.1	0.4	1.9
16. Playing football	5.7	2.0	1.6	0.5	0.1	0.1	0.0	1.7
17. Playing soccer	3.9	2.3	1.9	0.8	0.1	0.0	0.0	1.6
18. Playing racquetball	2.4	1.0	0.9	0.6	0.3	0.1	0.0	0.9
19. Downhill skiing	1.3	0.7	0.7	0.4	0.4	0.1	0.0	0.6
20. Waterskiing	0.7	0.5	0.5	0.1	0.2	0.0	0.0	0.4
21. Cross-country skiing	0.0	0.2	0.4	0.3	0.3	0.0	0.1	0.2

Source: CDC, 1998.

TABLE 1.3. Frequency of Activity Participation in the Past Two Weeks, United States, 1998 (Number of Times)

	Age Group							
Activity	18-24	25-34	35-44	45-54	55-64	65-74	75+	Total
1. Walking for exercise	5.8	5.6	6.1	6.5	7.3	8.2	8.6	6.5
2. Gardening or yard work	3.1	2.9	3.2	3.4	4.2	4.6	4.9	3.6
3. Stretching exercises	6.6	6.5	6.6	7.4	8.2	8.2	8.6	7.0
4. Weight lifting	5.6	5.5	5.3	5.8	6.2	6.5	6.8	5.6
5. Bicycling	3.9	4.1	3.7	4.5	5.0	6.0	6.4	4.3
6. Jogging/running	5.0	4.3	4.7	5.1	6.3	6.8	5.3	4.8
7. Stair climbing	5.4	5.4	5.7	8.0	9.1	8.9	8.1	6.5
8. Aerobics	4.5	4.1	4.7	4.4	5.0	5.8	4.7	4.5
9. Playing basketball	3.5	2.7	2.7	2.7	2.7	3.3	1.0	3.0
10. Swimming	3.1	3.3	3.3	3.7	4.5	5.9	5.4	3.7
11. Playing golf	1.9	2.1	2.0	2.3	3.3	3.6	3.3	2.4
12. Bowling	1.7	1.5	1.8	2.0	2.4	2.8	3.1	1.9
13. Playing baseball/softball	2.4	2.5	2.7	3.0	2.5	2.3	1.0	2.6
14. Playing volleyball	2.5	1.9	1.9	2.1	1.9	1.5	1.0	2.2
15. Playing tennis	3.1	2.0	2.2	3.3	3.7	4.4	3.6	2.8
16. Playing football	2.5	2.2	1.9	2.8	2.0	1.0	0.0	2.3
17. Playing soccer	2.9	2.6	2.6	2.6	2.5	1.0	0.0	2.7
18. Playing racquetball	2.2	2.0	2.4	2.5	3.7	6.5	0.0	2.3
19. Downhill skiing	1.4	1.4	2.0	2.1	1.9	1.9	2.0	1.7
20. Waterskiing	1.8	1.6	2.8	1.0	1.6	0.0	0.0	2.0
21. Cross-country skiing	0.0	3.5	2.9	2.5	2.6	2.0	1.6	2.9

Source: CDC, 1998.

pate. However, whereas the peak frequency age for walking is in the oldest age group, frequency in stair climbing peaks in the younger fifty-five to sixty-four group.

These data form the basis for the activity growth projections outlined in the following section based on demographic change alone. It is worth noting, once again, that the data in Table 1.3 are conditional on the data in Table 1.2, so the two tables must be combined to obtain the frequency results.

RESULTS

Leisure futures were calculated for the next two decades for the activities in Tables 1.2 and 1.3 based on a change in demography using population projections developed by the U.S. Census Bureau. In these population projections, annual population growth in the United States is projected to average approximately 1 percent, although growth will gradually decline over the period, reflecting the aging of the U.S. population over this period.

The boom, bust, and echo profile that characterizes the U.S. population continues to move up the population pyramid in these projections. The well-known baby boomer generation born between 1946 and 1964 in the United States were aged thirty-six to fifty-four by 2000. Twenty years later, at the end of the projection period, they will be aged fifty-six to seventy-four. Their children, the so-called Echo Boom, were mainly born in the 1980s, thus they will be reaching their twenties in the 2000s and their thirties over the 2010s. Growth rates and relative rankings of the leisure activities will be impacted as the various demographic groups move through their life course over the projection period.

Growth rates for the "medium" population growth scenario are presented in Table 1.4 for both participation rates and frequency. To facilitate their interpretation, Table 1.5 shows these growth rates relative to population growth over the period. (In terms of Equation 1.2, Table 1.5 shows $g(N_j)/g(P)$.) This is a useful index of the relative impact of aging on growth. The absolute impact is measured by the difference $g(N_j)–g(P)$ as shown in Equation 1.2.

From 2000 to 2005 only walking and gardening show above-average growth. When frequency of participation is included, these two

TABLE 1.4. Leisure Activity Growth, United States, 2000-2020

Activity	2000-2005		2005-2010		2010-2015		2015-2020	
	Partici-pation*	Fre-quency	Partici-pation	Fre-quency	Partici-pation	Fre-quency	Partici-pation	Fre-quency
1. Walking for exercise	1.14	1.24	1.12	1.24	0.96	1.12	0.85	1.02
2. Gardening or yard work	1.19	1.33	1.16	1.34	1.04	1.27	0.94	1.15
3. Stretching exercises	0.99	1.12	0.98	1.08	0.77	0.86	0.66	0.72
4. Weight lifting	0.81	0.87	0.83	0.89	0.58	0.64	0.46	0.50
5. Bicycling	0.89	1.03	0.93	1.10	0.81	1.00	0.72	0.89
6. Jogging/running	0.67	0.78	0.67	0.74	0.35	0.38	0.22	0.23
7. Stair climbing	0.98	1.29	0.95	1.19	0.73	0.87	0.61	0.68
8. Aerobics	0.73	0.75	0.79	0.81	0.58	0.64	0.47	0.54
9. Playing basketball	0.55	0.63	0.59	0.65	0.30	0.28	0.17	0.12
10. Swimming	0.87	0.97	0.87	1.06	0.74	1.02	0.66	0.92
11. Playing golf	1.06	1.29	1.14	1.45	1.02	1.38	0.87	1.14
12. Bowling	0.86	0.99	0.94	1.07	0.73	0.94	0.59	0.81
13. Playing baseball/softball	0.40	0.41	0.48	0.45	0.32	0.28	0.26	0.24
14. Playing volleyball	0.56	0.66	0.62	0.68	0.29	0.25	0.13	0.05
15. Playing tennis	0.90	1.22	0.92	1.21	0.69	0.86	0.52	0.59
16. Playing football	0.59	0.71	0.61	0.69	0.24	0.21	0.09	0.02
17. Playing soccer	0.42	0.44	0.46	0.47	0.23	0.22	0.17	0.14
18. Playing racquetball	0.75	0.84	0.70	0.78	0.27	0.39	0.09	0.20
19. Downhill skiing	0.77	0.80	0.74	0.64	0.42	0.32	0.26	0.21
20. Waterskiing	0.41	0.12	0.45	0.08	0.39	0.28	0.36	0.48
21. Cross-country skiing	0.87	0.70	0.59	0.53	0.44	0.45	0.47	0.48
Total population	1.09		1.08		0.91		0.81	

*All calculations based on % per year.

Note: Calculations by the author based on Tables 1.2 and 1.3.

TABLE 1.5. Leisure Activity Growth Index, United States, 2000-2020 (Population Growth = 100)

Activity	2000-2005		2005-2010		2010-2015		2015-2020	
	Partici-pation*	Fre-quency	Partici-pation	Fre-quency	Partici-pation	Fre-quency	Partici-pation	Fre-quency
1. Walking for exercise	104	113	104	114	105	123	106	126
2. Gardening or yard work	109	122	107	124	114	139	116	143
3. Stretching exercises	91	102	90	100	84	94	81	90
4. Weight lifting	74	80	77	83	64	70	57	62
5. Bicycling	82	94	86	102	89	110	89	110
6. Jogging/running	62	72	62	69	38	42	27	28
7. Stair climbing	90	118	88	110	79	95	75	84
8. Aerobics	67	69	73	75	64	71	59	67
9. Playing basketball	51	58	55	60	33	31	21	14
10. Swimming	79	89	80	98	81	112	82	114
11. Playing golf	97	119	106	135	112	151	107	141
12. Bowling	79	91	87	100	80	103	73	100
13. Playing baseball/softball	37	38	45	42	36	31	33	29
14. Playing volleyball	51	61	57	63	32	28	16	7
15. Playing tennis	83	112	85	112	75	94	64	73
16. Playing football	54	65	56	64	26	23	11	3
17. Playing soccer	38	41	42	44	25	24	20	18
18. Playing racquetball	69	77	64	72	29	42	12	25
19. Downhill skiing	71	74	68	60	46	35	32	26
20. Waterskiing	38	11	42	7	42	30	44	59
21. Cross-country skiing	80	65	55	49	48	49	59	59

**Note:* Leisure activity growth divided by population growth (× 100).

activities are joined by stretching, stair climbing, golf, and tennis. Population aging has a large impact on the growth of the last three activities. At the bottom of this list in terms of growth is waterskiing, playing baseball or softball, and to a lesser extent playing soccer. These are all young persons' activities which are impacted negatively by the aging U.S. population.

These results largely continue between 2005 and 2010, by which time gardening and golf are the fastest-growing activities. When frequency of participation is factored in, golf outpaces gardening as the fastest-growing activity. The aging baby boomers are making golf a booming "industry" in the United States in the first decades of the new millennium. Walking, stair climbing, and tennis also experience above-average growth in the frequency results. It is interesting to note that when frequency is not included, stair climbing and tennis have below-average growth. Another activity, bicycling, also experiences a move from below- to above-average growth as a result of population aging.

These results continue largely unchanged into the second decade of the new millennium. Golf and gardening remain the big winners from demographic change, followed by walking, swimming, and bicycling. The big losers are all the sports activities near the bottom of the list.

Over the entire period, walking, gardening, bicycling, and swimming gradually improve their relative positions, while the positions of stretching, jogging/running, stair climbing, and most sports gradually get worse. These relative positions remain unchanged under alternative population projections.

CONCLUSION

Population aging presents challenges and opportunities for business and government. Leisure trends also reflect these demographic changes. Using a framework that isolates the impacts of demographic change (including population aging) and incorporates life-course behavior, this chapter explores the impacts of demographic change on leisure futures. The framework is illustrated using data from a 1998 U.S. national health survey that includes both information on leisure activity participation and, conditional on participation, the frequency (or intensity) of participation.

The results reflect the aging of the U.S. population, especially the large baby boomer generation born between 1946 and 1964. The fastest-growing leisure activities on the list of twenty-one activities over the first two decades of the new millennium are walking for exercise and gardening or yard work. The slowest-growing leisure activities on the list are all sports activities (playing basketball, baseball/softball, volleyball, football, soccer, and racquetball).

Incorporating frequency (or intensity) of participation introduces interesting nuances in the results. Leisure activities such as golf and tennis move from below-average growth to above-average growth. For these activities, frequency increases with age into the early retirement ages (sixty-five to seventy-four), so population aging results in greater growth than if the frequency data are omitted from the analysis. On the other side, activities for which frequency decreases with age, such as waterskiing, suffer even more as a result of population aging.

These results have important implications for both businesses and governments. In general, aging populations change their leisure choices over time from active sports activities to less-active recreation activities. Construction and maintenance of facilities to support these leisure trends, whether in the private or public sectors, need to be adjusted accordingly. For example, aging populations favor walking trails over running tracks and tennis over volleyball courts. In addition, the range of merchandise sold in support of these activities will change over time. Opportunities abound for businesses that incorporate these future leisure trends into their strategic plans.

REFERENCE

Centers for Disease Control and Prevention (1998). National Health Interview Survey: Public use data release (computer file). Conducted by Division of Health Interview Statistics, National Center for Health Statistics, Hyattsville, MD, October 2000. Available at <http://www.cdc.gov/nchs/nhis.htm>.

Chapter 2

Concerns and Considerations About the Future of Youth Leisure: An International Perspective

Linda L. Caldwell
Cheryl K. Baldwin

INTRODUCTION

This chapter has two main purposes. First, we will discuss the leisure behavior and experience of youth from a world perspective. Second, and more important, we will raise questions about the future of youth based on these observations.

Two policy initiatives on children and youth provide a foundation for this chapter. The World Leisure and Recreation Association (WLRA) recently formed the Working Group for Children and Youth and developed a general framework for its work, with concomitant goals and objectives. Much of the working group's efforts and ideas are reflected in this chapter. We also adopt a public policy perspective on youth recreation developed by the Canadian Policy Research Networks and Canadian Council on Social Development. The Canadian Council developed four hypotheses about how youth learn through recreation (Laidlaw Foundation, 1999, in Canadian Policy Research Networks, Inc. and Canadian Council on Social Development, 2001). These hypotheses are as follows:

1. *Human development:* The absence of structured recreation for youth negatively affects the long-term socioeconomic human development of youth as adults.

2. *Civic competence:* The absence of involvement by youth in interpersonal recreation activities affects an individual's future civic competence and also affects the quality of democracy.
3. *Insufficiency:* Significant numbers of youth are not participating in recreation activities at levels sufficient to support their human development and future civic competence.
4. *Inadequacy:* Nonparticipation by youth in recreation and arts activities can be related to the inadequacy of existing public systems dealing with the provision of youth recreation.

Taken together, the WLRA and Canadian policy statements assert that leisure is a basic human right in need of support and protection and that leisure can play an important role in the healthy development of youth and communities. For the developmental benefits of leisure to be fully realized, carefully designed experiences and structured opportunities must be accessible and then fully accessed. Society must make an investment in youth recreation so that future socioeconomic, democratic, and personal benefits associated with leisure are achieved.

The ideas encompassed in these hypotheses are consistent with and further elaborated in one theory of human development, the ecological systems theory (EST) (Bronfenbrenner, 1979). EST conceptualizes the influences that support and enhance an individual's healthy development and suggests that there are four broad systems of influence on a youth as he or she develops: macro, exo, meso, and micro. At the middle are those influences that are most direct and immediate and operate in what is called the microsystem. These are factors in the youth's immediate environment that influence a youth directly, such as activities; interpersonal relationships with peers, parents, teachers, coaches, and clergy; and roles a youth takes on during his or her development (such as being a sibling, a worker, a student, and so on). At the next level (mesolevel) are influences on the youth caused by the relationships between the microsystem influences. Examples include the relationship between parents and peers, or home and recreation center. The exosystem relates to factors in the community that influence a child at a political level, such as recreation and park systems. Here there is no direct influence, but opportunities and type of community indirectly influence the youth. Finally, and very important to this presentation, is the most diffused level—the cultural context (macrolevel).

This theoretical framework for human development is the basis for formulating a series of key questions for research on the character and importance of leisure. How do youths throughout the world *use* their leisure time and what variations do we see at the individual, community, and cultural levels? How do youths *experience* their leisure time? What factors characterize optimal and less than optimal leisure experiences?

These are not trivial questions, nor are they simple questions. How youths spend their time influences subsequent growth and development as a human being and as a citizen. Larson and Verma (1999) observed that economists consider time to be "human capital," and likewise they suggested that for youths, time is a capital resource. Although time spent on activities such as education (school) is easily seen as productive and instrumental to the transition to productive adulthood, time spent in leisure and social activities is typically not seen that way, even though these are critical developmental contexts. Larson and Verma (1999) state, "A society that structures its youths' time to provide them chances for developing social and emotional competences is making a long-term investment in the overall maturity and mental health of its adult population" (p. 702). However, knowing what youths do is not enough. Leisure is more than filling time, and the meanings and experiences associated with what is done in free time are often more important that what one does. Also important to this discussion is examining the nature of the leisure experience since positive experiences are critical to one's personal satisfaction and well-being.

Unfortunately, little consistency occurs across studies in categorizing what youths do in their free time. In this chapter terms and activities used by the researchers in their respective reports or documents are used. Although this will not allow exact comparisons across studies or populations, it will provide a snapshot of time use for that group and culture. How youths experience free time and what aspects of experience are important are also inconsistently and often poorly defined. This state of affairs is reflective of the fact that research on youth leisure is still in its infancy. As youth leisure garners increasing research attention, these issues surrounding time use and leisure experience are likely to be addressed.

We will next present case studies of five countries: South Africa, Togo, Australia, Sweden, and Chile. These countries were chosen because the first author has some familiarity with them and they illustrate the points we would like to raise. We regret in particular that we were not able to discuss Asian and Southeast Asian countries. We have omitted a discussion of North American youth not because the same problems do not exist (they do), but because much of the available research focuses on these populations and we felt it more important to expand the scope of this chapter.

CASE STUDIES

South Africa

Little research has been conducted about the leisure of youths in South Africa, although there are three studies to consider. A pre-apartheid study, The Youth Centre Project, investigated the leisure prospects of black urban youths aged sixteen to twenty-four years (Møller, 1991). Wegner (1998) completed a master's thesis on the relationship between leisure boredom and substance abuse among high school students in Cape Town. Finally, Statistics South Africa conducted a population study of how South Africans spent their time, which included some information on youths. Combined, these studies offer interesting insight into the leisure time and leisure experiences of youths.

Time Use

Among ten- to nineteen-year-old South African youth, 24 percent of males and 20 percent of females spend their time in leisure activities (socializing, watching TV, listening to radio, other mass media use, and other social and cultural activities). Females watch more TV than males (26 percent of their leisure time versus 22 percent). Males spend 48 percent of their leisure time in other social and cultural activities (e.g., games, indoor and outdoor sports, spectator sports, and arts and hobbies) compared to girls, who spend only 35 percent of their time in these activities (Budlender, Chobokonane, and Mpetsheni, 2001). Møller (1991) found that black South African youths spent most of their time in social interaction and conversation, followed by television watching, listening to music, and sporting activities—soccer in particular.

Experience

One indicator of the quality of leisure experience is leisure boredom. Given the passive leisure activities that dominate the time use statistics it is not surprising that for youths in South Africa leisure is associated with boredom. In Møller's (1991) study, one-quarter to one-third of the youths reported "excessive boredom and restlessness." In addition, "pure" leisure activities were not as valued by youths as those that might be considered "semileisure" (education and moneymaking activities). Møller attributed this finding to the fact that South Africa is considered a developing country, where pure leisure is perceived to be only for the privileged class.

There are also interesting demographic differences in the leisure experience. Wegner (1998) found that girls in her study were more bored than boys, and in grades eight and eleven, black students were more bored than white students. White male grade-eleven students had the least amount of boredom. Unfortunately, students who drank alcohol were less bored than those who did not drink.

These basic findings about time use and experience, as well as the gender and racial differences associated with them, raise a number of issues about opportunity. Wegner hypothesized that boys were less bored than girls because boys had more opportunities available to them and society encouraged them to be more active. As seen in the Statistics South Africa data, boys spend much more of their time engaged in sports and active activities, which characteristically provide social connectedness, excitement, and being away from the home. The reason blacks might have reported high degrees of boredom is complex and likely related to vestiges of apartheid and/or socioeconomic status, which is highly correlated with race in South Africa (Wegner, 1998).

Togo

While findings in South Africa provide some insight on societal influences related to gender and race, research in Togo reveals the subtle way that cultural beliefs and economic hardship shape opportunity and access.

Time Use

Youths in Tomegbe, a small rural village of approximately 4,000 in Togo (Africa), indicate that leisure may not be a concept which holds much currency. Most youths are not involved in organized activities: 39 percent of youths are not involved in *any* organized activities, and 60 percent participate in activities only if run by the school. The main form of entertainment is listening to music (84 percent of youths), while 74 percent report dancing each week for one or more hours, and 44 percent report watching TV each week for one or more hours. Some participation in unstructured activities occurs: 59 percent report doing a hobby, and 49 percent read four or more hours per week. Although these statistics might lead one to think that youths are somewhat engaged in leisure activities, data from focus groups with youths and youth chiefs in the village present a slightly different picture of the character and value of leisure experiences (Adubra et al., 2002).

Experience

Consider the following quotations taken from a focus group conducted with the youth representatives (e.g., youth chief) in the Adubra and colleagues study:

> Apart from folk drumming and dancing with Agbeyeye, sometimes, very occasionally, some people will bring generators and come to show some videos in the village. Due to a lack of available electricity, there are no entertainment centers. Only a few individuals in the village who have the means to afford a generator set their generators in motion for a night to show films on TV. They use their own houses (a tiny room in the house) and sell tickets at their doors.
>
> RESEARCHER: How about the girls?
>
> FOCUS GROUP PARTICIPANT 1: They play ampe.
>
> R: Is that it?
>
> FG1: Even for ampe, it is now forbidden.
>
> FG2: Wait a minute. That rule was to prevent playful life for girls. They are in school and instead of studying they play ampe. . . . The rule is to allow the girls to have more study time.
>
> R: Is there a rule forbidding boys to play soccer during study time?
>
> FG2: No. But then, when school is over the boys are free to go practice in the evening. During class time nobody from school would practice.

After further discussion, someone said,

> Ampe game involves thinking, too. You have to check your partner and think what foot to push forward to turn her on. Other things like the toy bamboo trucks that the kids construct are of the same value. They are the premises of engineering thinking of the kids. But we don't value those things. We only see them as jokes, and already from the beginning of the vacations, the chiefs say: no way, those things cannot be seen in the village. I was asking those women if today, with the new civilization age, it's still necessary to regulate those things whereby the kids could develop their creative skills. So for me, that too is something important that is worth discussing at some point later in the village. You know sometimes you see some of the toys these kids make with some styles, which proves that the kid has a resourceful mind oriented toward mechanics. *And you kill that spirit.* The vacation time, which should be the time by excellence for freedom, you want the kids to go to farm and come back home in the evening to lie down for the night.

A follow-up response was:

> That's true. What my brother says is absolutely right. What a child can fabricate can really impress sometimes. My little child once made a toy car. I beat him and went to the farm. To my big surprise, when I came back, I saw a white man dragging the thing, playing with the toy. The white man asked him . . . how he managed to invent that car. So all those things we need to reconsider our negative attitudes toward those indigenous ways of expressing our skills in childhood.

Next are comments from a focus group conducted with youth who had dropped out of school.

R: What do you do for fun stuff?

FG1: Well they play drums and folk-dance music and we go there.

FG2: It's true there's no more fun these days because of the economic crisis, but whenever there's some celebration in the village you go there too and enjoy yourself like everybody. But these occasions are no more common. People are unhappy. There's no more money. Akpesse.

FG3: Like last year, we would form teams and play cards, and that was fun.

R: And you girls, what do you do? [Silence. No girl came up with an activity.]

FG2: The girls come to watch soccer. They also play ampe. And very often, too, they fight!!! [laughter]

R: Fight for fun or fight, real fight?

FG2: All kinds, but real fights mainly. . . . Like when they work or chat and there's a small dispute, they settle it by fighting. And we gather to watch. That's entertaining, isn't it?

R: Do they show movies in the village?

FG3: No, but very rarely. And they're not encouraged. . . . They come from Kpalime or Kuma. And they do it in Mr. X's house . . . they show us shootings, fightings, and some Nigerian evangelization films, etc.

Community Attachment

One way that structured leisure activities can influence youths is to provide experiences in the community which engage them with caring adults and civic leaders. These experiences can often foster a sense of civic engagement and community attachment. However, in Togo a survey of all youths in school indicated that only 2 percent of them expected to continue to live in their village when they grew up, and none expected to work in the village. Furthermore, 58 percent of them felt people in their village could not be trusted, and 46 percent felt that people are not willing to help their neighbors. On the other hand, 62 percent felt that they could turn to adults other than their parents for help. The following dialogue helps clarify these findings.

R1: Here in Tomegbe, do you know a place where you could go and people would talk to you and show you how to carry yourselves in society, in the community, in public? Are there places like that, or are there activities you could participate in to acquire these types of knowledge?

FG2: Here in Tomegbe, it's not common. There are no places you could visit and indirectly learn how to become confident and knowledgeable about what's happening in the world around us. You need to go out of the village. Even for learning your trade there's nobody you can work with to feel sure that you've learnt something superior and could practice it and gain respect. . . . You need to leave . . .

FG5: To acquire those skills you need to approach the elders, follow them, and watch how they do things.

FG3: For example, there are people here, they don't like going out to mingle with others and learn how to be in community. Those people they can't learn these skills. But if you go out and participate in activities with other youth in the village you may learn other things.

R2: What activities do you see as capable of fostering these skills?

FG1: Like when they call for community work, you can join people, and by working with them you listen to what they talk about and see how they do things.

FG8: Some people create groups and association for gardening, etc.

Australia

Time Use

According to the Australian Bureau of Statistics, of children aged five to fourteen, 29 percent were involved in either playing a musical instrument, singing, dancing, or drama outside of school hours. Twice as many girls than boys participated in these activities. Of the cultural activities selected, playing a musical instrument was most popular, followed by dancing, singing, and drama, respectively. In regard to formal lessons, dancing had the highest occurrence (93 percent) followed by playing a musical instrument (75 percent), drama (69 percent), and singing (57 percent).

By comparison, 59 percent in the same age group were active in organized sports after school hours (66 percent of boys and 52 percent of girls). Furthermore, 32 percent of the boys participated in more than one sport compared with 20 percent of the girls.

It is important to note, however, that of children aged five to fourteen years, 30 percent did not participate in any organized sport or cultural activity outside of school. Furthermore, almost half of the children born overseas in non-English-speaking countries were not involved in these activities, and almost half of the children living with a single unemployed parent participated. Thus, in addition to differences in leisure participation based on the demographic characteristics of race and gender, immigrant status and parental employment appear to have an effect.

Experience

Although participation rates are relatively high for some youths in Australia (white males and females in respective activities), high levels of leisure boredom are reported among some youths. Patterson, Pegg, and Dobson-Patterson (2000) hypothesized that leisure boredom was related to gender and place of residence (rural versus urban). They attempted to find out why such high levels of depression (and consequent suicide) and alcohol abuse occur among Australian youth, particularly in rural New South Wales. Rural females experienced higher levels of boredom than male youths in rural areas and males and females in urban areas. In 1992, Jones observed that in rural Australia fewer activities were available for girls compared with boys. Although recreation facilities offered sports to boys, girls were not typically interested and therefore had no activities to physically and mentally engage in.

Chile

An ongoing study about youth in Santiago, Chile, examined leisure opportunity, community attachment, and civic engagement (Martinez et al., in progress). Interviews with community leaders and youths indicated that although all youths had high aspirations and interests, many encountered institutional barriers that were related to social class structures. The particular group a person belongs to seemed to dictate opportunity.

In the upper-middle and upper-class communities, individual families and households were responsible for the social and leisure activities of youths. Among lower socioeconomic groups, a more collective approach to youth needs was taken, although the support for youth agencies to assist in this endeavor is lacking. Youths felt that community spaces neglect them, and the quantitative data support this. Of the 580 youths surveyed, about half reported that they wished they knew more about free time activities in the community (and 32 percent were unsure). About 30 percent felt that the community lacked things for them to do, and 17 percent were not sure. These findings did not vary by gender.

Time Use and Experience

Almost 70 percent of the youths reported doing their "favorite" leisure activity to develop skills, and virtually everyone did their activity because they enjoyed it. At the same time, 23 percent did their favorite activity because there was nothing else to do, and 21 percent did it because parents expected them to. By contrast, when asked why they participated in the activity they did most frequently, 32 percent reported doing it to develop skills, 44 percent enjoyed the activity, and about 68 percent had nothing else to do.

Many youths in the Santiago area used their leisure time to help others and participate in other civic types of activities. Almost 36 percent participated in or helped a charity organization one to five times, 28 percent led or helped with a children's group one to five times, 36 percent helped their friends or classmates three or more times, 36 percent volunteered at a school event one to five times, and 33 percent helped an organization associated with environmental causes one to five times.

Almost 50 percent felt people in their neighborhood were willing to help others, and 33 percent felt that people in their neighborhood could be trusted (35 percent were not sure).

Sweden

Mahoney and Stattin (2000) looked at youth participation in structured (organized) activities versus participation in Swedish youth recreation centers. These centers first appeared in the 1900s in response to concerns over lack of leisure opportunities for youths to spend their free time in the evening and were an alternative to spending time on the streets. Currently, these centers are not well staffed, there is high staff turnover, and the staff does not provide much guidance or structure (Mahoney et al., in progress).

Findings indicated that youth who were regularly involved with the Swedish youth recreation centers are more antisocial and reported more fights, property offenses, substance abuse, and police arrests. The authors advocated that centers not be shut down, but saw them as a unique opportunity for prevention. They believed that youths who participate in high-risk activities have self-selected these environments, and with careful structure, opportunity for skill building, and adult guidance, perhaps youths can be assisted and their energies channeled.

CRITICAL QUESTIONS AND ISSUES FOR THE FUTURE OF YOUTH LEISURE

Our brief snapshot of youth leisure in five countries suggests that worldwide the leisure behavior and experience of youth varies, although many similarities exist. Although many youths are being provided and take advantage of leisure opportunities, in every country there is also an inequitable distribution of resources. Lobo and Olson (2000) make a compelling statement that relates to leisure of youths worldwide:

> There is a certain irony to the image of children at pleasure as presented in contemporary leisure management and planning textbooks, when compared to the reality of the millions of children from throughout the world for whom leisure has no practical meaning. . . . In the underbelly of every society are children who have little opportunity to personally come to understand and appreciate leisure and recreation, for their concerns are immediate and governed by the biological imperatives required to survive. (p. 5)

The four hypotheses generated by the Canadian Policy Research Networks, Inc. and the Canadian Council on Social Development challenge governments and individuals worldwide to consider how leisure opportunity is provided, who is able and chooses to take advantage of the opportunities, what the short-term and long-term personal and societal benefits are of such participation, and what happens when leisure is not possible or is experienced negatively. Ecological systems theory helps to understand variations in how free time is spent and in the quality of the leisure experience at different levels of ecological systems (micro, exo, meso, and macro), as well as the interconnections among various levels of influence that affect opportunity provision, participation, and experience. The following discussion incorporates these challenges and additional theories to raise questions about the future of youth and leisure.

TIME USE, EXPERIENCE, AND HUMAN DEVELOPMENT

The human development hypothesis suggests that leisure can positively influence youth development. Free time use descriptive statistics provide a sense of what types of activities most youths are undertaking. However, knowing the ways youths spend their time does not necessarily provide information about what benefits accrue, to whom, and under what conditions. For example, although sport participation for boys was common across most of the cases, sports cannot be definitively labeled developmentally good or bad, although the assumption of many people is that sport activities are good. We also need to better understand outcomes associated with participation in various activities based on gender, race, sexual orientation, disability, and so on. Outcomes accrue differentially, but much more research is needed to address this issue. Therefore, important questions to pursue are the following: What types of activities, under what conditions, are associated with developmental benefits? What extent of participation—how long and at what intensity level—is optimal? For example, does volunteering once a week, one hour per week, for twelve weeks with an environmental group suffice? Do optimal levels differ by age, gender, and life circumstance? Why do many youths choose to watch TV or play computer games rather than do something physically or mentally active? Answers to these questions would begin to offer strong empirical support for the concerns reflected in the insufficiency hypothesis, which points out that despite adequate resources, many youths do not participate in activities, even when opportunity exists. Western research on youths from developed nations suggests that long-term participation, which includes increasing challenges to one's skill level, is critical for a youth to reach his or her full developmental potential in the activity (Bronfenbrenner and Morris, 1998; Larson, 2000). However, more detailed specification and more information on these factors are needed.

Both structured and unstructured activities are important. Although much discussion occurs in Western literature about the value of structured leisure over unstructured leisure, it is not clear for whom and under what circumstances structure or lack of it produces good outcomes. Informal family leisure, singing, dancing, and games are very important developmental contexts for some youths, in particular for those who do not have access to other community opportunities. Whether music and dancing serve as the basis for important social interactions, cognitive skills, and physical activity or are diversions from boredom for youths are important issues that underlie the developmental relevancy of leisure.

As discussed, time use is only one part of the picture—*what one experiences during free time is as important as what one does.* The evidence of boredom in leisure across cultures suggests that a deeper examination is needed of both informal and formal contexts. The research in Sweden by Mahoney, Koutakis, and Stattin (in progress) suggests that opportunities for structured and unstructured leisure need to better meet the needs and interests of youths. It is also important to understand how personal needs and characteristics, structure, activity, and experience intersect to produce optimal experiences for youths.

CIVIC AND SOCIETAL BENEFITS

The civic competence hypothesis suggests that one important developmental outcome associated with leisure, particularly structured contexts, is building the capacity of youths to take future leadership roles, enhancing civic and community development and fostering social cohesion. The level of engagement in volunteering and use of leisure to build skills found in the Chile case demonstrates that some societies support this sense of community. Also, there is some evidence of youths in newly democratic or developing countries participating in pro-social activities. Unfortunately, most surveys or statistics largely ignore the civic engagement facet of leisure time use, suggesting that research and attention should be given to this topic. Although research documents the positive pro-social outcomes associated with extracurricular activities (e.g., Eccles and Barber, 1999), we do not know what it is about these activities that promote pro-social behavior, nor is pro-social behavior well defined. Furthermore, extracurricular activities are available to only a subset of youths—either due to structural barriers (e.g., money and transportation) or societal norms (e.g., blacks in South Africa or girls in Togo should not participate, *even* if the opportunity existed). Structured contexts are important but not equally allocated.

OPPORTUNITIES FOR PARTICIPATION AND PROVISION OF SERVICE

While the insufficiency hypothesis suggests that youths are not taking full advantage of opportunities to engage in constructive leisure pursuits, the inadequacy hypothesis encourages consideration of the amount of public resources devoted to leisure. Ecological systems theory suggests this phenomenon be examined on multiple levels. Perhaps immigrant parents in Australia feel excluded from society and restrict their children's participation in community programs. Or, as illustrated in Chile, perhaps opportunity varies by class and it is the middle- and upper-class families who ensure access to leisure. The fact is, that unless culture, gender, and socioeconomic status privilege a youth, opportunities for developmentally productive leisure are lacking. Neither the United States nor other countries seem to be able to avoid this reality. The question of who should be responsible for youth policy as it relates to leisure, youth service provision, and civic engagement is a rare discussion. In South Africa, for example, government-sponsored recreation services may sporadically exist to serve the needs of the dominant culture. Otherwise, leisure-related services are typically provided by an NGO (nongovernmental organization). Although many of these agencies are excellent, are well staffed with professionals, and are long-lived, the opposite is true as well.

It is also important to better understand how people with limited economic and social resources view leisure. In the Togolese village of Tomegbe, as well as in the geographic area surrounding Cape Town, South Africa, leisure is not a valued part of life for many. Unemployment rates and opportunities for meaningful jobs impact youth leisure in many ways. Many parents place greater value on their child's support on the farm and getting a good education than on his or her creative play. Furthermore, long-established societal norms and cultural beliefs may constrain parents and society from promoting engagement of youths in meaningful leisure activities. As illustrated in the comments of the youth chiefs interviewed in Togo, although they felt that activities afforded important experiences such as fostering creativity and problem solving among youth, societal norms were such that such engagement was not actively promoted.

CONCLUSION

In conclusion, leisure is a basic human right. If society believes in the first hypothesis, that leisure makes an important contribution to healthy development, then the study and support of culturally appropriate mechanisms for leisure that allows every child access to personally meaningful leisure is essential. Ecological systems theory states that change at one level alone will not likely be effective. Youths need to be guided and educated to fully experience leisure and its benefits. Families, communities, governments, and NGOs must all contribute to the provision of opportunities for constructive and meaningful leisure. Most important, opportunity for positive experience must be equitably allocated.

REFERENCES

Adubra, E., Adubra, L., Caldwell, L., Perkins, D., and Smith, E. (2002). Youth capacity building in rural Togo: A community analysis. Research in progress funded by the Children, Youth, and Family Consortium, The Pennsylvania State University, University Park, PA.

Bronfenbrenner, U. (1979). *The ecology of human development.* Cambridge, MA: Harvard University Press.

Bronfenbrenner, U. and Morris, P. A. (1998). The ecology of developmental processes. In *Handbook of child psychology, Volume 1: Theoretical models of human development,* Ed. R. M. Lerner. New York: Wiley, pp. 993-1028.

Budlender, D., Chobokonane, N., and Mpetsheni, Y. (2001). A survey of time use: How South African women and men spend their time. Pretoria, South Africa: Statistics South Africa. Available at <http://www.statssa.gov.za>.

Canadian Policy Research Networks, Inc. and Canadian Council on Social Development (2001). Four hypotheses about the public policy significance of youth recreation: Lessons from a literature review and a data analysis on "Learning through Recreation." Ottawa, Canada: Family Network of Canadian Policy Research Networks.

Eccles, J. S. and Barber, B. L. (1999). Student council, volunteering, basketball, or marching band: Which kind of extracurricular involvement matters? *Journal of Adolescent Research,* 14, 10-43.

Jones, D. (1992). Book review of "No space of their own: Young people and social control in Australia" by Rob White. *The British Journal of Criminology,* 32(3), 393.

Larson, R. (2000). Toward a psychology of positive youth development. *American Psychologist,* 55, 170-183.

Larson, R. and Verma, S. (1999). How children and adolescents spend time across the world: Work, play, and developmental opportunities. *Psychological Bulletin,* 125(6), 701-736.

Lobo, F. and Olson, E. (2000). Leisure services and children at risk: Against all odds. *Journal of Park and Recreation Administration,* 18(1), 5-18.

Mahoney, J. L. and Stattin, H. (2000). Leisure activities and adolescent antisocial behavior: The role of structure and social context. *Journal of Adolescence,* 23, 113-127.

Martinez, L., Cumsille, P., Caldwell, L., Perkins, D., Smith, E., and Flanagan, C. (in progress). The youth that care framework. Research in progress, funded by the Children, Youth, and Family Consortium, The Pennsylvania State University, University Park, PA.

Møller, V. (1991). Lost generation found: Black youth at leisure. Durban, South Africa: Youth Centre Project. South Africa.

Patterson, I., Pegg, S., and Dobson-Patterson, R. (2000). Exploring the links between leisure boredom and alcohol use among youth in rural and urban areas of Australia. *Journal of Park and Recreation Administration,* 18(3), 53-76.

Wegner, L. (1998). The relationship between leisure boredom and substance abuse amongst high school students in Cape Town. Unpublished master's thesis, University of Cape Town, South Africa.

Chapter 3

A Leisure Lifestyle Study of Generation X in New Zealand

Sarah Todd
Rob Lawson
Juergen Gnoth

INTRODUCTION

The present study describes the leisure behavior of a distinct age group of eighteen- to twenty-five-year-olds that emerged in a consumer lifestyle study conducted in New Zealand in 2000 (Todd, Lawson, and Jamieson, 2001). It is a replication of a study conducted in 1995 (Todd, Lawson, and Faris, 1998) which, after clustering the data on a number of psychographic and personality variables, describes seven distinct market segments. In replicating this study in 2000, a distinct group of consumers emerged which is significantly characterized by the high proportion of eighteen- to twenty-five-year-olds associated with it, namely, the "young pleasure seekers."

In the literature, a debate exists as to whether cross-sectional studies of leisure behavior are as meaningful when compared to analyses of overall patterns or orientations toward activities (Raymore, Barber, and Eccles, 1999). Although there may be many reasons for why one chooses one or the other technique, both deal, essentially, with techniques of stratification. Which one is chosen largely depends on the actual goal of the study. In any case, however, similar to Lawson (1988) who refers to the family life cycle as a means of stratifying the consumer market, it can be argued that the concentration on an age cohort will never be able to totally extricate itself of other contemporary influences. Indeed, there are "trends working over time such as changes in general social norms, national income levels or technology" (Lawson, 1988, p. 29) that one needs to consider when attempting to describe and explain one's findings. Thus, when describing this distinct group of New Zealand consumers, a psychographic picture and profile of consumption behavior of a cohort emerges that was not significant in the previous study. However, it can be understood and described within the context of the changing economic, technological, and social environment that exists in New Zealand.

The concept of lifestyles, psychographics, and AIOs (attitudes, interests, and opinions) are often used interchangeably as measures or techniques (Todd, Lawson, and Faris, 1998). In effect, they are operational measures that supersede views expressed in demographic, behavioral, or socioeconomic measures when describing consumer behavior. The change came about through the increasing diversification of consumption behavior that could not be (exclusively) linked to demographic variables or the concept of class (Weber, 1948). In the present study, the use of psychographics as backgrounders helps to enrich our understanding of the particular ideological atmosphere in which this cohort's leisure consumption takes place.

BACKGROUND

New Zealand is essentially comprised of two major islands, home to some 3.8 million people, and is situated in the southwest Pacific. As a former British colony, it has an emerging, unique character that sets it apart from its old motherland but puts it closer to its old rival and neighbor, Australia, some three hours away by plane. The country is also developing considerable pride in its multicultural heritage which, apart from the original immigrants, the Maori, now also comprises other Pacific Islanders as well as Asians in addition to the predominant European settlers.

New Zealand's economy is traditionally commodity based, and the farming industry is still the major foreign exchange earner. However, since 1985, the country forcefully changed its dependency on agriculture and tried to diversify as well as add value to traditional produce through processing lamb, beef, milk, and timber. Tourism, boatbuilding, software, and other technology-based industries are also emerging as valuable employers and exporters. After a painful number of years that brought social change to a country which prided itself as an egalitarian society, the country is slowly emerging from a long period of economic hardship.

In reporting on the 1995 lifestyles study, we noted that the early 1990s had seen a continuation of many new technological developments which were fundamentally changing the values, lifestyles, and consumption behavior of many New Zealanders. That trend continued into the second half of the decade, although arguably fewer innovations had the same widespread impact on our daily lives as did the VCR and microwave in the 1980s. Perhaps the most profound changes in technology relate to communications. The Internet and cellular phones in particular have revolutionized the freedom and price of communications, including the way we are able to complete all aspects of purchasing, from information searches to actual payments and transfer of money. Internationally, New Zealanders have been at the forefront in the adoption of these technologies, even though our location and small population has made the provision of some infrastructure such as broadband facilities slow to appear. Other new technologies that have come into our homes in the past few years, such as home entertainment systems and flat-screen televisions, are essentially improvements and replacements for previous items as opposed to new items fundamentally affecting the way we behave as consumers.

Furthermore, since the early 1990s, "loyalty schemes" made strong inroads to New Zealand in order to capture increasing numbers of consumers who have grown to be more fickle and less consistent in their product choices. Fast-food outlets, both national and international, have mushroomed, as has the use of prepared meals and meals consumed in restaurants. The late 1980s and early 1990s saw, in general, a radical opening of consumer markets through the abolishment of import taxes across all products, turning New Zealand into a truly open market and exposing its economy to global competition. The rapid change from what appeared to be a rather content and sports-oriented culture toward a technology and consumer product-oriented culture very much characterized the segments found in the 1995 study of New Zealand lifestyles. Seven major lifestyle segments were identified:

1. *Success-driven extroverts* (16.4 percent) were characterized as ambitious and self-oriented, in favor of many of the changes that

had been made at a political level. They valued free enterprise and sought an exciting, urban lifestyle.

2. *Educated liberals* (9.7 percent) had similar levels of high education and income to the success-driven extroverts and also enjoyed variety and diversity in their lives. However, they were notable for their social concern. Progressive and egalitarian, this group was less happy with many of the changes occurring in New Zealand society.
3. *Active "family values" people* (15.5 percent), as the name suggests, had a strong family and community focus. Generally positive about the New Zealand of the early 1990s, they appeared to hold relatively traditional principles.
4. *Pragmatic strugglers* (14.7 percent) were a new group to emerge in the 1995-1996 study and reflected the changes in government policy (with increased "user pays," a policy move toward users of services, such as health care, increasingly paying more of the charge, rather than it being levied across all taxpayers as a general rate) as well as trends toward more single-parent families. The survival of those families was their prime focus, with determination and conservative political attitudes characterizing those in this group.
5. *Social strivers* (13.0 percent) were a conformist group, very outwardly directed in both their attitudes and consumption behavior. Not well resourced, they felt life was a struggle and that they were getting a raw deal.
6. *Accepting midlifers* (17.1 percent), a new group and the largest identified in 1995-1996, were both the least opinionated and the least active of all segments identified. They appeared relatively content with their life and accepting of the status quo. Preferring to observe life, rather than partaking, sums up this group.
7. *Conservative quiet lifers* (13.5 percent) are the oldest segment, often retired or widowed with conservative views. They are homebodies, reflective, and often nostalgic.

METHODOLOGY

The methodology of the 2000 lifestyle study was strongly influenced by the 1995 findings. Particularly the materialistic tendencies in consumption behavior convinced the authors that this arising characteristic needed to be considered and, in addition to a number of tested scales regarding shopping and consumption attitudes, we also included Richins's (1987) materialism scale. Apart from replicating the original scales we also added scales which reflected the changing behavioral, political, and social trends that had occurred over recent years, especially as a new cohort, Generation X, made its impact felt.

Each question from the previous survey was individually examined and its ability to accurately differentiate across segments was evaluated. Those questions that failed this test were discarded. The new questionnaire was pretested prior to its final distribution and, in total, 514 individual questions were deemed applicable:

- Sixty-two attitudinal questions relating to social and political issues
- Fifty-nine questions regarding personality and family attitudes
- 108 questions relating to shopping and consumption attitudes, including consumer sentiments, materialism, compulsive buying, frugality, and opinion leadership scales among others
- Forty-two questions comprising Schwartz's (1992) revised value instrument
- 130 questions about behavior, including media, holidays, activities, and eating habits
- Ninety-seven questions regarding ownership of products, including motor vehicles, finance, cooking appliances, and other household items
- Sixteen demographic questions

The study then involved a nationwide postal survey of 10,000 New Zealanders, aged eighteen and over. The addresses were obtained from the New Zealand Post household postal address directory. The questionnaire was administered during October and November 2000. Of these 10,000 survey forms, 9,778 reached the individuals involved and 3,710 were returned, equating to a 38 percent response rate.

Comparing the sample to the 1996 New Zealand census statistics on age, ethnicity, marital status, employment situation, and house ownership resulted in the detection of some underrepresentation of those aged sixty-five years and older as well as a slight overrepresentation of people renting. Although adjustments were made for these and other minor differences, they need not concern us here, as we are focusing on the young pleasure seekers only.

For the clustering procedure we used K-means on SPSS (version 10) for Windows, especially developed for clustering large numbers of cases. As the purpose of the groupings was primarily to differentiate on the basis of motives and opinions, attitudinal and personality questions (excluding Schwartz's value questions) were used as input variables. A number of cluster solutions were considered to arrive at the optimal solution. Seven was deemed to be the best fit in terms of clear differentiation across all groups, which was tested for by comparing the mean scores of all input variables through analyses of variance as well as cross-tabulation on nominal-type variables. It also aided the consistency of comparison with the previous data.

RESULTS

Before focusing on the targeted cohort of this study, it may be of interest to summarize the findings of the 2000 survey and introduce the segments found in order to generate a larger frame of reference. Overall, New Zealanders appear less positive about life in New Zealand than they did in the 1995-1996 study. There is more agreement with the suggestions that one needs to go overseas to get ahead, that most of what is good is borrowed from overseas, and that life abroad is more interesting. In a similar vein, New Zealanders appear more open to foreign input, with fewer indications that too many foreigners are living in New Zealand; the suggestion that we need a larger population is more likely to be agreed with. With regard to political policy, there is an indication that more should be spent on the police and defense, as opposed to more spending in the areas such as health and education.

Big business also seems to be perceived in a more positive light, with less agreement with the suggestion that government has allowed business to make more profit, and more agreement that little corruption exists in New Zealand business. In line with this pro-business sentiment, environmental groups are also seen as causing too many delays to development.

In line with the more negative view being taken of New Zealand as a place to live, there is also increased dissatisfaction expressed with life at an individual level. The traditional Kiwi attitude toward doing it yourself appears to have declined in popularity (despite the number of TV programs currently devoted to such activities), as does the appeal of natural living and striving for better things. Overall, individuals are more likely to agree with the suggestion that they get a raw deal compared with others, to see their work as less interesting, and to describe themselves as less outgoing than previously.

Reinforcing the findings of 1995-1996, New Zealand families indicate that they spend less time together and describe themselves as not being as close as they were. This may well be a reflection of increasing numbers of divorces in New Zealand, with indications also that marriage is outdated in its current form. The trend away from eating meals together has strengthened, and people spend less time at home in general. These trends do not appear to necessarily be welcomed, however, with increased importance attributed to children's position in parents' lives.

Time away from children and family appears to be imposed rather than what is desired, with more people indicating they would rather spend an evening at home. In line with this sentiment, as well as possibly being a reaction to the number of mothers now in the paid workforce, there is increased agreement with the suggestion that working women do not spend enough time with their children. Nor does all this increased pressure appear to be for financial gain, with greater numbers i licating that their family is not as well off financially as last year.

Regarding consumption issues and possibly due to increased expectations because of technological developments, product quality is not seen to have consistently improved over the years, and although prices are acknowledged as reasonable, there is also less satisfaction overall with prices paid. Service quality, an area often considered to be a negative part of the New Zealand shopping experience, does appear to have improved, with increased numbers agreeing that they can usually receive assistance in stores when they require it. Eating is an important part of our culture and our social lifestyles, and New Zealanders appear to be consuming more exotic foods, no doubt partly a reflection of increased ties with Asia.

Several of the 1995 groups are still clearly recognizable in the seven segments to result from the 2000-2001 survey. However, perhaps not surprisingly, the demographic characteristics of some groups have changed, as the population ages. This is particularly the case for the educated liberals, who are very much a value-driven group; while clearly holding the same principles, they appear older than the same group in 1995-1996. The older group identified in the first study (conservative quiet lifers) appears now to have split into two, one being better resourced than the other. Nor is it surprising to see the emergence of a new group, namely the young pleasure seekers, reflecting many of the characteristics of the much talked about Generation X. The active "family values" people have not emerged as a separate group this time, but some of their identifying characteristics are evident in other groups. In particular, older members appear to have moved into the new traditional values segment, and some family groups who have fallen on harder times financially and socially may be in the slightly changed social strivers group.

The success-driven extroverts, then, are still very much in evidence, and there appears to be little difference from the group described in 1995-1996. There is a slight reduction in the size of this segment though (now 13.2 percent), which is a reversal in the trend seen from 1989 to 1995-1996.

As noted, the educated liberals (10.3 percent) also appear to be very much the same group as previously identified, although now slightly older than before (most between thirty and forty-nine years of age) and also with a wider range of marital status evident.

The pragmatic strugglers (11.8 percent) are still present. A notable change in this group is the presence of more older members. They also appear more inclined to indicate they are getting a raw deal and slightly less inclined to believe that they are going to get out of their present financial and social position.

Traditional values (18.8 percent) is one of two older groups identified in this current study. As mentioned, they undoubtedly comprise some of the former active "family values" people grouping and share many attitudes with the success-driven extroverts, although they are more traditional in some of the opinions expressed. The better-resourced members of the former conservative quiet lifers are also thought to have moved into this group.

The accepting midlifers (19.4 percent) are still the largest segment and share many identifiable characteristics with the previous group of the same name. However, demographically there is a change, with more older, retired households evident.

Social strivers (13.1 percent) are still evident, and it is possible that some of the less well-off active "family values" people have moved into this group. Overall, they still demonstrate the same conflict between what they want and what they can attain, as well as a conflict between attitudes and actual behavior. However, the opinion that they are getting a raw deal and are struggling is not so strongly expressed as it was in 1995-1996. It is possible that those less well-off members of this group in the first study have moved into the pragmatic strugglers segment this time.

The young pleasure seekers (13.5 percent) are a different group from any previously identified, but their emergence is in line with social trends evident worldwide. They are young and primarily living for today, with few opinions on social and political issues and an emphasis on hedonic consumption.

In conclusion then, the seven groups identified in this recent study reflect trends such as an aging population and the growth of a young market that is strongly consumption oriented. The identification of two older groups indicates that it is no longer enough to treat the "gray" market as one, but rather that recognition should be made of the differing resources older people have at their disposal, as well as their heterogeneous opinions and behaviors. "Middle" New Zealand appears to have further diminished, with differences increasingly evident between those who have the wherewithal to cope in modern society and those who do not.

The young pleasure seekers turn out to be a group that is closely associated with, or even represents, the New Zealand version of Generation X. They express few opinions regarding social issues and exhibit high levels of materialism and consumption. They indicate that they would be happier if they could afford more, expressing relative agreement that money can buy happiness. They are less likely to describe themselves as cautious shoppers, agreeing that they are not disciplined about money and have trouble delaying or resisting purchases.

Members of this group are more likely to have bought something to make themselves feel better, spend any money left at the end of the pay period, make only minimum credit card payments, and have written checks knowing there was not enough money to cover them. They agree that others would be horrified if they knew of their shopping habits and also indicate that they have thrown away products that are still useful, with little agreement that they reuse items.

In part due to their age, family does not figure highly in this group's life, with an indication that they do little as a family in general and are less likely to eat as a family. In line with this last comment, nibbling has taken over from set meal times, there is little planning of the evening meal, and many prepared meals are consumed. Health does not figure highly. Foods are chosen for taste rather than nutritional value.

Financially, this group is more likely to have rent-to-own purchases, borrowers'/credit card insurance, loan/overdraft, and retail charge cards. Print media consumed is varied. They watch TV frequently, and radio music consumption is high. They own more than one TV, and they use computers, play electronic games, and e-mail more than other groups. They are unlikely to use public transport to go to work or study, but rather to walk to save time because they usually live close. They are either single or living with a partner, often in apartments with some three other income earners, and they work full-time in clerical or skilled positions or study.

Activities they participate in include computer games, e-mail, text messaging, and buying products off the Internet. They are more likely to have been to sports events, played rugby/soccer/hockey, and gone tramping/camping. In part because they are the least likely group surveyed to own a house, they are also the least likely to have worked in the garden or vegetable garden which, traditionally, is considered a major pastime in New Zealand. They are far less likely to attend church or religious activities or to go to club meetings, but are slightly more likely than average to attend locally held art events. They are average purchasers of lottery tickets and bet on horses and sports events slightly more than average, but are less likely to do arts or crafts or knitting.

The young pleasure seeker buys an average amount of books as compared to other segments, but reads fewer fiction books and far more magazines. They are slightly more likely to have written a letter to a friend or relative recently and far more likely to have e-mailed or text-messaged them. They are slightly more likely to have played a musical instrument recently and the most likely to have listened to pop/rock music, but are far less likely to have listened to classical, country, or folk music. They are also slightly less likely to have gone fishing or boating, gone jogging or to aerobic classes, or to kept fit/lost weight than average. They are less likely to play golf and far less likely to play lawn bowls than average, but tend to go to movies, theaters, and ballets more often. They are less likely than average to recycle glass, plastic, cardboard, or aluminium cans.

This segment clearly enjoys shopping the most of all segments, while trying to earn loyalty points and shopping for specials more. They like brands and personal attention in shops and try to be innovative when introducing new brands and products to their friends. Distinctly more than average (but less than social strivers), they like to share information about products with friends.

DISCUSSION

The profile of the young pleasure seekers shows a distinct attitude toward leisure activities of all types. We also include here purchasing, consuming, and talking about products. Although they are similar to their compatriots in loving team sports, both actively and as passive observers, their strong level of materialism, frequent shopping, and brand consciousness permeates their leisure orientation.

Overall, this group has just left its nest and is in the transitional phase of settling down into an instrumental activity such as study or work (Greene, Wheatley, and Aldava, 1992). The adolescent/young adult phase is a strong feature of this group, and, at that age, they enjoy a relative freedom from more enduring obligations and responsibilities. There is a certain playfulness with which they consume products and services, how they spend money without apparent thoughts for tomorrow, satisfy cravings for variation; and ask for instant gratification. It causes the phase of "experimentation with the adult role" (Iso-Ahola, 1980) to appear materialistic and dependent on technology. This group has neither strong political views nor any historic and defining life experiences similar to those held by the baby boomers.

The young pleasure seekers turn out to be a group that is closely associated with or even represents the New Zealand version of Generation X. Although not identical to their U.S. counterparts, their features indicate "arguably the first fully postmodern cohort . . . and they are the product of their culture and of their place in history" (Sacks, 1996, p. 110). Their consumption is conditioned by watching television ("tele-conditioned") (Kottack, 1995), and they are seemingly consuming products as ends in themselves, for which they often find nothing but criticism (Wilson, 1998).

When trying to address the notion and need for sustainable consumption, a United Nations Environment Program/United Nations Scientific and Cultural Organization (UNEP/UNESCO) report (2000) states that "young people [the exact age group addressed here] do understand the importance of the issue but are not necessarily aware of the effects of their own purchases on the environment and their consciousness does not necessarily lead to action" (2000, part II). Although the present lifestyle study of the youth cohort aged eighteen to twenty-five signals a kind of leisure pursuit that is group oriented, technology related, brand distinct, instantly gratifying, and materialistic, the more general observations that point toward well-educated and environmentally conscious (though not active) future adults allows one hope that the general orientation will be, socially and arguably economically, a productive one.

REFERENCES

Greene, A.L., Wheatley, S.M., and Aldava, J.F. (1992). Stages on life's way: Adolescents' implicit theories of the life course. *Journal of Adolescence Research,* 7(3):364-381.

Iso-Ahola, S.E. (1980). *The social psychology of leisure and recreation.* Dubuque, IA: Wm. C. Brown Company.

Kottack, C.P. (1995). Television and cultural behavior. In Petracca, M.F. and Sorapure, M. (Eds.), *Common culture: Reading and writing about American popular culture* (pp. 155-164). Englewood Cliffs, NJ: Prentice Hall.

Lawson, R.W. (1988). The family life cycle: A demographic analysis. *Journal of Marketing Management,* 4(1):13-32.

Raymore, L.A., Barber B.L., and Eccles, J.S. (1999). Leisure behavior pattern stability during the transition from adolescence to young adulthood. *Journal of Youth and Adolescence,* 28(1):79-103.

Richins, M.L. (1987). Media, materialism, and human happiness. *Advances in Consumer Research,* 14:352-356.

Sacks, P. (1996). *Generation X goes to college: An eye-opening account of teaching in postmodern America.* Chicago: Open Court.

Schwartz, S.H. (1992). Universals in the context and structure of values: Theoretical advances and empirical tests in 20 countries. *Advances in Experimental Social Psychology,* 25:1-65.

Todd, S., Lawson, R., and Faris, F. (1998). A lifestyle analysis of New Zealand consumers. *Asia-Pacific Journal of Marketing and Logistics,* 10(3):30-47.

Todd, S.J., Lawson, R.W., and Jamieson, T. (2001). *New Zealand beyond 2000.* Dunedin: Consumer Research Group, University of Otago.

United Nations Environment Program/United Nations Scientific and Cultural Organization (2000). Expert Workshop on Youth, Sustainable Consumption and Life Styles, UNESCO Headquarters, Paris, November 6-7.

Weber, M. (1948). Class, status, party. In Gerth, H. and Mills, C.W. (Eds.), *From Max Weber* (pp. 180-195). London: Routledge.

Wilson, J.L. (1998). Generation X: Who are they? What do they want? *NEA Higher Education Journal,* 9(Fall):9-18.

SECTION II: THE GLOBALIZATION OF LEISURE OR REDISCOVERING SLOWNESS?

The trends of growing globalization and specialization are considered to be not only the driving forces behind economic growth, but also the reason for the ever-increasing acceleration of society. Speed, however, also has negative effects on both private and professional life, such as increased violence, disparities in income, and health problems. Over the past few years "slowness" has thus developed as a new trend to counteract globalization: The Slow Food movement opposes international fast-food chains, Slow Cities become an antipode to the dazzling metropolis. New working-time models emerge as an expression of the growing importance of flexible time use and the value of leisure time.

Gabriele Morello discusses in his contribution the spatiotemporal perspective of consumer and managerial behavior. In light of shrinking space and scarce time due to globalization, leisure producers and consumers perceive and shape time to fulfill their personal goals. Tight schedules during working hours and the pressure to fill free time with as many activities as possible put major constraints on the autonomy of individuals. Karlheinz Woehler presents the rediscovery of slowness during vacations as a solution for the lost ability of humans to organize their own free time. Rafael Matos describes the potential of so-called slow tourism in Alpine regions as a niche product. Slow tourism around antiquated pleasures, such as walking and flower-viewing excursions, is introduced as an antipode to fast and stressful (mass-) tourism products. Finally, John R. Kelly's investigation of the interrelation of leisure investment, supply, and demand in a global context rounds off Section II.

Chapter 4

Spacing and Timing in Leisure Activities

Gabriele Morello

SCENARIO

One generic scenario for the coming years is largely accepted. Technological progress, information and communication technologies, higher levels of education, managerial know-how, increasing exchange of goods and services, innovation, and organizational change will continue to be the driving forces of economic growth and social development. On the negative side, conflicts, violence, inequalities, poverty, and ecological injuries will continue to plague vast areas of the world. Hopefully, such aspects will gradually be brought under control in the process of modernization.

Fewer people will be engaged not only in manual and physically demanding work but also in office jobs. In Europe, the working time of employees already accounts for less than 10 percent of their lifetime. Intellectual, flexible, and creative work will grow. Unemployment will remain more or less constant, and the labor market will increasingly consist of temporary and unstable positions, abrupt job moves, and more home-based work.

Production and consumption of goods and services related to the leisure sector, which already account for about 20 to 25 percent of the world gross product, will continue to rise both in absolute and relative terms. Leisure time and *loisir* will constitute a bigger portion of the time budget of people of all ages.

Physical motion, virtual communication, and the electronic "e"-world are the factors behind the demise of distance, time compression, and multitasking. Mobility will increase: "The modern subject is a subject on the move" (Urry, 1995, p. 141). People will also become mentally more dynamic, moving from a sense of locality to a sense of globality. In a postmodern vision, space appears to shrink and time horizons tend toward an "eternal present" (Virilio, 1994).

Work and leisure will be increasingly interconnected. In the most advanced societies, the traditional distinction between working time and free time has already become blurred, being enriched by a multitude of interests and occupations. Ideally, the new lifestyles will be characterized by increasing autodetermination, a decline in predetermined packages of work and free time, and a gradual overcoming of the distinction between spectators and actors of free time.

THE STUDY OF LEISURE ACTIVITIES

Whatever the rhythms and the details of this scenario, the growing importance of leisure time can be taken for granted. It is therefore important to deepen our knowledge of the behavioral traits of leisure activities, with special reference to travel and tourism as relevant components of new ways of life.

In recent years, leisure activities have been observed and analyzed from many angles. In the study of consumer behavior related to vacations, for instance, learning objectives, travel motivation, destination choices, and user and nonuser models have been considered from different viewpoints. The image of different destinations, decision processes, pre- and postpurchase reactions, package tourism, and customer loyalties, perceptions, and expectations have been scrutinized, through both qualitative and quantitative research. The supply side is also being examined. Which kind of entrepreneurs—both private and public—are most interested in investing in the leisure industry, and why? What managerial tasks are involved? What organizational measures, professional talents, and training are required for the successful implementation of the projects?

All types of tourism are studied. From trekking and climbing in the Austrian Alps to Caribbean cruising, from archaeological tours in Egypt to camping in New Zealand, the various subsectors of leisure activities (cultural tourism, senior tourism, congress tourism, health tourism, etc.), as well as all travel-related patterns and profiles, are currently under scrutiny at both national and international levels. A recent publication edited by Pechlaner and Weiermair (2000) is a collection of articles on the subject, linked to marketing strategies.

What seems to have received less attention until recently, and hence can be considered innovative in the panorama of studies on the subject, is a spatiotemporal perspective of consumer and managerial behavior. This perspective refers to the way that different actors in the leisure industry—producers, distributors, and consumers—perceive and mold space and time in pursuit of the fulfillment of their goals. Given the relevance of attitudes toward space and time in different cultures, this chapter will present the issue and some cases related to it, originating from studies conducted in various countries.

SPACE AND TIME

In order to explore the underlying factors that shape leisure futures, a spatiotemporal approach must start with a discussion on the fundamentals of the subject. Leaving aside philosophical debates on metaphysical issues and keeping in mind that according to modern science space and time are somehow linked in an indivisible unity, both realities can be discussed on the basis of at least two meanings which we shall call Space 1 and Space 2, and Time 1 and Time 2.

Space 1 refers to the unlimited n-dimensional extension, in which all material objects are located. It comprises the simultaneity of all tangible and virtual places, within and outside our own globe. The ancient Greeks had a specific term for this abstract dimension of space: *chôros*. Similar to the concept of infinity, from the standpoint of geometry it has been defined as an entity where the surface is everywhere and the center nowhere. With reference to our planet, this type of space has already been almost entirely conquered. In the words of a French social researcher:

> Planet Earth almost no longer offers any Terra Incognita. Space, as seen by the individual today, has become unified, globalized space, although there are pockets of smaller spaces where expansion and contraction take place according to ethnicity. This space is imposed on him. In fact, with today's progress in means of transportation and information technologies, this space is increasingly difficult to escape. Mastery of space induces an excess of space and leads to its temporalization. (Daucé, 2001, p. 234)

On the basis of this kind of thinking, it has already been anticipated that people would consider time rather than geography as the next frontier, indicating that life would extend from day into night, with all the consequences that this might produce in urban structures and organizational aspects of work and leisure. Even if this forecast has not fully materialized, the tendency toward multifunctional places where different groups and different motions mingle seems valid. Changes in the spatial scale of mobility, temporalization of space, and *rasender Stillstand* (applied to those travelers who fly from one place to another without even indulging in physical exercise) are all new aspects of Space 1 modernity.

Space 2 has a more concrete connotation. It refers to the human sensation of objects, perspectives, and horizons linked to meaningful places and contextual localization. To distinguish this meaning of space from *chôros,* the Greeks called it *topos* (from which we get topic, topography, topology, etc.). Innsbruck—like Paris, London, etc.—is a *topos*. A specific monument, an ethnic restaurant, a private residence are all *topoi.* As Moles and Rohmer (1978) put it, the building of a place, or a "here-point," consists of isolating a point in space with walls that are not simply brick walls but can be made of any element, physical or not, capable of creating an identity. Architects and designers, as well as marketing and communication experts, are at ease in developing identities of this kind. Positioning a product is part of their job. The whole story of the battle for the mind of the consumer is based on the shift from Space 1 to Space 2, a theme that should be of particular interest for developers of the travel and tourism industry.

The ancient Greek language also had two terms for time. *Kronos* conveyed the idea of chronological time, objective time, clock time, i.e., successions in the eternal, ongoing march of time. Whether *kronos* is linear or circular, how the arrow of time proceeds in its endless movement, and whether this movement is absolute or relative are topics concerning this type of time, which intrigued Heraclitus and Plato, Aristotle and Saint Augustine, Newton and Einstein, to name only a few. Authoritative scholars have suggested the term "chronosophy" for the study of this kind of time (Fraser, 1981). More simply, we call it Time 1.

Kairos, on the other hand, meant a specific time, the time of a given opportunity, of the propitious moment. This we call Time 2, to indicate subjective time, mental time, personal time. It implies the ways and means by which men and women of all ages perceive and use time. This varies throughout time itself, in events as well as in the meanings of words ("now" on the stock exchange is today, in fashion it is a season, in demographics it is a decade . . .). Time 2 is social time. It is social because humans, who by definition live an in-time existence, always use time to control, regulate, order, and synchronize their social life, which they structure and measure. In terms of cognitive processes, time presupposes a view of time which is always formulated both individually and collectively (Adam, 1986). In the words of Kant: *"Du selber machst die Zeit, das Uhrwerk sind die Sinne"* ("You make your own time; the senses are the source").

It is mostly to Space 2 and Time 2 that we refer to in our own research. However, in dealing with spacing and timing, Space 1 and Time 1 may also be involved.

SPACING AND TIMING

In classical thought, space and time—separated or interconnected—are considered as entities per se, independent of human will. According to another approach, space and time can be "constructed" (expanded, compressed, collapsed, etc.) by human beings. The words *spacing* and *timing* are used to indicate the latter approach. It can be applied to numberless situations, evolving within different landscapes and timescapes. The painter's term *landscape* refers to a picture representing a given scenery, as distinct from a portrait or a still life depicting objects. A timescape is made of recognizable time areas, with permeable borders—*private* and public time, past, present and future time, home time and work time, etc.—all of which exist within a geography of space.

In recent years, spacing and timing have been largely associated with and have given rise to a culture of immediacy, quickness, rapid obsolescence, and continuous innovation. Polychronicity (doing several things at the same time) has tended to prevail over monochronicity (doing, sequentially, one thing at a time). Multipresence, supported by information and communication technologies, has increased interaction, interdependence, and contextual mobility. From the standpoint of business, aggressive behavior has moved from an environment in which the big fish eat the small fish to an environment in which the fast eat the slow. The ability to be ahead of and faster than other organizations has usually been considered an advantage in guaranteeing survival and growth in the competitive arena. At an industrial level, the strategy of velocity is founded on sound economic principles, and time value can well be seen as a competitive tool (Brondoni, 2001). Time-based strategies are linked to the possibility of reducing the time of market response through the improvement of company performance with regard to time aspects such as punctuality, respecting delivery times, reengineering, technical innovation, and new product development. Flexibility of production and logistic processes usually spell a reduction in fixed investments, a compression of material handling costs, and an improvement in productivity (Borghini, 2000).

The culture of speed, however, is not valid always and everywhere. Excessive anticipation of customer demand has generated more than one failure, both in the industrial area of tangible goods and in the offering of services. The slow food movement as opposed to fast-food restaurants is a case in point. At a social level, time pressure and excessive mobility ("space overdose") has proved to be harmful and unbalancing for many individuals.

To state that business strategies are linked only to second-order derivatives (acceleration of change) is too simplistic and reductive. Organizations construct time spans and space semantics of their own (Butler, 1995). Space and time are considerably richer dimensions, with many more possibilities for acting than simply concentrating on becoming faster. In complex structures, modern systems theory (MST), which portrays organizations as social systems operating on a dynamic mode of ongoing communicative and coordinated processes, seems to offer more articulated models to cope with the multidimensional facets of changing environments.

> According to MST, social systems are faced with environmental complexity, which implies that they have to be selective and partly ignorant in order to handle that complex environment. In other words, organizations are not able to deal with the environmental "world" as a whole—they therefore have to reduce environmental complexity to a workable level so that their members can act upon it. By doing this, systems inevitably establish a difference (i.e., a boundary) between themselves and the environ-

> ment. As a result, each system itself remains complex, but it is always less complex than its environment. The continuing existence of the system is secured by permanently maintaining or reproducing the system's boundary. (Noss, 2001, p. 4)

If this approach makes sense in general terms, it makes even more sense in the area of leisure activities, which by definition encompasses many types of tourism and recreational pursuits characterized by slowness, relaxation, and tranquil contexts. The maintenance (and creation) of such an atmosphere in many *topos* is a vital side of tourism.

Coming back to the notion of spacing and timing, one should thus think of them as a set of creative possibilities to act not only in one spatiotemporal direction, but along many possible alternatives: here/there, near/far, fast/slow, before/after, compression/expansion, etc. In contemporary studies of social time, this broader view on a more articulate use of space and time seems to follow two streams of analytical interest: (1) the general notion of Space 1 and Time 1, as well as the attitudes people manifest toward different landscapes and timescapes, and (2) the components of Space 2 and Time 2, with the objective of mastering space strategies, such as local versus global, and time strategies, such as time awareness, orientation, anticipation, postponement, rhythm, succession, and synchronization.

EXAMPLES AND CASES

A few cases in which the "broader view" of spacing and timing have been applied in the leisure industry are described in this section. They involve three different areas of spatiotemporal perceptions, namely (1) the use of space and temporal typologies in marketing strategy; (2) the assessment of time perceptions in different cultures; and (3) a "dynamic" presentation of financial data.

Space and Temporal Typologies

Psychographic analysis has proven that people can be divided into different categories, according to their prevalent time orientation. Although past, present, and future always fluctuate and interconnect in the human mind, post-Jungian psychologists have found that some individuals are prevalently oriented toward the past (feeling types), others toward the present (sensation types), others toward the future (intuitive types), while others give equal importance to all three dimensions (thinking types). A strong correlation seems to exist between each of these types and specific behavioral characteristics. Past-oriented or feeling types tend to privilege personal experiences and memories; they are conservative, sociable, easily emotional, and brand loyal. Present-oriented or sensation types spend most of their mental time in current day-to-day reality; they are hedonists, self-assured, and extroverted impulse buyers. Future-oriented or intuitive types are attracted by innovation, risk, and adventure. For thinking types, past, present, and future have equal value; they are characterized by coherence, continuity, and logic, and they tend to order events in a systematic structure.

It is highly likely that these characteristics also influence all personal and social determinants of leisure behavior (holiday choice, desires/needs, expectations, range of travel opportunities, etc.). For instance, feeling types should be destination loyal, hotel loyal, travel agency loyal, etc. Museums, monuments, and historical sites would be their main interests. Sensation types would be moved by "wanderlust" and "sunlust," to use Gray's terms (1970). Intuitive types would tend to seek novelty and adventure, and thinking types may find satisfaction in a rich travel experience and well-organized arrangements.

At an operational level, a space/time-based segmentation has recently been used in promoting Sicilian tourism and Sicilian wine. Sicily, the largest island in the Mediterranean and traditionally advertised for its mild climate, natural beauties, and cultural heritage, annually produces about 10 million hectaliters of wine. Vineyards are scattered throughout the island. In the offer for a special destination package which follows the wine routes of Sicily, a strategic alliance between wine producers and tourism promoters has been implemented, with satisfactory outcome.

Figure 4.1 shows the quantitative results of exploratory research conducted on a sample of 211 subjects, asked to complete a test aimed at unraveling their attitudes toward three concepts: (1) Sicily, (2) Sicilians, and (3) wine from Sicily. Measurements indicate the affective distance between temporal types (past-, present-, future-oriented groups) and the elicited concepts. Scores could have ranged from –3 (very negative feelings) to +3 (very positive feelings).

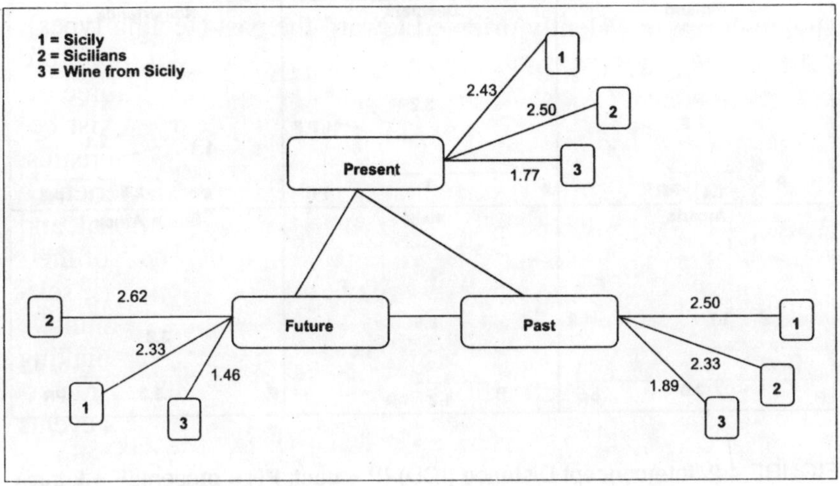

FIGURE 4.1. A Market Segmentation Based on Temporal Typologies

This can be considered a typical case in which Space 1 (undefined Sicilian territory) has been changed into Space 2 (the wine routes) and targeted at groups with different time perceptions. This approach, previously used in designing a marketing strategy for Sicilian wine (Morello, 1993), is currently being employed by the Regional Council for Tourism.

Time Perception in Different Cultures

Cultural differences in attitudes toward time are an accepted fact. These differences apply both to such basic aspects as attitudes toward the past, the present, and the future, and to specific components of attitudes toward space and time, such as the proximity or remoteness of one concept to another that characterizes the perception of different groups. Figure 4.2 reports interconcept distance (ICD) data originating from semantic differential exercises conducted in the 1980s (Morello, 2001).

The triangles show that for South Africans at the time of data collection (one week before Nelson Mandela was released from prison) the future was considered just around the corner. Also in Denmark and Austria, the future was seen as near to the present, while in Italy,

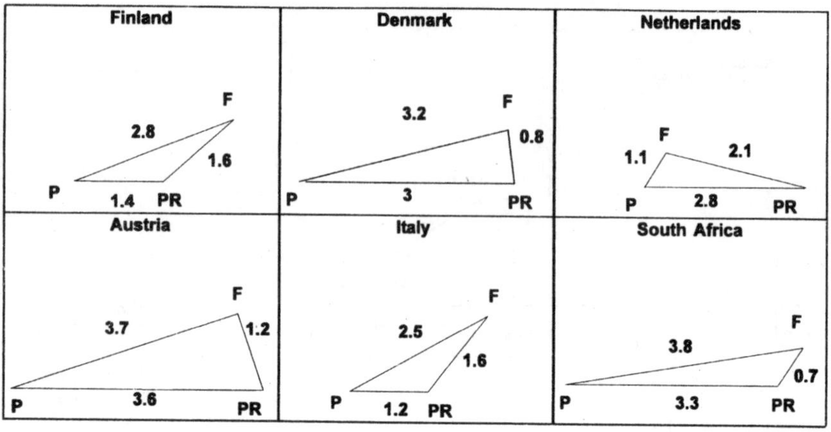

FIGURE 4.2. Interconcept Distance (ICD) (P = past; PR = present; F = future)

Finland, and even more so in the Netherlands, it was perceived as more distant.

Because all the countries at issue have a prominent tourism sector and partake in the scenario described at the beginning of this chapter, information of this kind can be gainfully employed in tourism strategies.

One Italian region actively pursuing a strategy of this kind is Trentino. In 2000, 4.5 million tourists visited the area, spending a total of 28 million days there. A report published by Provincia Autonoma di Trento (2002) sheds light on the strong and weak aspects of local tourism and on the reactions of the population toward tourists.

The results of having just applied the same ICD measurements of time perceptions to a selected group of top managers from Trentino indicate that, although they have a strong affective feeling toward the past, they consider the future to be very near to the present, like the South Africans, the Danish, and the Austrians did a couple of decades ago.

Financial Management

Another application of spacing and timing comes from financial management, an area which plays a critical role in the tourism sector. Specific frameworks of financial information can be devised that measure and monitor business conduct, with the aim of facilitating adaptability and sustainability. One such system, which Snaith and Walker (2001) call a dynamic financial management (DFM) radar chart, aims at capturing past, present, and future information through an all-embracing illustration of business performance.

As shown in Figure 4.3, the simultaneous presentation of dynamic net contribution (DNC) of working capital, dynamic net assets (DNA), and dynamic cash movement (DCM) presents financial management with a composite set of options, which facilitates the decision process and speeds up communication within the organization. Spacing and timing are involved in the construction of the chart, and especially in planning, implementing, and controlling the ensuing business undertakings.

CONCLUSION

The two basic dimensions that characterize the biological experience of all human beings—space and time—are a neglected area in

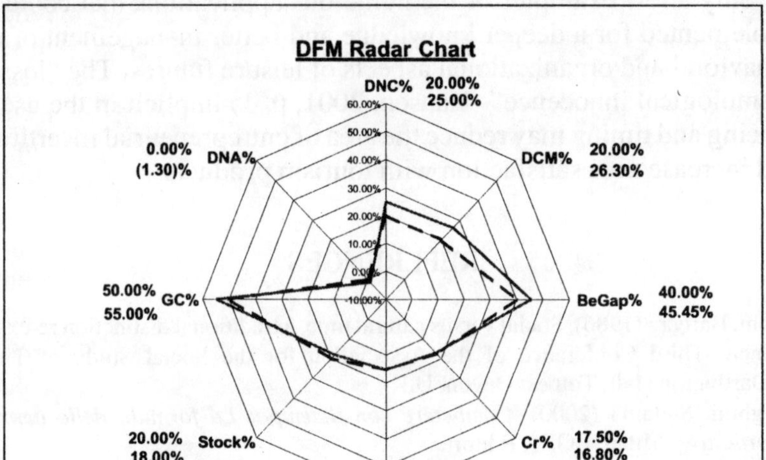

FIGURE 4.3. DFM Radar Chart
Note: DNC = dynamic net contribution; DCM = dynamic cash movement; BeGap = break even gap; Cr = creditor; Dr = debitor; DNA = dynamic net assets

the study of leisure activities, and even more so the dynamic concepts of spacing and timing, a methodological challenge in management and in the social sciences. The application of such concepts to problems encountered in travel and tourism—both on the demand and the supply side—would constitute a valuable contribution to the development of the industry.

This statement becomes even more valid if one examines the cross-cultural side of the topic, given the differences in values, beliefs, and behaviors that distinguish social environments and global scenarios. A recent review of cross-cultural issues in the area of tourism confirms "first, that evidence about cross-national differences does exist; second, that these differences can be observed and recorded; and third, that these observed differences have a significant bearing on the behavior of both consumers and marketing decision makers" (Pizam, 2000, p. 400).

This chapter advocates that innovation in the cross-cultural study of travel and tourism should take place through further study of spacing and timing. The cases illustrated in the last section of this chapter are only a few examples of the numerous applications that could be implemented for a deeper knowledge and better management of the behavioral and organizational aspects of leisure futures. The "loss of cosmological innocence" (Hansen, 2001, p. 1) implicit in the use of spacing and timing may reduce the area of entrepreneurial incertitude and increase user satisfaction with tourism products.

REFERENCES

Adam, Barbara (1986). Social versus natural time, a traditional distinction re-examined. Third Conference of the Association for the Social Study of Time, Dartington Hall, Totnes; Devon, U.K.

Borghini, Stefania (2000). *Competere con il tempo: La formula delle imprese proattive.* Milan: EGEA Editori.

Brondoni, Silvio (2001). Time compression and time value as a competitive strategy. In Caseby, Dawn (Ed.), *Time and management,* ISIDA Study and Research Series number 16 (pp. 343-354). Palermo: Fabio Orlando Editore.

Butler, Richard (1995). Time in organizations: Its experience, explanations and effects. *Organization Studies,* 16(6): 925-950.

Daucé, Bruno (2001). The influence of contraction of time and distance on the way we consider places. In Caseby, Dawn (Ed.), *Time and management,* ISIDA

Study and Research Series number 16 (pp. 233-249). Palermo: Fabio Orlando Editore.

Fraser, Julius Thomas (1981). *The voices of time.* Amherst: University of Massachusetts Press.

Gray, H. Peter (1970). *International travel: International trade.* Lexington, MA: Heath Lexington Books.

Hansen, Niels Viggo (2001). Where does spacing and timing happen? Two movements in the loss of cosmological innocence. International Conference on Spacing and Timing: Rethinking Globalization and Standardization, November 1-3, 2001, Palermo, Italy.

Moles, Abraham and Rohmer, Elizabeth (1978). *Psychologie de l'espace.* Paris: Casterman.

Morello, Gabriele (1993). *Ricerche e strategie di marketing per il vino Siciliano,* ISIDA Study and Research Series number 11. Palermo: Fabio Orlando Editore.

Morello, Gabriele (2001). Time orientation across cultures: A comparative study in Italy, Cuba and Spain. In Caseby, Dawn (Ed.), *Time and management,* ISIDA Study and Research Series number 16 (pp. 81-100). Palermo: Fabio Orlando Editore.

Noss, Christian (2001). Beyond velocity: Competition, inter-organizational timing, and the relevance of organizational time constitution. International Conference on Spacing and Timing: Rethinking Globalization and Standardization, November 1-3, 2001, Palermo, Italy.

Pechlaner, Harald and Weiermair, Klaus (2000). *Destination management: Fondamenti di marketing e gestione delle destinazioni turistiche.* Milan: Touring Editore.

Pizam, Abraham (2000). Cross-cultural tourist behaviour. In Pizam, Abraham and Mansfeld, Yoel (Eds.), *Consumer behavior in travel and tourism* (pp. 393-411). Binghamton, NY: The Haworth Press.

Provincia Autonoma di Trento (2002). *Verso l'ospitalità evoluta: Essere accoglienti per essere competitivi.* Trentino, Italy: APT del Trentino.

Snaith, Bill and Walker, Jane (2001). Dynamic financial management: Managing tomorrow today. In Caseby, Dawn (Ed.), *Time and management,* ISIDA Study and Research Series number 16 (pp. 135-157). Palermo: Fabio Orlando Editore.

Urry, John (1995). *Consuming places.* London: Routledge.

Virilio, Paul (1994). *The vision machine.* London: Indiana University Press.

Chapter 5

The Rediscovery of Slowness, or Leisure Time As One's Own and As Self-Aggrandizement?

Karlheinz Woehler

INTRODUCTION

A number of scientists assert that Western populations both race along and dissolve with the world (see, e.g., Reheis, 1998). "Acceleration" is the prevalent keyword to characterize the current social composition. Buying, hearing, or seeing something *immediately,* being at another place, knowing about other people and other things, and being informed about and talking to others are no longer difficult from either a technical, social, or cultural point of view. Time is no longer an issue. Immediately does not only mean that people get—or could get—what they want at once, but also implies that oblivion is immediate as well. Restated, almost everything can easily be discarded and replaced in order to redirect attention to other achievable wishes. Innovation is the new buzzword: Everything becomes outdated the moment it is consumed. Product life cycles constantly shorten.

For an economy that strives to accept this challenge, time must no longer be an obstacle. This implies that the human being as part of the workforce is exposed to the pace of a "just in time" economy (Hildebrandt and Linne, 2000). People are constantly both actor and subject of happenings, which means they strive to make things move and thus produce events (this is the etymological meaning of "to happen").

However, does much happen and, in particular, does it happen that fast? Does speed determine our daily routine? The French novelist and essayist Bruckner, for example, describes in his book *Condemned to Happiness: Modernity's Curse* (2001) "the bitter-sweet epic of dreary everyday life." The fast world flashes by, while everyday life is determined by a "tremendous lethargy." As things constantly revolve day after day, nothing new happens, adding triviality and stress to people's lives when they cannot find their ringing mobile phones. The application of Far Eastern relaxation exercises is expected to guarantee that nothing happens. Bruckner says that one does not live, but lasts. Duration is the opposite of acceleration and speed; lasting stands for constancy and durability.

Both (empirically verified) points of view—here the monotonous "nothing happening" and there the fast "something is going on all the time"—are drawn on to assign leisure time a status which allows the postmodern human being to freely organize time. This is not surprising, as there is one fact connecting both perspectives. The fast and constant (daily) life is determined by a rather strict organization of time. Personal self-fulfillment, however, requires a slackening of this strict time management during leisure time, whose healing power has been rediscovered in the postmodern age.

THE FORMATION OF PERSONAL TIME

It was not until the Modern Age, and especially the Age of Enlightenment, that the concept of each individual possessing his or her own time was attributed general value and thus became a component of social life. In previous times, nonworking time was not only regulated by institutions such as the church, aristocracy, employers, and other organizations of social status, but such time also did not have a future. Life and the constitution of society remained unchanged, and there were no chances of improvement. Redemption of the present time was promised to occur in the afterlife. People in the Middle Ages could imagine a better life only as former "places in time" (for instance, as a new Jerusalem) or as a location in the present. This location is utopian, not within the existing society (regarding such utopias, see, e.g., Burnier, 2000). Since the Modern Age, the perception of other societies or social conditions has led to a comparison of the prevailing present era with former ones, revealing any development and progress.

Conceiving progress and development as characteristics of a society means that time becomes a crucial factor for changes in social life (Luhmann, 1997, p. 997). In the eighteenth century, time was no longer seen as a patiently abided state, but instead as a rationally used resource to shape an improved future society. Without being able to follow the different ramifications of the usage of time (Wendorf, 1985), it can be stated that from then on the individual became a symbol of social development. The individual is believed to incorporate the past, the future, and thus the resulting present. As a result, human individuals took responsibility for organizing their own lifetime (for critics, see Schäfer, 1993, p. 82ff). As time investments require rational decision making (i.e., taking both goals and means into consideration) humans became aware of the importance of time for self-consciousness and individuality.

To emphasize the fact that human beings hold and control their own time inevitably causes tension between the individual on one side and social structures on the other side. Institutions freeze the present; they bring time to a rest (Gehlen, 1986, p. 16). The human striving to break free of institutional bonds—bonds that are always time bonds—is logically consistent according to the perspective of "temporalizing" one's own life. Integrating individuals into institutions is questioned to the extent to which it presents an obstacle to individual self-fulfillment, in other words, to the extent to which it determines the usage of (life) time. The quality of time spent within institutions declines if this time fails to promote the individual or to contribute to the well-being of the individual. Detachment from traditional social bonds, and thus unlimited responsibility for one's own life planning, is inconceivable without the ability to manage one's own time (Beck, 1986).

LEISURE TIME AS AN INSTITUTION

One bond, besides social bonds of family and school, is almost impossible to break, namely, the economic or industrial time regime. Participating in economic progress or wealth (i.e., in the better life) has created and still creates a "steel case of bondage" for human beings (Weber, [1921] 1985, p. 835). This bondage forces individuals into production and working processes which are continually intensifying, accelerating, and adapting due to technical innovations and changing market conditions. The more the social progress is determined by wealth, in terms of consumption figures, the more employees and employers must comply with a rational order of time, which derives from the efficient production of goods. Efficiency makes goods fully ("democratically") marketable and purchasable. The time required for the production and distribution of goods determines the working time. Only those who can share in the economic wealth can act within the pattern of time dictated by the economy, and so can those who generate income from this economic time pattern.

The modern age transformed the so far irregular into a regular time that could be precisely measured and assessed due to its linearity (clock time). Time has become a scarce commodity that influences the whole society, which in return is responsible for the prerequisites and maintenance of the economy of time (socialization of time within family, school, administration, hospital, military, etc.). Today everyone knows that individual development opportunities and wealth depend on economic providers of work and thus time. The price for the dissociation from nature and the resulting role of the individual as an organizer of his or her own (life) time is a new dependence on or bond with time. This structural tension introduces time as a disposable factor into social consciousness, and time—as opposed to natural time—becomes an autonomous, structuring rule for social functions (Luhmann, 1985, p. 253). During the nineteenth century, working life and leisure were demarcated and attributed different, peculiar elements of time orientation. Leisure time was henceforth seen as an individually determined use of time, while working time is a nonautonomous use of time determined by the industrial time regime. This demarcation between work and leisure time causes a lack of time, because both subsystems place demands on the time of the other field (Luhmann, 1985, p. 526).

As soon as particular usages of time are assigned to specific subsystems, the result is not only a lack of time and the related valuation of time, but also the necessity of timing between both subsystems, i.e., the interdependence of work and leisure time. From the last third of the nineteenth century until today, the degree to which unions, parties, and employers have associated the amount of nonpurposefully used time (leisure time) with wealth, and to which they have considered it as an improvement of living standards, a quantitative increase in leisure time could and still can prevail only as long as reduced working time—and thus more leisure time—still allows individuals to maintain the efficiency of the economic system. Such an increase in productivity can be achieved only if labor as a production factor advances by technological progress and improved education. The fact that leisure time (daily leisure time, free weekends, vacations, and retirement) could be established as an institution and that a lasting quantitative increase is still possible depends on the compatibility of leisure time and working time. There is no doubt that the reduction of working time was (and still is) enforced by collective bargaining policy, which is achievable only if it does not contradict economic welfare (Rinderspacher, 2000, p. 60). The predominance of company holidays, school holidays, and working time over one's own rhythm of time emphasize the interdependency of both fields. This interdependency implies that leisure behavior is not allowed to be a burden to the world of work and thus is not really an autonomous institution.

In modern society, leisure time is a well-defined system, or rather an institution with high specialization. Specialization means that functions alien to the system, such as politics or economics, are deliberately ignored to dedicate leisure time to nothing but self-fulfillment. Leisure time becomes quality time and provides room for individual development and values without requiring any justification (see Gross, 1999). Boundless possibilities of action lead to a diversity of leisure lifestyles with different leisure time activities. During leisure time, human beings are free of control and can thus experience true development and shape their own lives. The institution of leisure time contributes to the formation of a social identity (Urry, 1994).

As the free evolution of man is one of the most prominent values of Western societies and is legitimately realized during leisure time, other social subsystems, including economy, education, culture, and politics, play only a secondary role in this context (see Featherstone, 1995, p. 75; Rojek, 1995). These subsystems are placed within the world of leisure, in which consumption and learning are staged as enjoyable, playful, and emotional experiences based on individual needs. Even work becomes leisure oriented because the working population can decide when work fits into daily life (see, e.g., Hildebrandt, 2000). Layering society with leisure-oriented values and semantics gives the impression that today's society is a leisure society:

each individual can decide what he or she wants, how he or she wants it, and when.

VACATION TIME

The modern concept of autonomous life planning, the self-regulated use of time, was incorporated within the leisure institution. Within the leisure institution it survives and persists, because human beings act according to this idea. Leisure time institutionalizes the subjective; its purpose lies in the utilization of "that agility, variety, and lack of consequences of the subjective" (Gehlen, 1961, p. 75, translation by the author). In order to realize the subjective, leisure time must not be subject to regulations or guidelines limiting the use of free time. Leisure time asks for time out from social time, with social time being a structurally and culturally developed time that collectively organizes and justifies the life and values of a society (Garhammer, 1999, p. 113). Does this imply that the accelerated use of time as the basic principle of social action is not effective during leisure time (Geissler, 1999, p. 57)? Are vacations also vacations from social regulations and systems?

Vacations are determined by speed and regulation. Although it is correct to attribute this to the characteristics of the leisure industry and its time regime, it does not provide any explanations. Vacations, similar to any other institution, provide tourists with directives and justifications for decisions (Gehlen, 1961, p. 69). Vacationers benefit from time savings because they do not need to organize their stay in terms of transport, accommodation, and catering (savings consist of transaction costs associated with the planning and realization of a holiday; see, e.g., Williamson, 1996). Booking a package holiday is thus nothing but time management, specifically, institutionalized patterns of time usage are applied to save scarce vacation time without giving up too much self-regulation.

Time is considered a scarcity during vacations. As the perception of vacation time is generally reduced to "time for oneself," tourists are pressured to use as much time for themselves as possible. Vacation is therefore attributed a special meaning, namely to spend leisure time wisely (Ryan, 1997). As opposed to everyday time, vacation time should be considered an investment or a commodity to determine the scope of what is possible. Vacations become a piece of art—the vacationer creates a "great time" and must indulge in activities (Adler, 1989; Campbell, 1995, p. 118).

In order to reach this stage of hedonistic time consumption, tourists need to search for alternative experiences. The costs of this search are time costs deducted from the vacation time budget. In order to minimize this inevitable time loss, time demands are placed on the space where vacation takes place (tourist space). Time claims within the tourist space mean that destinations are expected to provide a great variety of attractions and entertainment (even in eventful city destinations; see Judd and Fainstein, 1999). It is well known that destinations react in a post-Fordistic way to these expectations; they not only offer an abundance of experiences, but also leave it to the vacationer to compose his or her holiday out of a large number of possibilities (Lash and Urry, 1994, p. 274; Büttgen, 2000). This implies that offers have to be standardized and the service process needs to be accelerated in order to ensure just-in-time delivery of any service the tourist might request. Living up to customers' time expectations requires not only a quantitative and qualitative broadening of offers, but also extended and more flexible times of service provision (longer seasons, twenty-four-hour services, etc.).

In conclusion, tourists can make use of a multioptional vacation landscape and choose from infinite options at any time. However, as vacationers do not know which experiences enable them to live up to their "real" identity, pressure increases to constantly realize different or additional activities and experiences (Gross, 1994). The effect is a lack of time during vacations which is experienced as speed. Tourists seek compensation for this lack of time combined with the desire for self-development and take advantage of premanufactured offers, i.e., package holidays. The result of many tourists following this behavioral pattern is "fast leisure": the pressure for individualization requires immediate, flexible provision of various options at any time. This can be guaranteed only if tourism products become detached from (unwieldy) space and make use of infrastructure (homogenization). As a result, vacationers suffer from new constraints of the leisure industry because vacation time is externally dictated. This is one paradox of free time. The other paradox is that vacationers seem to be forced to use time in a certain way to live up to the expectation of self-fulfillment at any cost.

SLOWNESS DURING VACATION

Time scarcity during vacations stems from the pressure to consume as many options (offers) as possible in order to find self-fulfillment. The fact that experiences can be made successively but not simultaneously creates a lack of time and a "fast-forward" consumption of standardized tourism products in destinations. Tourists lose their time autonomy, and holidays are no longer a contrast to daily life, without any room for real self-fulfillment. Reducing stress during vacations would mean approaching vacations more slowly and with more joy. The solution is not to preach relaxation and contemplation as the ultimate goal of leisure time. The structural roots of postmodern vacation time, however, provide a starting point to unshackle tourists from time constraints without denying their wish for self-fulfillment.

The countermovement to fast, accelerated vacation time has already started. In order to restore vacationers' own self-controlled time, and to keep them motivated to stage their own personality, vacation time must become free of time pressure. Institutionalizing different forms of time allows for the incorporation of slowness into vacation time (Nowotny, 1989, p. 52). The tourism phenomenon of using as many offers as possible in rapid sequence can be partially abolished if (1) the individual vacation space ("natural" space constitution) and/or (2) the vacationer in his or her physical constitution ("natural" human constitution) are the starting point and the leading rule for vacations (see, e.g., Crouch, Aronsson, and Wahlström, 2001). A different option to achieve slowness (in addition to speed) would be to synchronize the "natural" time of people and space with the time structure of historically grown leisure tourism. Incorporating "natural" time also allows the integration of other social functions into the program of vacation time (which corresponds to dedifferentiation; see, e.g., Rojek, 1995).

The "wellness trend" and the trend for "sustainable" tourism illustrate the specific meaning of this integration. Both trends are examples of "slow leisure." Although some wellness programs could be completed very quickly, wellness usually takes time because well-being results only from sensuous immersion. Sustainable tourism follows the same principle, because the experience of the given space also requires sensuous immersion. In both modes of using leisure time, one's own body (and mind) and physical performance are the source of meaning for life. The vacationer's identity, what he or she is or could be, is determined by his or her physical constitution expressed through "slow" holiday offers. Other systems (health and environment) may also benefit from this type of vacation time. Moreover—besides combining one's own pleasure with business—this means little time commitment and planning, as it is completely open when and how both of these "bodies of nature" (people and space) can be sensuously experienced.

REFERENCES

Adler, J. (1989). Travel As Performed Art. *American Journal of Sociology,* 94, 1366-1391.

Beck, U. (1986). *Risikogesellschaft: Auf dem Weg in eine andere Moderne.* Frankfurt a.M.: Suhrkamp.

Bruckner, P. (2001). *Verdammt zum Glück: Der Fluch der Moderne.* Berlin: Aufbau-Verlag.

Burnier, M.-A. (2000). *Les Paradis Terrestres: 25 Siècles d'Utopies de Platon à Biosphère 2.* Paris: Florent Massot.

Büttgen, M. (2000). Einsatz von Mass Customization zur Erlangung von Wettbewerbsvorteilen. *Tourismus Journal,* 4, 27-49.

Campbell, C. (1995). The Sociology of Consumption. In Miller, D. (Ed.), *Acknowledging Consumption: A Review of New Studies.* London: Routledge, pp. 96-126.

Crouch, D., Aronsson, L., and Wahlström, L. (2001). Tourist Encounters. *Tourist Studies,* 1, 253-270.

Featherstone, M. (1995). *Undoing Culture: Globalization, Postmodernism and Identity.* London/Thousand Oaks/New Delhi: Sage.

Garhammer, M. (1999). *Wie Europäer ihre Zeit nutzen: Zeitstrukturen und Zeitkulturen der Globalisierung.* Berlin: Edition Sigma.

Gehlen, A. (1961). *Urmenschen und Spätkultur: Philosophische Ergebnisse und Aussagen.* Wiesbaden: Athenäum Verlag.

Gehlen, A. (1986). *Urmenschen und Spätkultur: Philosophische Ergebnisse und Aussagen.* Wiesbaden: Aula.

Geissler, Kh.A. (1999). *Vom Tempo der Welt: Am Ende der Uhrzeit.* Freiburg/Basel/Wien: Herder.

Gross, P. (1994). *Die Multioptionsgesellschaft.* Frankfurt: Suhrkamp.

Gross, P. (1999). *Ich-Jagd.* Frankfurt: Suhrkamp.

Hildebrandt, E. (2000). Einleitung: Zeitwandel und reflexive Lebensführung. In Hildebrandt, E. and Linne, G. (Eds.), *Reflexive Lebensführung: Zu den sozialökologischen Folgen flexibler Arbeit.* Berlin: Edition Sigma, pp. 9-45.

Hildebrandt, E. and Linne, G. (Eds.) (2000). *Reflexive Lebensführung: Zu den sozialökologischen Folgen flexibler Arbeit.* Berlin: Edition Sigma.

Judd, D.R. and Fainstein, S.S. (Eds.) (1999). *The Tourist City.* New Haven/London: Yale University Press.

Lash, S. and Urry, J. (1994). *Economies of Signs and Space.* London: Sage.

Luhmann, N. (1985). *Soziale Systeme,* Second Edition. Frankfurt a.M.: Suhrkamp.

Luhmann, N. (1997). *Die Gesellschaft der Gesellschaft.* Frankfurt a.M.: Suhrkamp.

Nowotny, H. (1989). *Eigenzeit: Entstehung und Strukturierung eines Zeitgefühls.* Frankfurt a.M.: Suhrkamp.

Reheis, F. (1998). *Die Kreativität der Langsamkeit: Neuer Wohlstand durch Entschleunigung,* Revised Second Edition. Darmstadt: Wissenschaftliche Buchgesellschaft.

Rinderspacher, J. (2000). Auf dem Weg in bessere Zeiten? Modernisierung zwischen Zeitsouveränität und Marktanpassung. In Hildebrandt, E. and Linne, G. (Eds.), *Reflexive Lebensführung: Zu den sozialökologischen Folgen flexibler Arbeit.* Berlin: Edition Sigma, pp. 47-98.

Rojek, C. (1995). *Decentering Leisure.* London/Thousand Oaks/New Delhi: Sage.

Ryan, C. (1997). "The Time of Our Lives" or Time for Our Lives: An Examination of Time in Holiday. In Ryan, C. (Ed.), *The Tourist Experience: A New Introduction.* London: Cassel, pp. 194-205.

Schäfer, L. (1993). *Das Bacon-Projekt: Von der Erkenntnis, Nutzung und Schonung der Natur.* Frankfurt a.M.: Suhrkamp.

Urry, J. (1994). Time, Leisure and Social Identity. *Time and Society,* 3, 131-151.

Weber, M. ([1921] 1985). *Wirtschaft und Gesellschaft,* Revised Fifth Edition. Tübingen: Mohr.

Wendorf, R. (1985). *Zeit und Kultur: Geschichte des Zeitbewußtseins in Europa,* Third Edition. Opladen: Westdeutscher Verlag.

Williamson, O.E. (1996). *Transaktionskostenökonomik,* Second Edition. Hamburg: Lit-Verlag.

Chapter 6

Can Slow Tourism Bring New Life to Alpine Regions?

Rafael Matos

Happiness is a butterfly, which, when pursued, is always just beyond your grasp . . . but if you will sit down quietly, may alight upon you.

Nathaniel Hawthorne

INTRODUCTION

After reviewing the importance of tourism and its underlying new trends, this chapter will outline the principles of slow tourism and analyze its potential development, in particular for mountain resorts of moderate altitude.

Tourism represents the largest single sector of the world economy, accounting for 8 percent of all exports, or, in terms of employment, for one job in every twelve. Its growth rate remains high and shows an almost constant upward trend since 1950. In 2001, the World Tourism Organization (WTO, 2003) recorded 693 million international arrivals with a total expenditure of $462 billion (excluding domestic tourism).

Tourism plays a particularly important role in the Swiss economy. In 2001, it represented 5.4 percent of gross national product (GNP)

This chapter was translated by Merrick Fall (Ecole hôtelière de Lausanne).

and, directly or indirectly, provided some 300,000 jobs. In 2000, Swiss tourism generated 13 billion Swiss francs, making it the third largest export industry (Swiss Federal Statistical Office et al., 2002).

Despite this almost continuous expansion, tourism in Europe is showing unmistakable signs of reaching a ceiling, in particular in comparison with new destinations. Europeans have an increasing tendency to split up their holidays. They may, for example, take an "exotic" trip and then a short break closer to home, such as a long weekend or a city trip. Changing trends in the economy and the world of work, as well as the development of transport, go a long way toward explaining such developments.

In the main tourism-generating countries, people have less and less time to travel, despite their often sufficient financial resources to do so, e.g., DINK (double-income, no kids) households. In Switzerland, the proportion of these households has increased substantially since 1990. They represented almost one-third of all households in 2003 (Swiss Federal Statistical Office, 2003). Holidays are shorter and tend to be more frequent and more intensive. New tourism products must compress the strongest sensations into the shortest possible time.

The traditional search for foreignness and difference is aggravated by the trend toward individualism and hedonism. A greater segmentation of tourist supply and demand can be detected, as well as a proliferation of particular niches, such as adventure tourism, wellness tourism, etc. The common underlying trend, however, is customers' search for the quality of the experience, its "uniqueness." The WTO refers to an evolution from a "service" economy to an economy of "experiences."

The acceleration within this cycle of evolution is unmistakable. At the same time, a search for a new balance between work, family life, and leisure time occurs. In this context, the idea of "downshifting" and the struggle against overwork (e.g., "karoshi" in Japan and the "burnout" syndrome) are starting to make a timid appearance.

Increasingly frequent reactions against a way of life based on performance and competition are perhaps the harbingers of a new tourist demand, based on values closer to nature and on the discovery of different natural and human environments. Such an approach could generate different forms of behavior, which would allow for slow, but deeper awareness, for a more authentic discovery of a locality, of its people, and of its culture. Such a trend would revolutionize tourism.

Environment and Tourism

In Western societies, a pristine natural environment is a precious asset. Europeans are increasingly conscious of the negative effects of mass tourism and turn toward ecotourism and close-to-home tourism.

For the time being, however, the continuous growth of tourist flow and its environmental consequences continue unabated. The physical results include air and noise pollution, the proliferation of concrete, the loss of biodiversity, and the degradation of landscapes. Mountain regions are particularly vulnerable to such phenomena. Moreover, global warming, which among other impacts increases the altitude of the snow line, threatens to have additional negative consequences on mountain regions of medium altitude. Considering "softer" tourist activities, which are less dependent on the climate and will be compatible with other forms of tourism, is a matter of urgency. In addition, the typical "snow package," which has been dominant for the past thirty years, no longer meets new aspirations, particularly visible in the case of an increasing number of summer tourists. At the same time, the globalization of the economy and the imperatives of open markets strongly penalize agriculture. These problems could to some extent be defused if agriculture is combined with a complementary tourist activity.

A Necessary Deceleration of Tourism?

The present value system of modern society is based on the economy, on the world of work, on extreme mobility, and on the constant need for information, and has imposed a breakneck pace on tourist and leisure activities. However, a paradigm shift has become visible, and sociocultural trends now encourage tourism and leisure activities that satisfy physical, emotional, social, and cultural needs. The trend is toward quality: need for inner vitality, search for meaning, willingness for interaction with others.

One of today's trends in the field of tourism is so-called slow tourism. This corresponds to the needs of a new tourist segment to give up fast, stressful tourism, in favor of an interlude of quiet serenity to recollect energies and genuinely enjoy the holiday. The theoretic concept of slow tourism subsumes the original idea of "wellness," developed in 1959 by the American doctor Halbert Dunn. His idea of "high-level wellness" is based on four pillars: a healthy diet, movement, relaxation, and cultural and spiritual renewal. In Switzerland, however, only a very limited number of tourist establishments offer such a product. Only 14 percent of wellness hotels offer a full range of services (Lanz Kaufmann, 1999).

Tourists might rediscover simple pleasures such as walking, the smell of flowers, tastes, "lonely peace" (Wordsworth, 1888), or beautiful landscapes. In search of tranquility and genuine relaxation, greater weight might be given to the original meaning of words such as "holidays" (holy days), "vacances" (in French empty days), or "recreation." This new vision of tourism includes not only accommodation (which must be simple), but also diet (healthy), leisure (peaceful), culture (local), services (provided in a peaceful atmosphere), and respect for the natural environment.

SLOW TOURISM: AN ANTIDOTE TO SPEED AND A PROMISING NICHE

Speed and Society, Speed and Work

Slowing down is the antithesis of "speed." The modern economy tends to impose its fast pace on society and nature. As a result, the rhythm of the seasons, of days of rest, and the alternation between night and day are respected less and less.

Everything is expected to be short and fast. Broadcasting reports last for no more than ninety seconds. A microwave oven allows users to cook a meal in three minutes. McDonald's promises to serve a hamburger in fifty-five seconds. As Klaus Backhaus and Kai Gruner (1994) point out, time has become *the* competitive factor. It is thus not surprising that time is the second-most popular subject of conversation after weather.

A growing number of consumers are now aware of this concern, and some interesting initiatives have emerged both in leisure and work. The number of *slobbies* ("slower but better working people") is gradually growing. Some managers advocate the creation of wellness rooms and of islands of calm. The financial services company

Ernst and Young has created a program known as "Life Balance," under the heading "Company Wellness." Employees who are relaxed and well motivated must surely be more creative and cost-effective than their overworked counterparts.

The Ecology of Time

Evidence indicates that this analysis of time is reflected in space, e.g., in urban environments. A symbolic example is the case of "Time Offices" emerging in Italy and elsewhere, where citizens can reconcile their life rhythms. One of the most promising experiments derives from the work of the Deutsches Institut für Urbanistik and the Bremen Time Laboratory, inspired by the work of Matthias Eberling. The idea of "Times of the City" is to create "breathing spaces" in urban environments, or "decelerated" areas. These *chronotopes* "protect" time and are hence complementary to *biotopes,* where natural spaces are protected. The project also aims at making natural rhythms visible in an urban environment by integrating daily and seasonal cycles into the stream of urban life. The first experiments have taken place in Bremen-Vegesack, Germany.

"Deceleration" in Action: Slow Food, Slow Cities . . .

Even software designers and contemporary philosophers are beginning to give some thought to the hectic acceleration of modern life. A striking example is the clock known as Long Now, created by Daniel Hillis, to be erected in the middle of the desert in Nevada. Now under construction, it will be based on four principles, namely accuracy, ease of maintenance, transparence, and longevity. The mechanism is designed to operate for 10,000 years, in particular because it will work slowly (www.longnow.org).

Literature and poetry have reflected this new awareness for quite some time. Famous examples are the pioneering manifesto *The Right to Be Lazy* by Paul Lafargue (*Le droit à la paresse,* 1880), and *The Art of Idleness* (*Die Kunst des Müssiggangs*, 1904) by Hermann Hesse. More recently there has been *Slowness: A Novel* by Milan Kundera (1994) and *Du bon usage de la lenteur* (*On the Good Use of Slowness,* 1998) by Pierre Sansot. Societies complement the movement. For example, in 1990 the philosopher Peter Heintel founded an "Association for Delaying Time" ("Verein zur Verzögerung der Zeit"), which now has 1,200 members.

Concrete initiatives, such as the Slow Food movement (www.slowfood.com) based in Bra, Italy, are gaining wide acceptance. Founded by Carlo Petrini in 1986 to offset the influence of fast food, Slow Food currently has 70,000 members in fifty countries.

The "philosophy of slowness," which underlies Slow Food, is by definition expressed in the dietary or culinary sphere. It advocates healthy food (quality rather than quantity), particular attention to flavor, local and regional products, and careful food preparation. This philosophy also supports tradition (adapted as necessary to the modern context), conviviality, and respect of seasonal rhythms. It aims to combine the cultural advocacy of hedonism, enjoyment, and conviviality with ecological commitment. However, Slow Food has not developed any genuinely "slow" concept for tourism or hotels yet.

The Slow Cities ("Città Lente") movement, founded in July 2000, derives in turn from Slow Food and plans to spread throughout Europe. Through the promotion of slowness, it aims to improve the quality of life in urban areas. Some seventy Italian cities and villages so far have committed themselves to regulate advertising signs and construction fences, to promote cycling, to support local restaurants and small shops, to combat noise pollution, and to create green spaces.

A number of other initiatives also illustrate the trend toward deceleration. A German travel agency, for example, has the evocative name "Slow Motion Tours" and follows the slogan "The Discovery of Slowness Instead of Travel on the Production Line." The spa town of Königsfeld, Germany (www.koenigsfeld.de), bases its marketing around the theme of *Eigenzeit* ("time for oneself"). The concept of this so-called *Time Resort* (*Zeit-Kurort*) was developed by the "time manager" Manfred Molicki. He argues that in the past time was naturally regulated by the flow of seasons, collectively (e.g., by church bells), or by government commercial regulations. Today, time is more flexible and time management is more precise ("just in time"), which creates a greater need for *Eigenzeit* and for places to act out this need.

Königsfeld uses this theme as a marketing tool: "There is more to time than what the clock says!" namely, *Eigenzeit,* although in practice only one week per year is genuinely devoted to the theme, when public lectures on the theme of time, concerts (in *tempo giusto*), and other time-related activities take place.

A Few Examples in Switzerland

A number of Swiss destinations explicitly mention the idea of decelerating daily life (German: *Entschleunigung*) in their promotional materials, although very little is put into practice. In Gstaad for example, its slogan, "Come up, slow down," finds hardly any practical application yet.

Matthias Kurt (Betelbergbahnen, <www.lenk.ch>) developed an interesting, but scope-limited idea based on slowness and created footpaths for hiking, excursions, etc., based on specific themes: the Marmot Trail, the Lynx Trail, the Zen Trail, the Alpine Flower Trail, etc. The associated promotional material communicates the concept of slowness: "Swap the future and the past," "Get in tune with the mountains."

The Suisse à Velo (Switzerland by Bike) foundation organized so-called SlowUp Days (www.slowup.ch), a scheme more strictly related to the theme of time. Once a year, traffic around the pilot area of Lake Morat is restricted to allow participants to travel by bike or any other means of transport using muscle power (human-powered mobility.) The first SlowUp event, on September 3, 2000, involved 30,000 people, while the second, on September 2, 2001, attracted 60,000. The 2002 and 2003 SlowUp editions included new locations—Lake Constance (Euregio SlowUp), Gruyeres, and Sempach. The intention is to make SlowUp one of the pillars of SchweizMobil. By 2007, SchweizMobil aims to integrate selected tourist destinations, public and private transport, accommodation, and restaurants in a global tourism concept covering the whole of Switzerland.

Finally, so-called "timeless hotels" are hotels which see no reason to explicitly communicate slowness, but rather put the concept into practice. Some of the most striking examples are Hotel Waldhaus (Sils-Maria), the Grandhotel Giessbach (near Brienz), the Hotel Riffelberg (Zermatt), and the Château Gütsch (in Lucerne). Other hotels use slowness implicitly, such as the Paxmontana (Flüeli-Ranft, Obwald), the Uomonatura Ecological Center (Acquacalda, Ticino), and a small number of monastic hotels in Switzerland. These monasteries allow their guests to spend a few days of contemplative life in quiet meditation to recharge their energies and to rediscover a sense of direction in life. The philosophy and the particular "product" of monastic hotels seems to come closest to the principles that underlie slow tourism, namely "soft" vitality and the search for meaning and emotional and cultural satisfaction.

SLOW TOURISM AND ITS PRINCIPLES

To be genuine, slow tourism must follow two essential principles: (1) "taking time" and (2) attachment to a particular place. Taking time means modification of the daily time relationship, specifically a different perception of nature and living in harmony with a place, its inhabitants, and their culture. The environment is not merely perceived by sight, but by using all five senses. Tourists must be able to change pace, to look rather than to see, to experience the area rather than to endure it.

In Tune with a Sense of Place

Such an approach to places consists of clearly defined criteria delivering well-being in a particular manner. The intention is to discover the particular characteristics of a place, whether through its topography, its cultural heritage, or anything of interest to live in harmony with the locality and its inhabitants, and to do so without falling into nostalgia for the past or into commercial kitsch.

One of the principles underlying such an approach is architecture, which must emphasize the specific characteristics of a place; any building should make use of regional materials. The work of the architect Peter Zumthor, in particular the wooden chapel of Sogn Benedegt (Sumvitg, Grisons, 1989) and the thermal spring baths at Vals (Grisons, 1996), are excellent Swiss examples of how to combine modern architecture with traditional materials without the errors of neotraditional architecture. The use of renewable energy is also an indispensable feature of this approach.

The Actors Concerned

To promote and successfully develop slow tourism, it is particularly important to inform, motivate, and involve all stakeholders and organizations directly or indirectly concerned. Consideration should above all be given to farmers who would have to adjust their way of living at a time of insecurity. A family farm could indeed decide to host paying guests, but this also implies extra work. With the development of a variety of "slow" initiatives under different headings, tourist offices are expected to act as coordinators. The managers of restaurants, shops, hotels, and alternative accommodations will also be highly involved. Slow tourism could contribute to the upgrading and rejuvenation of the local industry, for example, by opening hotels based on the concept of slowness, also known as Slowtels. Other tourism stakeholders are the owners and managers of regional heritage sites, local artisans, tourist guides, and mountain guides. It becomes obvious that the acceptance of slow tourism among the local population is a sine qua non, as indeed is the involvement of local societies and associations. Tourism must embrace greater local participation.

The objective must be to define slow tourism in practical terms. The preparation of a code of conduct, job descriptions, and a charter setting out the criteria for slow quality might encourage the implementation of slow tourism and promote the introduction of different initiatives to coordinate the various tourist products.

For regions interested in investing in slow tourism, it is important to stress that slowness is not synonymous with backwardness and has no negative image effect. On the contrary, slow tourism aims to combine slowness, time for living, and quality of life with modernity and contemporary technology. Authenticity is not incompatible with technology (Kappeler, 2000). Slowness could indeed be an effective marketing concept.

Sociocultural, Environmental, and Economic Aspects of Slow Tourism

From an economic point of view, it is more beneficial to upgrade—if possible—existing products rather than to create a whole range of new products. Local products and slow or traditional methods of transport need to be promoted, and natural assets, including rural housing, should be better used. It is also easier to coordinate existing tourist products in terms of avoiding overlap and competition in favor of possible synergies and development of complementary products.

Moreover, slow tourism needs to encourage visitors to stay longer in order to make the concept feasible. Longer duration of stay would also make it easier for tourists to relate to the local population, which would be beneficial for both sides in terms of reciprocal understanding.

The concept of sustainable development, which includes economic, environmental, and social sustainability, should be perceived as a pillar of the philosophy of slow tourism. This new trend provides fertile ground to promote education about the natural environment. In combination with its sociocultural dimension, this represents one of its most interesting characteristics of the slowness concept.

CONCLUSION

Mountain regions should invest in the growing interest in softer forms of tourism and in the development of short-haul holidays. Slow tourism can be one way for Alpine tourism to offer a wider range of tourist products and to protect the natural environment. Hansruedi Müller (1998, p. 229) explicitly suggested that "mountain tourism should promote slowness." Such a deceleration, including a change to different forms of transportation and new zones of tranquility, would undoubtedly help to improve the quality of the holiday experience.

Although the rediscovery of "slowness" receives a fair amount of attention, many people might find it difficult to accept the ideas of "slowing down" their life rhythm, given the modern perception of time. Slow tourism will only gradually become part of daily life. Furthermore, the confidentiality and marginality of slowness suggest that slow tourism should initially be based on high quality. In medium altitude Alpine and peri-Alpine regions, the only surviving local offerings will be those of high quality. In this sense, slow tourism and its Slowtels could offer a viable alternative to winter sports and contribute to sustainable development. Edmond Hervé (2001, p. 1) reminds that "time is at the heart of life: it is legitimate for us to give thought to its existence and its use."

REFERENCES

Backhaus, K. and K. Gruner (1994). Epidemie des Zeitwettbewerbs. In B. Backhaus and H. Bonus (Eds.), *Die Beschleunigungsfalle oder der Triumph der Schildkröte* (pp. 19-46). Stuttgart: Schäffer-Poeschel.

Hervé, E. (2001). *Temps des villes.* Paris: Rapport.

Kappeler, B. (2000). Schluss mit dem Alpen- und Tellenmythos: Der Schweizer Tourismus braucht ein neues Schweizbild—eines, das mit der Wirklichkeit dieses Landes übereinstimmt. *Weltwoche,* 31 (August 3).

Lanz Kaufmann, E. (1999). *Wellness Tourismus: Marktanalyse und Qualitätsforderungen für die Hotellerie.* Berne: Forschungsinstitut für Freizeit und Tourismus der Universität Bern.

Matos, R., Adamo, A., Brodard, S., Guindani, S., Pfarrer, R., Rosset, R., and Turiel, A. (2001). Faisabilité de centres touristiques basés sur le slow tourism dans les régions de moyenne montagne en Suisse [co-financement Commission pour la technologie et l'innovation, CTI]. Le Chalet-à-Gobet: Ecole hôtelière de Lausanne, Lausanne Institute for Hospitality Research.

Müller, H. (1998). Les vacances en montagne: Rétrograde ou à la mode? In International Commission for the Protection of the Alps, *1er Rapport sur l'état des Alpes: Données, faits, problèmes, esquisses de solutions* (pp. 226-230). Schaan: CIPRA.

Swiss Federal Statistical Office (2003). Eidgenössische Volkszählung 2000: Starkes Wochstum der Privathaushalte, verlangsamter, Wandel der Familienformen. Press release, September 2. Available at <http://www.statistic.admin.ch/news/pm/0350-0307-50.pdf>.

Swiss Federal Statistical Office, GastroSuisse, hotelleriesuisse, Swiss Tourism Federation, and Switzerland Tourism (2002). Le tourisme suisse en chiffres. FST: Berne.

Wordsworth, W. (1888). Prospectus to the Recluse. In *The Complete Poetical Works of William Wordsworth.* London: MacMillan and Co.

World Tourism Organization (2003). *Tourism highlights 2003.* Madrid: WTO.

Chapter 7

Leisure Investments: Global Supply and Demand

John R. Kelly

INTRODUCTION

How is it possible to look ahead in an environment of change, complexity, and conflict? The premises of micromarket analyses of demand err in ignoring the macrocontexts of global capitalism. Economic megaperspectives include capitalist investment that drives supply, investment biases that produce imbalances, and the commodification of leisure. The future promises little change in macrolevel investment even when micromarketing becomes more sophisticated and segmented. Capital will continue to be concentrated and create markets of style and consumption-based immediate return. Finally, market rather than individual alternatives are proposed.

Stability is overwhelmed by change, both superficial and profound. The assumption of safety is exploded. Social models seem absurd in their presumed systemic rationality. Cultures are in a global whirl; they are not islands of personal and social security. The only safe premise about leisure, or anything else, is that it is part of a dynamic world which is complex and conflicted. Our little markets, even in the vast enterprise of global tourism, ride in the ocean of the "perfect storm" that has powers outside our conventional instruments of measurement.

HOW, THEN, CAN WE EVEN BEGIN TO LOOK AHEAD?

When the focus is on economic investment, the traditional economic approach is to analyze markets. The stress is on demand—historic, current, and projected. In leisure, presumably predictable factors such as population estimates, income distribution, and behavior trends are combined into demand projections. Warnings about economic contexts of recession and erratic growth, cataclysmic events, and technological innovation are largely set aside when it comes to forecasting demand and making investment judgments.

Most often, familiar methods are applied despite their imperfections. For example, in *Recreations Trends and Markets,* a colleague and the author have taken twenty-five-year participation trends based on yearly studies of over 20,000 U.S. households to identify growth, stable, and declining market segments. The model focuses on two factors: demographic and supply trends. For example, the growth of older cohorts and the progress of the baby-boomer cohort through the life course change the sheer size of age-identified market segments. Changes in gender access and orientations have created women's engagement in some activities, while the rapid increase in provisions for casino gambling has impacted participation rates across demographic categories. The most rapidly increasing activities with substantial participation are thus age-related walking, supply-based gambling, and golf that reflects both age and supply.

The approach seems relatively simple: take demographic projections and supply trends of capital investment patterns and combine them with participation trends into some coherent graphs. The approach can be useful in identifying markets and investment opportunities. It may also be wrong, or at least misleading.

Why? First, there are limits in resources, including time and space. For example, most golfers live in urban areas where land is increasingly scarce and costly. The development of golf courses within a viable driving time of potential golfers is limited by geography. Even walking is limited by urban limits of safe and accessible environments and the low rates of public investment in walkways. Second, every activity is subject to a life cycle. The familiar concept of a product life cycle can be applied to all new leisure activities. Historical studies of gambling in the United States have found cycles of rise and fall. In leisure, an activity life cycle makes the application of linear growth trends deceptive and, for investment, dangerous. There are no exceptions: every market has limits and cycles, and in the end reaches saturation. Approved market-trend analysis is useful but limited.

These are only the limits *within* the assumptions of the microlevel demand model. For example, the factor of diverse and variable cultures must also be considered. Leisure is a matter of style, symbolic display, and identity presentation. However, market analysts are not without resources. The aim is, after all, to assess demand in terms of market segmentation, not just gross demand. One response is to identify markets by cultures, more commonly referred to as styles, to combine more traditional demographics with measures of values and style.

For example, airlines and hotel chains sponsor a proprietary repeated study of tourism based on a complex analysis of patterns of values with lifestyles or patterns in a method developed at Stanford Research International. Markets are segmented by more than location and income. Travel styles are based on personal identities, decision-making strategies, social connections, and even emotions, loves, and fears. Markets are identified by a sophisticated analysis that also provides a basis for marketing and promotion.

Another example in the United States, a demand analysis called "Claritas," identifies "lifestyle enclaves" that are based on residential neighborhood and family composition as well as traditional income, education, and ethnic elements. Central to the typologies are styles of consumption and leisure. Demand is assessed in terms of cultures, in which leisure consumption is embedded in the geographical location of stylistic enclaves. Leisure demand is not just a residual consumption category, but rather a central element in patterns of interests, social and cultural skills, the symbolic meanings of consumption to the significant social enclave, and previous investments in culture and relationships as well as material goods. It seems complex, but computer software can sort such multiple factors in mere minutes and seconds. This program focuses on localized and culture-specific symbol systems. Note that again the attractive cultural symbols for effective marketing are part of the demand package.

This is all based on the old economics of capitalism with the basic premise that "demand creates supply" in an efficient market. My fundamental argument is that revisionist economists have effectively turned this model upside down. In order to even begin to look to the future, it is necessary to take quite a different view of capitalist investment and markets.

Any compartmentalized mode of forecasting is discredited by the macroforces of global capitalism. The revised analysis begins with a sweeping view of the world in which the future of leisure and tourism exists.

1. The world economy, subject both regionally and globally to economic cycles of growth and recession, affects different market segments differently. Populations remain stratified, although with dramatically different proportions, from the central to peripheral economies. On a mesolevel, multilayered international corporations create products that cross old borders. The corporations are the economic elites who control most investment capital with policies that seek to stabilize investment returns. There is the growing "new class" of research, development, and finance technocrats who are considered essential to productivity and, consequently, to profit. There is the "middle mass," increasingly employed in the service sectors with skills that can be learned quickly and who are, therefore, replaceable. Finally there are the poor, a few days away from destitution, in percentages ranging from 5 to 80 percent across the international economic spectrum. Cycles and stratification, along with other dynamic factors, are the context in which markets grow and die.
2. Conflict has many dimensions. Cultural conflict between local and regional cultures seeks to preserve historic symbols, myths, customs, and other elements fundamental to community continuity and all the forces of marketed global culture through mass media. Social conflict exists between those striving to maintain traditional identities and those who would appropriate global values, styles, and material goods. Religious conflict manifests, often with centuries of history. Economic division is found between the affluent and the poor, as well as political conflict between those with power to command economic assent, often called "imperialists," and those who can join in the global economy only on dependency terms. There is reception and resistance, celebration and terrorism, integration and segregation, and even war. If this is indeed "one world," it is a world torn and divided.
3. Dual sets of images command attention if not action. The symbols of affluence, economic progress, technological advance,

and material comfort abound. At the same time visual symbols emerge of poverty, starvation, displaced peoples seeking refuge, rampant disease usually associated with poverty, and children maimed by machetes and mines.

4. Desperate programs of self-protection and containment ensue. On large scales they are military, devoted to displays of destructive power designed to fight yesterday's wars. On smaller scales, walls are topped with razor wire and broken glass, gates with uniformed guards, closed borders, and electronic screening. Less dramatic are the resources and opportunities closed by the market means of admission fees, privatization, and social norms. The excluded and the disinherited are always present. At the high end in leisure and tourism, wealth can buy privacy, protection, restricted access, and the conquest of distance. At the low end, crowding and exclusion are found.

The consequences of all this are warnings to tourists of increasing theft in most destination cities, direct threats to travelers' safety when even money and the right passport cannot buy safety, and wars that are no longer distant events fought by the poor. Even the compassionate in the West have seen the world in "we-they" terms. Now in so many ways "we" are "they." Neither endless markets nor cheap religion offer real assurance.

How can we focus on leisure and tourism as though all this was a separate world? How can we be so narrow as to believe that neat micromarketing models of "reasoned actors" can provide visions of the future? How can we separate anything from this dynamic, complex, and conflicting environment?

The answer, of course, is that we cannot. And we should not, both because leisure and tourism exist in this world and because we are human beings trying to make sense of our lives and work and love in this real world.

MEGAPERSPECTIVES

It can be suggested that even to begin to look ahead, we need to begin with megaperspectives rather than micromodels and supply rather than demand. While many models pretend no world exists out there, and that human actors balance benefits and costs and are reasoned actors without emotion, this chapter will try to offer a framework for looking ahead at the uncertain and the problematic.

The basic framework is economic, but with a variety of symbols and meaning embedded. Also, challenging every generality are counter cases and conflicting perspectives. First, in a capitalist economic matrix, investment drives supply. The old classical economic dictum implied that demand creates supply. J. K. Galbraith and other revisionist economists have demonstrated that in a condition of mass markets and media promotion, supply creates demand. That is the meaning of marketing and the imperative of capital investment. Especially in markets based on discretionary spending, to justify investment a plan must be developed for creating a market.

Environments of water, mountains, or forest create demand for resource-based outdoor recreation. Compare participation rates in the Pacific Northwest to the Netherlands. The proliferation of legal casino gambling in thirty-eight of the United States has made gambling rates soar. Ten-deck cruise ships have drawn the middle mass to a once-exclusive activity. Investment and marketing have produced resort destinations where tourism has become the main business.

There are, however, limits. Natural environments may be so degraded by heavy use that they lose their appeal to the discriminating. Markets become saturated. Thirty new cruise liners in a few years led to the bankruptcy of at least one major cruise line even before September 11, 2001. Income and wealth distribution places limits on markets, especially for high-end opportunities. Note the number of bankrupt retirement resort developments in the American Southeast. The activity life cycle of leisure suggests that no market trends are linear. Many leisure markets have a short life span when based on fads or fashions. No "insatiable consumer" is out there providing an infinite market for anything. Supply can create demand, but not without limits. Cycles occur as sports, gambling, and even destinations rise and fall in popularity.

Without supply there is no demand. When shoreline is all private or tickets to the theater start at over $100, effective demand is stifled. Further, in leisure, there is no demand from necessity since at any given time and place anyone can just not do it or can do something less costly or demanding. Supply creates demand, but that demand is limited by space, costs, distance, and the nature of the activity itself.

Second, the capitalist system produces an investment bias. The essence of capitalism is that it rewards investment capital first and labor second. An added bias exists toward short-term return on investment that applies constant pressure on corporate management.

In a global economy with almost instantaneous electronic transfer of capital, the entire process comes under the pressure of immediacy. Investment in a world-scale economy requires interlocked control not only of money but also of all the resources required to produce a commodity, be it a tractor or heli-skiing. In international tourism, for example, investment requires political involvement through congressional and parliamentary lobbying, state-corporate cooperation, or outright bribery and graft.

The investment imbalance gives priority to those enterprises that offer the greatest repeated return. Gambling, of course, is leisure capitalist perfection, and thus we have Las Vegas. Investment goes to entertainment with fees for each event, theme parks with both entry costs and secondary sales, ski resorts where lift tickets are only a beginning for repeated food and drink, evening entertainment, and endless boutiques with high prices for unlimited shopping. The priority is for a high rate of return as in gambling, sex industries, and entertainment.

The related demand for low taxes leaves the public sector with little money to develop walkways, protect forest paths, set aside beaches, or preserve mountainsides. It leaves relatively little for activities with durable equipment, and the call for investment in developing skills is greater than the disbursement of money. It privileges entertainment over engagement, fashion over durability, and commodities over community. The "opportunity costs" when investment is limited mean that Mirage Resorts builds another "Bellagio" or "New York-New York" in Las Vegas while a rain forest is slashed for fuel or a wetland is filled for housing.

Workers face consequences as well. In leisure and tourism, workers become a cost of production with wages to be kept as low as possible, especially in developing economies or when illegal migrants can be exploited. Most leisure employment is temporary, low wage, and insecure.

The primacy of investment return also produces divided markets. Oversupplied upscale markets entice the affluent who can purchase special environments, attentive service, utter convenience, and protection from crowding and crime. The mass markets are advertised for those with limited resources but a desire to experience at least a little of that world of glamour at the price of crowding and predetermined experience. Finally, the exploitative markets remain for the poor to keep them available for their low-wage and leftover employment. Currently, the world economic recession skews leisure and tourism supply even further toward the upscale.

Other biases are present in this investment imperative. Traditional cultures are appropriated as folk festivals become standardized shows for the transient tourist. See how the folk elements of Carnival have been transformed into routinized tourist attractions in Rio and elsewhere. In the Pacific, see the hotel luau or the Maori display of music and dance.

The consequences are an oversupply of the upscale, a standardization of mass markets, and the exploitation of powerless indigenous labor who are frequently excluded from the very resources that now draw paying visitors. Technology has made this possible—jets, computers, communication networks, and the flow of capital. The information superhighway becomes a supermarket. The sunset becomes an attraction. The symbols of community and culture become a show. All this is no accident. It is not the design of evildoers. It is the consequence of a system of investment.

Third, leisure becomes something for sale, a phenomenon referred to as the "commodification of leisure." We buy experience, rent sunsets, are lifted by helicopters to mountaintops, and purchase people—for viewing or companionship or even sex. Commodification suggests that the meaning and value of leisure comes to be identified with the purchase, possession, and control of material goods. Instead of being an instrument of engagement, the latest golf clubs or ski togs become essential to the sport. Possibly we believe we are more satisfied when we spend more. Add to this a resurgence of Veblen's idea of "conspicuous consumption" in leisure and the centrality of leisure spending to status symbolism. This symbolism is universal in media, especially television, and not just advertising. Most television programming identifies the "good life" with costly leisure environments. These images, wherever produced, are global in impact.

Marx labeled this preoccupation with possession "commodity fetishism." Whatever the vocabulary, the wedding of the market with style and fashion attempts to produce unquenchable desire. There is desire not only for things but also for appearances, not only fashionable costumes but the bodies they adorn, not only transport but statements of status. Changing style requires the continual replacement of items that are otherwise still serviceable.

Changes in leisure for women may serve to illustrate this process. The early period of the women's movement was largely a battle for opportunity. Not only sports but also other closed environments were slowly and grudgingly opened, usually in response to political pressure. In the West that battle has been largely won. Women are now recognized as a major market segment and courted for their purchasing power. A presence that was at first permitted is now sought. Does this signify victory in the gender struggle?

In the market sector where 97 percent of leisure spending occurs, earlier resistance of women to being commodified themselves is now being transformed by media marketing. The emphasis on opportunity, access, engagement, self-determination, and the power to determine their own identities seems often to be transformed from feminist to feminine. Examine critically the images of women on television, even in work settings. A return is evident to feminine fashion, bodily shape and display, and defining women by the gaze of men. The commodification of women's bodies is renewed now not by patriarchal power but by the market. Feminism's arena of resistance may shift from access to the market. Advertising images of leisure now are more likely to feature the shaped and dressed bodies of women than their actions.

Here as in the former "counterculture" period, the market soon appropriates liberation. Protest becomes fashion. Self-determination becomes freedom to shop. Entire lines of retail shops adopt the labels and logos of cultural resistance. The market is more than a response to demand. Rather, it reshapes the culture into symbolic products that have "sign" value more than use value. In time our symbols are for sale, our ideas become sales slogans, and our individuality is a niche market. Labels and images are everything. Now every travel package that involves walking over 100 meters or leaves the tour bus is called "adventure tourism." Market segmentation is refined to employ diverse symbols to sell the products of corporate investment. Sometimes it seems that everything is for sale, even people.

THE FUTURE

The implication of these factors for the future of leisure and tourism is mainly a point of perspective. Looking ahead calls for global perspectives and mega-analysis. The central issues have already been introduced.

First is the nature of investment in determining supply. There is no reason to expect that the investment bias will be substantially altered. In developed economies somewhat increased attention may be given to environmental preservation and conservation management. Public reviews of plans for forests and other natural resources may lessen the market emphasis on rapid return on investments. In societies such as the United States, with its implicit ideology that the market sector should bear responsibility for as much of leisure opportunities as possible, there is not likely to be a major shift in resources toward the public sector. Further, international corporations have such a distance between decision-making bodies and local interests and environments that policies are not likely to give greater weight to particular local conditions and unique natural resources. The casino will continue to attract more funding than the walkway, the mall more than the neighborhood park. Investment return will remain the first criterion for investment. The supply bias is directed toward the upscale in a recession and toward protected venues by terrorism.

Second, the market sector will employ increasingly sophisticated methods of identifying consumers and their particular leisure-related identities. Markets will become more and more segmented in terms of symbolic values, subcultures, and situated styles. Marketing will not just respond to desires but will create them. The marriage of advertising with electronic entertainment will present pictures in which fulfillment is based on leisure commodities. The diversity and reduced costs of the media will enable product promotion to become more accurately focused on particular consumer groups to re-create their ever-changing symbols of social identity.

Third, as the market sector always does, some kinds of leisure goods and services will be oversupplied. Saturated markets will be the inevitable outcome of responding to what appear to be growth markets. Further, because of the investment bias, upscale markets tend to become saturated first as wealth attracts investment. The market never knows when to stop until the signs of bankruptcy turn sunrise industries into sunsets. For the middle-mass markets, there are cycles in most activities, such as gambling and perhaps the cruise industry, which turn once-profitable enterprises into marginality or failure. All this may be abruptly accelerated by traumas of terrorism or regional conflict that impact the attraction of many leisure and tourism possibilities. September 11 has become a vivid reminder that in leisure markets the possibility always exists that people may choose to *not do it*. There is no necessity in leisure markets.

Fourth, leisure markets will remain deeply divided, although there might be some reallocation of wealth and gradual increases in wage levels for some sectors. Corporations will continue to consider labor as a cost of production to be reduced and dismissed in order to maintain profit levels. More of the population is employed in services that yield low wages and high insecurity. Investment rather than employment will produce a higher proportion of wealth, making it increasingly difficult to move from marginality to affluence.

Fifth, there is no indication that the concentration of investment capital and consequent economic power will decrease. Return on investment will continue to flow to a few centers of capital. Peripheral regions, economic sectors, and workers will continue to be exploited, especially in conditions of dependency. When the governments of developing countries can be bought by corporate largesse, effective resistance from the marginal and the poor seems unlikely. Even in the democratic United States a literal shuttle between Wall Street and the federal ministries in Washington ensures that state policy will be designed to support investment.

Sixth, the central control of global media further limits visions and messages that might threaten the overall system. Especially television, which commands most leisure time, promotes a commodified vision of life. Even folk cultures become routinized tourist attractions rather than centers of deeply grounded creative change.

Finally, the union of media with the marketing of fashion and symbols of cultural identity will continually re-create markets for leisure goods and services that are based on the investment imperative. The aim is to renew markets on schedules which respond to market analysis that takes account of distance, costs, activity patterns, cultural identities, and the dampening of cycles through media promotion.

In short, there seems to be little reason to expect anything other than more of the same. Cycles of rise and fall will occur in specific markets and activities, in addition to localized loss of attraction due to the degradation of resources and crowding, fads that come and go quickly, saturated markets and bankruptcies, the impact of new technologies, and traumatic events that may alter even long-established patterns of behavior. However, as long as global capitalism dominates, the investment imperatives of supply and the creation of demand will continue.

Of course, this may be viewed in two ways. One is that the market remains the most efficient and responsive mechanism of supply. Despite miscalculations and occasional overallocation, the market economy is creating a vast world of diversity, wonder, opportunity, and excitement for a significant part of the world population. The challenge is to enlarge the markets and meet desires. The opposing view is that the system is biased in ways which exploit resources, energy, and people, and the supply is based on investment rather than some vision of human possibilities.

ALTERNATIVES

Are there alternative scenarios? Are there possibilities of change and resistance? Can the system be redirected toward greater openness so that resources are directed toward human growth, expression, and even community and creativity?

One set of proposals on the demand side is essentially oriented toward individuals. The recommended response is for individuals to change their consumption habits, reduce work commitments with consequent reductions in income and professional advancement, examine energy usage and waste, and develop lifestyles that give greater priority to relationships, environmental immersion, and leisure based on personal investments rather than commodity and entertainment purchase. This individual change, sometimes called "downshifting," leaves the economic climate of global marketing unchanged. It does not challenge the system except insofar as a few people reduce their consumption levels.

There is, of course, nothing wrong with individual resistance on that level. Although it may ease the "work and spend" pressures for a few higher-income households, it does little or nothing to change the market supply system. Further, it has limited relevance for those with little or no discretionary income. Its symbolic value is limited, especially when those who claim to be downshifting still have three cars in the driveway, second homes, and plans for international travel. "Downshifting" means that one of the cars has only four cylinders, the second home is in some natural area rather than a megaresort, and the next trip is labeled as "green" or "adventure." It is hardly surprising that most neighbors are unaware of the value shift.

More important, a few thousand or even 100,000 downshifters will have little or no impact on the investment patterns of global capitalism. Earth-colored clothes just become a new brand or even chain of boutiques. Upscale safaris move to air-conditioned tents, and helicopters fly green tourists into the backcountry. The market is ready for any lifestyle change if it provides a viable new market segment. A few alterations in symbols, labels, and images may occur, but the supply system goes on its merry way. Further, the marketing media remain directed toward high-return enterprises that can be offered with glamorous commodified images.

It would be more significant if resistance might have some impact on the system. Are there ways in which leisure and tourism investment can be redirected to alternative forms of supply? Can the system be subverted so that it promotes different kinds of opportunities?

No doubt such efforts can be identified. The problem is that they are overwhelmed by the massive and powerful investment-media combines of the so-called "leisure industries." Space here will not allow a proposal for a set of business plans or integrated campaigns. However, it is possible to at least suggest some areas in which a different investment system might be developed. Indications suggest that such a system can produce viable returns on well-planned investments.

1. Political programs and policies are required. From the ground up, policies that begin to change the investment imbalance need support. The assumption has to be attacked that voters always prefer low taxes rather than public investments which significantly enhance the quality of life. The market is not always more efficient. Further, once crucial resources are remanded to the market, they can seldom be restored for long-term conservation. Many indications suggest that political constituencies no longer see leisure resources as trivial and natural environments as limitless. The first step is political organization and courage.

2. In the complex matter of culture, considerable research demonstrates that many people have created small worlds of leisure in which they find community, expressive outlet, and long-term satisfaction. In cultures of creative community, there is the social reinforcement to combat mass global marketing. In some areas, it is even possible to re-create elements of folk culture that tie people together and to their environment. Subcultures of high personal investment and low financial investment can begin locally and become symbols of another way. They provide communities of reinforcement, not just individual resolve.
3. Education is crucial. Considerable evidence indicates that skill in the arts, sports, and other skill-based leisure has its most enduring beginning in school programs. Every effort should be made to support programs, in and after class and preferably voluntary, that open an awareness of opportunities for lifelong investment and provide a confidence in an ability to learn. Such programs, unlike current elite sports and arts programs, should be inclusive rather than exclusive, to widen confidence in competence. This program requires subverting current programs of directing schools more and more toward skills of economic productivity and perhaps even away from the seductive computer as the solution to all educational issues. Again, it means beginning to redress the investment imbalance to invest money in the children we claim are so important.
4. Investment possibilities are available within the current market structure. The author's aforementioned study of 103 activities found several that are growing, but from a small base and with limited potential. These "niche markets" can provide a viable investment return when developed carefully from a good participation base and located at or near attractive resources. Some activities are based on special skills, some on special environments, and many combine the two. They *always* involve skills and challenges rather than quick thrills or entertainments, and they always involve access to resources. In tourism, such niche markets are based on local investments and special cultural or environmental resources. They often, as in Costa Rica, involve government policy and economic support. The point is that they are more than relabeling current mass marketing, such as adding an "educational" component to a gambling cruise or retail ports.

Although it is beyond the scope of this chapter to even begin to explore such niche markets, it is important to notice that they exist within the capitalist system when identified and supported. A common problem in many countries is that tax incentives go to "corporate socialism" rather than truly free enterprise.

5. The media offer both the heart of the problem and possible resistance as they deluge viewers with images of affluent commodified leisure, which is unlikely to change. However, electronic developments now give the possibility of more variety and diversity. Some may come from satellite channels that boost the numbers of the providers. Some may come in mainline programming as creative writers and producers are given the chance to do something different in order to address the problems of entertainment saturation and boredom. The technologies provide the opportunities for diversity that introduce and reinforce the activities of high personal investment, alternative environments, and subcultures of creativity and community. They can open new possibilities for those who have come to recognize that the world of mass entertainment can be rather lonely and empty.

These and other possibilities are more than individual resistance. They admit the problem of supply creating demand and attempt to address the supply issue. In doing so, they expose the limits of the current market mall of leisure with its glorification of symbolic price and possession. They create venues of self-investment rather than consumption. They focus on self-creation rather than product development. They are, if you will forgive the term, "existential" in recognizing that we create our lives by what we do.

Such a subversive and yet creative program could begin to lead to new patterns of financial investment, new valuation placed on special resources, and even new political movements. Greater value would be placed on economic initiative rather than conformity, on political systems that open real personal freedom rather than become chained to corporate markets, and on real cultural diversity rather than market-appropriated symbols. I would even argue that, considering the alternative, such a program could be a market response to being and becoming human.

SECTION III: (INTER)CULTURAL LEISURE BEHAVIOR

Leisure, especially tourism, merges different aspects of culture. First, each consumer is embedded in the culture of his or her home country, which influences individual behavior, self-perception, and social roles, and also develops a holiday/travel culture closely linked to his or her home environment. Leisure behavior is hence strongly influenced by cultural aspects of the home region, as Chapters 8 and 9 in this section illustrate.

Given that Asia will emerge as the leading leisure market in the future, John Ap provides some insights into Asian leisure behavior. The focus is on how the collectivist nature of Asian society, the concept of face, and the Asian hierarchy of needs mold leisure behavior. Joan Sureda and Josep-Francesc Valls studied the leisure styles of German, French, Italian, British, Spanish, and Portuguese leisure consumers. The survey results crystallized eight different European leisure types, their preferred activities and main characteristics, as well as which of these leisure types is most common in each of the countries.

Second, each host region has its own culture. This culture not only influences interaction with visiting tourists, but also provides the basis for cultural tourism. Cultural tourism in the broader sense refers to any travel activities aimed at experiencing the history, cultural heritage, and lifestyle of the host country. As an example, Francis Lobo discusses the relationship of cultural tourism within the leisure paradigm in Australia.

Chapter 8

Intercultural Behavior: Glimpses of Leisure from an Asian Perspective

John Ap

INTRODUCTION

Scholarly research and the literature in leisure has been led and dominated by scholars and researchers from the West. The body of leisure literature has indeed bloomed, and this has provided a solid base upon which to develop our knowledge of one of the world's leading industries. In the tourism sector for example, the World Tourism Organization's Tourism 2020 Vision report forecasts that growth in tourism arrivals over the next twenty years will be concentrated in Asia for both inbound and outbound travel. Moreover, as the affluence of Asian countries increases and greater awareness of the need for quality of life emerges among Asians, greater attention and focus on Asia and its markets is expected. It will be important for leisure researchers, marketers, and providers to be aware of the issues to consider when providing leisure services in an Asian context. Although leisure and recreation has reached a relatively mature stage in Western society, leisure as an integral part of one's life is not as widely embraced in Asia. Thus, the region represents a challenge and also a major potential area of growth for the leisure industry.

Given that Asians will emerge as the leading leisure consumers over the next twenty years, a number of questions are raised for consideration. They are as follows:

- What are the nature and characteristics of Asian consumers?
- How does the collectivist nature of Asian society impact leisure behavior?
- What is the role of face in Asian society?
- How does the Asian hierarchy of needs differ from Western needs?
- To what extent would Western concepts of leisure apply in an Asian context?
- What are some of the issues to consider when providing leisure services for Asians?

In examining these questions, the work of Hellmut Schütte, who is prominent among Western scholars in Asian consumer behavior, is referred to frequently in this chapter. Another book worth reading is John Naisbitt's *Megatrends Asia* (1998) which provides an insightful and macro overview of Asia and its impact on the world. The title of this chapter hints that it refers to "glimpses" of leisure from an Asian perspective. One must recognize that Asia covers an extensive area and many countries. The Asian consumer is not simply one huge homogeneous market. It is heterogeneous, and Fitzgerald (1997) especially warns about generalizations in cross-cultural situations. This chapter can provide only some glimpses of leisure behavior among Asians from one part of Asia, namely East Asia, which has been influenced primarily by Confucianism and the Han Chinese culture. The glimpses provided are also based upon the author's observations and experience living in this part of Asia during the past ten years.

In dealing with cross-cultural research, Schütte (1999, p. 37) states that

> Culture has a profound impact on how individuals perceive who they are, what they are allowed to do, and what their role is as a member of society. These perceptions are often so thoroughly internalized that they are difficult to express explicitly but they are revealed through behavior such as consumption.

When comparing Asian values with those of the American culture, for example, Hitchcock (1994, cited in Naisbitt, 1998) noted that although values appear to be universal, they do differ in terms of importance and priority (see Table 8.1). From an Asian perspective, these differences do reflect certain assumptions that guide their behavior.

TABLE 8.1. Top Personal and Societal Values Between Asians and Americans

Asia	America
Top personal values	
Hard work	Self-reliance
Respect for learning	Hard work
Honesty	Achieving success in life
Self-discipline	Personal achievement
Self-reliance	Helping others
	Honesty
Top societal values	
Orderly society	Freedom of expression
Harmony	Personal freedom
Accountability of public officials	Rights of the individual
Openness to new ideas	Resolve conflicting political views through open debate
Freedom of expression	Thinking for oneself
Respect for authority	Accountability of public officials

Source: Adapted from Naisbitt, 1998, p. 73.

Two profound impacts that are thoroughly internalized in Asian society are collectivism and face, which are discussed in the next section.

COLLECTIVISM AND FACE

Individualism and personal achievements are typical characteristics of Western society, whereas Asian societies are fundamentally collectivist in nature. Collectivism is grounded in Confucianism, which calls for behavior such as respect for elders and authority, loyalty, filial piety, and reciprocity in human relationships. Thus, throughout Asia collectivism is an overriding and unifying belief across most societies and would apply in countries such as China, Japan, Korea, Taiwan, Singapore, Hong Kong, and Macau. This certainly has obvious implications for Western-style approaches to leisure service provision where individualism is more prominent.

Collectivism expresses itself in a number of ways (Schütte, 1999):

- *Belongingness:* Asians demonstrate concern for acceptance as well as anxiety about exclusion in which individual desires are secondary to those of the group. The sense of belonging is an anchor for self-identity, which in turn demands loyalty to the group.
- *Reciprocity:* Rules concerning reciprocity are more formal and binding than in the West and reflect the importance placed upon relationships and social ties. Gift giving is the most tangible means of cultivating *guanxi* (i.e., connections) in Chinese cultures or fulfilling *on* or discharging *giri* in Japan.
- *Self-esteem:* Asians are taught values of modesty and self-effacement, in contrast to the West where children are encouraged to be assertive and self-assured. This does not mean that Asians lack self-respect, but they do not assume they automatically deserve to regard themselves with esteem in comparison with others.
- *Group conformity:* Strong pressure is placed on the individual to conform to group norms, and those who deviate from the norm may be treated as outsiders.
- *Status:* Asian societies are hierarchical and have high power distance compared to Western societies. "Asians are always conscious of their place in the group, institution, or society as a whole, and of the proper behavior, dress, and speech corresponding to status" (Schütte, 1999, p. 39). In this regard, conspicuous consumption is very evident among the image- and status-conscious Asians who have to portray the "right" image. They are also extremely aware of the need to maintain their own dignity (or face) and that of others.

Accompanying the concept of collectivism is the role and influence of the family. In most Asian societies, the family has a very pervasive influence on the lives of each member, and the extended family system, while providing a support network, also places additional obligations on its members. Filial piety and respect must be shown to elders and/or senior family members, and during important festivals, custom would dictate that certain familial obligations should be met. For example, on the eve of the Chinese Lunar New Year, celebrations start with the family reunion dinner where every member of the family is expected to be present. Over a two-week period one is also expected to visit friends and relatives. Such customs have implications on what one can or cannot do, especially during the traditional three-day public holiday period set aside to welcome the new year. Thus, one is not necessarily free to pursue leisure activities as one pleases.

The aforementioned concept of face is a complex and important aspect of Asian society that impinges on behavior. Bond and Hwang (1986) describe six types of face behavior in Chinese society: enhancing one's own face; enhancing other's face; losing one's own face; hurting other's face; saving one's own face; and saving other's face. Face not only deals with the individual or group concerned, but also with saving or protecting the face of other parties involved—even that of an adversary. The concept of face highlights the importance of adopting a nonconfrontational or consensus approach when dealing with Asians. This is in direct contrast to the common Western way of doing things, which is to be individualistic and, at times, confrontational.

When treading in the delicate area of status and face, the non-Asian is advised to adopt a cautious approach and not to rush into things. If there is uncertainty in the situation, it is better for the Asian host to direct you, as he or she will certainly know the status situation of the various members in a group. Non-Asians should be aware that when they make a mistake, an Asian will not necessarily inform them that a mistake has been made, because of politeness and an effort to save face. Thus, the importance of status and giving face needs to be dealt with sensitively.

An understanding of the nature and various aspects of collectivism and face serves as a useful guide in knowing how to deal with Asians and is critical if one is to successfully interact with them. Besides the pervading influence of collectivism and face, other issues to consider are Asian hierarchy of needs and the role and meaning of leisure for Asians.

ASIAN HIERARCHY OF NEEDS

In Western motivation literature, most are familiar with Maslow's (1970) hierarchy of needs—physiological, safety, belonging, prestige, and self-actualization. The hierarchy provides a means to identify and assess what motivates the individual to satisfy his or her needs. A major premise of the hierarchy is that an unfulfilled need creates tension within the individual and reduction of this tension is what motivates behavior. Physical needs represent the lower-order needs, while sociopsychological needs represent the higher-order needs. Lower-order needs must be satisfied before any higher-order needs emerge. According to Schiffman and Kanuk (1994), it is assumed that with Maslow's hierarchy of needs, dissatisfaction is a strong motivator of behavior.

Although Schütte and Ciarlante (1998) indicate that Maslow's hierarchy is particularly suited to Western culture,

> It is debatable whether self-actualization as a personally directed need actually exists for the Asian consumer. Instead, it may be a socially directed need reflecting the desire to enhance an individual's image and position through contributions to society. Among the collectivist cultures of Asia, the idea that personal needs are the highest level of needs would be neither readily accepted nor regarded positively by others. Indeed, the emphasis on achieving independence, autonomy and freedom characteristic of the individualistic value system of Western cultures is visibly absent from Asian cultures. In the Asian context, socially directed needs are considered those of the highest level. . . . As a consequence, the highest level of satisfaction is not derived from the actions directed at the self but from the reactions of others to the individual. Therefore, a more accurate hierarchy of needs in the Asian context is one which eliminates the personally directed self-actualization need and instead emphasizes the intricacies and importance of social needs. What Maslow has identified as the social needs of belonging and prestige can be broken down into three levels: 1) affiliation, 2) admiration, and 3) status. (p. 92)

As reflected in Figure 8.1, status represents the highest level need for Asians, followed by admiration which is earned through acts that demand the respect of others, while affiliation refers to the acceptance of an individual as a member of a group (Schütte and Ciarlante, 1998). Accompanying status is the need to exhibit some degree of conspicuous consumption. In Singapore, for example, they refer to

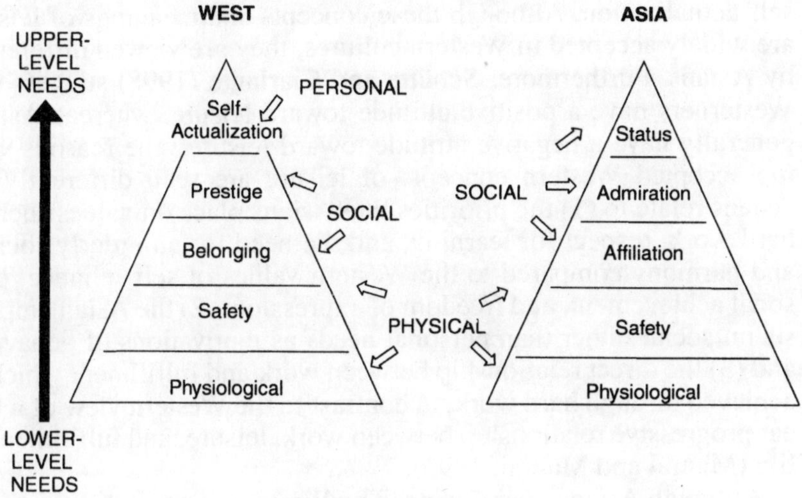

FIGURE 8.1. Maslow's Hierarchy of Needs and the Asian Equivalent (*Source:* Adapted from Schütte and Ciarlante, 1998, p. 93.)

the four Cs of success as having a career, condominium, car, and club membership. The notion that social needs are the dominant motivators of behavior in Asian cultures is congruent with the concepts of collectivism and face and, in fact, are manifestations of these phenomenon.

THE CONCEPT AND MEANING OF LEISURE: AN ASIAN PERSPECTIVE

In a recent review of the leisure experience literature, Lee (1999) highlighted the importance of park and recreation service providers as facilitators of the "leisure experience." From a Western perspective, leisure experiences are multifaceted and feature different levels of intensity such as flow. Csikzentmihalyi (1993), for example, describes the notion of flow as an intense experience characterized by total absorption in the activity one is engaged in, feelings of freedom, and decreased awareness of time. In terms of Maslow's hierarchy of needs, flow has been described as an activity that fulfills the need of self-actualization. Although these concepts and meanings of leisure are widely accepted in Western cultures, they are viewed differently by Asians. Furthermore, Schütte and Ciarlante (1998) suggest that Westerners have a positive attitude toward leisure, whereas Asians generally have a negative attitude toward leisure. The reasons why the accepted Western concepts of leisure are seen differently by Asians relate to (1) the priorities that Asians place on values such as hard work, respect for learning, and the need for an orderly society and harmony compared to the Western values of self-reliance, personal achievement, and freedom of expression; (2) the Asian emphasis on social rather than personal needs as motivations of behavior; and (3) the direct relationship between work and fulfillment which is achieved through hard work, in contrast to the Western view of a linear progressive relationship between work, leisure, and fulfillment in life (Manrai and Manrai, 1995).

Although Asians are influenced by Western ideas, it does not necessarily mean that they embrace Western values. This sentiment was reinforced by Tay (2001) who commented that

> The [Asian] region may be absorbing Western influences, but it is not going to end up as another MacDonald's franchise. . . . Rather, the increased links with the United States and the West will likely result in hybrids that abandon traditional Asian forms while still insisting on a difference from the West. (p. 74)

Thus, it is essential for leisure service providers to understand what is "the Asian way."

As far as motivations are concerned, Schütte and Ciarlante (1998) noted that motivations which would be particularly embraced by Asians for leisure activities are group engagement, learning, and status elevation. Group engagement would certainly reflect the collectivist nature and family orientation of the Asian culture. Learning is an important motivator given that Confucianism stresses the importance of self-improvement through education. Learning provides a justification to engage in leisure activity. This phenomena was demonstrated when the Hong Kong media reported on the findings of a local survey on what types of toys parents purchased for their children and the reasons why they purchased particular toys. The majority of parents selected toys on the basis of their educational value and not simply for fun and enjoyment. Furthermore, a study by Wong

(1996) found that one of the most important elements which attracted people to a local and well-known theme park in Hong Kong, Ocean Park, was the educational component.

The amount of time available for leisure even in modern Asian societies is also limited due to the fact that family and social obligations must be met. Although the lunar new year provides a few days off for most workers, the custom of having the family reunion dinner and visiting family and friends prescribes what one can actually do and leaves little time for the pursuit of individual leisure activities.

For the average person in Asia, leisure time is regarded as a luxury. Hence, for the majority, many are struggling simply to survive and satisfy their basic needs. Most Asian countries contain a large working and lower class, and although an emerging middle class has acquired some affluence, they are still in the minority and are quite thrifty. Asians are well known for their industriousness and efficiency. However, this is masked by the fact that Asians work longer hours than their Western counterparts, with many working a five-and-a-half or six-day workweek, and with unpaid overtime a common practice. It was only recently that workers in China and Japan were given a five-day workweek, and this was in response to factors such as mounting pressure to create more jobs, union pressure, and slowing down overproduction. Because leisure is not afforded much priority, one also finds that national studies of leisure and recreation patterns or behavior are noticeably absent in Asia. If leisure-related studies at the national level are conducted, they will be found in the areas of sport and tourism, which are able to claim legitimacy for health and economic reasons, respectively.

In light of this discussion, one realizes that the Western concept and meaning of leisure do not necessarily apply in the Asian context. However, with Asia emerging as a major world player in the future, the Western leisure service provider must develop an understanding of Asian cultural values and their perspectives of leisure if they are to capitalize on Asia as a potential market.

IMPLICATIONS FOR LEISURE SERVICE PROVISION

Collectivism, face, and the overriding importance of social over personal needs impinge upon Asian behavior in many ways. For the leisure service provider, in developing an awareness, understanding, and sensitivity of Asian culture and behavior, an understanding of the complexity of collectivism and face is essential. Recognizing that the Asian culture is heterogeneous, care must be exercised not to stereotype Asians. For example, among Chinese, differences exist among them depending upon their dialect and country of residence. Tsang (1998), in particular, raises this point, and Fitzgerald (1997) warns against making generalizations about cultural groups.

When establishing business contacts, making a cold call is not the most appropriate way of making contact, and wherever possible, one should use an intermediary to make the initial contact on your behalf. This is particularly important in China, where one needs to establish *guanxi* or connections. Also, identifying and making contact with the key person of the appropriate status may be difficult, but once the appropriate person has been identified, it can certainly open doors.

Asians expect to develop rapport and reciprocation, and there is need for patience because dealing with Asians can be frustrating to the uninformed Westerner. At times, they may not provide an immediate or direct answer in order to save face or even protect your face. Another matter to consider is that some Asians, such as those from China, Japan, and Korea, may not give a direct "no" as an answer. Thus, when you hear the words "We will see what we can do," "We will do our best," or "We will look into the matter," it is an indirect way of saying no. Again, such replies are provided to save your face and avoid any embarrassment on your part, especially if your request cannot be met.

As Asians do not subscribe to the same meaning and experiences of leisure that Westerners have, leisure providers need to have an understanding of what motivates Asian leisure behavior. In planning any leisure strategy for the Asian market, Schütte and Ciarlante (1998) suggest that one should

1. tailor facilities and services for group or family activities;
2. promote educational and learning experiences so that participants can justify having fun and pleasure;
3. present visible signs of achievement such as certificates to enhance the participant's status; and
4. provide souvenirs that can be shared with or purchased for those back home.

In addition, the author also recommends that

1. activities which encourage active participation or interaction should be carefully thought through to either avoid or minimize loss of face and
2. activities and opportunities which raise one's self-esteem and enhances one's status should be facilitated.

Consideration of these suggestions will certainly give leisure providers and marketers some direction as to what needs to be done to tap into the Asian leisure market. One dilemma that service providers must address is the following question: To what extent does one have to tailor or customize a Western-based product for the local culture? There is no definitive answer to such a question and one would have to rely on sound market research data, if available, sound judgment, as well as the input and opinions of local marketers.

In considering the implications examined in this chapter, it is recognized that there are many issues to consider and, at best, it may be difficult to take all these implications into consideration and/or successfully implement the suggestions provided. The local situation and heterogeneity of Asian society could also compound the development of a good understanding of the Asian culture.

CONCLUSION

In conclusion, this venture into the Asian culture in the context of leisure behavior will hopefully raise the level of awareness and understanding of Asian values and their way of thinking. An appreciation of the issues and implications will certainly help to overcome or, at least, address the problems a service provider is likely to face when providing leisure services. The contents of this chapter are very much limited to the experience of the author who is an overseas-born Chinese and Western-educated academic based in Hong Kong. Any errors and oversights remain the responsibility of the author, and despite this cautionary warning, the insights obtained for the reader will hopefully provide a greater understanding of intercultural leisure behavior between the Asian and Western cultures.

REFERENCES

Bond, M. and Hwang, K.H. (1986). The social psychology of Chinese people. In Bond, M. (Ed.), *The Psychology of the Chinese People* (pp. 213-266). Hong Kong: Oxford University Press.

Csikszentmihalyi, M. (1993). *The Evolving Self: A Psychology for the Third Millennium.* New York: Harper Perennial.

Fitzgerald, H. (1997). *Cross-Cultural Communication for the Tourism and Hospitality Industry.* Elsternwick, Australia: Hospitality Press.

Hitchcock, D. (1994). *Asian Values and the United States: How Much Conflict.* Washington, DC: Center for Strategic and International Studies.

Lee, Y. (1999). How do individuals experience leisure. *Parks and Recreation,* 34(2): 40-46.

Manrai, L. and Manrai, A. (1995). Effects of cultural context, gender and acculturation on perception of work versus social/leisure time usage. *Journal of Business Research,* 32(2): 115-128.

Maslow, A. (1970). *Motivation and Personality,* Third Edition. New York: Harper and Row.

Naisbitt, J. (1998). *Megatrends Asia.* New York: John Wiley and Sons.

Schiffman, L. and Kanuk, L. (1994). *Consumer Behavior,* Fifth Edition. Englewood Cliffs, NJ: Prentice Hall.

Schütte, H. (1999). Asian culture and the global consumer. In Kellog, I. (Ed.), *Mastering Marketing: Complete MBA Companion in Marketing* (pp. 37-43). London: Financial Times.

Schütte, H. and Ciarlante, D. (1998). *Consumer Behavior in Asia.* London: Macmillan Press.

Tay, S. (2001). Don't cry for Asia. *Newsweek Special Edition: Issues Asia,* July-September, p. 74.

Tsang, E. (1998). Inside story: Mind your identity when conducting cross-national research. *Organisational Studies,* 19(3): 511-515.

Wong, E. (1996). A study of educational value in a theme park with reference to a case study of Ocean Park. Unpublished final year dissertation. The Hong Kong Polytechnic University.

Chapter 9

Cultural Tourism and the Leisure Paradigm: The Australian Experience

Francis Lobo

INTRODUCTION

This chapter examines the relationship of cultural tourism within the leisure paradigm in Australia. Tourism is placed within a framework in which the leisure experience is realized at a distance from the normal home environment. Contrasts and similarities are stated between casual and serious leisure on the one hand and mass and cultural tourism on the other. The characteristics of the arts—high and popular—are differentiated and Australian research on each is discussed. The second section of this chapter focuses on the Australian context that profiles patterns of participation in cultural activities. This is followed by patterns of domestic and international participation in cultural tourism. Economic implications are briefly dealt with. The chapter shows that the National Culture/Leisure Industry Statistical Framework to track Australian data provides cultural organizations important information for planning purposes.

UNDERSTANDING LEISURE AND TOURISM

Leisure is a complex phenomenon with three primary elements—time, activity, and experience. Brightbill (1963) refers to leisure as discretionary time, beyond that required for existence or subsistence. It is time used according to our own judgment and choice. The second aspect of leisure refers to the types of activities engaged in, sometimes referred to as recreation activities. Roberts (1983) maintains that an important aspect of leisure practice is "play." Play is separated from other types of occupations by a combination of time, place, and rules. Play is limited in space and time, as its rules take on spatial and temporal elements in order to demarcate them more fully. Thus "playing" games has boundaries, areas on which play proceeds and rules which govern the conduct of play. The third element of leisure is the "leisure experience," which is chosen for its own rewards. It is pleasurable and satisfying. Thus, perceiving leisure merely as specific occupations may be misleading, because what is a leisure activity for one person, may be a chore for others. The view of leisure as freedom to choose an occupation which is intrinsically satisfying and bounded by time, place, and rules is further construed as being socially beneficial and desirable. This is a traditional stance and perceived by many as having universal benefit for society. However, it is a view that is challenged by leisure theorists, who see other forms of leisure as being distinctly antisocial and detrimental to the health and well-being of individuals.

Godbey (1989) refers to certain leisure forms as antileisure. They include activities that are undertaken compulsively, as a means to an end, as a necessity, with externally imposed constraints, with considerable anxiety, or with a high degree of time consciousness, minimum personal autonomy, and narrowing self-actualization and authentication. Occupations within antileisure include vandalism, abuse of drugs and alcohol, other forms of substance abuse, violent activities, and certain types of sexual behavior. These are activities usually performed in discretionary time, which presents a leisure paradox to those who believe that leisure should benefit society.

According to Urry (1990), tourism is a departure from everyday experience. He describes tourism as experience and as a free-time activity that contrasts with the daily routine and which can chiefly be identified by means of "signs" bringing significance to the attention of the tourist (for example, beauty, romance, nature). Cohen (1979) presents a framework in which types of leisure experience are realized away from the daily routine.

Cohen (1979) follows a theoretical reasoning in which he proceeds from the degree to which tourists let go of the orientation of their everyday world and focus on the Other and the unknown. He arrives at five variations in orientation, which are well known in the literature and have been given considerable attention. The first mode he describes as *recreational,* in which individuals step outside the normal and the ordinary in search of entertainment. The next possibility is the *diversionary* mode, in which a person breaks out of the stress of everyday life for a moment. The third form of experience he calls the *experiential* mode, which proceeds from the awareness that ordinary life lacks richness and those more authentic experiences of social life, culture, and nature must be sought elsewhere. The fourth mode is *experimental.* Alienation here deeply affects individuals who are in danger of losing themselves in everyday life and who make the effort to rediscover themselves in another context either in nature or a social world that is foreign to them. The fifth and last is *existential*. Here the persons have the feeling that they are living in the wrong place at the wrong time. This estrangement from ordinary life is so strong that a better world is sought elsewhere, in the tourist location and, if possible, on a permanent basis.

An important part of Cohen's argument is based on Turner's (1973) distinction between *center*—the environment and values that form the casualness of the everyday world—and the *center-out-there,* an orientation point situated outside the culture of the home environment. This shift in orientation comes, according to Cohen, both from an alienation from everyday life and from an interest in the Other. The form of this distinction is that it is simple and well reasoned. It gives full value to elements such as search and escape, whereby the tourist is brought into action through motives that concern the "self" or the social world. An illustration of Cohen's modes of tourist experience is presented in Figure 9.1.

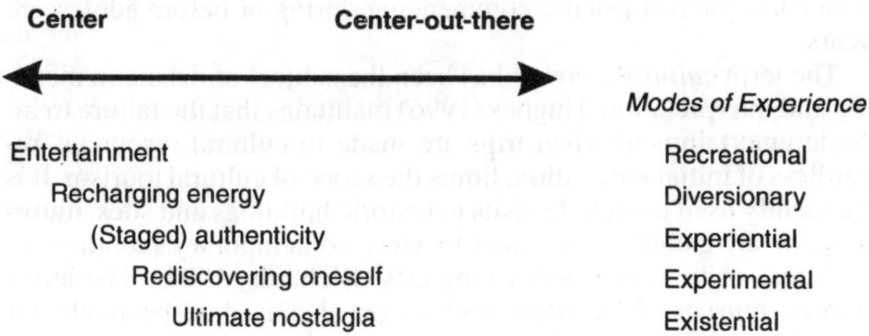

FIGURE 9.1. Cohen's Modes of Tourist Experience (*Source:* Adapted from Cohen, 1979.)

Within the domains of leisure and tourism various forms exist which differentiate one from another in the nature and characteristics of the experience. Thus the relaxation, recuperative, and diversionary functions of leisure are contrasted with more committed forms. In tourism, various prefixes to the word "tourism" cover subdomains and special interests. Forms of leisure and tourism are therefore discussed in the next section in order to focus more precisely on the essence of this chapter.

LEISURE AND CULTURAL TOURISM

For simplicity, leisure is often distinguished between casual and serious forms. Casual leisure is described as being immediately, intrinsically rewarding, a relatively short-lived pleasurable activity requiring little or no special training to enjoy (Stebbins, 1997). Examples of casual leisure are taking a stroll in the park, watching a fireworks display, or simply watching television for relaxation. Serious leisure is defined as the systematic pursuit of an amateur, hobbyist, or volunteer activity sufficiently interesting and substantial in nature for participants to build a career acquiring and expressing a combination of its special skills, knowledge, and experience (Stebbins, 1992). Serious leisure is distinguished from casual leisure through qualities separating the former from the latter (Stebbins, 1997). These qualities are discussed later in the chapter, but the developmental features of serious leisure have enabled sportspersons, musicians, dancers, singers, hobbyists, and actors to develop careers for themselves with early interest usually commencing during or before adolescent years.

The term *cultural tourism* has been the subject of debate in meaning and interpretation. Hughes (1996) maintains that the failure to include entertainment when trips are made to cultural resources, regardless of initial motivation, limits the scope of cultural tourism. It is frequently used to include visits to historic buildings and sites, museums, or art galleries, and also to view contemporary paintings or sculpture or to attend performing arts (Richards, 1994). The terms *historic tourism* and *heritage tourism* are also used, respectively, for describing visits to buildings and sites (Smith, 1989) and trips to natural history attractions and performing arts (Prentice, 1993). The term *arts tourism* is used by Myerscough (1988) to cover museums and art galleries. For those tourists who wish to experience culture as a distinct way of life, Smith (1989) uses the term *ethnic tourism.* For Williams (1988), cultural tourism does not include live entertainment, but works and practices of intellectual, spiritual, and aesthetic development. What remains, according to Storey (1993), is popular culture, which includes live entertainment.

Cultural tourism finds a niche in Cohen's model in Reisinger's (1994) definition, which places it as a form of experimental tourism based on the search for and the participation in new and deep cultural experiences of an aesthetic, intellectual, emotional, or psychological nature. Using Reisinger's position, Stebbins (1996) states that many people who tour for cultural reasons can be understood as pursuing a singular form of serious leisure known as cultural arts and hobbies.

Urry (1994) observes that the enhancement of self-image is especially significant for tourists in the postmodern age. He asserts that identity is formed through consumption and play and that people's social identities are increasingly formed not through work, whether in the factory or the home, but through patterns of consumption of goods, services, and signs. Tourism according to Urry has become a main pattern of consumption. Stebbins (1997) points out that Urry fails to note that tourists' identities can vary with the type of tourism. He places mass tourism alongside casual leisure and cultural tourism as a form of serious leisure. Other authors (see, e.g., Hall and Weiler, 1992) have also commented on rewards from special interest tourism. The main rewards are self-actualization, self-gratification, and enhancement of self-image.

Stebbins (1997) substantiates why cultural tourism generates distinctive identities. He states that all serious leisure, cultural tourism included, is rooted in six distinguishing qualities separating it from casual leisure. First, the occasional need to persevere typically generates positive feelings about the activity. Second, participants find a nonwork career in the endeavor, shaped by its own special contingencies, turning points, and stages of achievement or involvement. Third, careers in serious leisure are also shaped by substantial personal effort based on specially acquired knowledge, training, or skill and, indeed, all three at times. Fourth, several durable benefits such as self-actualization, cherished experiences, self-gratification, and enhancement of self-image accrue from serious leisure. The fifth quality is the unique ethos and social world that grows up around each instance of serious leisure. The sixth quality flows out of the preceding five: participants in serious leisure tend to identify strongly with their chosen pursuits.

The importance of the economic aspects of cultural tourism cannot be understated for countries around the world. Definitions, therefore, have tended to be inclusive of mass and cultural tourism, casual and serious leisure. In Australia, for instance, cultural tourism relates to those travelers who want to experience, understand, and appreciate the character and culture of a place. It is about people traveling for cultural motivations, such as to visit historical sites or to attend festivals or the performing arts (Australian Bureau of Statistics [ABS], 1997a). The leisure arts feature prominently, but again there are structural differences within the leisure framework and between types of art forms, which deserve comment.

LEISURE AND THE ARTS

Leisure theorists have assigned the arts the highest importance and value as an element within human society (Volkering, 1998). For Huizinga (1970) the arts are a superior form of play. In poetry, music, and dance, play is "innate" (p.182) and the visual practitioner in striving to achieve the ultimate masterpiece is driven by "agonistic impulse" (p. 194) to "challenge a rival to perform some difficult, seemingly impossible feat of skill" (p. 194). The arts offer access to pure leisure which provides creative experiences and processes that offer optimum pleasure predicated on a high level of engagement, an absence of time, choice, and structural constraints, and maximum freedom of choice (Gunter and Gunter, 1980). According to Kelly and Godbey (1992), the arts are confirmation of the essentially creative function of leisure. They state that the connection between leisure and creation is more prevalent in the arts than any other form of activity. Leisure is the context for such creative activity, play is the action dimension of leisure, and creation is the producing element.

The leisure significance of the arts may be evaluated from "flow" theory. The term *flow* represents a state in which people become totally involved in an activity and experience loss of self-consciousness, distortion of time perception, focused concentration, enjoyment, and a perception of control over outcomes (Csikszentmihalyi, 1990).

Volkering (1998) states a number of reasons for suggesting the importance of flow theory for optimal experience in the arts. First, flow theory applies to the arts creator and the arts perceiver—artists and audiences—and therefore offers a unified theoretical framework for the explication of the human experience of the arts. Second, flow theorists maintain that the arts have a more than usual capacity to engender optimal experience. If this is so, the validity of flow theory as a leisure paradigm can be evaluated through employing research data regarding the responses and attitudes of arts audiences. Third, flow theory connects optimal experience with a range of social benefits that closely resemble the outcomes which, according to cultural theorists, arise from intrinsic involvement in the arts. To the extent that arts policies are designed to achieve these outcomes, flow theory offers a framework for evaluating the effectiveness of initiatives for the support of the arts.

Australian research into the public use of art galleries has established that only frequent visitors with a special interest in art find their visit "a pleasurable leisure experience" whereas "people who rarely visit galleries" derive less pleasure from their leisure experience of art. Bennett (1994) documented fully the attitudes and preferences of attenders and nonattenders of public art galleries. The data suggest that the majority of arts "perceivers" require little from their leisure experience which moves them from their established comfort zone (Volkering, 1998).

In contrast to the higher arts, the popular arts are widely accessible, thrive on innovation, and are dynamic in their form and presentation. They provide pleasure, power, and satisfaction, rather than higher-order satisfactions and outcomes on which flow theory is predicated (Volkering, 1998). The discussions on theoretical underpinnings of forms of leisure and tourism will be followed by cultural participation patterns of Australians in recent years.

AUSTRALIAN CULTURAL PARTICIPATION

Similar to many countries around the world, Australia has experienced an economic downturn in the manufacturing industries and a growth in service-oriented industries. As most cultural activities are service oriented, important questions pertaining to the scope and extent of cultural participation were left unanswered. This was not only in regard to participation, but also for employment as well. To this end, Australia set up a National Culture/Leisure Industry Statistical Framework based on the 1986 UNESCO Framework for Cultural Statistics. It was established because Australia lacked reliable, well-organized, and accessible statistics on culture/leisure activities. The adoption of the framework has permitted various organizations that collect culture/leisure statistics to do so on a consistent basis. The classification contains the following sectors: national heritage; museums; zoological and botanical gardens; literature; libraries and archives; music; performing arts; music and performing arts services; visual arts; film and video; radio; television; community activities; education; festivals and administration; and sport (ABS, 1997a, p. 98).

A household survey (ABS, 1997b) found that 4.7 million people were involved in cultural tasks in the previous twelve months. This was one-third (32.8 percent) of the population. Of these 4.7 million people, about 2.6 million were involved in a hobby capacity only—the activity was solely for their own use or the use of their family. Consequently, about 2.2 million people undertook the tasks as a work activity. Two-fifths (40.2 percent) of the people who did culture-leisure work received payment.

In recent years private organizations have also undertaken surveys to determine participation rates of Australians in cultural activities. Hirons (1999) reports on market research by Brian Sweeney and Associates into artistic interests of Australians in December 1997. The survey attempted to determine attendance at twenty-two different arts and entertainment activities based on 1,500 random telephone interviews. The survey was conducted over the five mainland Australian state capitals and Canberra. In each city, a fifty-fifty male-female split was obtained. All interviewees were within the sixteen to sixty-five year age group and quotas were set so that one-third of the respondents were aged sixteen to twenty-nine, one third thirty to forty-four, and one-third forty-five to sixty-five. Among several questions asked was "Which of these (activities) do you ever visit or attend?"

Patronage levels of the twenty-two arts and entertainment categories canvassed in the survey are shown in Table 9.1. Commercial cinema was by far the dominant entertainment pursuit, with just over eight in ten metropolitan residents having ever attended, followed by

TABLE 9.1. Activities Ever Attended

Activities	Percent (%)
Cinema (mainstream)	84
Art galleries (public)	55
Theme parks	55
Public exhibitions	54
Live theater (drama)	54
Live bands	53
Rock concerts	51
Museums (science/natural history)	50
Musicals	50
Arts/music festivals	39
Theater (amateur)	34
Other concerts	33
Cinema (art house)	30
Sporting halls of fame	26
Commercial dance	26
Classical musical recitals	25
Art galleries (private)	24
Children's theater	18
Opera	17
Contemporary dance	17
Ballet	16
New Age festivals	12

Source: Adapted from Brian Sweeney and Associates, cited in Hirons, 1999.

public art galleries, theme parks, public exhibitions, live theater, live bands, rock concerts, museums, and musicals.

The data presented were based on a "once ever visit or attendance." Yearly attendance patterns show reduced rates of attendance, but the rankings are not much different. The ABS (1997a) reported on cultural trends in Australia from a household survey undertaken in March 1995 of people fifteen years and over. The counted population of Australia at the time was 17,892,400; the survey covered about 14.1 million people aged fifteen and over. The numbers and percentage rates of people attending cultural venues are presented in Table 9.2.

TABLE 9.2. Persons Attending Cultural Venues: Twelve Months Ending in March 1995

Venue/activity	Number of people attending	Percentage of total population
Art gallery	3,134,100	22.3
Museum	3,905,600	27.8
Animal and marine parks	4,966,000	35.3
Botanical gardens	5,410,500	38.5
National, state, or local library	5,403,100	38.4
Popular music	3,790,700	26.9
Classical music	1,081,300	7.7
Theater	2,336,300	16.6
Dance	1,407,500	10.0
Opera or musical	2,722,100	19.3
Other performing arts	2,634,400	18.7
Cinema	8,733,800	62.1
Sporting events	6,237,800	44.3

Source: Australian Bureau of Statistics 1995, 1996.

Most Australians had attended at least one cultural venue during the year ended March 1995. The data illustrated, for example, Australians' huge interest in sports by the fact that 44.3 percent attended a sporting event in the twelve months prior to March 1995.

The survey also showed that many Australians were interested in flora and fauna. About two-fifths (38.5 percent) had visited a botanical garden at least once in the previous twelve months, while about one-third (35.3 percent) had been to an animal or marine park (including one-fifth of the population who had visited zoos).

Australians were also frequent users of libraries—almost two-fifths (38.4 percent) of the population aged fifteen years and over had been to a national, state, or local library in the previous twelve months and, of these, over half had visited the library more than five times during the year.

Most Australians were interested in the heritage of their country, and this is reflected in the large number that visited museums. Over a quarter (27.8 percent) of the population had visited a museum in the previous twelve months, with about half of these (46.3 percent) making at least two visits during this period. Attendance rates were highest for parents with children under fifteen years (33.2 percent) and for full-time students aged fifteen to twenty-four years (34.0 percent). Attendance rates at the performing arts ranged from 7.7 percent for classical music to 19.3 percent for opera/musicals.

The data show the extent to which cultural activities impact Australians. Large proportions participate in a wide range of cultural pursuits. Although sporting events and popular culture figure highly in participation rates, the higher arts of dance, theater, and opera/musicals range between 10 and 20 percent, which contribute adequately to the maintenance of the arts industry.

CULTURAL TOURISM

Tourism in Australia is supported domestically and internationally. Cultural tourism is regarded as being important to the economy, and statistics are maintained for domestic as well as international tourism.

In 1995, the ABS (1997a) conducted a survey on attendance at cultural venues. In part it measured the magnitude of domestic cultural tourism by Australians, as it questioned people on whether they had visited cultural venues while staying at least forty kilometers away from home. As the people had to spend at least one night away from home to be asked these questions, the data excluded the cultural activities of day-trippers.

A total of 10,250,000 (72.9 percent) Australians aged fifteen years and over spent one or more nights at least 40 km away from home in the twelve months to March 1995. Of these, only 47.4 percent visited one or more cultural venues while they were away. Table 9.3 shows that the most popular cultural venues attended while away were animal parks, botanical gardens, cinemas, and museums.

A survey conducted by the Bureau of Tourism Research (BTR) in the September quarter of 1995 examined the purchase of arts and crafts by international visitors aged fifteen and over. During the interview period 2,279 visitors were questioned about their shopping experiences in Australia. It found that about one-half (49 percent) of these visitors bought at least one item that they identified as being art or craft. Most purchases were items which could be easily carried in

TABLE 9.3. Domestic Cultural Tourism

Venue/activity	Percent (%)
Art galleries	10.9
Museums	15.2
Animal parks	17.6
Botanical gardens	17.0
Libraries	3.3
Popular music	6.5
Classical music	1.4
Theater	3.1
Dance	2.1
Opera/musical	5.2
Other performing arts	2.1
Cinema	16.5

Source: Australian Bureau of Statistics, 1995.

hand luggage. The visitors' expenditure for the three-month period was estimated at $50 million, which meant that international visitors' annual spending on arts and crafts were in the order of $200 million. Frequencies of purchases and proportions of visitors buying arts and crafts are listed in Table 9.4.

Handcrafted clothing was bought by almost one-fifth (18.0 percent) of international visitors to Australia aged fifteen and over as shown in Table 9.4. Those who bought handcrafted clothing spent an average of $162 on these items during their visit. Purchasers of leather items also spent a significant amount of money, but the proportion who bought leather goods was small (9.2 percent). Overall satisfaction levels with the shopping experience was measured on the range, availability, cost, and quality of goods purchased. Responses indicated that satisfaction levels were high on a very dissatisfied to very satisfied 1 to 4 Likert scale. Mean satisfaction scores ranged from 3.1 for the cost of art and craft goods to 3.8 for service in shops. The range and quality of goods scored 3.7 each as satisfaction measures. Availability of Australian goods was scored at 3.4 (BTR, 1995, p. 4). It was concluded that the satisfaction results were very pleasing.

The BTR (1995) survey also asked international visitors about entertainment venues they had visited while in Australia. Table 9.5

TABLE 9.4. Visitor Purchases and Average Expenditure by Category

Purchase category	Number who purchased	Proportion of total visitors (%)	Average expenditure (all visitors)	Average expenditure (shoppers)
Paintings, drawings, or prints	41,300	5.5	$5	$83
Sculpture	8,000	1.1	$1	$59
Wood or furniture	57,800	7.6	$5	$67
Ceramics, pottery	29,600	3.9	$2	$55
Glass	10,500	1.4	$1	$66
Handcrafted clothing	136,700	18.0	$29	$162
Other textiles	19,600	2.6	$4	$154
Metalwork	4,800	0.6	*	$60
Leather	69,500	9.2	$15	$163
Other handicrafts	30,500	4.0	$4	$100

*less than $1

Source: Bureau of Tourism Research, 1995.

TABLE 9.5. Visitor Attendance at Entertainment Venues and Average Expenditure

Venue	Attendance (%)	Average expenditure ($)
Nightclubs, discos, or karaoke	10	5.60
Museums or art galleries	18	1.70
National parks	27	1.10
Historic sites or houses	13	0.30
Cinemas or movie theaters	13	4.70
Theater, opera, or ballet	7	3.70
Classical music	1	0.20
Contemporary music	2	0.70
Sporting venues	5	2.10
Adventure activities	8	17.20
Theme or amusement parks	15	3.80
Animal parks, zoos, or aquariums	32	4.10
Adult entertainment	2	2.20
Other entertainment	13	4.20

Source: Bureau of Tourism Research, 1995

shows that the most commonly visited venues were animal parks, zoos, and aquariums as well as national parks. A small proportion (8 percent) of international visitors undertook adventure activities such as scuba diving and white-water rafting, but the average expenditure per person was far in excess of expenditures in other entertainment categories.

The study by the BTR (1995) was able to determine the current state of the visual art and craft market as viewed by international visitors. Not all aspects of the study have been highlighted in this chapter; however, the wide-ranging questions asked on the type of purchases, the places purchases were made, expenditure on various categories of art and craft goods, satisfaction with aspects of art and craft shopping, and details of entertainment are conducive in profiling the cultural market in Australia.

CONCLUSION

Cultural tourism, domestic and international, is an integral part of the leisure paradigm. Its significance and place in Australia is recognizable by definitions that delineate the scope and extent of cultural tourism. Research into participation, satisfaction, and expenditure patterns support attempts made by the government to promote this form of tourism. The establishment of the National Culture/Leisure Industry Framework has enabled cultural organizations to have well-organized and accessible statistics, which lay the foundations of sound planning for the future. Earlier in the chapter the place of tourism in the leisure paradigm was established, with similarities observed between mass tourism and casual leisure on the one hand and cultural tourism and serious leisure on the other. The arts, too, were differentiated between higher and popular forms, with the former being more exclusive with smaller rates of participation and the latter more inclusive, supported by large proportions of Australians.

REFERENCES

Australian Bureau of Statistics (1995). *Attendance at Selected Cultural Venues,* March. Cat. no. 4114.0. Canberra, Australian Capital Territory: Author.

Australian Bureau of Statistics (1996). *Sports Attendance,* March 1995. Cat. no. 4174.0. Canberra, Australian Capital Territory: Author.

Australian Bureau of Statistics (1997a). *Cultural Trends in Australia: A Statistical Overview*. Canberra, Australian Capital Territory: Department of Communication and the Arts and ABS.

Australian Bureau of Statistics (1997b). *Work in Selected Culture/Leisure Activities, Australia, March 1997*. Cat. no.6281.0. Canberra, Australian Capital Territory: Author.

Bennett, T. (1994). *The Reluctant Museum Visitor: A Study of Non-Goers to History Museums and Art Galleries*. Sydney, Australia: Australia Arts Council.

Brightbill, C.K. (1963). *The Challenge of Leisure*. New Jersey: Prentice-Hall Inc.

Bureau of Tourism Research (1995). *Cultural Tourism in Australia: Visual Art and Craft Shopping by International Visitors*. Canberra, Australian Capital Territory: BTR and Department of Communication and the Arts.

Cohen, E. (1979). A phenomenology of tourist experiences. *The Journal of the British Sociological Association,* 13(2): 179-201.

Csikszentmihalyi, M. (1990). *Flow: The Psychology of Optimal Experience*. New York: Harper and Row.

Godbey, G. (1989). Anti-leisure and public recreation policy: A view from the USA. In F. Coalter (Ed.), *Freedom and Constraint* (pp. 74-86). London: Comedia/ Routledge.

Gunter, B.G. and Gunter, N.C. (1980). Leisure styles: A conceptual framework for modern leisure. *Sociological Quarterly,* 21: 361-374.

Hall, C.M. and Weiler, B. (Eds.) (1992). Introduction: What's special about special interest tourism. In *Special Interest Tourism* (pp. 1-14). New York: Wiley.

Hirons, M. (1999). Australians: Artistically inclined? *Australian Leisure Management,* December 1998/January 1999, pp. 56-59.

Hughes, H.L. (1996). Redefining cultural tourism. *Annals of Tourism Research,* 23(3): 707-709.

Huizinga, J. (1970). *Homo Ludens.* London: Granada.

Kelly, J.R. and Godbey, G. (1992). *A Sociology of Leisure.* State College, PA: Venture.

Myerscough, J. (1988). *The Economic Importance of the Arts in Britain.* London: Policy Studies Institute.

Prentice, R. (1993). *Tourism and Heritage Attractions.* London: Routledge.

Reisinger, Y. (1994). Tourist-host contact as a part of cultural tourism. *World Leisure and Recreation,* 36(2): 24-38.

Richards, G. (1994). Developments in European cultural tourism. In A. Seaton, C. Jenkins, R. Wood, P. Pieke, M. Bennett, L. MacLellan, and R. Smith (Eds.), *Tourism: The State of the Art* (pp. 366-376). Chichester, U.K.: Wiley.

Roberts, K. (1983). *Youth and Leisure.* London: Allen and Unwin.

Smith, V. (Ed.) (1989). *Host and Guests* (Second Edition). Oxford: Blackwell.

Stebbins, R.A. (1992). *Amateurs, Professionals and Serious Leisure.* Montréal and Kingston, Canada: McGill–Queen's University Press.

Stebbins, R.A. (1996). Cultural tourism and serious leisure. *Annals of Tourism Research,* 23(4): 948-950.

Stebbins, R.A. (1997). Identity and cultural tourism. *Annals of Tourism Research,* 24(2): 450-452.

Storey, J. (1993). *An Introductory Guide to Cultural Theory and Popular Culture.* London: Harvester Wheatsheaf.

Turner, V. (1973). The center out there: Pilgrim's goal. *History of Religions,* 12(3): 191-230.

Urry, J. (1990). *The Tourist Gaze: Leisure and Travel in Contemporary Society.* London: Sage.

Urry, J. (1994). Cultural tourism and contemporary tourism. *Leisure Studies,* 13(4): 233-238.

Volkering, M. (1998). The arts and optimal experience: Theory, practice, policy. In H.C. Perkins and G. Cushman (Eds.), *Time Out? Leisure Recreation and Tourism in New Zealand and Australia* (pp. 310-326). Auckland, New Zealand: Addision Wesley Longman.

Williams, R. (1988). *Keywords: A Vocabulary of Culture and Society.* London: Fontana.

Chapter 10

A Comparison of Leisure Styles in Germany, France, Italy, Great Britain, Spain, and Portugal

Joan Sureda
Josep-Francesc Valls

INTRODUCTION

Analysis of European leisure consumption patterns over the past few decades reveals that social criteria—economic, demographic, and even behavioral—fail to explain observations well. By contrast, an analytical approach which employs psychographic criteria (i.e., consumer lifestyles and personalities which are reflected in people's values, activities, interests, and opinions) provides a great deal of valuable information on consumer behavior. This information is of inestimable value when it comes to planning and marketing tourism/leisure products and destinations. This study is based on the hypothesis that certain values are common to consumer groups which strongly influence their buying decisions.

To verify this hypothesis, the results obtained from a survey of 4,800 Europeans belonging to six European Union (EU) member states were analyzed. These data provided information on the way Europeans structure their holidays, their use of free time and where they spend it, their preferences (and the factors underlying them), their attitudes about work and leisure, and the breakdown of their spending. This information allowed us to establish a set of eight leisure styles for the European population surveyed by the study.

This chapter first reviews the literature that led to the adoption of a psychographic segmentation approach and then goes on to describe the basic features of the eight European leisure styles revealed by the study. The chapter concludes by looking at lifestyle trends in the countries examined and puts forward a hypothesis regarding their convergence on a European scale.

METHODOLOGY

A structured survey was administered by telephone (random dialing) to a sample of 4,726 European citizens over the age of fifteen. The sample was stratified by country, age, and sex. The following sample sizes were obtained for each country:

Germany	822
Spain	811
France	702
United Kingdom	799
Italy	797
Portugal	795

The questionnaire consisted of various sections covering sociodemographic characteristics, the importance given to various leisure activities, habits regarding the use of free time, preferences regarding tourism activities and destinations, as well as questions covering respondents' satisfaction concerning both the amount of their free time and what they did with it.

The following information was used to identify leisure styles:

- Respondents' preferences concerning various types of leisure activities (twenty-one items measured on a scale of 0 to 10)
- Evaluation of the importance of certain features considered when choosing leisure activities (twenty items on a five-point scale)

The following results were obtained after analyzing the main components from each of these scales:

- *Leisure activity preferences:* The following nine aspects were identified which, taken together, explain 73 percent of the total variance:
  1. sports,
  2. entertainment and fun,
  3. culture and education,
  4. educational activities,

5. relaxation/hedonism,
6. socializing,
7. passive multimedia,
8. sun and beach, and
9. open air.

- *The importance of leisure activity characteristics:* Six aspects were identified under this head which, taken together, explain 61 percent of the total variance:
  1. fun/parties,
  2. innovation/effort,
  3. social/group,
  4. fashion,
  5. cheap, and
  6. individual.
- *The process involved in identifying leisure styles:* Both sets of criteria were used in classifying data to establish leisure typologies. The process involved in obtaining these typologies was as follows:

  First stage: A hierarchical classification algorithm using the Ward method and Euclidean distance was employed. This allowed us to analyze solutions with different numbers of groups and test how closely the results fit the data.

  Second stage: Valid clusters or groups identified during the first stage were then classified using an algorithm employing moving means in which the previous solution provides the starting point for the next cycle. This allowed us to refine the typology and avoid some of the problems implicit in the use of hierarchical algorithms.

The aforementioned analysis was used on 75 percent of the total sample, the remaining 25 percent being employed to validate the results obtained. The whole process yielded eight leisure styles encompassing the survey respondents. We shall now describe the salient features of these eight leisure styles.

LIFESTYLES AS A CRITERION FOR SEGMENTATION IN THE LEISURE AGE

Geographical, economic, sociodemographic, and even behavioral criteria provide valuable data concerning purchasers' attitudes. However, these criteria are inadequate when it comes to analyzing consumers' attitudes toward leisure. This shortcoming has been aggravated by significant shifts and apparent contradictions in Europeans' behavior with regard to free time. Changing levels of welfare, better education, greater information, and new attitudes toward work and leisure have no doubt played a part in this process—hence the need for a new methodological approach. One needs to bear in mind that the most important factor determining which leisure products are purchased is their capacity to provide customer satisfaction (Valls, 2000).

From this point of view, personal satisfaction—or self-realization—is strongly linked to one's scale of personal values. These values are therefore of enormous importance when making decisions regarding leisure activities (e.g., planning a cultural itinerary; visiting a city/natural park/fitness center/theme park; organizing a journey; booking a hotel or a flight). These scales of values group together consumers from different geographical areas, income levels, social class, age, and education levels. The consumer conduct exhibited by these groups is much more strongly linked with an individual's life aims (Adler, 1929) or the symbolism of objects and moral values (Lazer, 1963). For Dubois and Rovira (1998), it is a question of reconciling the advantages of statistical surveys with the uncertainty involved in better understanding consumer attitudes and behavior.

In the early 1970s, Joseph Mazanec reintroduced the use of psychography in Europe and segmentation by lifestyles in analyzing consumers of tourism and as a tool in planning tourist destinations (Mazanec, 1993). As Lambin (1995) states, segmentation by lifestyles provides a more human depiction of consumers which goes beyond narrow sociodemographic profiling by including information on values, activities, interests, and opinions. Kotler (Kotler, Bowen, and Makens, 1997) added that this kind of segmentation facilitates the task of defining the market.

The Escuela Superior de Administración y Dirección de Empresas (ESADE) Centre for Tourism Management* has been working on the application of leisure styles since 1997 (leisure styles refer to consumers' lifestyles, which affect their choice of leisure activities). This work builds on a line of research explored by Mazanec and on Yankelovitch's control system and the VALS (Value and Lifestyles

---

*The authors are affiliated with this center.

Segmentation) approach. The ESADE research was first applied to the Spanish population over a period of three years (Sureda and Valls, 1997, 1998, 1999) and subsequently expanded to include the six European countries included in the latest survey (Sureda and Valls, 2001): France, Italy, Germany, Portugal, the United Kingdom, and Spain.

DESCRIPTION OF EUROPEAN LEISURE STYLES

Eight leisure styles were identified from the nine factors included in the survey. The leisure styles are described in this section.

Hedonists

The hedonists group comprises people whose preferred activities involve entertainment/fun, sports, and socializing and who are not interested in educational and outdoor activities. They are more strongly motivated by fun and following the crowd than by innovation, effort, and individual activities. The average age of people in this group is relatively young (thirty-six). Men (58 percent) outnumber women; 40 percent are single; professional and educational level are mid-range (students, clerical, and sales staff). The education profile is primary (19 percent), secondary (43 percent), and vocational training. This group splits into three virtually equal parts when it comes to taking either one, two, or three holiday periods per year.

Leisure activities are mainly carried out with friends, followed by family and partners as a close second. This leisure style predominates in France and the United Kingdom and represents 12 percent of the European population (Figure 10.1)

E-Freaks

The e-freaks group comprises people who like a wide range of activities involving entertainment/fun, multimedia, educational, and "sun and beach" activities. They are more strongly motivated by fun, by following the crowd, and by innovation and effort than by socializing and groups. The average age of people in this group is younger than in the first group (thirty). The group is almost evenly split be-

"Hedonists" (12%)

	☺	☹
Preferred activities	Entertainment and fun Sports Socializing	Educational activities Open air
Characteristics of preferred activities	Fun/parties Fashion	Innovation/effort Individual

Demographic variables **Age:** Under 24 (38%), 25-34 (19%), average = 36
Gender: Men (58%), women (42%)
Marital status: Single (40%)
Occupation: Students (16%), clerks, sales staff
Education: Secondary (43%), primary (19%), vocational training (17%)
Income: Middling

Holiday periods One period = 37%
Two periods = 29%
More than two = 34%

Leisure budget 23% of total budget

Satisfaction Fairly + Very satisfied = 79%
Little + Not at all satisfied = 9%

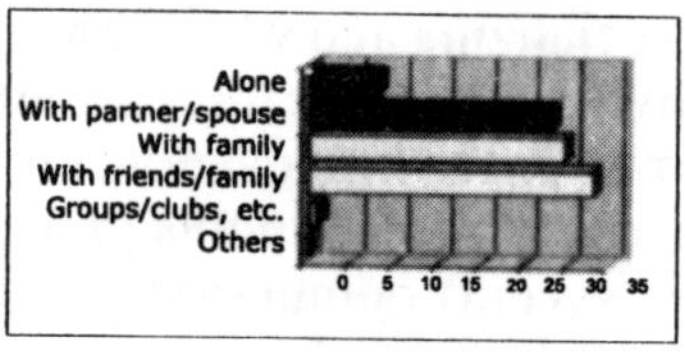

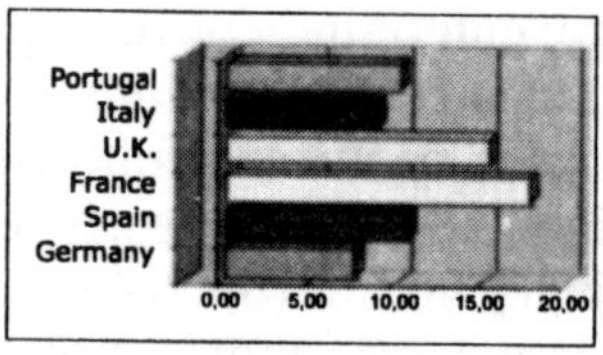

FIGURE 10.1. Hedonists

tween men (49 percent) and women (51 percent). It is the leisure style which features the highest proportion of single people (63 percent); professions are similar to those in the first group (students, clerks, and sales staff); educational levels are also similar, with 55 percent of respondents educated to secondary school level. Income levels are midrange. Almost half (44 percent) of those in this group take their holidays in more than two periods.

Leisure activities are mainly carried out with friends, with partners coming a very distant second. This leisure style predominates in Italy and Germany and represents 12 percent of the European population (Figure 10.2).

"E-freaks" (12%)

	☺	☹
Preferred activities	*Many activities:* Entertainment and fun Multimedia Educational activities Sun and beach	Socializing
Characteristics of preferred activities	Fun/parties Fashion Innovation/effort	Social/group Individual

Demographic variables
Age: Under 24 (45%), 25-34 (27%), average = 30
Gender: Men (49%), women (51%)
Marital status: Single (63%)
Occupation: Students (24%), clerks, sales staff
Education: Secondary (55%), vocational training (14%), short degree (15)
Income: Middling

Holiday periods
One period = 29%
Two periods = 27%
More than two = 44%

Leisure budget
27% of total budget

Satisfaction
Fairly + Very satisfied = 78%

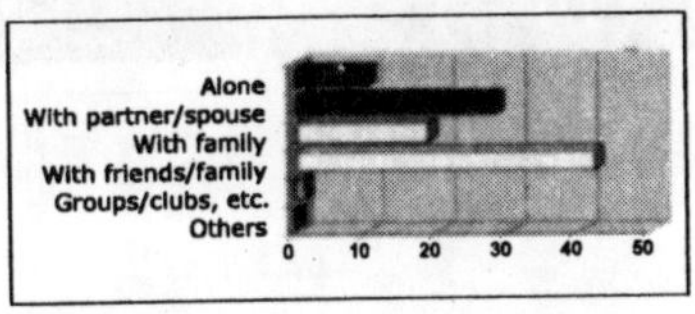

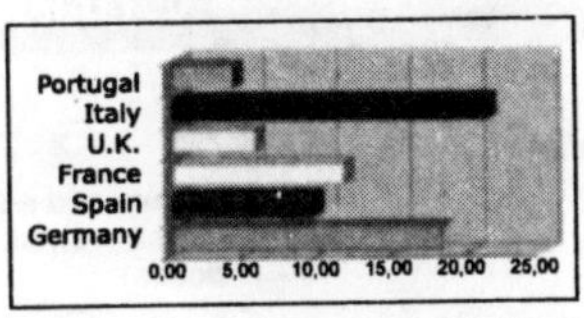

FIGURE 10.2. E-Freaks

Workaholics

The workaholics group comprises people whose preferred activities largely involve culture and education (albeit in small doses). They are motivated by innovation and effort and tend to follow the crowd. The average age of people in this group is older than in the preceding two groups (forty-four). Men (54 percent) outnumber women (46 percent); there are slightly more married people (53 percent) than singles; the leisure style is widely spread between various professions and educational levels (businesspeople, self-employed professionals, clerical and sales staff; graduates and those with vocational training). Income levels are in a higher bracket. They split their holiday periods between one (37 percent) and more than two periods (38 percent) per year.

Leisure activities are mainly carried out with partners. Holidays with family and alone trail a significant distance behind. This leisure style is well represented in Germany and can also be found in France. This leisure style represents 14 percent of the European population (Figure 10.3).

Social Freaks

The social freaks group comprises people whose preferred activities involve socializing, sun and beach, relaxation, hedonism, and entertainment/fun. They are not interested in sports and multimedia. They are motivated by fun/parties and socializing, and they follow the crowd. They are interested in individual activities but show no interest in innovation and effort. The average age of people in this group is

"Workaholics" (14%)

	☺	☹
Preferred activities	Culture and education (albeit in small doses)	Leisure is not a priority
Characteristics of preferred activities	Innovation/effort	Fun/parties Fashion

Demographic variables
Age: 25-34 (23%), 35-44 (20%), average = 44
Gender: Men (54%), women (46%)
Marital status: Married (53%)
Occupation: Businesspeople, professionals, clerks, sales staff
Education: Long degree (18%), short degree (16%), vocational training (17%)
Income: Higher

Holiday periods
One period = 37%
Two periods = 25%
More than two = 38%

Leisure budget
19% of total budget

Satisfaction
Fairly + Very satisfied = 75%
Little + Not at all satisfied = 9%

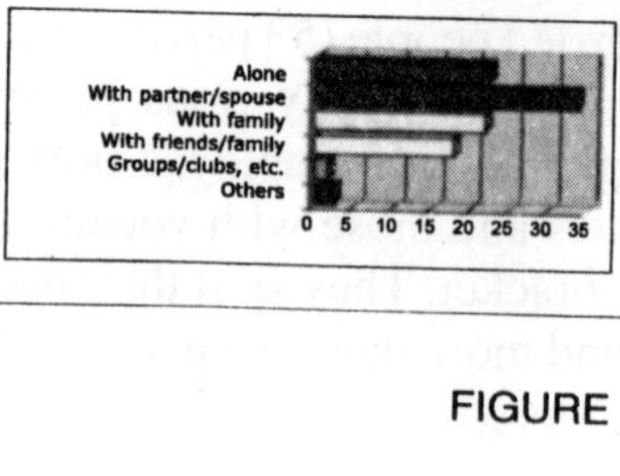

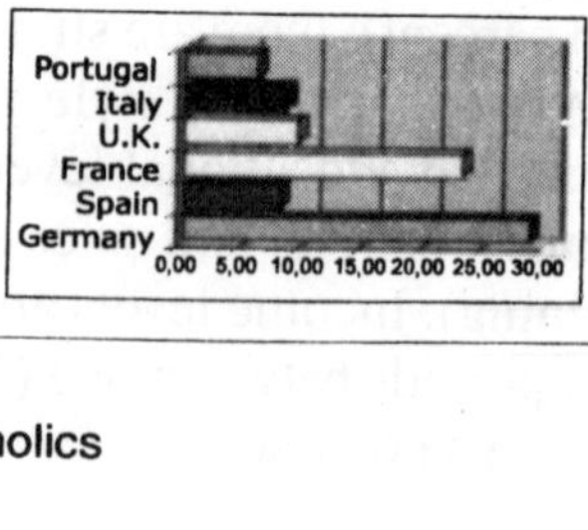

FIGURE 10.3. Workaholics

forty-four. Women (70 percent) outnumber men (30 percent); most of them are married (68 percent); profession and educational level are midrange (clerical and sales staff, service staff, pensioners); education is predominantly secondary (41 percent). Primary and vocational education account for 22 percent and 17 percent, respectively. Income level is midrange. They split their holiday periods in a similar fashion to those in the workaholic leisure style (i.e., in one period and three or more periods, with the former [40 percent] predominating).

Leisure activities are mainly carried out with family and with partners. This leisure style is well represented in Italy, with Germany and the United Kingdom trailing some distance behind, and it covers 13 percent of the European population (Figure 10.4).

"Social freaks" (13%)

	☺	☹
Preferred activities	Socializing Sun and beach Relaxation/hedonistic Entertainment and fun	Sports Multimedia
Characteristics of preferred activities	Fun/parties Social/group Individual	Innovation/effort Fashion

Demographic variables **Age:** 25-34 (19%), 35-44 (21%), 45-54 (16%), average = 44
Gender: Men (30%), women (70%)
Marital status: Married (68%)
Occupation: Clerks, sales staff, service staff, pensioners
Education: Secondary (41%), primary (22%), vocational training (17%)
Income: Middling

Holiday periods One period = 40%
Two periods = 24%
More than two = 36%

Leisure budget 19% of total budget

Satisfaction Fairly + Very satisfied = 77%
Little + Not at all satisfied = 12%

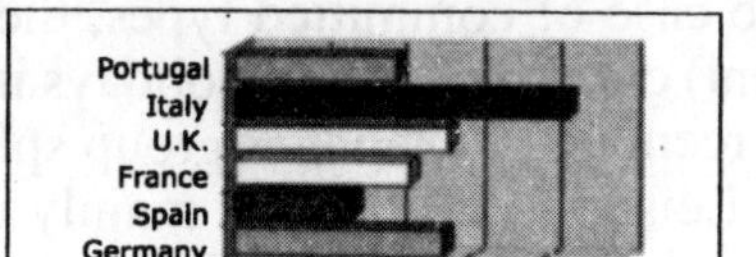

FIGURE 10.4. Social Freaks

Committed Types

The committed types group comprises people whose preferred activities involve relaxation, hedonism, sport, the open air, educational, and cultural activities. They are not interested in entertainment/fun or multimedia. They are motivated by innovation and effort, socializing, and cheap activities. They are not motivated by individual activities, fun/parties, or following the crowd. The average age of people in this group is forty-one. Men (53 percent) and women (47 percent) are almost evenly matched; most of them are married (64 percent); there is a wide range of professions, and the educational level is mid- to low range (secondary [32 percent], primary [27 percent], and vocational training [17 percent]); income level is midrange to low. Almost half of this group (45 percent) spend their holidays during just one period per year.

Leisure activities are carried out with the whole family, followed by those with partners. This leisure style is much more strongly represented in Spain than in any other of the countries in the study (Figure 10.5).

Routine Types

The routine types group comprises people whose leisure is split between sports, education, and passive multimedia. They are not interested in relaxation, hedonism, and culture. They avidly follow the crowd, carry out their leisure pursuits on an individual basis, and dislike cheap activities. The average age of people in this group is relatively young (thirty-nine). Men (57 percent) outnumber women; 56 percent are married; profession and educational level are midrange (students, clerical, and sales staff), with primary, secondary, and vocational education accounting for 21 percent, 39 percent, and 17 percent of respondents, respectively. Income levels are midrange. As in the case of committed types, the majority of routine types (45 percent) concentrate their holidays in just one period. However, a higher percentage of the latter group split their holidays into two periods.

Leisure activities are mainly carried out with partners, followed closely by family. This leisure style is well represented in Portugal, followed by Italy and the United Kingdom. Routine types represent 21 percent of the European population and constitute the largest single group (Figure 10.6).

"Committed types" (8%)

	☺	☹
Preferred	Relaxation/hedonism Sports Open air Educational activities Cultural	Entertainment and fun Passive
Characteristics of preferred activities	Innovation/effort Social/group Cheap	Individual Fun/parties Fashion

Demographic variables **Age:** 25-74 (75%), average = 41
Gender: Men (53%), women (47%)
Marital status: Married (64%)
Occupation: Extremely varied
Education: Secondary (32%), primary (27%), vocational training (17%)
Income: Middling to low

Holiday periods One period = 45%
Two periods = 24%
More than two = 31%

Leisure budget 20% of total budget

Satisfaction Fairly + Very satisfied = 70%
Little + Not at all satisfied = 10%

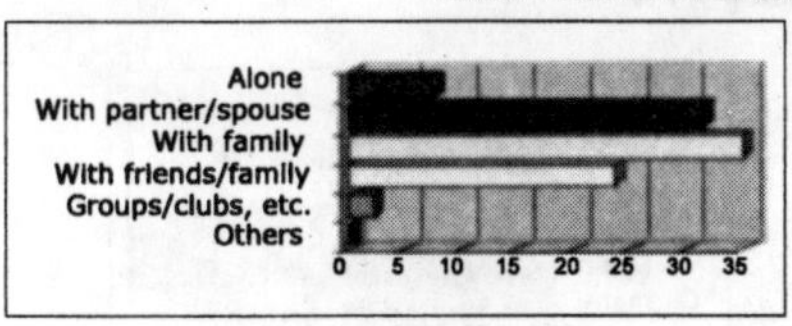

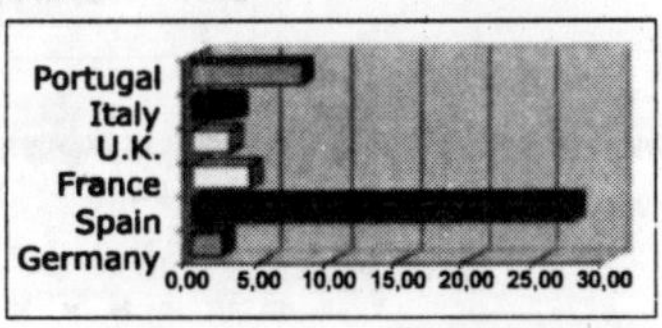

FIGURE 10.5. Committed Types

Well-Established Types

The well-established types group comprises people whose preferred activities involve culture and socialization. They are not interested in relaxation, hedonism, or sun and beach. They are motivated by social/group factors, innovation, and effort rather than by cheap activities and following the crowd. The average age of people in this group is somewhat higher (fifty). Women (56 percent) outnumber men; married people predominate (72 percent); professional and educational levels are higher (pensioners [22 percent], professionals and technicians, businesspeople; long- and short-degree graduates [17 percent and 14 percent, respectively], secondary education [36 percent], and vocational training [17 percent]). Income levels are higher.

"Routine types" (21%)

	☺	☹
Preferred activities	Low level of activity Sports Educational activities Passive	Relaxation/hedonistic Cultural
Characteristics of preferred activities	Fashion Individual	Cheap

Demographic variables **Age:** 16-54 (79%) (widespread), average = 39
Gender: Men (57%), women (43%)
Marital status: Married (56%)
Occupation: Students, clerks, sales staff
Education: Secondary (39%), primary (21%), vocational training (17%)
Income: Middling

Holiday periods One period = 45%
Two periods = 29%
More than two = 26%

Leisure budget 19% of total budget

Satisfaction Fairly + Very satisfied = 77%
Little + Not at all satisfied = 7%

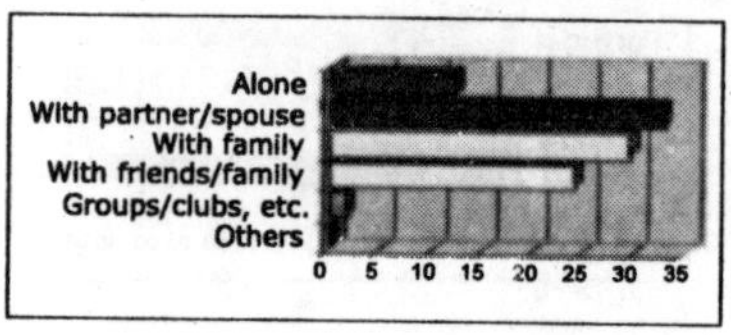

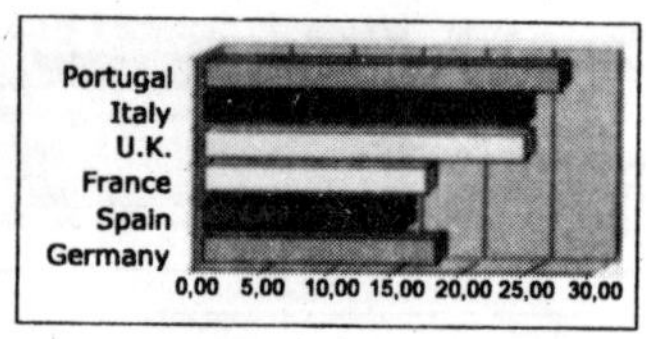

FIGURE 10.6. Routine Types

Most split their holiday periods between one (39 percent) and more than two periods (41 percent) per year.

Leisure activities are mainly carried out with partners, followed by the family. This leisure style is well represented in Spain, followed by the United Kingdom, and represents 10 percent of the European population (Figure 10.7).

Passive Types

The passive types group comprises people whose preferred activities involve passive multimedia (watching TV) and family social relations. They are not interested in entertainment/fun, educational ac-

"Well-established types" (10%)

	☺	☹
Preferred activities	Cultural Socializing	Relaxation/hedonistic Sun and beach
	☺	☹
Characteristics of preferred activities	Social/group Innovation/effort	Cheap Fashion

Demographic
Age: Over 45 (61%), average = 50
Gender: Men (44%), women (56%)
Marital status: Married (72%)
Occupation: Pensioners (22%), professional and technical staff, businesspeople
Education: Long degree (17%), short degree (14%), secondary (36%), vocational training (17%)
Income: Higher

Holiday periods
One period = 39%
Two periods = 20%
More than two = 41%

Leisure budget
16% of total budget

Satisfaction
Fairly + Very satisfied = 79%
Little or not at all satisfied = 7%

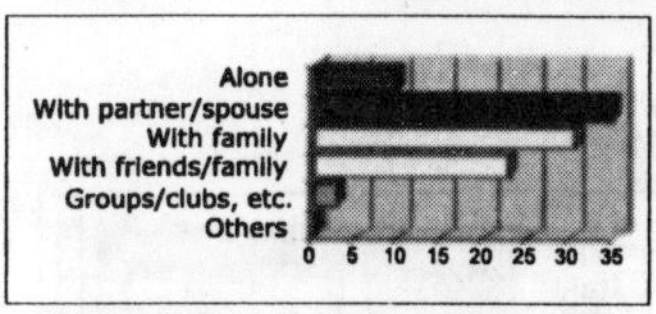

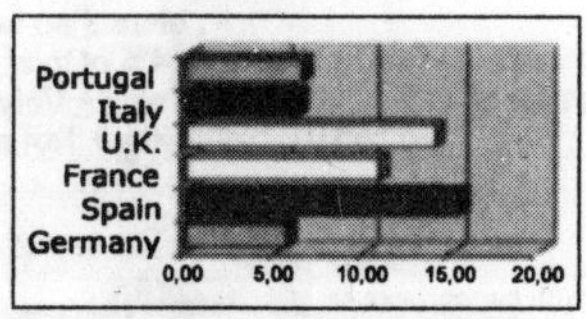

FIGURE 10.7. Well-Established Types

tivities, or sports. They are most strongly motivated by social groups and cheapness rather than by innovation and fun/parties. The average age is relatively old (fifty-seven), and there are more women (62 percent) than men; 67 percent are married and 16 percent are widowed; this leisure style has a high percentage of pensioners, and the educational level is low: primary (46 percent), secondary (26 percent), no formal education (12 percent). Income levels are low, and 58 percent of this group spends holidays in just one period a year.

Leisure activities are mainly carried out with family, with partners coming a very distant second. This leisure style is well represented in Portugal, with the United Kingdom trailing some distance behind, and represents 11 percent of the European population (Figure 10.8).

"Passive types" (11%)

	☺	☹
Preferred activities	Passive multimedia Socializing	Entertainment and fun Educational activities Sports
Characteristics of preferred activities	Social/group Cheap	Innovation/effort Fun/parties

Demographic variables **Age:** Over 65 (47%), average = 57
Gender: Men (38%), women (62%)
Marital status: Married (67%), widowed (16%)
Occupation: Retired (38%)
Education: Primary (46%), secondary (26%), no formal education (12%)
Income: Lower

Holiday periods One period
Two periods
More than two = 18%

Leisure budget 14% of total budget

Satisfaction Fairly + Very satisfied = 56%
Little + Not at all satisfied = 15%

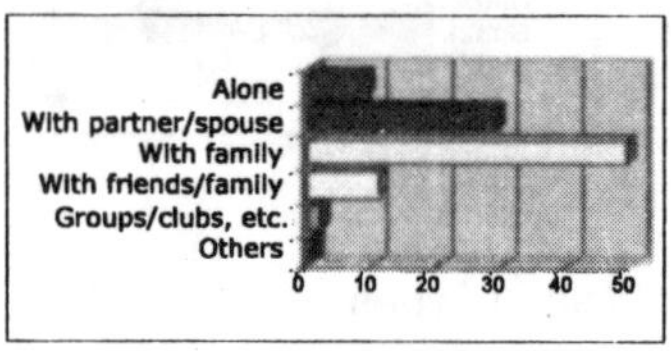

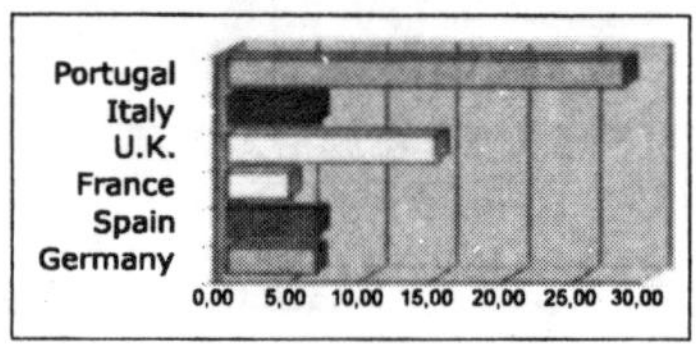

FIGURE 10.8. Passive Types

FACTORS IMPEDING HOMOGENIZATION OF RESULTS

The makeup of leisure styles in each country showed considerable variations. The relative weight of each of the groups identified varied from country to country.* This result indicates that substantial underlying differences still exist between countries and that these have repercussions on leisure and tourism. Our study tried to pin down these differences and analyze their impact on consumer behavior. The work-

*Chi-squared test between both variables led to rejection of the hypothesis that these were independent (chi-square = 1192.780, df = 35, sign = 0.000).

ing hypothesis was that these differences could be grouped and handled by considering the following three major dimensions:

1. *Economic dimension:* disposable income, annual budget earmarked for leisure
2. *The form holidays take:* number of holiday periods per year, total number of days holiday, work timetable
3. *Cultural dimension of leisure:* the importance given to leisure, the importance of leisure in relation to work, willingness to reduce income to obtain more free time

The first case consisted of quantifying these dimensions from the survey responses. The indicators employed for each of these dimensions yielded the following results: Carrying out a factorial correspondence analysis* on each of the indicators yielded standardized quantitative indices for each of these dimensions. Analysis of the behavior of these indices in each country (Table 10.1) revealed significant differences between the means in each case.

Analyzing the behavior of these dimensions as a function of leisure styles still revealed differences, but these were smaller than in the previous case. In fact, an exhaustive CHAID (chi-squared automatic interaction detector) used for providing potential predictors for

TABLE 10.1. Holidays, Economic, and Cultural Indicators

Country	The form holidays take	Economic dimension	Cultural dimension
Germany	.1639	.3201	.4345
Spain	–.2089	–.3471	–.2207
France	–.0247	.1657	.0641
United Kingdom	.0810	.2798	.3205
Italy	.1620	.0546	–.0705
Portugal	–.1784	–.4595	–.5326
Total	.0000	.0000	.0000
F (sign)	22.368 (.000)	95.481 (.000)	114.026 (.000)

*The categorical nature of some of the indicators was the reason why this technique was adopted.

the dimensions in each nation surveyed found the country to be the best predictor in each case.

These results led us to hypothesize that the lack of homogeneity in the leisure styles in each country might be ascribed to the different makeup of leisure styles in each nation. The persistence of these differences in the near future might pose a serious hurdle to homogenization of European leisure styles. Looking on the bright side, the lessening of these differences would produce gradual convergence of leisure style structures in the countries surveyed.

Analyzing graphs A and B in Figure 10.9 reveals a certain correlation between cultural and economic dimensions (r = 0.496), with clear distinctions between countries in these respects. A comparison of both graphs provides a visual representation of the structure of leisure types in the countries surveyed. The lower left quadrant corresponds to less wealthy countries, which also happen to have less developed leisure cultures. Portugal and Spain belong in this category. The prevalent leisure styles in this quadrant are the passive and committed ones. A similar analysis reveals a greater presence of e-freaks and workaholics in Germany.

A similar phenomenon can be seen when analyzing the relationship between economic dimension and the form holidays take (correlation r = 0.185). Although this correlation is less apparent than that discussed in the preceding paragraph, there is nonetheless a strong link between a country's economic dimension, the form holidays take, and the structure of leisure styles (Figure 10.10).

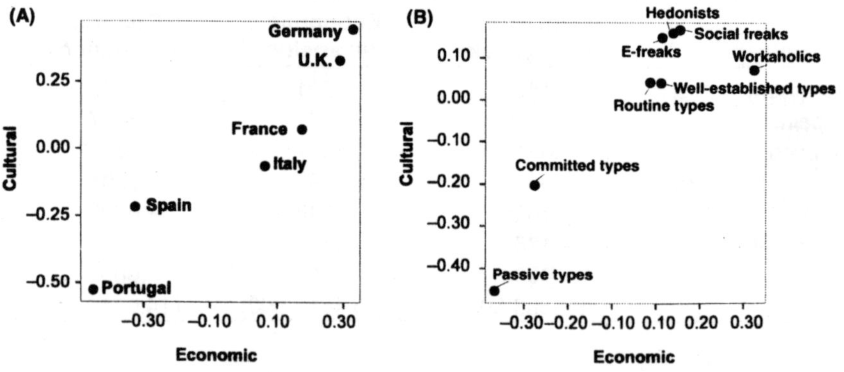

FIGURE 10.9. Structure of Leisure Types in the Countries

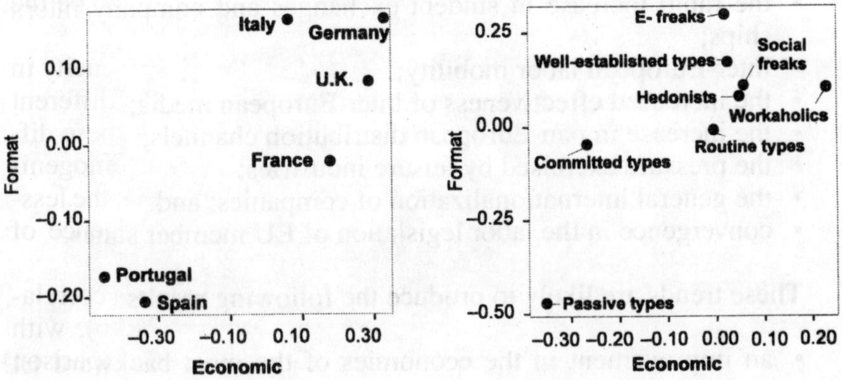

FIGURE 10.10. Structure of Leisure Types in the Countries

In any event, this approximation and the variables concerned do not rule out analysis of the differences between various countries or consideration of the hurdles to greater homogeneity in leisure styles. Differential factors of a cultural, geographic/climatic, political, or religious kind may underlie the attitudes and behavior of European citizens. If this is the case, the chances of removing national influence on leisure patterns are remote.

TRENDS

In the previous section, we analyzed the factors that explain the existing differences between leisure patterns in the countries surveyed. The development of the EU and recent trends strongly suggest that economic convergence between member states is inevitable and their economic differences will steadily shrink over time.

In addition, we believe that the current spate of social, labor, legislative, and cultural developments in Europe will speed up the rate at which differences between EU member states shrink (particularly with regard to leisure culture and the form in which holidays are taken). Some of the processes at work in evening out these differences are as follows:

- the rapid increase in student exchanges and company internships;
- inter-European labor mobility;
- the increased effectiveness of inter-European media;
- the increase in pan-European distribution channels;
- the pressure exercised by leisure industries;
- the general internationalization of companies; and
- convergence in the labor legislation of EU member states.

These trends are likely to produce the following results:

- an improvement in the economies of the most backward EU countries (i.e., a leveling up);
- growth in the leisure culture (leveling up); and
- development of more advanced holiday formats;

Figure 10.11 shows anticipated trends indicating a gradual decline in the passive, routine, and committed leisure styles and growth in the others. These groups, as seen in previous sections, are particularly important in Spain and Portugal. In other words, the leisure patterns in Europe will increasingly come to resemble those of the most economically and culturally advanced EU countries.

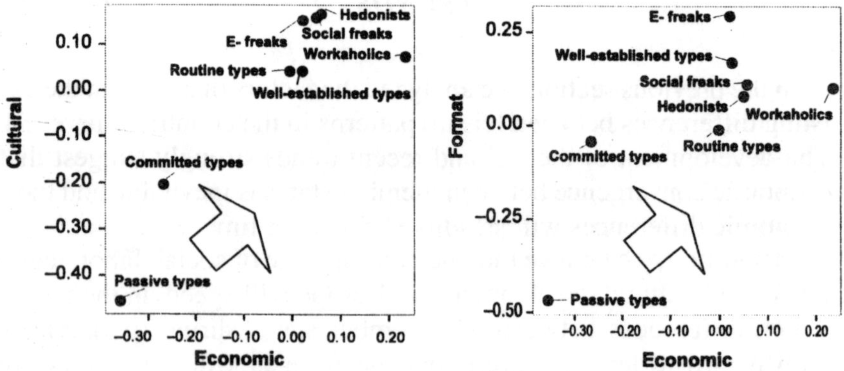

FIGURE 10.11. The Trends of Leisure

CONCLUSION

1. Psychographic segmentation criteria are the most appropriate ones for analyzing the leisure behavior of European consumers, providing the best insights into purchasing patterns. This is so because such criteria take into account leisure consumers' values, interests, and opinions—all vital aspects when one considers that the end pursued by the client is personal satisfaction and self-realization.
2. Each one of the eight leisure styles identified in the study represents a well-differentiated psychographic group, reflecting a particular holiday pattern and use of free time; activity preferences (and the factors underlying them); attitudes toward work and leisure; and a given spending pattern. These data are indispensable for planning tourism/leisure products and destinations.
3. The structure of leisure styles varies between countries. There are various hurdles to homogenization of leisure styles in Europe, including social, economic, demographic, and cultural differences. Even attitudes toward leisure itself vary considerably. However, other factors foster homogenization of leisure styles. These include the following:
   - the rapid increase in student exchanges and company internships,
   - inter-European labor mobility,
   - the increased effectiveness of inter-European media,
   - the increase in pan-European distribution channels,
   - the pressure exercised by leisure industries,
   - the general internationalization of companies, and
   - convergence in the labor legislation of EU member states.
4. The differences in the structure of leisure styles in member states will gradually disappear as conditions in EU countries (i.e., social, economic, demographic, and cultural ones) become more similar. In this process of change, the passive, routine, and committed leisure styles will steadily lose ground to the rest.
5. Despite this process of homogenization, each country will maintain some specific features with regard to leisure types (given that these are the product of climate, geography, culture, and attitudes toward leisure in general). Such differences are almost impossible to erase.

REFERENCES

Adler, Alfred (1929). *The Science of Living*. New York: Greenburg.

Dubois, Bernard and Alex Rovira (1998). *Comportamiento del consumidor*. Madrid: Prentice Hall.

Kotler, Philip, John Bowen, and James Makens (1997). *Mercadotecnia para hotelería y turismo*. Mexico City: Prentice Hall.

Lambin, Jean Jacques (1995). *Marketing Estratégico*. Madrid: McGraw-Hill.

Lazer, William (1963). Life-Style Concepts and Marketing. In Greyser, S. (ed.), *Toward Scientific Marketing*. Chicago: American Marketing Association, pp. 130-139.

Mazanec, Josef A. (1993). *Estilos europeos comparados*. Barcelona: ESADE. II Simposio Internacional Turismo ESADE.

Sureda, Joan and Josep-Francesc Valls (1997). Ociotipos españoles. Study presented at the ESADE VII Simposio Internacional Turismo y Ocio, Barcelona.

Sureda, Joan and Josep-Francesc Valls (1998). Ociotipos españoles. Study presented at the ESADE VIII Simposio Internacional Turismo y Ocio, Barcelona.

Sureda, Joan and Josep-Francesc Valls (1999). Ociotipos españoles. Study presented at the ESADE IX Simposio Internacional Turismo y Ocio, Barcelona.

Sureda, Joan and Josep-Francesc Valls (2001). Ociotipos europeos comparados. Study presented at the ESADE X Simposio Internacional Turismo y Ocio, Barcelona.

Valls, Josep-Francesc (2000). *Gestión de empresas de turismo y ocio*. Barcelona: Ediciones 2000.

SECTION IV: CHANGING PATTERNS IN LIFESTYLE AND IMPLICATIONS FOR LEISURE BEHAVIOR

Discussing leisure futures means above all making future leisure and tourism behavior, which is as multifaceted as the palette of new lifestyle trends, attainable. Tomorrow's consumers have high expectations of travel and leisure products: free time needs to provide both relaxation and thrill; people no longer want to buy products or services but experiences; work, leisure, and education seem to merge into one purchasable bundle; adventure and relaxation as well as fun and health consciousness are no longer contrasts.

Andreas Reiter gives an innovative overview of the boundless range of lifestyle orientations of the new hybrid consumer and provides a number of examples how merging industries succeed in creating lifestyle products.

An abundance of new wellness centers and hotels as well as rediscovered traditional spas show that the newfound health and body consciousness is the predominate lifestyle trend of the new millennium. Wolfgang Nahrstedt provides evidence for the new wellness boom and illustrates the development of the European health system into a new global, leisure-oriented health and wellness society. The physician Wolfgang Schobersberger, in collaboration with Sven Greie and Egon Humpeler, investigate the potential of Alpine health tourism and analyze the medical benefits of holidays at moderate altitudes.

The wellness trend is not the only example of how changing lifestyles manifest themselves in new leisure and tourism products: Roland Scheurer discusses the opportunities of traditional tourism destinations to follow the example of theme parks and create experiences rather than service bundles. Richard Perdue uses the case of Colorado to illustrate how the changing lifestyle diversity of tourism stakeholders shapes the face of the ski industry. Simon Hudson, Donald Getz, Graham Miller, and Graham Brown research how sporting events may help a host destination attract tourism.

Lifestyle trends are closely related to changes in mobility. Thomas Bieger and Christian Laesser examine the travel behavior of Alpine tourists and show that mobility patterns are an expression of preferred leisure activities and travel habits. Maria Carla Furlan, Sabrina Meneghello, and Valeria Minghetti approach the mobility issue from a different perspective by discussing how a greenway in rural areas can benefit from the trend toward green tourism.

Chapter 11

The Hybrid Consumer of Leisure Squeezed Between Fun Maximization, Chill Out, and the Radical Search for Inner Values

Andreas Reiter

Who would you like to be for the next twenty-four hours?

Patek Philippe advertising slogan

INTRODUCTION

We live in a world of constant change. In this world, traditional creators of identity such as profession, family, nationality, etc., lose their importance. Expectations that the leisure and consumption industry will provide a curing effect rise accordingly. Deconstruction in both professional and private everyday life is followed by reconstruction in leisure. Leisure *experiences* more than ever turn into tinkering with one's own identity. A holiday escape becomes a journey of self-exploration, and that implies *drudgery* with one's ego.

But where is the line between working time and leisure time? In our twenty-four-hour economy, the transition between work and leisure, fun and information processing, is smooth. The less free time people have, the more they try to squeeze into it—*maximum kicks in minimum time*. Postmodern experience junkies are not content to live *one* life—they prefer to live several lives at once. The happiness dealers of the leisure industry must constantly boost their customers' doses.

In the future, happiness will be sought only in the extremes—where it is extremely loud and where it is extremely quiet. The need for thrills increases as much as its negation: the (sensual) staging of nothingness/nonentity. The slogan is no longer either-or but both-and. The hybrid set of customer values reflects the multitasking phenomenon of today's information society. Consumers act touchy, despotic, they refuse any target segmentation, and they irritate providers—despite customer relationship management—with their complex desires:

> No one wants our drilling machines; customers want holes in the wall.

In our networked and transparent/lucent markets, consumers hold more power than ever. They know everything (about providers); they want everything and at once. They want tension and relaxation, frenzy/ecstasy and inner peace, bundled in one package. Tour operators work on increasingly complex programs for their all-inclusive holiday resorts. Cookery courses with leading chefs are as much part of packages as soccer training with famous Champions League players. Paradoxicalities become standard: the individual package tour, designer clothes at a bargain. "Retreat into the metropolis" was the advertising slogan of Chicago, Illinois, or consider "Zurich, downtown Switzerland." Both claims dissolve bipolar thinking and reduce with ease the complexity of this world.

Successful suppliers/providers react to hybrid customers with similar strategies. They offer a complex lifestyle world to their customers; they are organized around processes and themes rather than around products. Hairdressers turn into holistic beauty providers (coiffeur and boutique), dessous shops into wine boutiques (Wein and Lingerie). The Swiss Coop Vitality shops (organic food, textiles, and beauty products) positioned themselves as a holistic "problem solver for health and beauty issues" (quite a bold venture in the sedate Swiss retailing business).

Hybrid markets continuously soften the line between individual industries, such as retailing and leisure (e.g., Urban Entertainment Center), catering and entertainment (Eatertainment). Trendy restaurants transmute into nightclubs after dawn; what is a cozy café during the day becomes a huge dance floor at night. Supermarket chains mutate to tour operators (e.g., Billa in Austria), discounters sell cars and computers (Aldi), banks and post offices are well-disguised drugstores, the coffee provider Tchibo sells city trips at bargain prices, and tourism-marketing organizations operate/act as single agencies (e.g., the tourism organization of the German state Schleswig-Holstein).

The most interesting growth and innovation potentials no longer lie within *one* single market but can be found where individual industries meet and converge. Enterprises must operate within networks and strategic cooperations, to enable each enterprise to focus on its core competencies and to offer one collaborative solution to the consumer. In tourism, *destination management* is the first step into the right direction. In my opinion, transnational marketing communities, such as Best of the Alps, will increasingly gain importance. They are the precursors of a future champion league in tourism, which will position itself with show and entertainment character, following the unrivaled example of the winter destination Aspen, Colorado. (Did you know that in Aspen your skis will be delivered to your favorite ski station while you are sleeping?) Consumers want to be surprised—most of them already have a boring everyday life. *Give them the kicks*.

The need for kicks and thrills, for borderline experiences, increases significantly and is more and more frequently let out via the body. Endorphins and body thrills are—besides drugs and esoteric goods—the number one catalysts to escape everyday life. Leisure creations become more and more often body creations. Leisure stages become body arenas, and this is equally valid for booming sporting events and street and love parades, for city marathons and the staging of subculture lifestyles. What seems to be pure fun at first sight (such as widely popular fun sports), what guarantees adrenaline boosts (extreme sports such as ice climbing, shark diving, skydiving, etc.)—in the end it is all part of searching one's identity, of searching a *different* experience. The body acts as slide, as a playground for our own identity.

A veritable bodymania with ever new versions is dispersing in the leisure market, and profitable niche markets are occupied—whether it be gentle running, trail running, or Nordic walking. One of five Swiss visits a gym, and one out of ten does so regularly. As many as 980,000 Austrians are into running, and 5 million Germans regularly tie their running shoes.

THE BODY AS A BRANDING TOOL

An individualistic society, which allows us to be exquisitely self-reflexive and to constantly engage with our small egos (the ego as a construction site), provides the perfect stage to carve our bodies and thus our logo. The body turns into a blue chip on the market for competition and attention—which is not completely unimportant in a society coined by an increasing number of (temporary) singles. Body and body design are more and more regularly a tool for social distinction. Here we have the chip-munching couch potatoes, there we have the well-being elite, here those who lose mobility, and there those who gain it.

"The body is becoming a phenomenon of choices and actions," Anthony Giddens said several years ago, and he is right. The more virtualization and gene technology enters our society, the more attention the real body receives. The more traditional strong men (such as tradesmen and blue-collar workers) and original physical strength vanish into thin air, the more they are aesthetically created—in the torture chambers of the fitness industry as well as on the cliffs of free climbers.

The feminization of society, of course, gently decelerates the staging of the body. Soft values such as pampering and work-life balance are more established and stimulate new leisure products and services. Who else will pamper all these singles, exhausted managers, and housewives close to a nervous breakdown, if not the wellness industry? The business world also discovered the importance of health and balancing programs with the company to increase employee motivation. That is corporate wellness—which encompasses a bit more than tolerating power napping in the office (in the new economy it was fashionable to place a sandbag next to one's desk to relieve piled-up power).

Today the term *wellness* has admittedly blurred and become a shell for a vast array of freeloaders (who release countless make-you-feel-good products from wellness socks to green tea window spray to ironing liquid with lavender). However, no doubt wellness is a socially required corrective, because it manages the collective need for deceleration and regression. The change agents of this development—namely women and the fifty-plus generation—will even further establish a holistic lifestyle in today's society.

Stimulated by feminization, men also develop a new body consciousness off the beaten track of sports and mechanistic body management. Approximately 70 percent of the male German population takes a shower or a bath once a day, and more and more discover the advantages of cosmetics and plastic surgery (in the United States every fifth patient of plastic surgery is male). Lately men also have their exclusive indulgence resorts. Burned-out achievers can, for example, spend 50 EUR per hour to enjoy a scalp massage in the Urban Healing Center in Antwerpen (the first wellness center in Europe for men only).

Pampering and attention—those are the vital deficits of a turbo-generation. In the light of our nonstop society, whose members are on round-the-clock standby, *immediate* deceleration strategies gain tremendous importance. The future belongs to leisure at the doorstep, *instant* leisure, following the slogan "We do it shorter and shorter, but more often." The attractiveness of indoor halls and center parks, ski-domes (currently two in Germany) and amusement parks in the commuter belt of large congested areas will not decline in the future.

Not surprisingly, as these experience quickies around the corner comply with the central customer value of "convenience" the importance of invested time for the quality judgment of leisure experiences for postmodern consumers grows steadily. A short trip promises a higher density of experiences, and thus a higher experience quality, and reduces the risk of potential disappointment (which is more likely with two weeks of a sun and beach holiday). The line of social demarcation is also clearly visible here: Those with money treat themselves with a two-day indulgence trip to the surrounding wine region, while the rank and file consume blockbuster movies in a multiplex.

While urban leisure locations appeal to a wide target audience, short trips in a narrower sense are quick escapes reserved for high-wage earners (in Austria the share of short trips is 8 percent, compared to 14 percent for trips between five and thirteen days). Almost 80 percent of Germans, however—and there is no doubt that they are the mainstream in European tourist behavior—still go on their two-week holiday at least once a year. Nevertheless, short trips will eventually trickle down to a broad audience with the usual time lag and fragment their leisure behavior even more. The encroachment of low-cost carriers such as JetBlue (catering on board are blue potato chips), Ryanair, Southwest, etc., will further add to this development.

Our society unmistakably displays a nomadic nature, above all in metropolitan areas. It is not a coincidence that the most popular meeting points are transit areas: lounges and hotel bars (who experience a worldwide revival/renaissance), where someone such as Philippe Starck can be found. Stressed urban professionals are provided with an infrastructure of *de*celeration just in time. In London, empty batteries can be recharged in multimedia energy rooms at the so-called energy bank; in Berlin you can loll in publicly accessible dormitories (which have the charming atmosphere of a boarding school dorm). Ladies indulge in day spas (in between two meetings), and afterward they dine like ancient Romans in fashionable Relax Restaurants: in a lying position, entirely relaxed, in a pile of cushions and pillows. . . . Motto: well seated, but not stuck.

Successful products are always problem solutions. The central problem of Western society: standard of living increases, but quality of life decreases. This is where the leisure industry kicks in as a pampering service provider. The need for regression is broadly rising—and water seems to be the perfect element to respond to it. Waterscapes are mushrooming everywhere, and so are pleasure parks designed around the central theme of "water," ranging from spas to a simulated Caribbean in center parks; from Hamams to Ethno Water Parks.

No other element has such an emotional connotation as water, and no other element is so loaded with myths. We hail from water and water accompanies us throughout our lives. Children, who are magically attracted to any variety of water from tiniest puddles to huge water slides, illustrate how much we depend on water drip feeding. The fact that the majority of tourists prefer a swimming holiday cannot be ascribed to the abundance of cheap sun and beach destinations—it is more about a collective/mutual regression: water allows you to immerse, to drift and float without worrying, like in your mother's womb . . . water becomes a psychotope. Leisure landscapes/sceneries more and more turn into water landscapes/sceneries. The leisure industry heavily occupies water as a theme: deep diving becomes increasingly popular, underwater hotels are on the lead, e.g., Jules' Undersea Lodge off the Florida shore. Cruises such as theme cruises with folk music stars and riverboat cruises boom (although they experienced a massive slump after September 11), and young people fancy fun cruises. The European fans of cruises also grow steadily (not only due to demographics), following the motto "Halve the speed and double your perception and awareness."

The leisure industry indeed faces a paradigm shift, a new boom of self-discovery: macerated by water in spas and wellness resorts, people more and more find themselves. The fun society breaks the mold of the nonsense container and starts with relish the long overdue search for inner values. In the future, experiences should not only offer fun and pleasure but also meaning and clues. One does not exclude the other, which has been proved by numerous hip-hop fans: they face the astringency of life and even manage to enjoy it.

The question of the meaning of life once again (not only since September 11) comes to the fore. Deficiencies of meaning have successively increased since the hedonistic 1980s. The demand for leisure products which transport meaning and hands-on/playful offers/solutions for self-identity will increase. "Who am I? Where do I go?"—are vital questions that people seek to answer above all in their leisure time. Only in their time off are people in control of their own time and can reflect in peace about touching things.

The door leading to a new spiritual era, in which hedonism and the question of a just life gain importance, is pushed open. This search for meaning stimulates new products such as holidaying in convents or monasteries (in Austria, "Klöstereich" is a well-positioned innovative product) and recycles traditional pilgrimages and study trips. Some temporarily drop out and take a sabbatical, others pilgrimage to Santiago de Compostela. City dwellers treat themselves with downtime, e.g., at an Alpine hut without running water and electricity. These are certainly niche products tailored for a selected few who are fed up with civilization, but they have a pull effect on the product portfolio of large tour operators. TUI, for example, successfully offers an array of simple Alpine huts ("Alpine hut 'Heinzenberg,' 1500 m above sea level, nearest train station 12 km, log-fire heating").

In their leisure time, consumers are in search of the rug that has been pulled out from under their feet. Do you know the happy feeling of townspeople when they walk in a meadow *barefoot*? Germany has barefoot parks, where people can walk around with bare feet and come to terms with themselves. Toni Strohhofer, adventurous owner of Germany's largest Autobahn roadhouse, built a "filling station for the mind," where day-trippers experience "what it feels like to cut a tree in order to carve a wooden bench."

The question of the meaning of life especially gains importance in middle age—in the face of the sooner or later dominating fifty-plus generation; this is a crucial challenge for new leisure products. Consumers are fed up with being two-legged marketing targets. They want to be taken for *real,* and they want to be touched and inspired. They perceive leisure providers as meaning providers, who manage to stage vital issues in startling theme parks.

"Discover what is relevant" is the slogan of the successful young travel track of the German weekly newspaper *Die Zeit.* A fasting week for managers in Aix en Provence promises not only "rejuvenation for skin and body cells," but also "steps to find the meaning of life and to counter existential frustration."

Undoubtedly, the thirst for clues and for the art of living grows. Museums and fans of culture boom in metropolitan areas and form the strategic center of city tourism. While a city trip to London meant a shopping trip a few years ago, people now also visit museums and art exhibitions, sniff at subcultures, and visit architecture exhibitions (Bilbao, Berlin-Mitte, etc.). The thirst for meaning merges with the thirst for experience. Or, to use the words that can be read in a designer boutique in Los Angeles: "Life is beyond price."

Chapter 12

Wellness: A New Perspective for Leisure Centers, Health Tourism, and Spas in Europe on the Global Health Market

Wolfgang Nahrstedt

THE EUROPEAN HEALTH SYSTEM ENTERS THE GLOBAL MARKET

The increasing popularity of the wellness concept in Europe since the 1990s shows that the European leisure and health resorts have entered the global market. After the eras of Roman thermae and European (national) spas, the European leisure and health system entered an era of leisure-based global health and wellness centers after the fall of the iron curtain in 1989. Wellness represents a new global approach to health and stimulates a more leisure-based health concept as well as the development of a new health-oriented leisure system. Wellness hotels and health tourism started this process; gyms, saunas, fun pools, and wellness centers followed and are still following. Traditional health resorts such as spas and hospitals fell into a crisis and therefore need to modernize their concepts. The wellness approach initiated a process of globalization which can be seen and used as an opportunity for the innovation and modernization of the European leisure and health resorts, spas, and tourism destinations.

Three Historic Periods

The history of the European leisure-based health systems is distinguished by the following three periods:

1. From holy springs to Roman thermae: Founding of the European spa culture (10,000 B.C.-500 A.D.).
2. From bathrooms ("Badestuben") toward (inter-)national spas: Democratizing the European spa culture as a leisure-based health system (Middle Ages until 1996).
3. Global perspectives for a new European leisure-based health system in the young/new millennium (since 1989): Globalization was enhanced by a globalized approach to health (WHO, 1948, as cited in Anderson, 1987), a broader understanding of health (Dunn, 1961), and a worldwide growth and differentiation of the leisure structures of wellness resorts (wellness hotels, wellness tourism, wellness offers in leisure centers, spas, gyms, fun pools, saunas, hospitals, etc.)

These three periods produced the following results:

- The first period from 10,000 B.C. to 500 A.D. developed the European leisure-based spa culture until the height (main period) of the Roman thermae.
- The second period from 500 to 1989 A.D. brought a democratization of the European spa and health culture in the nineteenth century. For example, every German worker was allowed to visit a spa every three years for four to six weeks, paid for by the social insurance system.
- The third period, however, will force spas and health resorts to overcome two contradicting trends, namely the worldwide growing leisure-based health orientation and the reduction of social support.

HEALTH CARE: BASIC INNOVATION FOR THE NEXT MILLENNIUM?

Support for the modernization of and the switch to a new, more leisure-based health system opens up a new field of research in economic science (see Figure 12.1). Health care will be the field of a new innovation for the next business cycle in the new millennium, following the basic assumption of the economic theory of long waves (Nefiodow, 1996). This raises the question of how European leisure and health systems should react. What trends among Europeans and

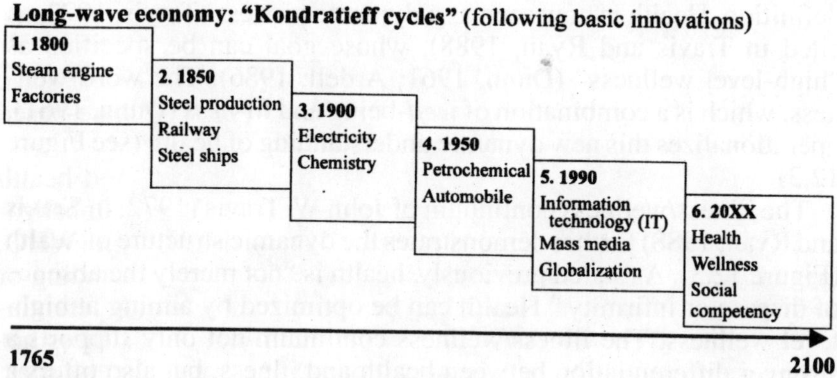

FIGURE 12.1. Health Care: Basic Innovation? (*Source:* Adapted from Nefiodow, 1996.)

international tourists can be observed? Which new health-oriented lifestyles will be developed?

THE WHO'S NEW DEFINITION OF HEALTH

At the heart of the wellness concept lies the WHO's new definition of health (Anderson, 1987, p. 5): "Health is a state of complete physical, mental and social well-being and not merely the absence of disease or infirmity."

Defining health as complete well-being is a reaction to higher life expectancy due to medical progress and, consequently, to the worldwide explosion of health costs. Good health for everyone asks each individual for increased self-responsibility for health care, but also for the financial investments for a healthy lifestyle. The WHO definition broadens the understanding of health, which becomes separated from disease and infirmity and is instead seen as a dynamic process. The WHO aims at providing the highest possible health standard for people all over the world, and thus increases global demand.

THE WELLNESS CONCEPT

The American physician Halbert Dunn developed the wellness concept in 1959 (Müller and Lanz, 1998; Lanz Kaufmann, 1999). This can be seen as a way to implement the new, broader WHO health definition. Health is now seen as a dynamic process (Travis, 1972, as cited in Travis and Ryan, 1988), whose goal can be specified as "high-level wellness" (Dunn, 1961; Ardell, 1986). The word wellness, which is a combination of *well*-being and fit-*ness* (Dunn, 1961), operationalizes this new dynamic understanding of health (see Figure 12.2)

The illness/wellness continuum of John W. Travis (1972; in Travis and Ryan, 1988) further demonstrates the dynamic structure of health (Figure 12.3). As stated previously, health is "not merely the absence of disease or infirmity." Health can be optimized by aiming at high-level wellness. The illness/wellness continuum not only supports a stronger differentiation between health and illness, but also offers a new perspective for illness, because high-level wellness is perceived a perspective for ill people:

> Wellness is best described as a way of life. It is a *lifestyle* that you, as an individual, create to achieve your highest potential for well-being. Your *lifestyle* consists of actions you are able to control, such as how you exercise, eat, manage stress, and perceive the environment. Achieving a high level of wellness involves continual striving for a more healthful way of living. (Ryan and Travis, 1981, cited in Kammermann et al., 1983, p. 1)

From a Knowledge to a Wellness Society

Wellness can be understood as a product of the knowledge society. On one hand, the knowledge society has enforced health dangers through a growing rationalization and mobilization of living conditions. On the other hand, the knowledge society has significantly increased understanding about the relationship between illness and health. The reasons for premature death and the possibilities to fight and overcome it have become better publicized throughout the world. Health education becomes essential as a basis for the development of

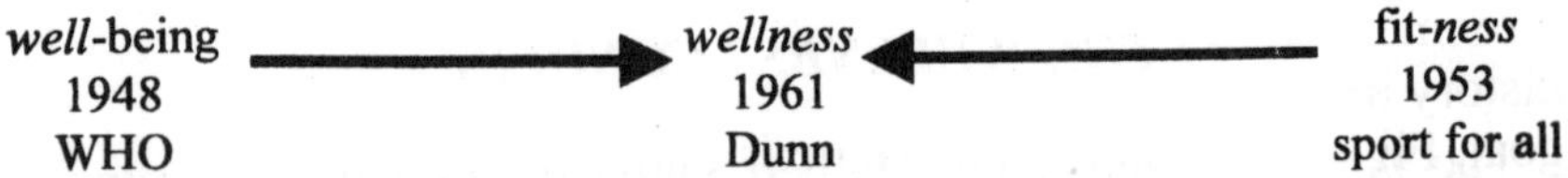

FIGURE 12.2. Wellness Word Development

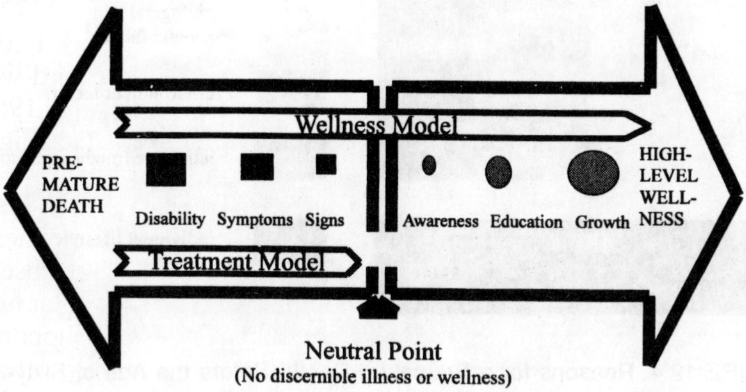

FIGURE 12.3. Illness/Wellness Continuum (*Source:* Adapted from Travis, 1972, as cited in Travis and Ryan, 1988.)

such a conscious lifestyle, especially because the individual lifestyle dominates as a main reason for premature death (Hertel, 2001) (Figure 12.4).

Fitness, Diet, Beauty, Soul, Mind: A New Lifestyle Profile for High-Level Wellness

Learning becomes necessary to develop one's own lifestyle in the direction of high-level wellness. The basic condition and the essential elements for a life of full health and optimal wellness must be clarified. The WHO health definition provides the first hints. The basic condition must be a "complete physical, mental and social well-being," and a wellness lifestyle has to concentrate at least on these three elements.

Fitness is thus one element for physical well-being on the way toward a high level of wellness; however, other elements such as good nutrition, beauty, relaxation, mental activity, social harmony, and environmental sensitivity must be added. The whole potential of human history in regional and global cultures should be used to achieve this goal. Figure 12.5 summarizes the elements required for such a comprehensive understanding of wellness and provides a basis for further development of the wellness concept.

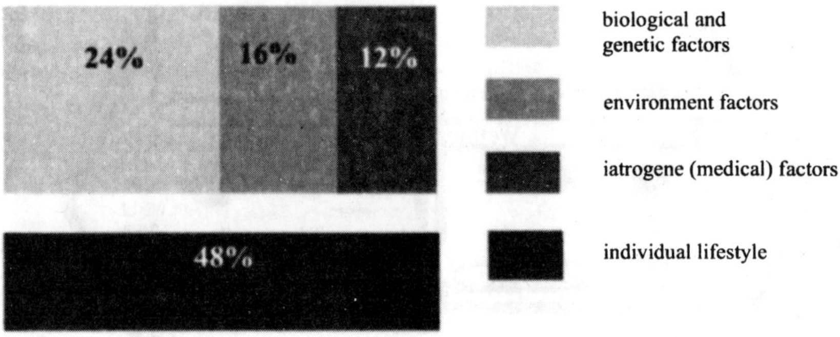

FIGURE 12.4. Reasons for a Premature Death (Before the Age of Sixty-Five Years)

Yoga, Ayurveda, Tai Chi: Globalization of the Health Culture

According to the WHO health definition, all peoples of the world should try to achieve the highest health levels attainable, leading to a gradual convergence of international health care approaches. The different approaches to health in the six or seven existing world cultures have come into more intensive interaction, e.g., Asian approaches such as traditional Chinese medicine, yoga, Ayurveda, tai chi, qi gong, reiki, and shiatsu with Western physical therapy. Meditation is already integrated as one example of elements for high-level wellness in Figure 12.5. The wellness concept tries to integrate these different approaches and thus requires a new metatheoretical effort for quality in understanding of future health care for all human beings.

Precise Wellness Structure Through Health and Wellness Tourism

The growth of health tourism with a strong element of wellness vacation has created a more precise discussion on the structure of wellness elements (Nahrstedt, 2001) (Figure 12.6).

Wellness Concept for Quality Management

Wellness resorts need a quality-management orientation tailored to the new health and wellness concept in order to strengthen their market position and to attract new target and lifestyle groups. The ba-

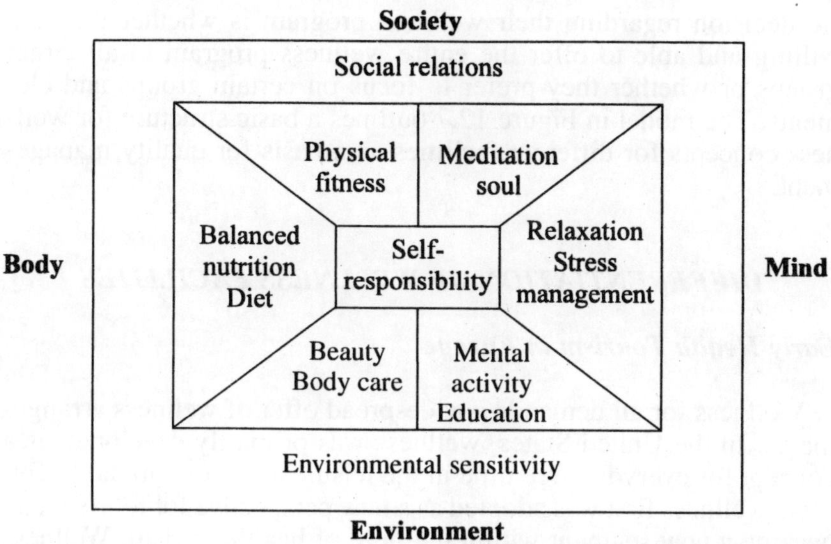

FIGURE 12.5. Elements for High-Level Wellness (*Source:* Nahrstedt, 2001.)

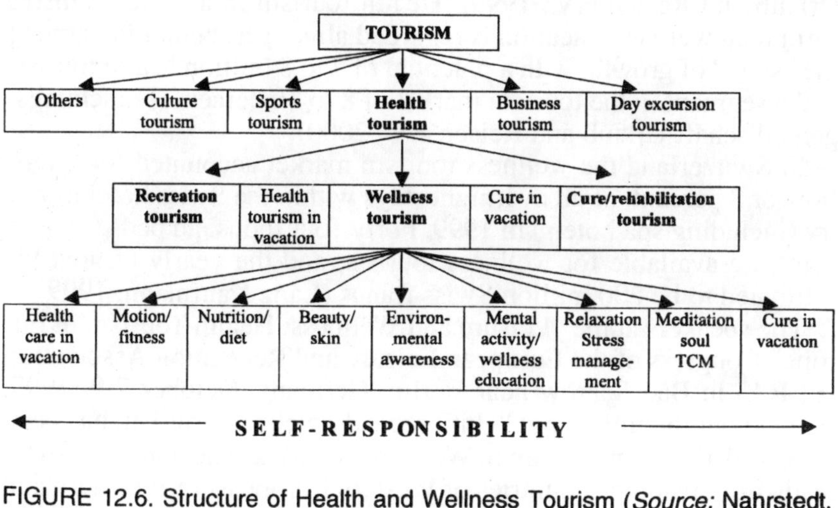

FIGURE 12.6. Structure of Health and Wellness Tourism (*Source:* Nahrstedt, 2001.)

sic decision regarding their wellness program is whether they are willing and able to offer the entire wellness program to all target groups or whether they prefer to focus on certain groups and elements. The model in Figure 12.7 outlines a basic structure for wellness concepts for different facilities as a basis for quality management.

DIFFERENTIATION OF WELLNESS FACILITIES

Early Health Tourism in Europe

Wellness for all demands a widespread offer of wellness arrangements. In the United States, wellness was primarily developed as a concept for everyday free time in the leisure and work arena. In Europe, wellness first was adopted as a new perspective for tourism and became a new segment within the field of health tourism. Wellness hotels have become the pacemaker in Austria and Germany since 1989, and tourism destinations and operators followed since the mid-1990s.

Approximately two-thirds of the German population consider doing something for health to be especially important. This was the result of the German Travel Analysis 1999 (Forschungsgemeinschaft Urlaub and Reisen e.V., 1999). Health tourism in a more intensive form than wellness vacation is regarded already as belonging among the "stars" of growth, with a potential of 7 to 8 million health tourists and a segment in the tourism market of 8 to 10 percent (Forschungsgemeinschaft Urlaub and Reisen e.V., 2000).

In Switzerland the wellness tourism market accounted for 1 million, or 3 percent, of all overnight stays within the Swiss hotel industry (including spa hotels) in 1999. Forty-four thousand beds (16 percent) are available for wellness tourists, and the yearly turnover is estimated to be 200 million Swiss francs (Lanz Kaufmann, 1999).

The speakers at the "Leisure and Wellness: Health Tourism in Europe" Congress of the European Leisure and Recreation Association (ELRA) in Bad Saarow near Berlin, Germany, October 7-9, 1999, pointed out the following: "Until recently wellness tourism has been observed as a phenomenon in Western countries. The dominant trend leads from resource countries of Western Europe toward Eastern and Southern target countries" (Joachim Scholz, German National Tour-

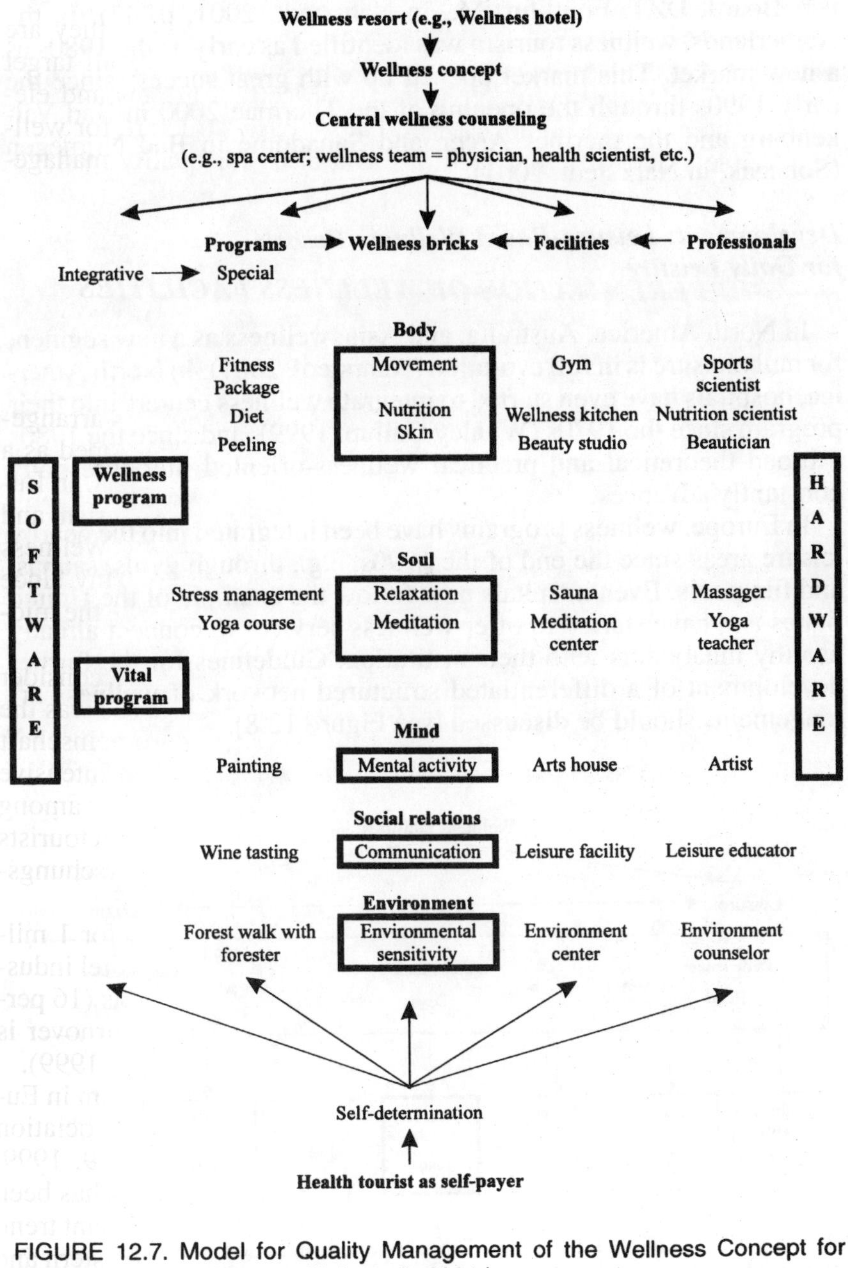

FIGURE 12.7. Model for Quality Management of the Wellness Concept for Different Facilities (*Source:* Nahrstedt, 2001.)

ism Board, DZT, Frankfurt/M., in Nahrstedt, 2001, p. 47). In the Netherlands, wellness tourism was identified as early as the 1980s as a new market. This market opened up with great success since the early 1990s through the opening of the Thermae 2000 in Bad Valkenburg and the thermes Arcen and Sanadome in Bad Nijmegen (Sobczak, in Nahrstedt, 2001).

Development: Leisure-Based Wellness Resorts for Daily Leisure

In North America, Australia, and Asia, wellness as a new segment for daily leisure is in full evolution (Nahrstedt, 2001). In North America, hospitals have even started to integrate wellness centers into their program since the 1970s (Whaley Gallup, 1999), and since the 1980s a broad theoretical and practical wellness-oriented literature body constantly advances.

In Europe, wellness programs have been integrated into the nearby leisure areas since the end of the 1990s, e.g., through gyms, saunas, and fun pools. Even hospitals now follow the example of the United States and have started to offer wellness services to connect already healthy inhabitants with their institution. Guidelines for the further development of a differentiated structured network of wellness arrangements should be discussed (see Figure 12.8).

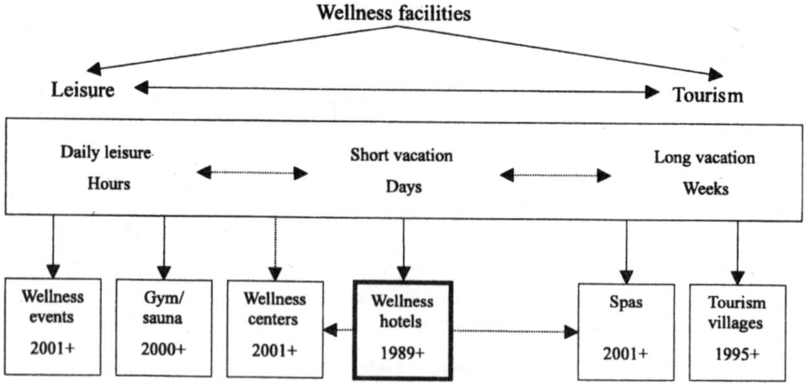

FIGURE 12.8. Wellness Facilities: Differentiation in Space and Time (*Source:* Adapted from Nahrstedt, 2002.)

TARGET GROUPS: FROM YOUNG FEMALES TO SENIOR CITIZENS AND MALES

The differentiation of the wellness facilities in space and time coincides with a dispersion of target groups. Although fitness was originally oriented toward young men, wellness was first accepted by young women. However, the wellness concept gradually became more and more accepted by men and senior citizens. The integration of wellness programs into gyms helped gain the acceptance of young men. The integration of wellness programs into saunas and wellness centers and wellness hotels into spas furthers acceptance by senior citizens.

SPAS: BETWEEN LEISURE AND TOURISM

Spas for All: The Workers Movement Entered the Spas (1884-1990)

Spas are a special example of the effect of the wellness concept in Europe, but they fell into a crisis after 1996. The reception process of the American wellness concept in Europe happened in tandem—not accidentally—with the change of the traditional European health concept and the social (financial) support system. The spas, as the traditional European leisure-based health system, had to adapt to these necessary changes, and not all spas succeeded. A short history of the German spas may help to understand their difficulties.

The social insurance laws of Bismarck (German chancellor, 1871-1890) made spas accessible to the working class. The workers movement caused an important result in Germany. Every worker obtained the right to stay in a spa for four to six weeks every three years for cures with therapeutic or prevention purposes. A new Roman era of spas began. It finished with the globalization of the world economy in 1989. A new era of a global leisure-based health culture including the spas has now started to develop.

The rising number of guests in the spa town Bad Kissingen, for example, demonstrates the dynamics of growth in the spa areas within the past two centuries. Due to social insurance laws from 1884, the guest numbers started to grow rapidly. Between the two world wars (1918-1939), the numbers stagnated on a high level. After World War II, during the period of the German economic miracle (1945-1970), the spas were restructured, the numbers continued growing, and health for everyone became reality (Specht, 1979).

The New Situation: End of the Postwar Era

When the iron curtain fell on November 9, 1989, the postwar era in Europe ended. Germany became unified and grew by 17 million new citizens, totaling more than 80 million inhabitants. The number of spas rose from 280 to 320. Of the approximately 1,500 spas in Europe (without Russia) today, more than 20 percent are situated in Germany. Approximately 13.5 million guests visited the 1,500 European spas (1994), and 10 million (75 percent) of them visited German spas. The approximately 13.5 million guests in European spas stayed approximately 150 million nights (average: 11.1 days), 116 million (approximately 80 percent) of them in German spas (ESPA, 1995). A statistic on the members of the European Spa Association (ESPA) gives similar numbers for 1995 (see Table 12.1). Germany, as one of ten members, represents 318 spas of 750 (42 percent), 74 percent of the visitors, and 97 percent of the registered nights.

In 1994 the 10 million visitors to German spas represented approximately 15 percent of the 80 million Germans, while the approximately 3.5 million visitors to the 1,223 spas in sixteen other European countries represented only 1 percent of 350 million Europeans. Until the early 1990s, visiting spas was regarded highly in Germany. Until the mid-1990s Germans were the most active spa visitors in the world. This led to a high standard of medical treatment and guest service within German spas. Spas in other European countries offer different advantages: Eastern European spas are cheaper, but Southern European spas have more sun, which means they also attract German guests.

Spa Crisis: Reduction of Social Support

Spas have encountered a serious crisis. The question now is how to overcome this crisis. What changes in health trends and lifestyle will occur as a consequence? What reaction to the European spas will be necessary? In 1996, the social health law was changed in many Euro-

TABLE 12.1. ESPA Member Spas and Health Resorts in Europe, 1995

Countries	Member spas	%	Spa visitors	%	Overnight stays	%
Belgium	2		5,000		1,170,267*	
Finland	31		500,000		500,000	
France	117		600,000			
Germany	318	42	9,400,000	74	111,000,000	97
Greece	52		370,000			
Italy	106		1,040,000			
Luxembourg	1		2,792		70,000	
Portugal	32		N/A			
Spain	71		400,000			
Switzerland	20		472,000		1,885,000	
Total	750	100	12,789,792	100	114,625,267	100

*1994

Source: Adapted from European Spas Association (ESPA), 1995.

pean countries, including Germany. The right of German workers to visit a "Kur" has been heavily limited. Now only every four (instead of three) years for three to five (instead of four to six) weeks subsidized visits to spas will be provided with reduced support. As a consequence, the number of overnight stays at many spas fell in 1997 by 30 percent or more (see Table 12.2). Clinics and hospitals had to be closed and thousands of jobs were lost (Deutscher Bäderverband e.V. [DBV], 1998).

The reduction of social support since the 1990s has forced spas and tourism destinations to develop health offers for self-paying guests, and thus create a new perspective of health tourism. An investigation conducted by our Institute for Leisure Science and Culture Work (IFKA) for the German Spa Association (DHV) in February 1999 demonstrated that 80 percent of the spas offer more than two health products for self-payers and 38 percent offer more than five (Nahrstedt and Brillen, 1999).

Foreign Guests: Looking for New Target Groups

As in Roman times and the nineteenth century, the origin of spa guests will become more international. In particular the German spa, with their high quality of medical health care, must fight for new target groups worldwide. Until the present day the share of international guests in German spas is very low, at less than 2 percent (1994: 1.3 percent; 1997: 1.4 percent, see Table 12.3) (DBV, 1995, 1998).

Also the spas must now enter the global leisure-based health market and compete to strive for guest groups worldwide in the new millennium: in Europe, in North America, and in Asia.

TABLE 12.2. Number of Guests and Nights in Western German Spas, 1977-1997

Year	Guests*	Nights
1977	5,637	82,459
1994	9,408	111,919
1997	9,066	93,291

*Length of stay minimum four days.

TABLE 12.3. Foreign Guests in German Spas: Number and Nights, 1977-1997

	Guests* (in thousands)			Nights* (in thousands)		
Year	Total	Int'l	%	Total	Int'l	%
1977	5,637	147	2.6	82,459		
1994	9,408	236	2.5	111,919	1,492	1.3
1997	9,066	251	2.7	93,291	1,307	1.4

*Length of stay minimum four nights.

WELLNESS IN THE NEW MILLENNIUM: RECOMMENDATIONS

The world has become a global village with a global leisure-based health system. Basic knowledge for a long life based on high-level wellness now is at worldwide disposal. Throughout the history of developed global cultures, (medical) treatments have been (theoretically) available. The network of health resorts offers all known treatments and wellness elements. High-level wellness could become available for all human beings. To this end, wellness programs will play a central role. A new global social health and wellness policy must be defined. Health and wellness for all should be guaranteed. Health education becomes essential. A self-directed lifelong learning process of wellness and a healthy lifestyle oriented toward complete well-being must be supported. Health resorts and health tourism will become important new forces in supporting wellness on a high level for all. A socially oriented wellness framework should be developed. The wellness resorts in all parts of the world should organize a social global marketing plan to present special wellness offers for all on the global health market.

The following summary of recommendations should further aid development of the European leisure-based health and wellness system to meet the demands of the global health market:

1. *Definitions:* Wellness and health resorts; wellness, health, leisure, and tourism associations; guest groups and service producers; leisure economy and health policy leaders should all agree on a common definition for wellness in health programs.
2. *Positioning:* Wellness should get the position of a new segment in health progams between "pure" recreation on the one hand and rehabilitation (e.g., as "Kur" in spas) on the other hand.
3. *Quality management:* Elements for wellness programs must be defined and qualified, especially offers for
   - body (movement: fitness, food: nutrition, skin: beauty);
   - soul (relaxation: stress management, meditation);
   - mind (culture, health education, and counseling), as well as social communication (socializing, events); and
   - environmental sensitivity (introduction to health and the environment, lectures on ecology, nature self-learning trails).
4. *Globalization:* The different health approaches of different cultures (e.g., TCM, yoga, Ayurveda) have to be transferred more precisely into the wellness programs.
5. *Benchmarking:* Benchmarking, learning from best solutions in the region and throughout the world, becomes essential for the further development of wellness programs.
6. *Target groups:* Regional as well as international target groups must be defined more precisely with regard to their wellness needs and their social situation.
7. *Marketing:* Marketing strategies for the wellness programs should be developed for (inter-)culturally and socially different target groups.
8. *Cooperative competition:* Quality standards for wellness programs should be optimized by the service producers in cooperation with the Wellness Commission of the European Union (EU), organized in collaboration with the relevant associations and ministries for health, leisure, and tourism (e.g., German Spa Association [DHV], German Tourism Association [DTV], German State Ministries on Health and Economy; SwissTourism Wellness Corporation, Swiss Spa Houses Association [VSK], Swiss Hotel Association; Austrian Tourism Association; Wellness Hotels Austria).

9. *Education and professionalization:* Wellness education for all becomes fundamental as part of health education within school and as lifelong self-directed learning. Lifelong self-directed learning of wellness elements supporting a healthy lifestyle of complete well-being should be elaborated upon. An adequate professionalization of wellness programs should be intensified by training of relevant personnel, by quality management of learning wellness institutions, through development of a new profile for wellness professionals (e.g., wellness trainer, counselor, manager), and through scientific research and evaluation.
10. *Health policy:* The wellness programs should be regarded as an innovative form of leisure-based health care, organized on a privately funded/self-funded principle. However, wellness programs should also be structured by the leisure and tourism industry rather than by health policy. Applying price differentiation, additional insurances, health education in and out of school, advertising, and recommendations helps to encourage wellness programs to become available to all groups of the population.

REFERENCES

Anderson, R.A. (1987). *Wellness Medicine.* Lynnwood, WA: American Health Press.

Ardell, D. (1986). *High Level Wellness.* Berkeley: Ten Speed Press.

Deutscher Bäderverband e.V. (DBV) (1995). *Jahresbericht 1994.* Bonn: REHA-Verlag.

Deutscher Bäderverband e.V. (DBV) (1998). *Jahresbericht 1997.* Bonn: REHA-Verlag.

Dohmen, G. (Ed.) (1997) *Selbstgesteuertes lebenslanges Lernen?* Bonn: Bundesministerium für Bildung, Wissenschaft, Forschung und Technologie.

Dunn, H.L. (1961). *High Level Wellness.* Arlington: RW Beaty.

European Spas Association (ESPA) (1995). *Spas and Health Resorts in Europe.* Bonn/Bruxelles: ESPA.

Forschungsgemeinschaft Urlaub und Reisen e.V. (F.U.R.) (1999). *RA 1999. Erste Ergebnisse. ITB 1999.* Berlin, Hamburg: Author.

Forschungsgemeinschaft Urlaub und Reisen e.V. (F.U.R.) (2000). *RA 2000. Erste Ergebnisse. ITB 2000.* Berlin, Hamburg: Author.

Hertel, L. (2001). Wellness. In Deutscher Heilbäderverband e.V. (Ed.), *Deutscher Bäderkalender* (pp. 164-172). Bonn/Gütersloh: Flöhmann-Verlag.

Kammermann, S., Doyle, K., Valois, R.F., and Cox, S.G. (1983). *Wellness R.S.V.P.* Menlo Park, CA: The Benjamin/Cummings Publishing Co.

Lanz Kaufmann, E. (1999). *Wellness-Tourismus: Marktanalyse und Qualitätsanforderungen für die Hotellerie-Schnittstellen zur Gesundheitsförderung.* (Berner Studien zu Freizeit und Tourismus 38). Bern: Forschungsinstitut für Fzeizeit und Tourismus der Universität Bern.

Müller, H. and Lanz, E. (1998). Wellnesstourismus in der Schweiz: Definition, Abgrenzung und empirische Angebotsanalyse. *Tourismus Journal* 2(4): 477-494.

Nahrstedt, W. (Ed.) (2001). *Leisure and Wellness: Health Tourism in Europe.* Eleventh ELRA Congress. Bielefeld: IFKA (IFKA-Dokumentation 21).

Nahrstedt, W. (2002). Wellness im Brennpunkt: Wissenschaftliche Betrachtung eines jungen Marktes. In B. Richter and M. Pütz-Willems (Eds.), *Wellness und Wirtschaft professionell und profitabel: Konzeption Finanzierung und Vermarktung von Spa-Projekten* (pp. 10-22) Augsburg: Willems.

Nahrstedt, W. and Brillen, H. (1999). Gesundheitstourismus—auf dem Weg ins Jahr 2005: Highlights der Kurexpertenbefragung '99. *Heilbad und Kurort* 51(9-10): 274-279.

Nefiodow, L.A. (1996). *Der sechste Kondratieff: Wege zur Produktivität und Vollbeschäftigung im Zeitalter der Information.* St. Augustin: Rein-Sieg-Verlag.

Specht, K.G. (Ed.) (1979). *Effektivität und Effizienz von stationären Heilverfahren in der Beurteilung von ärztlichen und nicht-ärztlichen Experten der Rehabilitation.* Nürnberg.

Travis, J.W. and Ryan, S.R. (1988). *The Wellness Workbook,* Second Edition. Berkeley, CA: Ten Speed Press.

Whaley Gallup (1999). *Wellness Centers: A Guide for the Design Professional.* New York: John Wiley and Sons.

Chapter 13

Alpine Health Tourism: Future Prospects from a Medical Perspective

Wolfgang Schobersberger
Sven Greie
Egon Humpeler

INTRODUCTION

If asked what is important in our society, the individual's wish for health still plays a central role. However, the definition of health has changed immensely over past decades. In 1948, the World Health Organization (WHO) defined health as "complete bodily, spiritual and social well-being."

Good health means much more than merely the absence of disease. However, attaining health according to the WHO definition is only partially possible and ultimately not achievable. Health includes the trio of body, mind, and spirit—the well-being of all three. The question is why, then, in our Western civilization is humankind still divided into these three parts even as the call for a holistic view gains momentum.

A MAGICAL TERM: WELLNESS

Well-being is closely associated with the term *wellness,* a combination of well-being and fitness. It is hardly possible to define wellness in a single sentence. Wellness describes physical activity combined with relaxation of the mind and intellectual stimulus, basically a kind of fitness of body, mind, and spirit, including the holistic aspect.

The objective lies in attaining personal, individual well-being under the strong influence of a subjective component equally dependent on individual expectations and an individual starting point—a kind of "finding yourself" in an age of megastress. Wellness is a constantly active process characterized by and living through its dynamic. Achieving well-being is a multilayered process of many phases. This process goes from becoming aware of non-well-being to clarifying possible improvements to eventual realization of improvements. The concept of well-being requires initiative and determination, everyone deciding for himself or herself whether to make a lifestyle change. Well-being can therefore be understood as a holistic philosophy of life. The ultimate goal can be aiming for temporary feelings of happiness as well as long-term contentment.

HEALTH AND WELLNESS TOURISM

Promoting health and well-being are goals of tourists and vacationers as well as part of market strategies of tourism providers. It is assumed on all sides that vacation in itself is healthy. How well-founded is this assumption of vacation as healthy? Is there hard scientific proof to confirm this supposition? "This billion dollar industry, tourism, flourishes with little basic research, since it satisfies fairly stable, periodically recurring needs" (Kagelmann, 1993, p. 34).

This quotation nearly preempts the previous questions. What is the international state of research in evidence-based medicine concerning vacation, health, and recovery? The following sobering result appeared after an international literature search in the largest scientific medical and social sciences database (Keul, 2000). Few publications link tourism with health. Our own analysis of the well-established medical database Medline showed that the search term "tourism 2001-2002" produced 123 publications, the combination tourism and wellness only revealing four. "Therefore, there can be no mention of tourism-health research on an international basis" (Keul, 2000, p. 48).

A very large discrepancy can be found here between existing promises from travel organizations and what has been proven in terms of studies. The consumer, i.e., the vacationer, thus assumes without further inquiry that the offer, and this automatically holds true for all wellness holidays, is necessarily beneficial to his or her health. There is no proof that the product "holiday for health," purchased with dear money, is as similarly effective as, say, medication. Can we, from a medical standpoint, simply watch all the offers in health tourism and the wellness field and count on their being effective and fitting? Clearly "no" is the frank and honest answer to this. In contrast to the numerous scientific tests in the spa industry domain (Hillebrand and Weintögl, 2001), we are still at the starting point concerning health tourism.

What does "health tourism" mean? According to Kaspar (1996, p. 55) "health tourism is the general term for a touristic sojourn with the aim of maintaining, stabilizing and regaining health, during which—in order to differentiate it from a normal holiday—health services form a focal and vital part." These can relate to various physical or psychological subcategories (medical checkup, beauty treatment, slimness, fitness, diet, etc.). In contrast, a wellness holiday is more hedonistic and based on enjoyment, relating less to individual goals and also being less medically oriented (Steinbach, 2000). Many elements of the integrated health holiday are included. Adventure, entertainment, and outdoor sports play important roles.

Expansion in health tourism, which has stagnated somewhat over the past few years, can be viewed as an increase in supply over demand. The results of a German travel analysis (FUR, as cited in Keul, 2000) show that between 1996 and 1998 approximately 8.2 million Germans chose health-oriented vacations (1998: 8.7 million; wellness holidays, 1.1 million; fitness holidays, 1.8 million; health holidays, 3.6 million; spa resorts, 2.2 million). However, these numbers have decreased slightly compared with the years 1993 to 1995. Therefore, it is important to create new highlights in these types of holidays, especially since the markets in the growth sectors of health and wellness tourism are coming closer and closer together. According to newest analyses (TUI study, as cited in Muhlhausen, 2001), 40 percent of all German citizens above age fourteen are basically interested in fitness, beauty, and spas.

On the medical side, some basic questions must be addressed to establish serious health tourism.

- Which health measures are effective in health tourism?
- What type of person can profit from which health measures?

- What would individual holiday planning be like?
- Where should the wellness holiday take place (e.g., mountain holiday versus vacation by the sea)?

Using the project AMAS 2000, we show a realistic way of combining well-founded medical research and touristic goals.

AMAS 2000: AN EXAMPLE OF SCIENTIFIC MEDICALLY ORIENTED HOLIDAY RESEARCH

AMAS 2000 is a research project, with the general objective of investigating the health aspects of a vacation in the mountains at various altitudes and comparing these with nearly identical holidays located in the valley. AMAS stands for "Austrian Moderate Altitude Study," and the number 2000 indicates that mainly sojourns at altitudes up to 2,000 meters were investigated. The main study was completed in the year 2000, and the results of the first part of the pilot project in Lech were published that same year.

Motivations for this study include the following:

1. In the years 1965 to 1972, systematic testing was carried out in Austria—in Kühtai in Tirol and in Obertauern in Salzburg—to determine the clinical and physiological importance of activity at moderate altitudes. This is closely associated with the names Inama and Halhuber (1975).
2. Austria has always played an important role in alpine medicine. Therefore, an idea already discussed and agreed upon in its outlines in 1988 in Davos by Berghold, Humpeler, and Schobersberger could almost automatically become reality. This idea found approval and resulted in the formation of the Austrian Society for Mountain Medicine in November 1988.
3. We are concerned by the discrepancy between the fact that yearly approximately 10 million people hike and ski in the mountains in Austria alone, that up to 40 million people visit the Alps every year, and that worldwide approximately 100 million spend holidays in altitudes around 2,000 meters, whereas extensive research results on this topic can hardly be found.

The topic of health will become a central theme in the future, and some authors even think that health in the holistic sense—bodily, spiritual, and social—will carry a new, long economic cycle in the twenty-first century (Nefiodow, 1997). The authors might also see the term alpine medicine defined in a somewhat broader sense than in the excellent editorial by Berghold (2000). Should every one of the millions of people who visit the mountains all around the world and spend their holidays hiking there be called an alpinist or mountain climber? Is alpine medicine really only there to explain the resultant damage from the strange behavior of these people or to try to limit such damage, or are mountain climbers really just the conquerors of the useless?

In any case, it is our opinion that evidence-based medicine in the areas of holiday medicine, health tourism (especially concerning mountain holidays), and the whole area of wellness should be required and that these topics should be discussed only by those competent in the field. Competence can be gained only if comprehensive studies conforming to strict scientific criteria are conducted.

Whenever health is recommended and advertised, proof of the studies upon which the advertisements are based should be required. The authors are strictly opposed to using the argument of health commercially without citing corresponding research results in advertising.

At this point it is important to note the fact that, after many years of discussion, diverse Austrian institutions have nonetheless supported our argument and agreed to medical research in tourism. This is particularly unique, as this was not a commissioned study, but a purely academic study, whose results were left absolutely open during the planning as well as the execution stages, thus allowing the authors to maintain absolute independence and freedom in all conclusions and publications.

Nonetheless, considerable funding is necessary to enable such a study, and so at this point we would like to thank all sponsors who supported the project AMAS 2000 (see Humpeler and Schobersberger, 2000).

As illustrated, there are numerous touristic medical reasons for the execution of the study, and it should not be forgotten that such projects make it possible to arrive at specific recommendations for tourists and those responsible for tourism. Also, doctors can determine who should be advised to spend a holiday in the mountains, how long he or she should stay, how he or she should behave there, what altitude is best for an optimal holiday, and also who should be dissuaded or should be advised to spend a holiday in the valley or at sea level.

Apart from these holiday medical aspects, there are also very solid scientific motivations as well as basic research, especially concerning questions of both altitude adaptation mechanisms and optimizing altitude training. Activity at higher altitudes requires altitude training, regardless of whether this is a young professional athlete or an older person who is not entirely fit. The decisive factor is the amount of exercise, i.e., the performance accomplished in relation to the endurance of the particular individual.

Why should we be concerned specifically with moderate altitudes (1,500-2,500 m)? Climatic changes play a special role in moderate altitudes, since the oxygen content of the blood is nearly identical with the supply in the valley even though mild hypoxia occurs. However, definite changes regarding adaptation mechanisms occur, mainly in the acute adaptation phase, which mean that possible negative effects of a mild lack of oxygen are all but overcompensated through countermeasures. The stimulus of a mild lack of oxygen thus leads to positive adaptation mechanisms in the organism.

In order to discuss a new way of thinking concerning altitude adaptation mechanisms, the study was conducted with people with metabolic syndrome, and the resulting study was titled "Influence of Moderate Altitude on Subjects with Metabolic Syndrome." There were two main reasons: First, excess weight, metabolic blood sugar and blood fat disorders, as well as elevated blood pressure and changes in the heart rate are not rare in the general population and are considered to be cardiovascular risk factors. To a certain extent, these trial subjects represent a mirror image of our society. Second, metabolic syndrome in humans exposed to moderate altitudes may be a model for investigating the additive effects of holidays plus moderate altitude.

This is about a network of negative correlations, whereby the active nervous system (heightened sympathicotonia) plays a pivotal role. The consideration was that throughout the exposure to altitude these heightened, sympathetic activities were slowed, reduced, and regulated, which ultimately would mean that an altitude exposure or activity at certain altitudes selectively blocks the sympathetic nervous system and thus may positively influence a whole set of risk factors in the cardiovascular system.

In order to address these complex questions, a very comprehensive study protocol was agreed to, whereby twenty-two men aged thirty-five to sixty-five years (average age fifty-five), chosen from the Tyrol area by the University Hospital of Innsbruck, participated in the pilot study in Lech. After an appropriate screening procedure the preliminary examinations took place in Innsbruck, followed by a three-week stay in Lech and Oberlech (Vorarlberg, Austria) with guided and pulse-controlled hikes between 1,500 and 2,500 m. During these three weeks the parameters in the study protocol were measured through both repeated blood sampling and noninvasive methods, and the study was brought to a close after a final examination upon return to valley altitude in Innsbruck.

Naturally, the approval of the study protocol by the ethics committee of the University of Innsbruck was obtained prior to the outset of the study.

The following areas were investigated:

- cardiovascular reaction (blood pressure measured at rest and under strain, twenty-four-hour BP and ECG records, ergometry);
- anthropometric data (body weight, body mass with analysis of muscle tissue, fat, and water);
- blood picture;
- state of well-being (neuropsychological testing); and
- further testing of internal organs (endocrinology and immunology).

Main Results of the Pilot Study in Lech

The decisive results were that after three weeks of moderate altitude exposure a considerable reduction in hypertension took place. We observed an improvement in fat metabolism, body weight was reduced by more than 2 kg without real dietary measures, the quality of red blood cells improved, and improvement of neuropsychological values occurred (e.g., positive life descriptions, quality of sleep) (for details see Schobersberger et al., 2000).

Significance of the Lech Study and Future Considerations

The great merit and importance of the Lech study was that through this pilot study both feasibility and safety could be tested for the first time and a series of very interesting results were found. What was, however, decisive with the Lech project is the fact that only through this study was the second part of the AMAS project made possible. Here, a moderate altitude study in Obertauern (Salzburg, 1,700 m) and a valley study in Bad Tatzmannsdorf (Burgenland, 200 m) were effected at the same time, and an additional pilot study as a substudy was carried out in Mauterndorf (Salzburg, 1,100 m). All of these studies, with eighty-five participants taken care of by a research team of thirty-six people, have been completed and some parts have been presented (Greie et al., 2003). The trend indicates confirmation of the Lech data, although we have very certainly also found positive effects with the participants in Bad Tatzmannsdorf.

FORECAST

Basic research in day-to-day medicine without application and usefulness is more an end unto itself and does not serve the final consumer. In the case of the AMAS 2000 project it was always our objective to structure the scientific facts in a transparent manner and then offer the results for the benefit of holiday-makers. Therefore, we have decided to integrate the knowledge gained from the AMAS study into a specific bookable holiday. We have succeeded in gaining the community of Lech am Arlberg, Austria, as a partner for this innovative venture. For the first time ever a hiking holiday of several weeks is on offer. It has been worked out and will be accompanied by the Research Institute for Leisure and Travel Medicine (IHS), based on the AMAS data (AMAS Welltain holiday, which consists of the combination of *well*ness and moun*tain*).

Using state-of-the-art medical and scientific sports technologies, we accompany the vacationer during a two-week hiking holiday whereby he or she is personally taken care of by specially trained sports scientists. The individual adjustment of the hiking vacation is made after a preliminary medical and scientific sports examination. The offer is a holistic one including bodily and mental relaxation units under the motto “feeling the mountains with all senses.”

Realizing the scientific part of AMAS 2000 in the vacationer-oriented AMAS Welltain holiday can be only the beginning of a long development process. Only in this manner can planned projects for the future, similar to AMAS 2000, obtain an optimal effect for the vacationer. We are particularly motivated to show that the individual and his or her health lie at the heart of this study, the discovery of optimal possibilities in preventive and rehabilitative medicine. We are great opponents of uncontrolled mass tourism in the mountains. The Alps should not replace the fitness studio or simply be derogatively looked down upon as sporting equipment, and we should always be aware of the special aspects of mountain vacations: pristine nature, the origin and beauty of the mountains, and flora and fauna. Hiking in the mountains becomes an adventure—all our senses are affected and at the same time we train muscles, our cardiovascular systems, and breathing as well as improve different metabolic parameters. The goal is for body and soul to regain harmony, and to practice research with this in mind is the ultimate intention of the IHS Research Institute. We are convinced that with AMAS 2000 an important start in addressing questions of holiday medicine in general has been made, particularly in gaining expertise in the medical questions of mountain and hiking vacations. We know very well that this can constitute only a beginning, as many unanswered questions will have to be further clarified through research.

REFERENCES

Berghold, F (2000). Was heisst eigentlich "Alpinmedizin"? Editorial. *Alpinmedizinischer Rundbrief,* 23 (August): 2-3.

Greie, S, Humpeler, E, Mittermayr, M, Fries, D, and Shobersberger, W (2003). Oxygen transport and erythropoiesis in tourists with the metabolic syndrome at altitude (1.700 m): Project AMAS-2000. *Hypoxia Medical Journal,* 3:10.

Hillebrand, O and Weintögl, G (2001). *Handbuch für den Kurarzt.* Wien: ÖÄK-Verlag.

Humpeler, E and Schobersberger, W (2000). Das urlaubsmedizinische Forschungsprojekt AMAS 2000. In Schobersberger, W, Humpeler, E, Gunga, HC, Burtscher, M, and Flora, G (eds.), Jahrbuch der Österreichischen Gesellschaft für Alpin und Höhenmedizin. Innsbruck: Raggl Digital Graphic and Print, pp. 23-32.

Inama, K and Halhuber, MJ (1975). *Der Herzkreislaufkranke im Hochgebirgsklima,* Volume 25. Frankfurt am Main: Schriftenreihe der deutschen Zentrale für Volksgesundheitspflege e.V.

Kagelmann, HJ (1993). *Tourismuswissenschaft.* München: Quintessenz.

Kaspar, C (1996). *Gesundheitstourismus im Trend: Jahrbuch der Schweizer Tourismuswirtschaft 1995/96.* St. Gallen: Institut für Tourismus und Verkehrswirtschaft, pp. 53-61.

Keul, AG (2000). Gesunde Reise-erholsamer Urlaub. In Keul, AG, Bachleitner, R, and Kagelmann, HJ (eds.), *Gesund durch Erleben? Beiträge zur Erforschung der Tourismusgesellschaft.* München, Wien: Profil Verlag GmbH, pp. 48-53.

Mühlhausen, C (2001). *Future Health.* Studie des VNR Verlags für die Deutsche Wirtschaft AG. Düsseldorf: Das Zukunftsinstitut.

Nefiodow, LA (1997). *Der sechste Kondratieff.* Rhein-Sieg: Verlag.

Schobersberger, W, Humpeler, E, Gunga, HC, Burtscher, M, and Flora, G (2000). *Jahrbuch der Österreichischen Gesellschaft für Alpin- und Höhenmedizin.* Innsbruck: Raggl Digital Graphic and Print.

Steinbach, J (2000). Das Marktpotential für den Gesundheits- und Wellnesstourismus. In Keul AG, Bachleitner R, and Kagelmann HJ (eds.), *Gesund durch Erleben? Beiträge zur Erforschung der Tourismusgesellschaft.* München, Wien: Profil Verlag Gmbh, pp. 73-83.

Chapter 14

Skiers, Ski Bums, Trust Fund Babies, Migrants, Techies, and Entrepreneurs: The Changing Face of the Colorado Ski Industry

Richard R. Perdue

INTRODUCTION

Service quality is a critical determinant of success in the tourism and leisure industries (Kotler, Bowen, and Makens, 1999; Perdue, 2000). In the Colorado resort industry, at least 80 percent of the guests are a direct result of service quality, either as satisfied repeat guests or first-time guests there as a result of a word-of-mouth recommendation. The "services marketing triangle" has been proposed as a foundation for understanding quality in service environments (Zeithaml and Bitner, 2000). This concept postulates that quality is a function of the interactions between a services firm and two populations—service consumers and service employees. Based on research conducted in the Colorado ski industry over the past ten years, this chapter contends that in resort environments this concept must be extended to examine the interactions between a resort and three populations—resort consumers, resort employees, and resort-community residents.

Historically, tourism service-quality research has focused on measuring consumer perceptions of quality and its impact on consumer satisfaction and revisit intentions (Fick and Ritchie, 1991; Yuksel and Yuksel, 2001). Market segmentation has been a major part of this research (Noe, 1999). Clearly, an enormous diversity exists in the characteristics and behaviors of leisure participants, diversity that significantly influences both consumer perceptions of service quality and satisfaction (Oliver, 1997). A broad portfolio of measures and techniques for segmenting this diverse population into more homogeneous groups has subsequently evolved, allowing us the opportunity to better understand segment motivations, expectations, and behaviors (Driver and Johnston, 2001).

Quality employees are the raison d'être of service quality in resort settings (Spiselman, 1995; Roos, 2002). Yet, for a variety of reasons, Colorado resorts are finding it increasingly difficult to attract and retain good employees (Ledgerwood, Crotts, and Everett, 1998). Consequently, the resorts have developed a variety of recruitment strategies aimed at both traditional and nontraditional employees. The result is an increasingly diverse employee population. The evidence clearly shows that resort consumer satisfaction is heavily influenced by employee satisfaction (Rust and Oliver, 1994; Brady and Cronin, 2001). To understand employee satisfaction, it is equally clear that segmentation strategies will facilitate an understanding of the diversity of employees, including their job motivations, expectations, and behaviors (Bowen, Schneider, and Kim, 2000; Brown and Dev, 2000).

Host-community residents significantly influence resort service quality. Four critical interactions between resorts and local residents have been identified: (1) local residents are the primary source of employees, (2) they commonly interact with resort guests in the host community and at the resort, (3) they can initiate antitourism behaviors which quickly and dramatically damage a resort's image, and (4) through the political process, they can impact public policy toward tourism development (Perdue, Long, and Kang, 1999). Although there is a significant body of research on host-community residents and their attitudes toward tourists and tourism development (Anderek and Vogt, 2000), this research has not been adequately extended to address the increasing diversity of resort-community residents. Over the past decade, many Colorado resort communities have experienced extraordinarily high population growth. A diverse mixture of people is migrating to the resort communities for a variety of different reasons, many of which are not related to work or employment. Again, segmentation strategies will facilitate understanding this diversity of residents and their attitudes toward both tourists and tourism development.

The purpose of this chapter is to describe a leisure-lifestyle segmentation of these three populations—guests, employees, and host-community residents—in Colorado ski resort communities. The chapter begins by describing lifestyle segmentation and the methodology used for this research. Eight major lifestyle segments are then described. The chapter concludes by discussing the implications of these lifestyle segments to resort development policy in Colorado.

LEISURE-LIFESTYLE SEGMENTATION

The concepts and methodologies of market segmentation are pervasive throughout both the services (Lovelock, 2001) and the tourism marketing literatures (Kotler, Bowen, and Makens, 1999). Tourism markets are routinely disaggregated into segments based on demographics, geography, behaviors, benefits sought, and a variety of other measures (Loker and Perdue, 1992). Fundamentally, the purpose of this process is to organize a heterogeneous population into more homogeneous subpopulations or segments in order to better understand, explain, and influence behavior. Ultimately, with the recent and dramatic advances in information technology, this process is being applied at the individual (N of 1) level (Darby, 1997). Further, in a classical Veblenian sense (Trigg, 2001), we are increasingly subject to "lifestyle brands" such as Tommy Hilfiger, Abercrombie and Fitch, Nike, Porsche, etc., wherein ownership and display of the brand communicates one's self-image and values (Helman and De Chernatony, 1999).

Recent advances in market segmentation have often combined several different types of measures into a summary concept. Lifestyle segmentation, as applied in the consumer behavior field, is such a summary concept (Swenson, 1990). Generally, consumer lifestyles are measured as a combination of consumer activities, interests, opinions, and demographics (Wilkie, 1986). Quantitative, factor and cluster analytic, qualitative focus group, and observational techniques have evolved as methodologies to identify lifestyle segments (Heath, 1996).

For the purpose of this chapter, lifestyle is defined as "the particular manner in which a person or group of people choose to live" (Cathelat, 1994), including their behaviors, interests, opinions, and demographic profiles. To further extend the concept of lifestyle, this chapter focuses on "leisure lifestyles," which incorporates the centrality of leisure preferences to the individual's life choices.

A wealth of research is found on the concept of lifestyles, not only in the consumer behavior literature, but also in the health, leisure, and deviant behavior literatures. Within the consumer behavior literature alone, literally thousands of lifestyle research citations occur. This extensive literature base is, in part, due to the robust nature of the lifestyle concept and its potential application to virtually any dimension of human behavior (Walters, 2000). It is also partly due to our constantly changing environment that creates opportunities for new lifestyle categorizations, primarily based on generational differences (Strauss and Howe, 1991) or on basic shifts in our collective behavior (Eaton, 1997). For example, the new buzzword is "technographics," which identifies lifestyle groups on the basis of information technology adoption patterns and literacy.

The popularity of lifestyle research is also a function of the intuitive appeal and face validity of different lifestyle acronyms. Because of our common mass media experiences (Englis and Solomon, 1995), we share an amazing level of agreement on what it means to be a Generation Xer, a baby boomer, a WOOF (well-off older folks), a DINK, a yuppie, or a redneck. Each of these terms implies a shared constellation of values, interests, and behaviors. Further, it seems that each new generation of lifestyle terms carries an increasing level of specificity. For example, consider the very popular PRIZM categories such as "Blue Blood Estates" versus "Public Assistance" or, my favorite, "Shotguns and Pickups" versus "Furs and Station Wagons." Although some decry the validity of these descriptors (Englis and Solomon, 1995), the existentialist perspective would argue that such acronyms and lifestyle descriptors allow us to efficiently organize and understand the complex environments of our everyday lives, thereby helping us to develop strategies for managing a multidimensional concept such as service quality (Walters, 1998). As such, the goal of this research has been to develop qualitative descriptors of the different lifestyle groups that comprise the consumers, employees, and host-community residents of the Colorado ski industry.

STUDY METHODOLOGY

This chapter is a summary of research conducted over the past ten years. For the skier populations, the associated research includes yearly on-site skier surveys and focus group studies, a panel study of the primary local skier market—the Colorado Front Range population which includes the Denver, Boulder, Colorado Springs, and Fort Collins metropolitan areas, and three major studies of the destination skier market conducted using mail or Internet survey methodologies. The employee studies include an annual employee opinion survey that has been conducted at four major resorts for the past seven years, focus groups, and qualitative interviews. The host-community resident studies include surveys conducted in seven resort communities over the past ten years. In addition, there have been ongoing participant observation studies, extended interviews with resort managers and community leaders, and continual analysis of industry and news media articles. Finally, extensive secondary analyses have been conducted of resort operating data, including financial reports, consumer satisfaction and complaint data, and guest history databases. This chapter draws upon the information from these various studies to illustrate the lifestyle diversity of the various key populations in Colorado ski resort communities.

COLORADO RESORT COMMUNITY LIFESTYLES

The central propositions of this chapter are (1) that service quality and resort management are a function of three critical populations: resort guests, resort employees, and host-community residents and (2) that each of these populations are increasingly diverse and must be segmented in order to understand their values, opinions, and behavior. This section describes eight segments: three resort employee groups, three host-community groups, and two resort guest groupings. This segmentation is not meant to be comprehensive; its purpose is to illustrate the diversity of these critical populations.

Employee Groups

Traditional Ski Bums

Probably the most recognized of the employee lifestyle groups is the traditional ski bum. They are young, typically male, from a reasonably affluent background, and relatively well educated. Many of them are taking a semester or year off from their university education to work at the ski resort. Others have just finished their university education and are working for a season at a ski resort before they "get serious" about their careers and enter the "real world." Importantly, ski bums often feel overqualified for the jobs they are being asked to perform. Various jobs, such as lift operations, tend to be repetitive and can be very boring. Furthermore, because of their affluent background, they seldom have experience working in frontline service occupations. As a result, many of them resent the nature of their jobs.

The ski bums love to ski. They work at a ski resort so that they can ski. Most of them rank the opportunity to ski as critical to their life satisfaction. Often they ski 100 days per winter, which equates to two out of every three days. Comparatively, the ski bums' jobs are relatively unimportant to them. Many change jobs several times over the course of the ski season, which is easy to do because of the high demand for employees in most resort communities. They are apt to catch the "powder flu," which is failure to show up for work on days with fresh powder snow on the mountains.

Traditional ski bums are very frustrating employees. They are not motivated by their jobs, their salaries, or career aspirations. They are there to ski. Work is secondary. If they do not like their current job, it is easy to quickly find another one. Many have high absenteeism levels. Resort managers must work extraordinarily hard to make the job fun and exciting to this group. Further, they have to make the employee feel involved in the resort.

Poor service quality can be a serious problem. Traditional ski bums often develop derogatory terms for resort visitors and develop an attitude of superiority, primarily based on their superior ski talent. In addition, because of their resentment toward their jobs, they frequently resent the special requests and questions of resort guests.

Interestingly, this group further divides into three groups. Most return to their homes, their education, and their planned careers after the ski season. However, some stay in the resort community and, over time, are promoted into management careers with the resort. These individuals often develop a very strong attachment to the resort community and its summer activities. A common saying in this group is "I came for the winter, but stayed for the summers."

A third group has evolved at upscale resorts such as Vail—the professional ski instructor. On a typical day at Vail Ski Resort, a relatively large number of skiers purchase private lessons, frequently as a means of avoiding lift lines. The professional ski instructor has evolved to serve this market. These individuals are highly evolved, are very close-knit, have their own language, and have a strong social structure based on seniority and ski ability. This group develops a strong sense of "insiders." Because gratuity income is especially important, they develop a strong sense of service quality for their clients. However, they also develop an equally strong sense of disdain for skiers who do not purchase lessons.

The New Ski Bum

A second group of ski bums has emerged over the past ten years. This group is almost the opposite of the more traditional ski bum. They are older, often over fifty. Many have taken early retirement from corporations or from military careers. They are reasonably affluent in that they have income from pensions and retirement funds.

They love to ski, but more important, they love to live in the resort towns. They become especially attached to the resort community and are often active in local programs and activities. Many of them enjoy the summers as much or more than the winters.

The new ski bums work in the resorts for the social opportunities of meeting other employees and guests and because it gives them a sense of belonging to the community. Although their jobs are important for income, they are even more important for the social and belonging opportunities.

They tend to be excellent employees. They are reliable, consistent, friendly, and far less derogatory in their attitudes toward resort guests. Obviously, they are more mature and more experienced.

However, the new ski bum is also very concerned about the effects that resorts have on the environment and the local communities. Quality of life and the cost of living in the resort communities are important issues to these individuals. They are likely to actively oppose resort development and expansion if they feel it will cause declines in local quality of life or increases in the cost of living.

Migrants

Getting and keeping quality employees is perhaps the greatest resort management challenge in Colorado, particularly for many back-of-the-house jobs such as housekeeping and maintenance. Over the past two decades, a dramatic growth has occurred in the number of migrant workers. Initially this group was comprised almost exclusively of people from Mexico. More recently, this group has experienced a strong surge in Eastern Europeans.

The Hispanic migrant workers enjoy a fascinating leisure lifestyle. They work extremely hard for six months and then spend the summers unemployed, enjoying their leisure back in Mexico. The resorts help them to attain a six-month work visa. During those six months, they try to work as many hours as possible, often working several different jobs and averaging in excess of eighty hours of work per week.

One of the potentially significant problems with the migrant employees is the nature of their work visas. The visa is actually granted to the resort. If the employee quits or is terminated from the resort job, the visa is revoked and the migrant must immediately return to his or her home country. This creates an opportunity for employee abuse and mistreatment.

The resorts feel that the migrant Hispanic workers are excellent employees. They show up for work every day. They will accept jobs that many traditional ski bums will not do. They want to work as many hours as possible and readily accept overtime assignments. Most do not ski and, consequently, never get the "powder flu." Contrary to the ski bums, they appreciate their jobs and rarely complain or cause problems with resort guests. However, they obviously require the resorts to develop both language and cultural sensitivity management skills.

In addition, the resort communities are required to acclimate to the Hispanic culture and presence, greatly increasing pressure and costs on such systems as housing, education, medical services, and public safety. Of particular note and concern to many resort community leaders and residents is the willingness of the Hispanic employees to live in overcrowded apartments, often having eight to ten people living in a simple two-bedroom apartment.

Because of the cost of living in resort communities, it is not uncommon for the migrant employees to live in other communities and commute either by car or by resort-provided busing. In a number of examples in Colorado, the employees are living in communities in adjacent counties. Because both local sales taxes and real estate taxes are levied at the county level, the adjacent counties do not benefit from the resort's commercial success. Yet these adjacent counties have to develop and pay for social services provided to the migrants, including bilingual education systems, medical services, and social welfare services. This often puts an enormous burden on the adjacent county public services and tax base.

Host-Community Resident Groups

Trust Fund Babies

A huge transfer of wealth is currently occurring in the United States. The Depression generation, born in the 1920s and 1930s, is dying. That generation is renowned for their work-oriented lifestyle and for their propensity to save money. My generation, the baby boomers, is inheriting this money. The baby boomer lifestyle tends to be characterized by a propensity to spend, often beyond our income as evidenced by high credit card debt, lack of home equity, and low savings rate. The baby boomers are much more oriented to their current life satisfaction and are not willing to defer leisure in favor of work. Thus, a very large sum of money is transferring from a work-oriented saving generation to a leisure-oriented spending generation. Estimates of the size of this wealth transfer over the next twenty years are as high as $3 trillion. As much as 5 percent of this money is being spent on vacation homes in and around resorts throughout the United States, leading to a massive buildup of resort condominiums and homes. Virtually every resort community in Colorado is currently experiencing massive development and redevelopment of vacation properties.

Dramatic increases in prices have resulted from this expansion. A single condominium in Beaver Creek sold recently for a record $7.8 million. One is under contract in Aspen for $7.5 million. Numerous homes and estates have sold for prices in excess of $20 million. The local residents who own property are benefiting from this price inflation. Renters or those wishing to buy property are being pushed out of the resort communities. For example, a recent study in Aspen, Colorado, concluded that a typical local employee would have to work twenty-seven full-time jobs in order to afford a home in Aspen.

Although many of these resort condominiums and homes are being purchased as vacation properties, a dramatic increase occurred in the number of very wealthy individuals either permanently or semipermanently living in the resort communities. I have titled this group "trust fund babies" in that their primary source of income is inheritance, in many cases leading to a population that does not need to work for income. The trust fund babies are a wealthy, mostly Caucasian, middle-age group that is extremely leisure oriented. They participate in skiing but also expect and are patrons of high culture and arts activities.

Importantly, the trust fund baby often views many of the resort communities almost as a private country club. They do not necessarily want resort expansion or large numbers of skiers. They live the ultimate leisure lifestyle and want a system that responds to their every wish and whim. Often they lack tolerance for less affluent groups, particularly the resort migrant employees. Conversely, they are often ridiculed by those other populations for conspicuous consumption, particularly for the size and opulence of their homes. The conversion of traditional agricultural and forested lands into their palatial estates is a significant political issue not only in the resort communities, but for the entire state of Colorado.

Techies

The "techies" are another group that has migrated into the resort communities in recent years. This group is affluent, middle aged, and highly educated. They work hard at jobs that are a combination of home offices, connected via the Internet to a remote corporation, and extensive travel to temporary job sites located throughout the world. For work, they need a combination of good air access and broadband Internet services. They can get these services in the resort communities. In addition, they have the leisure lifestyle and quality of life they seek. Although they work many hours, those hours tend to be bundled. They also tend to have bundled leisure time when they participate not only in the resort ski and summer activities, but also in the entertainment and related activities available in resort communities.

In the United States, real estate taxes are the primary source of funding for social welfare services such as education, public safety, parks and recreation, and medical services. Many Colorado resort communities have a large vacation home real estate base. For example, in Routt County (Steamboat Springs), Eagle County (Vail, Beaver Creek), Summit County (Keystone, Breckenridge, Copper Mountain), Pitkin County (Aspen), and San Miguel County (Telluride), the majority of the private property is owned by nonresidents; frequently these properties are occupied only a few weeks of the year. This creates a large tax base for a relatively small resident population. As a result, many resort communities have extraordinarily excellent schools, medical services, recreation facilities and services, arts and entertainment, and public safety programs. Because of the mobility of their jobs, the techies can easily live in the resort communities and benefit from this quality of life.

As with the trust fund babies, techies do not depend on resort success for their income. Their primary focus is maintaining and enhancing the local quality of life, which is not necessarily based on the local economy, particularly in the short term. The resorts need to be able to demonstrate how their expansion and operations benefit the local quality of life to gain the support of this group.

Entrepreneurs

A recent study conducted in the area surrounding Yellowstone National Park found that 40 percent of the local business owners had visited the area first as tourists, loved the area, and subsequently moved to the region and either started or purchased a business (Snepenger, Johnson, and Rasker, 1995). The ski resort communities of Colorado have also experienced this phenomenon. A growing population segment of entrepreneurs have moved to the region and started businesses because of their desire to live in an area that suits their leisure lifestyle. They are middle aged and relatively affluent, but they need their companies to be successful to be able to afford life in the resort communities.

This group experiences high frustration levels. Because of the shortage of employees, they tend to work long hours, often to the detriment of their leisure participation and the leisure lifestyle that originally attracted them to the area. Many entrepreneurs view the resorts both as business partners and as competitors. Because most of their businesses focus in some way on tourism, the resort's success in attracting tourists to the area directly impacts their own success. However, the resorts are aggressively trying to retain a greater revenue share of visitor expenditures by offering a broad range of products and services. Further, the resorts compete with the entrepreneurs for employees. Consequently, the entrepreneurs support resort expansion in any business category other than their own, and they are adamant in their wish for the large resort corporations to build and finance employee housing.

Guest Groups

As would be expected, enormous diversity occurs within the resort guest population, diversity that could be described at several levels of specificity. The following focuses only at the first level, the key differences between the "local skiers" and the "destination skiers."

Local Skiers

The local skiers are generally young, Caucasian, relatively affluent, and well educated. They live in the metropolitan communities on the Front Range of Colorado and commute by personal car to the ski areas, primarily for day trips on weekends. These individuals view skiing as a part of their normal recreational activities as opposed to a deserved vacation experience.

The local skiers' participation is heavily driven by value. They tend to be very price sensitive and try to get the best value possible, so that they can ski as often as possible. Local skiers are able to buy heavily discounted season passes. While the resorts may charge as much as $60 for a daily lift ticket, unlimited season passes are available to local skiers for less than $300. Still, the local skiers commonly feel that the resorts overcharge for other products, particularly food and beverages and equipment. Many see the resorts as being too profit oriented, too focused on the more lucrative destination skiers, and not sensitive to their needs.

The local skiers commonly develop derogatory attitudes and opinions of the destination skiers. In a paradoxical sense, they love to be tourists but generally dislike other tourists. It is not uncommon for conflict and arguments to occur between the local and destination skiers. The destination skiers are frequently inexperienced and unskilled. Consequently, the local skiers see them both as a potential hazard and as a subject of ridicule.

The greatest frustration for the local skiers is the heavy traffic on Interstate 70, the primary access between the metropolitan Front Range and the ski resorts. Locals feel that the resort should help pay for proposed multibillion-dollar improvements of the highway, but would adamantly oppose lift ticket price increases to pay for such road improvements.

Local skiers generally oppose resort expansion both because of traffic concerns and environmental protection. Although many of them own resort real estate, the ongoing rapid expansion of the resort communities is a major environmental concern, particularly the development of large "trophy home" estates owned by wealthy nonresidents.

Destination Skiers

Other than their geographical residence, the destination skiers are demographically similar to the local skiers. They also tend to be young to middle aged, Caucasian, and relatively well educated. Although their mean income is significantly greater than the local skiers' incomes, the median incomes are generally similar. Motivationally, they are fundamentally different. Instead of viewing skiing as a normal weekly recreational activity, they are on a ski vacation and want a memorable experience. The common attitude is "I work hard; I'm on vacation, and I deserve the best." As a result, the destination skiers tend to be less price sensitive but are still angered by the discrepancy between local and destination skier prices.

The destination skier is sensitive to crowding both in the ski lift lines and in the resort cafeterias. The local skiers commonly bring at least part of their lunch to the resort with them and purchase part from the resort cafeterias. The destination skier resents such local skiers when the cafeterias are crowded and lack seating, particularly given that they commonly spend what most consider to be high prices for their food and beverages.

Interestingly, the destination skier bifurcates into two subgroups. One subgroup is novelty seeking and has a "belt-notch mentality." They are trying to ski as many different resorts as possible, which creates a significant competitive advantage for resort areas such as Summit County, Colorado, where seven ski areas are located within an hour's drive.

Conversely, the other destination skier subgroup is loyal to a particular resort, often visiting it both in the winter and summer seasons. These individuals purchase resort condominiums and real estate that the resort subsequently manages for them as a rental property. This transition from "loyal guest" to "owner" results in dramatically higher service quality expectations.

IMPLICATIONS AND CONCLUSION

Thus, extreme lifestyle diversity exists within Colorado resort communities, impacting virtually all aspects of resort development, management, and marketing. As an example, on the issue of subsidized employee housing, trust fund babies and techies are generally opposed due to fears of its impact on their lifestyles. Entrepreneurs are hugely in favor but expect the large resorts to finance and develop the housing. The traditional ski bums and migrant workers favor housing development but are concerned about housing restrictions, particularly the migrant workers' concerns regarding occupancy restrictions. The new, older ski bums are less favorable due to fear of its potential impact on their own housing investment; NIMBY (not in my backyard) is a key issue to this group. Destination skiers generally favor employee housing, as it will probably result in better service. Local skiers oppose employee housing over environmental concerns and generally hold negative attitudes toward resort expansion. Effectively managing resort expansion and operations in such a contradictory policy environment is extremely difficult.

Management Implications

Given this complex policy environment, it is critical that resort managers

1. Understand the diversity of the leisure environment, considering not only guests but also employees and local residents, going beyond survey research and conducting focus group and observational research to understand the lifestyles and values of the different groups.
2. Understand the key concerns and motivations of each lifestyle group.
3. Develop expansion plans, management strategies, and marketing campaigns with a clear understanding of the needs and concerns of the different lifestyle groups.
4. Monitor the satisfaction of each group with the resorts' actions and programs.

Research Directions

Segmentation research in tourism and recreation has focused heavily on quantitative methods. Still, it would be extraordinarily difficult to design a survey that would capture the population variance described in this chapter. Clearly there is a role for both quantitative and qualitative research programs. As such, the following research directions are proposed:

1. A role exists for long-term observational studies to describe the diversity of leisure lifestyles.
2. Understand and recognize at least three populations that characterize the leisure/tourism setting—the consumers, resort employees, and the host-community residents. Only through the interactions of these three groups can we begin to understand the true diversity of tourism and leisure settings.
3. Understanding the various demonstration effects—the relationships between the various groups in the resort setting—is important to understanding the dynamics of service quality. The attitudes of the various groups toward one another are critical.
4. Move beyond traditional satisfaction and attitude studies, whether it be consumer or employee satisfaction or host-community resident attitudes, to understand the dynamics of the relationships between a resort and its publics.

REFERENCES

Anderek, K. and Vogt, C. (2000). The relationship between residents' attitudes toward tourism and tourism development options. *Journal of Travel Research,* 39(1): 27-36.

Bowen, D., Schneider, B., and Kim, S. (2000). Shaping service cultures through strategic human resource management. In Swartz, T. and Iacobucci, D. (Eds.), *Handbook of Services Marketing and Management,* pp. 439-454. Thousand Oaks, CA: Sage Publishing.

Brady, M. and Cronin, J. (2001). Customer orientation: Effects on customer service perceptions and outcome behaviors. *Journal of Services Research,* 3(3): 241-251.

Brown, J. and Dev, C. (2000). Improving productivity in a service business: Evidence from the hotel industry. *Journal of Service Research,* 2(4): 339-354.

Cathelat, B. (1994). *Socio-Lifestyles Marketing.* Chicago: Probus Publishing.

Darby, I. (1997). The meaning of lifestyle. *Marketing,* 92(8): 21-22.

Driver, C. and Johnston, R. (2001). Understanding service customers: The value of hard and soft attributes. *Journal of Service Research,* 4(2): 130-139.

Eaton, B. (1997). "Technographics" may be the new research buzzword. *Marketing News,* 31(19): 8.

Englis, B. and Solomon, M. (1995). To be and not to be: Lifestyle images, reference groups and the clustering of America. *Journal of Advertising,* 24(1): 13-28.

Fick, G. and Ritchie, J.R.B. (1991). Measuring service quality in the travel and tourism industry. *Journal of Travel Research,* 30(2): 2-9.

Heath, R. (1996). The frontiers of psychographics. *American Demographics,* 18(7): 38-43.

Helman, D. and De Chernatony, L. (1999). Exploring the development of lifestyle retail brands. *Service Industries Journal,* 19(2): 49-68.

Kotler, P., Bowen, J., and Makens, J. (1999). Marketing for hospitality and tourism, Second edition. Upper Saddle River, NJ: Prentice Hall.

Ledgerwood, C., Crotts, J., and Everett, A. (1998). Antecedents of employee burnout in the hotel industry. *Progress in Tourism and Hospitality Research,* 4: 31-44.

Loker, L. and Perdue, R. (1992). A benefit based segmentation of a nonresident summer travel market. *Journal of Travel Research,* 30(1): 30-36.

Lovelock, C. (2001). *Services Marketing,* Fourth Edition. Upper Saddle River, NJ: Prentice Hall.

Noe, F. (1999). *Tourist Service Satisfaction. Advances in Tourism Applications,* Volume 5. Champaign, IL: Sagamore Publishing.

Oliver, R. (1997). *Satisfaction: A Behavioral Perspective on the Consumer.* New York: McGraw Hill.

Perdue, R. (2000). Service quality in resort settings: Trends in the application of information technology. In Gartner, W. and Lime, D. (Eds.), *Trends in Outdoor Recreation, Leisure and Tourism,* pp. 357-364. New York: CABI Publishing.

Perdue, R., Long, P., and Kang, Y. (1999). Boomtown tourism and resident quality of life: The marketing of gaming to host community residents. *Journal of Business Research,* 44(3): 165-178.

Roos, I. (2002). Methods of investigating critical incidents: A comparative review. *Journal of Service Research,* 4(3): 193-204.

Rust, R. and Oliver, R. (1994). Service quality: Insights and managerial implications from the frontier. In Rust, R. and Oliver, R. (Eds.), *Service Quality: New Directions in Theory and Practice,* pp. 1-20. Thousand Oaks, CA: Sage Publications.

Snepenger, D., Johnson, J., and Rasker, R. (1995). Travel stimulated entrepreneurial migration. *Journal of Travel Research,* 34(1): 40-44.

Spiselman, A. (1995). Visionary Ritz-Carlton takes TQM to new level. *Hotels,* October: 45-46.

Strauss, W. and Howe, N. (1991). The cycle of generations. *American Demographics,* 13(4): 24-33.

Swenson, C. (1990). *Selling to a Segmented Market: The Lifestyle Approach.* Westport, CT: Quorum Books.

Trigg, A. (2001). Veblen, Bourdieu and conspicuous consumption. *Journal of Economic Issues,* 35(1): 99-115.

Walters, G. (1998). Three existential contributions to a theory of lifestyles. *Journal of Humanistic Psychology,* 38(4): 25-40.

Walters, G. (2000). *Beyond Behavior: Construction of an Overarching Psychological Theory of Lifestyle.* Westport, CT: Praeger Publishing.

Wilkie, W. (1986). *Consumer Behavior.* New York: John Wiley.

Yuksel, A. and Yuksel, F. (2001). Measurement and management issues in customer satisfaction research: Review, critique, and research agenda. *Journal of Travel and Tourism Marketing,* 10(4): 47-80.

Zeithaml, V.A. and Bitner, M.J. (2000). *Services Marketing,* Second Edition. New York: McGraw Hill.

Chapter 15

Theme Park Tourist Destinations: Creating an Experience Setting in Traditional Tourist Destinations with Staging Strategies of Theme Parks

Roland Scheurer

EXPERIENCES: A NEW PRODUCT OF A FUTURE EXPERIENCE ECONOMY?

Experience gastronomy; experience hotels; experience shopping; worlds of experiences; eating, drinking, driving, flying experiences—experiences are the keyword of actual leisure and tourist promotion. Is this a new concept in leisure and tourism? Since the early days of leisure and tourism people have traveled to particular locations to experience natural or human-made attractions that provided a pulling power and motivation to visit (Milman, 1993). Therefore, experiences are not a new concept in the leisure and tourism market.

The importance of experiences in society has grown. By 1992 the sociologist Schulze (1993) was already speaking of an experience society. The results of several sociological studies show that the importance of work declined while valence of leisure and consumption grew. In general, hedonistic, outward-oriented values such as companionability, fun, and extroverted lifestyles grow more and more important while work and liability-oriented values such as discipline, diligence, and thriftiness fade.

Pine and Gilmore (1999) speak of an experience economy that is developing. In the experience economy, the economic process is perceived as the creation of experiences by staging products and services for the consumer. Work is theater and every business a stage. This process can go to such lengths that the experience is no longer only an additional value for promoting a product. The experience, rather, becomes the central offer people are looking for, and the product itself is reduced to an additional feature, i.e., the permission to take part in a special experience setting. Food in themed restaurants, for example, can be an addition in the specific themed area of the gastronomy experience. No longer will products and services be sold, but—similar to the entertainment industry—participation or entrance fees will be charged.

Leisure and tourist industry theme parks are an already existing example for this new process. In exchange for an entrance fee they offer a setting with many different staged experiences. Visitors seem to be very happy with their stay, and the theme park industry worldwide has grown from 225 significant theme parks (U.S. parks with > 500,000 visitors and worldwide significant parks) with a total of 300 million visitors and $7 billion turnover in 1990 to 340 significant parks with 545 million visitors and $13.8 billion turnover in 1999 (Altenhöner and Friedrich, 2000).

On the other hand there is the development of "traditional" leisure and tourist offers such as museums, zoos, or tourist destinations (especially in Switzerland). Declining numbers of visitors, stagnant receipts, bad utilization figures, and corresponding financial difficulties are some of the main problems in these offerings. In order to fulfill the changing requirements of demand, some traditional museums and zoos have successfully begun to apply elements of theme parks in their offers (see Bäumler, 2001).

EXPERIENCE SETTING: THE FUTURE CONCEPT FOR TRADITIONAL TOURIST DESTINATIONS IN THE EXPERIENCE ECONOMY?

Theme parks aim to create an atmosphere of another place and time and usually concentrate on one dominant theme, around which architecture, landscaping, costumed personnel, and different facilities for entertainment, distraction, recreation, or physical activity, such as rides, shows, food service, and merchandise, are coordinated. Because the different facilities in a theme park all belong to the same enterprise, everything is coordinated to create an overall experience—a special setting for the visitor. Visitors of theme parks enter an artificial world created purely for commercial reasons. Is the comparison with traditional tourist destinations in the Alps therefore entirely impossible? Are the differences too fundamental? The question is wrong, because the contrast of artificial and genuine (or authentic) does not exist in tourism. In modern tourism the world has always been artificially arranged for visitors (Romeiss-Stracke, 1999). The real space has been touristified (Wöhler, 2000). Therefore, authenticity never existed in modern tourism. Regarded from this point of view, the so-called artificial experience worlds of theme parks are only a radical, consistent, and obviously successful further development (Romeiss-Stracke, 1999).

Of course, there are still differences between theme parks and traditional tourist destinations.

- One main difference is the *spatial relationship*. Wöhler (2000) explains in his concept of constructed spatially relations that a Lüneburger Heide tourist destination can be copied and staged anywhere in the world as a "Lüneburger Heide"-world of experiences with all its cultural attractions. But only in the Lüneburger Heide itself are these cultural attractions bound with the space. Therefore, traditional tourist destinations usually offer attractions that are bound up with the local space (landscape, culture). Theme parks, in contrast, are not bound within the specific space (they are in this sense artificial)—they can be built anywhere where requirements meet (good traffic connections, a sufficient population within a two-hour arrival, etc.).
- A theme park is an *enterprise*. All facilities (restaurants, rides, hotels) are planned and coordinated by the same management to create an overall experience. Most Alpine tourist destinations, in contrast, developed more slowly and without coordination—they are grown, not centrally planned. For this reason tourist destinations usually consist of independent, small and medium-sized, historically complex, and interlaced units. No service chain operates to create an overall visit impression. Therefore, a gap between the individual unit (restaurant, hotel) and the whole destination can be observed.
- In theme parks we have visitors and employees, which act in a direct economic relationship. Traditional tourist destinations also embrace inhabitants with no direct economic relationship with tourism.

These differences are mainly caused by the differences in the structure of "artificial experience worlds" (theme parks) and "grown experience worlds" (tourist destinations).

Comparing the results of motivational research in theme parks and tourist destinations (Bill, 1997; Scherrieb, 1997; Forschungsgemeinschaft Urlaub und Reisen [FUR], 2000; Lässer and Bieger, 2000), Table 15.1 shows that not many differences exist between people visiting theme parks and people visiting traditional tourist destinations.

Despite the structural differences between theme parks and traditional tourist destinations, the further considerations of this chapter will regard theme parks as a radical, consistent, and obviously successful further development in tourism. Theme parks offer the visitor a complete setting for experiences that corresponds to the future requirements of leisure and tourist offers in the concept of an experience economy. Theme park settings are thus considered as a model for experience settings in future tourism.

EXPERIENCE SETTINGS IN THEME PARKS

In this section the concept and core elements of experience settings in theme parks will be explained.

Experiences

Concerning some of the numerous descriptions of experiences (Husserl, 1901; Schöndorf, 1995; Schulze, 1993; Geser, 1996; Hartmann, 1996), experiences can be defined as consciously or unconsciously perceived, subjective involuntary personal processes which

TABLE 15.1. Motives in Theme Parks and Destinations

Motives of visitors in theme parks	Motives of visitors in tourist destinations
Spending time with family or friends	Spending time with family or friends
Fun and entertainment	Experience natural or human-made attractions
Escaping daily life	Escaping daily life
Relaxation and convenience	Wellness, relaxation, and convenience
Well-being in nice environment	Making own spontaneous decisions

become knowledge once they have been reflected upon. Thus experiences are subjective personal processes (Figure 15.1). While a certain incident for one person might be a novel experience, for another person it is just a normal incident, because he or she already has knowledge of this incident by experience.

Perception

For further discussions on the topic of stimulating experiences, the term perception is central. The phenomenon of perception is generally the subject of psychological research, which focuses on the individual as recipient of environmental stimuli (Figure 15.2). Perception therefore means the process and the result of converting stimuli. The result is a copy of the objective/real environment and the person's inner being (Hartfiel and Hillmann in Kampschulte and Schneider-Sliwa, 1997). Perception of a real environment is a subjective process, i.e., not every reality is transmitted in an equal copy. Therefore, the more activities a person is undertaking in a certain space, the more accurately he or she realizes the setting.

Atmosphere

Schober (1993a, p. 336) defines atmosphere "as the emotional effect of a spatial defined situation." Synonyms are ambience or setting. An atmosphere is created through all the stimuli in the defined situation. In addition to the emotional effect, an atmosphere also possesses a "request character," pointed out by Lewin (1951), and can therefore stimulate a particular behavior. Therefore, not only the individual's inner being but also the environment has a great influence on

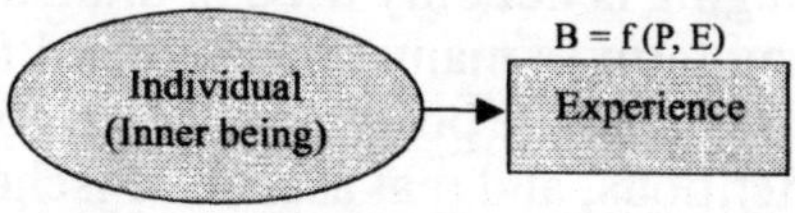

FIGURE 15.1. The Individual in the Experience Setting Concept

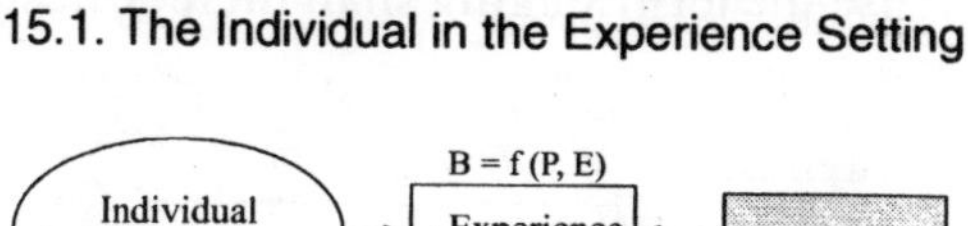

FIGURE 15.2. Perception in the Experience Setting Concept

experiences. Lewin (1951) formulated the field theory, which says Behavior = f (Person, Environment): All actions are influenced by the field in which they take place. Analysis must be based on the situation as a whole and must consider the dynamic interchange between parts of the system. Life space, the total subjective environment that each of us experience, the person, and the environment are viewed as one constellation of interdependent factors (Figure 15.3).

Barker (1968), one of Lewin's students, views the environment largely as an influence on people's behavior. Barker outlined the behavior setting as a unit of the environment which has both structural and dynamic aspects. He defines behavior settings as units of the environment that have relevance for behavior.

A behavior setting is made up of one or more standing patterns of behavior which happen to individuals. Barker exemplifies the behavior setting concept in relation to the design of supermarkets in which people are led to use specific paths from the entrance to the cashier.

Despite some criticisms, Zeisel (1981) considers Barker's ecological psychology approach as the single most valuable formulation on environment and behavior. Therefore, this approach is the origin of the following concept of experience settings. The term will be referred to as behavior setting, however, because the environment in theme parks is designed to create experiences it is renamed experience setting.

Staging

The term *staging* originated in the theater field and stands for the total preparation for the performance of a play. Today's general definition of staging accompanies the new definition of the theater term. Today the term staging is not only used in dramatics but has also advanced to a leading term in many other cultural fields. In this broad sense staging aims at creative processes, which correlate in a specific way imaginary, fictitious, and real aspects (Fischer-Lichte, 1998). In this aesthetic sense the term staging shall include aesthetic work in its

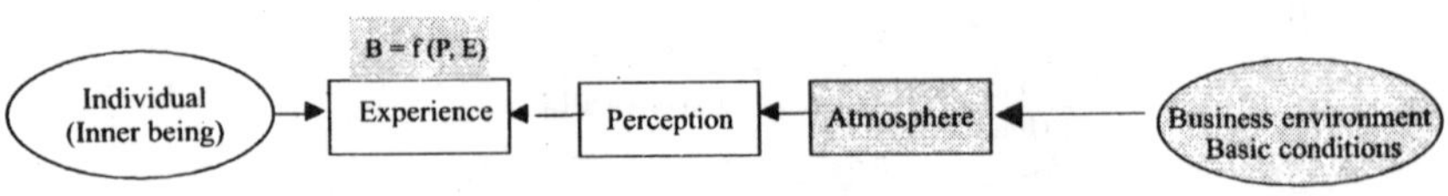

FIGURE 15.3. Atmosphere in the Experience Setting Concept

total broadness, i.e., not only artistic productions in a narrower sense but also the fields of design, fashion, and town and landscape planning (Figure 15.4).

Staging As the Instrument to Create an Experience Setting

Staging tries to create a certain atmosphere that stimulates visitors' experiences. Therefore, staging in this chapter is defined as an instrument for specific creation or intensification of an experience setting for a specific target group with different elements in consideration of business environment and basic conditions. Business environment includes the other management factors of theme parks, e.g., financial capacity and promotion. Basic conditions are economical (income), ecological (climate, weather), social (needs), and juridical factors influencing the staging process.

Key Elements of Successful Staging in Theme Parks

In a research process including evaluation of secondary literature and interviews with theme park experts, we found the following success factors of the product design in theme parks: theming, attractions, architecture/design, quality factors, cleanliness and kindness, management of visitor flows, visitor orientation, all-inclusive price system, and renewal/extension. These factors can be summarized in the following key elements (Figure 15.5):

1. The *main theme* is the starting point of the staging process. It is used to unify the structure and organization of the park through constant visual statements. Theming also means reduction; not all aspects of a theme can be considered. The main theme is synonymous with the story in a theater staging.
2. In the *staging concept* the concrete performance of the main theme is planned. It is important to find the core of the theme, expectations, and images visitors have in their heads.
3. *Attractions* are the focused stimuli of the staging process. There have to be core attractions (rides, shows, games) and supporting attractions (restaurants, souvenir shops, and so on) for all visitors, especially all members in families.
4. *Stage design* supports the theming performance and helps to create an atmosphere field with a consistent stimuli theme. It in-

cludes scenery, architecture, landscape, and also employees in a theater setting (cleaning personnel, for example). *Stage design* has the function of background stimuli in the atmosphere of the experience setting.

5. *Management of visitor flow* ensures that basic needs (security, information, orientation, hunger, thirst, personal needs) of visitors are always satisfied so that higher needs, such as experiences, can occur, as well as lengthening and intensifying experiences by applying dramaturgy (see Schober, 1993b) .
6. Former experiences and expectations of *visitors* act as residual stimuli. In contrast to a traditional theater staging, the visitors in theme parks are part of the staging and must therefore be considered.

CONCLUSION

Traditional leisure and tourist offers are already confronted with changing requirements of demand, i.e., experiences grow more important. Pine and Gilmore's (1999) concept of the experience economy sees experiences as the product consumers are looking for in the future. Therefore, traditional leisure and tourist offers must apply successful experience strategies to be competitive in the future. Theme parks are a model of future product design in leisure and tourism. Different traditional leisure and tourist offers such as museums and zoos have already started to copy strategies of theme parks. In traditional tourist destinations there is often a gap between the single units of the destination (hotels, restaurants) and the setting of the destination as a world of experiences. Although there are structural differences between theme parks and traditional tourist destinations, theme parks offer successful staging strategies to create an experience setting that can also be applied in traditional tourist destinations.

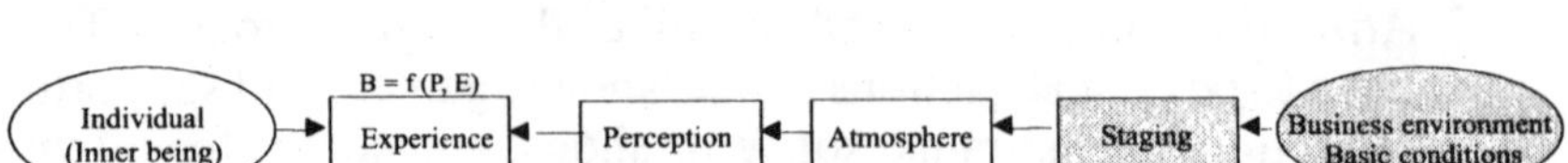

FIGURE 15.4. Staging: The Instrument to Create a Visitor-Oriented Atmosphere in the Experience Setting Concept

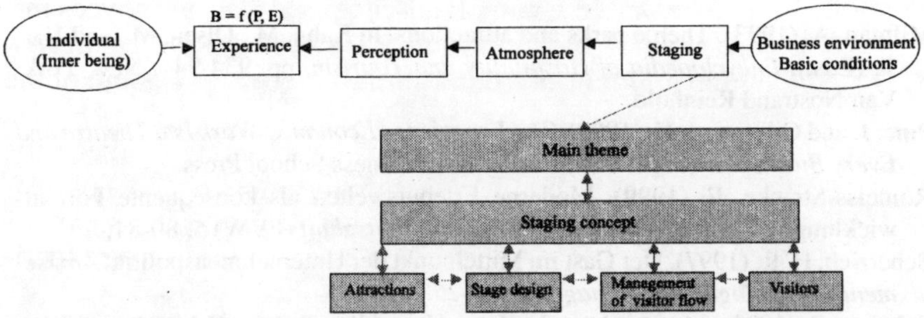

FIGURE 15.5. The Key Elements of Successful Staging in the Experience Setting Concept

REFERENCES

Altenhöner, N. and Friedrich, S. (Eds.) (2000). Bericht zur Branchensituation. Available at <www.themata.com>.

Barker, R. (1968). *Ecological Psychology.* Stanford, CA: Stanford University Press.

Bäumler, C. (2001). Edutainment und Museen. *Spektrum Freizeit* 23, 111-117.

Bill, Ch. (1997). *Freizeitparks in der Schweiz.* Bern Lizentiatsarbeit am Forschungsinstitut für Freizeit und Tourismus (FIF), Universität Bern.

Fischer-Lichte, E. (1998). Inszenierung und Theatralität. In Willems, H. and Jurga, M. (Eds.), *Inszenierungsgesellschaft,* pp. 85-115. Opladen: Westdeutscher Verlag.

Forschungsgemeinschaft Urlaub und Reisen (FUR) (2000). *Die RA-Trendstudie—Von der Vergangenheit in die Zukunft, langfristige Entwicklung des Urlaubsreiseverhaltens der Deutschen aus 30 Jahren Reiseanalyse.* Hamburg: Author.

Geser, H. (1996). *Elementare soziale Wahrnehmungen und Interaktionen—ein theoretischer Integrationsversuch.* Universität Zürich. Available at <http://www.geser.net>.

Kampschulte, A. and Schneider-Sliwa, R. (1997). *Das Image von Basel—Steuerungsinstrument für die Stadtentwicklung?* Beiträge zur Stadt- und Regionalforschung Band 16. Basel: Geographisches Institut, Universität Basel.

Hartmann, H.A. (1996). *Freizeit in der Erlebnisgesellschaft: Amüsement zwischen Selbstverwirklichung und Kommerz.* Opladen: Westdeutscher Verlag.

Husserl E. (1975). *Fünfte logische Untersuchung über intentionale Erlebnisse und ihre "Inhalte."* Hamburg: Meiner.

Lässer, Ch. and Bieger, T. (2000). *Reisemarkt Schweiz 2000, Kurzfassung.* St. Gallen: Institut fur öffentliche Dienstleistungen und Tourismus (IDT-HSG), Universität St. Gallen.

Lewin, K. (1951). *Field theory in social science: Selected theoretical papers,* edited by Dowin Cartwright. New York: Harper and Brothers.

Milman, A. (1993). Theme parks and attractions. In Kahn, M., Olsen, M., and Var, T. (Eds.), *Encyclopedia of Hospitality and Tourism,* pp. 934-944. New York: Van Nostrand Reinhold.

Pine, J. and Gilmore, J. H. (1999). *The Experience Economy: Work Is a Theatre and Every Business a Stage.* Boston: Harvard Business School Press.

Romeiss-Stracke, F. (1999). Moderne Erlebniswelten als konsequente Fortentwicklung des Tourismus. *Fremdenverkehrswirtschaft* (FVW) 5, 80-81.

Scherrieb, H. R. (1997). Der Gast im Mittelpunkt der Unternehmenspolitik. *Amusement Technologie and Management* 4, 25.

Schober, R. (1993a). Atmosphäre. In Hahn, H. and Kagelmann, H.J. (Eds.), *Tourismuspsychologie und Tourismussoziologie,* pp. 331-334. München: Quintessenz.

Schober, R. (1993b). (Urlaubs-)Erleben, (Urlaubs-)Erlebnis. In Hahn, H. and Kagelmann, H.J. (Eds.), *Tourismuspsychologie und Tourismussoziologie,* pp. 137-141. München: Quintessenz.

Schöndorf, H. (1995). Erlebnis und Wirklichkeit. In Heckmair, B., Michl, W., and Walser, F. (Eds.), *Die Wiederentdeckung der Wirklichkeit: Erlebnis im gesellschaftlichen Diskurs und in der Pädagogischen Praxis.* München: Sandmann Verlag.

Schulze, G. (1993). *Die Erlebnisgesellschaft,* Fourth Edition. Frankfurt a.M.: Campus Verlag.

Wöhler, Kh. (2000). Konstruierte Raumbindungen—Kulturangebote zwischen Authenzität und Inszenierung. *Tourismus Journal* 4(1), 103-116.

Zeisel, J. (1981). *Inquiry by Design: Tools for Environment-Behavior Research.* Monterey, CA: Brooks/Cole.

Chapter 16

The Future Role of Sporting Events: Evaluating the Impacts on Tourism

Simon Hudson
Donald Getz
Graham Miller
Graham Brown

INTRODUCTION

Despite the increasing popularity among destination management organizations (DMOs) for bidding on and hosting sporting events, research related to the evaluation of their impacts on tourism remains inadequate. This exploratory study seeks to add to this limited body of knowledge by questioning the DMOs of three countries in respect to three key issues, with the ultimate goal of developing theory and methods for improving the value of events to destinations. The three key issues requiring further examination are as follows:

1. *Goals for bidding on and hosting sporting events:* Little is known about the specific goals for hosting and bidding on events. Goals for destinations in hosting events can be compared to those sought by sponsors of events. Getz (1997) listed a number of such goals, including heightened visibility, image enhancement, and direct sales. For a destination, goals may be to increase future visitation (Hall, 1992), to improve the image of the city or country (Brown, 2000), or to disperse tourism activities in a wider region (Morse, 2001).
2. *Research conducted to measure the achievement of these goals:* Even less is known about how (or if) destinations or tourism organizations measure the achievement of these goals. A limited

amount of research exists regarding the impact of events on the awareness and image of the host destination (Ritchie and Smith, 1991; Nebenzahl and Jaffe, 1991; Kang and Perdue, 1994), and much debate has ensued over research methodology for evaluating the effectiveness of media coverage (Speed and Thompson 2000; Hudson, Getz, and Miller, 2001).

3. *The extent of event leveraging:* Event leveraging represents a subtle but significant advance on the study of event impacts (Chalip and Green, 2001) and is concerned with what is done or what can be done to obtain desired impacts from an event. There is much more to be learned about how events can be used to affect destination image, overall visitation, and visitor spending. The success of previous sporting events, such as the Barcelona Olympic Games, has drawn attention to the strategic value of events. For example, in the Bahamas, an events management company has been given the task of developing events that show the natural beauty of the islands to the world (Smith and Jenner, 1996). Both Chalip and Green (2001) and Morse (2001) have described how Australian tourism organizations implemented a series of strategies and tactics designed to enhance the tourism benefits to be obtained from the 2000 Olympic Games.

THE STUDY

Objectives

The objectives of this research study were to

1. understand the goals for DMOs when hosting sports events;
2. understand the research conducted to measure the achievement of these goals; and
3. understand the strategic action taken to maximize tourism benefits, in particular those relating to media coverage.

Method

A research instrument that could achieve these objectives was developed and piloted with tourism organizations in Canada. The questionnaire was divided into five key areas. The first part asked respondents the degree of importance of twenty-one goals when hosting a sports event. These goals were developed from previous literature and from the pilot study. Second, respondents were asked about research they had commissioned related to the achievement of their event-related goals, such as visitor expenditure surveys, visitor counts, recognition tests, etc. The third part of the questionnaire asked respondents to indicate what particular strategic actions they undertake in order to maximize the tourism benefits of hosting sport events. The list of seven possible actions was again based on past research and included such activities as familiarization tours, event packages, and building sport facilities. Respondents were then asked what strategic actions they undertake related specifically to media coverage, such as video profiles for incorporation in broadcasts, signage on the site, etc. The final part of the questionnaire asked whether they allocated funding for marketing (and impact research), as well as what particular sport events they hosted in 2000.

In the United Kingdom, the questionnaire was mailed during August 2001 to all London boroughs, county councils, metropolitan councils, district councils, and unitary authorities in England (389 local authorities in total). Seventy-eight positive replies were received, giving a response rate of 20 percent. In Australia, questionnaires were sent to 140 event tourism organizations, the list taken from *Who's Who in Meeting and Events,* 2000 edition, and thirty-three completed surveys were returned (23 percent). In North America, 300 surveys were sent to visitor and convention bureaus (a list was obtained from the International Association of Convention and Visitor Bureaus [IACVB]) and sport development organizations (a list was provided by the National Association of Sports Commissions). Forty-seven completed surveys were returned (16 percent). The 158 surveys were analyzed using SPSS for Windows.

Results

Table 16.1 shows the degree of importance of twenty-one goals when hosting a sports event for the three different respondent areas. For the sample overall, the most important goals (on an importance scale of 1 to 5) are to attract media coverage (mean = 4.31), maximize economic impact (mean = 4.30), and generate demand for hotel rooms (mean = 4.11). However, there were some significant differ-

TABLE 16.1. Goals When Hosting Sports Events

Goals	Mean Scores for Importance				
	Total sample ($n = 158$)	United Kingdom ($n = 78$)	Australia ($n = 33$)	North America ($n = 47$)	p-value*
To attract media coverage	4.31	4.27	4.39	4.32	ns
To maximize economic impact	4.30	3.94	4.61	4.70	< .001
To generate demand for hotel rooms	4.11	3.65	4.30	4.72	< .001
To increase the awareness of the resort/city/region as a tourist destination	4.09	3.95	4.21	4.23	ns
To increase tourist numbers while hosting the event	3.99	3.72	4.21	4.30	.0181
To stimulate the desire or intent to travel to the area	3.98	3.71	4.24	4.26	.0135
To stimulate repeat visits	3.92	3.72	4.21	4.06	ns
To increase tourist numbers after hosting the event	3.73	3.64	4.03	3.68	ns
To stimulate civic pride of local residents	3.67	3.97	3.24	3.47	.0012
To stimulate high-yield visitors while hosting the event	3.70	3.22	4.42	3.98	< .001

To extend the tourism season	3.56	3.24	3.85	3.89	.0181
To assist in branding the destination	3.56	3.32	4.16	3.53	.002
To increase local participation in sports	3.48	3.82	3.12	3.17	.0023
To change the tourist profile (e.g., average length of stay)	3.44	3.18	3.85	3.60	.0265
To attract sponsorship revenue	3.46	3.26	3.85	3.51	ns
To stimulate high-yield visitors after hosting the event	3.45	3.14	4.03	3.55	.0011
To change the image of the destination	3.40	3.47	3.18	3.43	ns
To increase cooperation between the stakeholders	3.39	3.42	3.46	3.28	ns
To disperse tourist activities in a wider region	3.34	2.86	4.39	3.38	.0170
To attract long-term investments (e.g., infrastructure)	3.39	3.40	3.52	3.28	ns
To enhance the destination's environment	3.23	3.17	3.33	3.28	ns

On a scale of 1 to 5 where 1 = not at all important and 5 = very important
*ns = not significant

ences in the responses from the various countries. For example, one-way analysis of variance between the groups showed statistically significant differences in the goal to disperse tourist activities in a wider region [$F(2,154) = 4.2097, p = 0.0170$]. This was an important goal for the Australians (mean = 4.39), and based on a post hoc test (SNK test) they were significantly more likely to pursue this goal than the U.K. or North American tourism organizations ($p < 0.05$). Stimulating high-yield visitors while hosting the event is also much more important to the Australians than the other two countries or regions (mean = 4.42, $p < 0.05$). In the United Kingdom, stimulating the civic pride of local visitors is relatively more important (mean = 3.97, $p < 0.05$), as is increasing local participation in sports (mean = 3.82, $p < 0.05$).

The second part of the survey asked respondents about research they had commissioned relating to the achievement of their sport event-related goals. Table 16.2 indicates that the Australians (55 percent) and the North Americans (53 percent) are significantly more likely to measure the achievement of sports event-related goals than the U.K. respondents (24 percent) ($\chi^2 = 14.32$, df = 2, $p < 0.001$). Over half of the Australian sample (52 percent) measure the impact of media coverage, compared to only 21 percent of North Americans and 14 percent of the British sample. Again, chi-square analysis showed a significant difference ($\chi^2 = 18.05$, df = 2, $p < 0.001$).

Table 16.3 outlines the type of research conducted by those that do commission it. The Australians, who appear to do more research than the other countries, tend to conduct visitor counts (54.5 percent) and visitor expenditure surveys during (57.6 percent) and after (33.3 percent) the event. The first two activities are also the most popular with the British and North American samples, but to a much lesser extent. As for measuring expenditure after an event, only 3.8 percent of the U.K. respondents and 10.6 percent of the North Americans commission such research. This tends to confirm contentions that most research on sporting events has been conducted prior to, during, or immediately after the event (Turco, Riley, and Swart, 2002), although it seems the Australians are more active in conducting expenditure surveys and tracking studies after the event.

The third part of the questionnaire asked respondents to indicate what particular strategic actions they undertake in order to maximize the tourism benefits of hosting sport events. On a scale of 1 to 4 where 1 = never and 4 = always, Table 16.4 indicates that the most popular

TABLE 16.2. Research Conducted by Each Country/Region

Who conducts research	**Total (n = 158) (%)**	**United Kingdom (n = 78) (%)**	**North America (n = 47) (%)**	**Australia (n = 33) (%)**
1. To measure the achievement of sports events-related goals	39	24	53	55
2. To measure the impact of media coverage	24	14	21	52

TABLE 16.3. Type of Research Conducted

Type of research conducted	Percentages (%)			
	Overall (*n* = 158)	**United Kingdom** (*n* = 78)	**Australia** (*n* = 33)	**North America** (*n* = 47)
Visitor/attendance figures/counts	32.3	19.2	54.5	38.3
Visitor expenditure surveys while hosting the event	27.2	14.1	57.6	27.7
Destination surveys	15.2	14.1	24.2	10.6
Visitor expenditure surveys after hosting the event	12.0	3.8	33.3	10.6
Opinion polls	10.1	6.4	24.2	6.4
Community perceptions/attitudes survey	10.1	3.8	27.3	8.5
Tracking surveys	7.6	0.0	27.3	6.4
Recognition tests	5.1	3.8	9.1	4.3
Recall tests (aided or unaided)	4.4	2.6	12.1	2.1
Focus groups	4.4	2.6	12.1	2.1
Persuasion tests via surveys	2.5	0.0	6.1	4.3
Roundtables	2.5	1.3	9.1	0.0

TABLE 16.4. Strategic Action Taken to Maximize Tourism Benefits

Action taken	Mean Scores				
	Total sample ($n = 158$)	United Kingdom ($n = 78$)	Australia ($n = 33$)	North America ($n = 47$)	*p*-value*
Build community support	2.88	2.72	2.94	3.11	.0336
Build event-management expertise	2.56	2.31	2.79	2.83	.0060
Create additional events around the main event	2.44	2.26	2.79	2.51	.0110
Develop event packages	2.33	1.97	3.15	2.34	<.001
Organize familiarization tours around the event	2.03	1.69	2.76	2.09	<.001
Develop pre- and postevent tours	1.82	1.43	2.58	1.94	<.001
Build sport facilities/infrastructure	1.78	1.64	2.03	1.83	ns

On a scale of 1 to 4 where 1 = never and 4 = always
*ns = not significant

activity overall was building community support (mean = 2.88), although, based on a post hoc test (SNK test), the North Americans (mean = 3.11) were significantly more likely to do this than their counterparts ($p < 0.05$). In fact, there were significant differences in responses to all the questions in this part of the survey. For example, one-way analysis of variance between the groups showed statistically significant differences in the strategy to organize familiarization tours [$F(2,155) = 18.618$, $p < 0.001$]. Just like all of the strategic actions, the U.K. respondents were significantly less likely to undertake such tours (mean = 1.69, $p < 0.05$). The most popular activity for the Australians was to develop event packages, and they were significantly more likely to develop these than the others (mean = 3.15, $p < 0.05$).

Respondents were then asked what strategic actions they undertake related specifically to media coverage, and Table 16.5 outlines the results. Again, on a scale of 1 to 4 where 1 = never and 4 = always, the key strategic action taken by all countries was having signage on the site of the event (mean = 2.95). Once again, the U.K. respondents were less likely to undertake the strategic actions related to media coverage. For example, one-way analysis of variance between the groups showed statistically significant differences in the activity of developing video profiles for incorporation in broadcasts [$F(2,155) = 22.3439$, $p < 0.001$]. For U.K. respondents this was their least likely activity (mean = 1.40), and a post hoc test (SNK test) indicated that the Australians were significantly more likely to develop such profiles than the other countries (mean = 2.58, $p < 0.001$). The second most popular activity for the Australians was working with media to increase exposure (mean = 3.24), and they were significantly more likely to do this than the other countries ($p < 0.05$). The North Americans, on the other hand, were significantly more likely to maintain an online presence during the event than the Australian or British respondents (mean = 2.98, $p < 0.001$).

The final part of the questionnaire asked whether they allocated money for events impact research and what particular sport events they hosted in 2000. Table 16.6 indicates that the Australians clearly allocate more funding for impact research—not surprising given the preceding results—with 58 percent of them responding positively to this question. On the other hand, U.K. respondents, perhaps surprisingly, are more likely to allocate money than the North Americans

TABLE 16.5. Strategic Action Taken Related to Media Coverage

	Mean Scores				
Action taken	**Total sample (n = 158)**	**United Kingdom (n = 78)**	**Australia (n = 33)**	**North America (n = 47)**	***p*-value***
Signage on site	2.95	2.69	3.30	3.13	.0041
Work with media to increase exposure (e.g., work with TV crews on site to ensure most beneficial camera angles are used)	2.71	2.38	3.24	2.87	.0006
Online presence	2.49	2.05	2.85	2.98	<.001
Pay to advertise	2.36	2.26	2.58	2.38	ns
Try to influence position of destination advertising within the broadcasts	2.25	1.87	2.88	2.45	<.001
Be a sponsor	2.17	2.00	2.30	2.36	ns
Video news release for TV news coverage	1.81	1.44	2.58	1.89	<.001
Develop destination video profiles or commercials for incorporation in broadcasts	1.75	1.40	2.58	1.74	<.001

On a scale of 1 to 4 where 1 = never and 4 = always
*ns = not significant

TABLE 16.6. Event Organizers That Allocate Money Specifically to Impact Research

Total sample (n = 158)(%)	United Kingdom (n = 78)(%)	Australia (n = 33)(%)	North America (n = 47)(%)
46	47	58	34

(47 percent versus 34 percent). Table 16.7 shows the average number of events held by each country or region and whether these events were international, national, or regional. One-way analysis of variance between the groups showed statistically significant differences in the number of international events held [F(2,155) = 29.2105, $p < 0.001$]. A post hoc test (SNK test) indicated that the Australians were significantly more likely to host such events (mean = 1.67, $p < 0.05$) than the British (mean = 0.35) or the Americans (mean = 0.49). Again, for the national events there were significant differences [F(2,155) = 20.5984, $p < 0.001$]. This time the North Americans (mean = 1.57) and the Australians (mean = 1.36) were significantly more likely to host such events than the British (mean = 0.40, $p < 0.05$). As for regional events, once again the U.K. respondents were significantly less likely to host them than their counterparts (mean = 0.37, $p < 0.05$). T-tests were conducted to explore any relationship between the type of events hosted and whether money was allocated for research. Not surprisingly, those respondents who hosted international events were more likely to allocate research money ($t = 2.99$, df = 156, two-tailed $p = .003$). However, there was no significant relationship between the allocation of money and the hosting of national or regional events. Analysis of the types of research conducted (see Table 16.2) indicated a significant relationship between the hosting of all types of events and the measurement of goals, whereas measuring the impact of media coverage was significant only for those hosting international and national events. Those hosting regional events do not necessarily conduct impact research.

DISCUSSION

Findings show that Australian DMOs are far more research active and there is more of a focus on tourism outcomes in Australia than in

TABLE 16.7. Average Number of Events Held by Country/Region in 2000

Type of event	United Kingdom	Australia	North America
International	0.35	1.67	0.49
National	0.40	1.36	1.57
Regional	0.37	0.76	0.77

the other countries. This is not surprising, as many of the people who received the questionnaire were in tourism departments or had some involvement in tourism (whereas in the United Kingdom the sample was local government authorities). The findings also indicate that the Australians are much more likely to host international events than the other samples. Finally, there is the possibility that the Australian tourism organizations have been positively influenced by the success of the Australian Tourism Commission in leveraging the Olympic Games of 2000. The Australian events sector now has a very high profile, as it is seen to be of national, strategic importance for developing tourism in the country.

The U.K. respondents are less likely to conduct most forms of research, but they do host relatively fewer events than the Australian or North American samples. Even though the North American respondents host more national or regional events than the Australians, they still conduct less research, especially in measuring the impact of media coverage of their events. They also undertake fewer strategic actions in order to maximize the tourism benefits of hosting sport events, and they allocate significantly less money for events research than the Australians.

LIMITATIONS AND FUTURE RESEARCH

The main limitation lies in the sample itself. The samples were different in both size and composition. The Australian sample was small (n = 33) and represented tourism departments likely to host sporting events. The North American sample was larger, but again was not a random sample, as respondents came from just two groups, CVBs and members of the National Association of Sports Commissions. In the United Kingdom, the sample was less targeted and represented London boroughs, county councils, metropolitan councils, district councils, and unitary authorities in England. Although they represented the largest number of respondents, they were less likely to host sporting events.

Despite the limitations, this was only an exploratory study and was the first part of a larger international research project to examine many interrelated issues. These include examining how destinations organize events to develop tourism and studying how consumers are affected by event media coverage. The long-term objective for most destinations sponsoring an event is to increase awareness levels, build on the image of the destination, and ultimately increase visitation levels in the winter. The assumption has been made that increased awareness and enhanced image will, over the longer term, provide a stronger competitive position and increased tourism receipts, but to the authors' knowledge, this hypothesis has not been subjected to empirical testing. Evaluating the impact of an annual major event on the decision-making process of tourists would test such a hypothesis.

REFERENCES

Brown, G. (2000). Emerging issues in Olympic sponsorship: Implications for host cities. *Sport Management Review,* 3: 71-92.

Chalip, L. and Green, B.C. (2001). Leveraging large sports events for tourism: Lessons from the Sydney olympics. In Moisey, R.N., Nickerson, N.P., and Andereck, K. (Eds.), *2001: A Tourism Odyssey* (pp. 11-20). Boise, ID: Travel and Tourism Research Association.

Getz, D. (1997). *Event Management and Event Tourism.* Elmsford, NY: Cognizant Communication.

Hall, C.M. (1992). *Hallmark Tourist Events: Impacts, Management and Planning.* London: Bellhaven Press.

Hudson, S., Getz, D., and Miller, G.A. (2001). The sponsorship of major events by destinations: Evaluating the impact on the decision-making process of the consumer. In Spotts, H.E., Meadow, H.K., and Smith, S.M. (Eds.), *Proceedings of the Academy of Marketing Science World Marketing Congress on Global Issues at the Turn of the Millennium,* Volume X. Cardiff, Wales.

Kang, Y-S. and Perdue, R. (1994). Long-term impact of a mega-event on international tourism to the host country: A conceptual model and the case of the 1988 Seoul Olympics. *Journal of International Consumer Marketing,* 6(4): 205-226.

Morse, J. (2001). The Sydney 2000 Olympic Games: How the Australian Tourist Commission leveraged the games for tourism. *Journal of Vacation Marketing,* 7(2): 101-107.

Nebenzahl, I.D. and Jaffe, E.D. (1991). The effectiveness of sponsored events in promoting a country's image. *International Journal of Advertising,* 10(3): 223-237.

Ritchie, J.R.B. and Smith, B.H. (1991). The impact of a mega-event on host region awareness: A longitudinal study. *Journal of Travel Research,* 30(1): 3-10.

Smith, C. and Jenner, P. (1996). Sponsorship in the travel and tourism industry. *Travel and Tourism Analyst,* 6: 64-79.

Speed, R. and Thompson, P. (2000). Determinants of sports sponsorship response. *Academy of Marketing Science,* 28(2): 223-236.

Turco, D.M., Riley, R., and Swart, K. (2002). *Sport Tourism.* Morgantown, WV: Fitness Information Technology, Inc.

Chapter 17

Future Living Conditions and Mobility: Travel Behavior of Alpine Tourists

Thomas Bieger
Christian Laesser

LEISURE AND TOURISM MOBILITY: A STRUCTURAL CONCEPT

Categories of Leisure Mobility

Leisure mobility can be divided into two or three main categories. According to the definition of tourism (Inskeep, 1991; Kaspar, 1996), traveling to a destination always involves mobility. This represents the first type of mobility, which can be categorized as interdestination mobility. It also has an impact on the second category, intradestination mobility, assuming that tourists arriving by car will use their car for further activities within the destination. Moreover, all other forms of mobility needed for access to leisure activities close to the area of living can be included (Müller et al., 1999). The third form of mobility includes mobility caused by sport activities (car racing, skiing, cycling) or cultural activities (sight-seeing on train trips), which are also highly dependent on mobility at home (Figure 17.1).

Leisure Mobility Model

A *leisure mobility model* (Figure 17.2) can be derived from the situational approach (Hägerstrand, 1970; Brög and Erl, 1983; Mentz, 1984; Hogrebe and Strang, 1994; Laesser, 1996; Bieger and Laesser, 2001). According to this approach, the need for mobility and its structure (modal split) is heavily influenced by (1) the socioeconomic

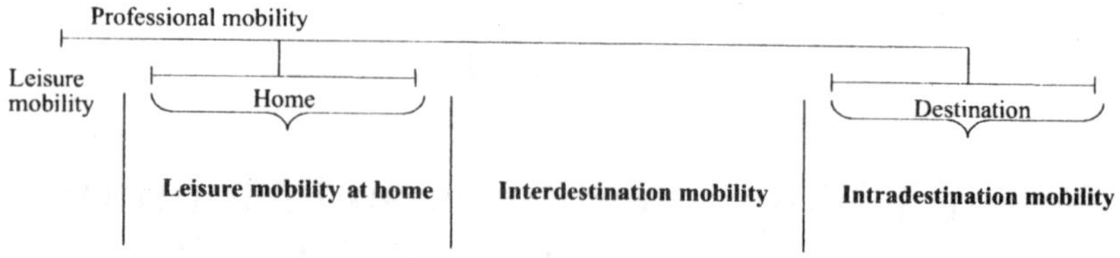

FIGURE 17.1. Mobility Typologies

predetermination of the mobility subject (i.e., user of a given means of transportation); (2) the form of leisure activity; and (3) the contextual factors of its consumption.

The volume of traffic varies with the activity, e.g., sports such as skiing require not only transport to the destination but also transport within the destination, such as cable cars (European Conference of Ministers of Transport [ECMT], 2000). Furthermore the location of the leisure activity and its distance to the place of living has an impact on the amount of mobility needed (Lawson, 2001). This shall be illustrated with cultural events. As most cultural events take place in town centers, it can easily be seen that different means of transportation will be used to get there and therefore different mobility patterns develop. Whereas people living in peripheral areas of a town will most probably rely on individual transport, people living downtown might use collective means of transportation to do the same kind of leisure activity. This generates different kinds of traffic flows.

Means of transportation offered also influences leisure behavior. The availability of a fast road, for example, will induce mobility, as this encourages people to use this additional capacity to travel not only faster but also more often (ECMT, 1998).

The *effects of traffic,* last but not least, affect housing conditions and relocation patterns. Due to the fact that originators of pollution often are not identical with the recipients, those effects become *external.* This in turn also influences the leisure behavior of both groups. In the tradition of a *leisure–living model* (Krippendorf, 1984), a loop back from traffic flows and infrastructure to leisure behavior and thus to mobility needs can be assumed.

This simple model can be taken as a basis for deriving various research questions and topics which are relevant for the future of leisure mobility:

- How do different forms of leisure activities influence mobility?
- Which trends in leisure mobility based on these relationships can be expected?
- How do different forms of leisure activities affect the modal split of traffic?
- What effects will traffic patterns have on living conditions and leisure behavior?
- What problems emerge? Is there room for improvement?

This chapter tries to develop hypotheses for discussion of these questions, drawing on empirical studies completed in Switzerland. Switzerland seems to be an interesting case study in many respects, as it has a *rich and affluent leisure market* at a comparatively highly developed stage (high market maturity), as well as a fairly high population density resulting in increased *sensitivity for problems emerging from traffic patterns.*

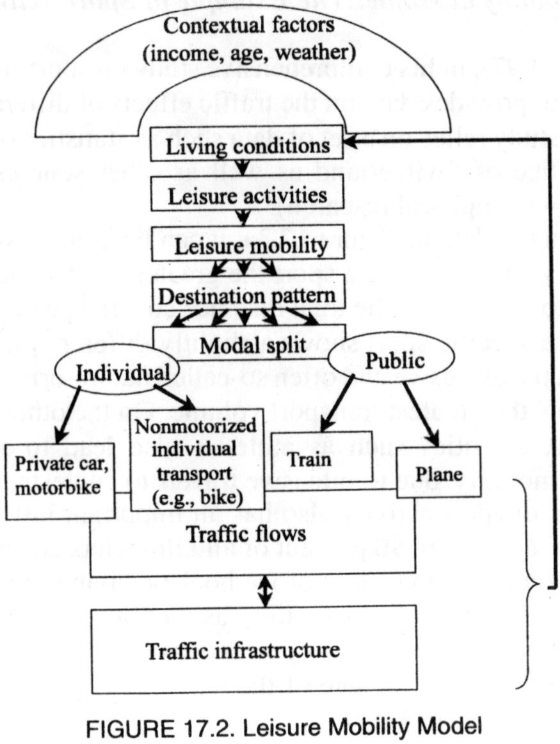

FIGURE 17.2. Leisure Mobility Model

THE INFLUENCE OF LEISURE ACTIVITIES ON MOBILITY

In Switzerland more than 50 percent of the overall traffic movements result from leisure activities (see Stettler, 1997). For more than 80 percent of kilometers driven, the private car is used.

The different forms of leisure mobility (please refer again to Figure 17.1) shall be illustrated by the following means:

- *Leisure mobility at home:* Sport activities-induced mobility patterns of Swiss people.
- *Interdestination mobility:* Tourism-induced mobility patterns of Swiss travelers.
- *Intradestination mobility:* Mobility patterns of Swiss tourists during their stay in the destination.

Leisure Mobility at Home: The Example of Sport Activities

Stettler (1997), in his comprehensive study on sports and traffic in Switzerland, provides data on the traffic effects of different forms of sport. The study relies on a set of data such as statistics of the federal statistic office of Switzerland as well as other sources (including Stettler's own empirical research).

Based on the data in Figure 17.3a, it can be hypothesized that the more trendy and exclusive a sport the greater the distance necessary to be able to execute it. The total distance covered per year by an enthusiast of a specific sport shows a slightly different picture (Figure 17.3b). Yet the exclusive and often so-called nature-oriented sport activities show the greatest transport volume. On the other hand, traditional sport activities such as athletics also lead to a significant amount of mobility, due to intensive travels to contests.

The type of sport activity also has an important influence on the modal split. More than 90 percent of all kilometers covered are done by car, especially in the cases of ice hockey, diving, golf, windsurfing, horseback riding, and shooting, as well as car and motorcycle sports. The share of public transport means is the highest for hiking, snowboarding (due to the age of the boarders), cycling, and mountaineering (Stettler, 1997).

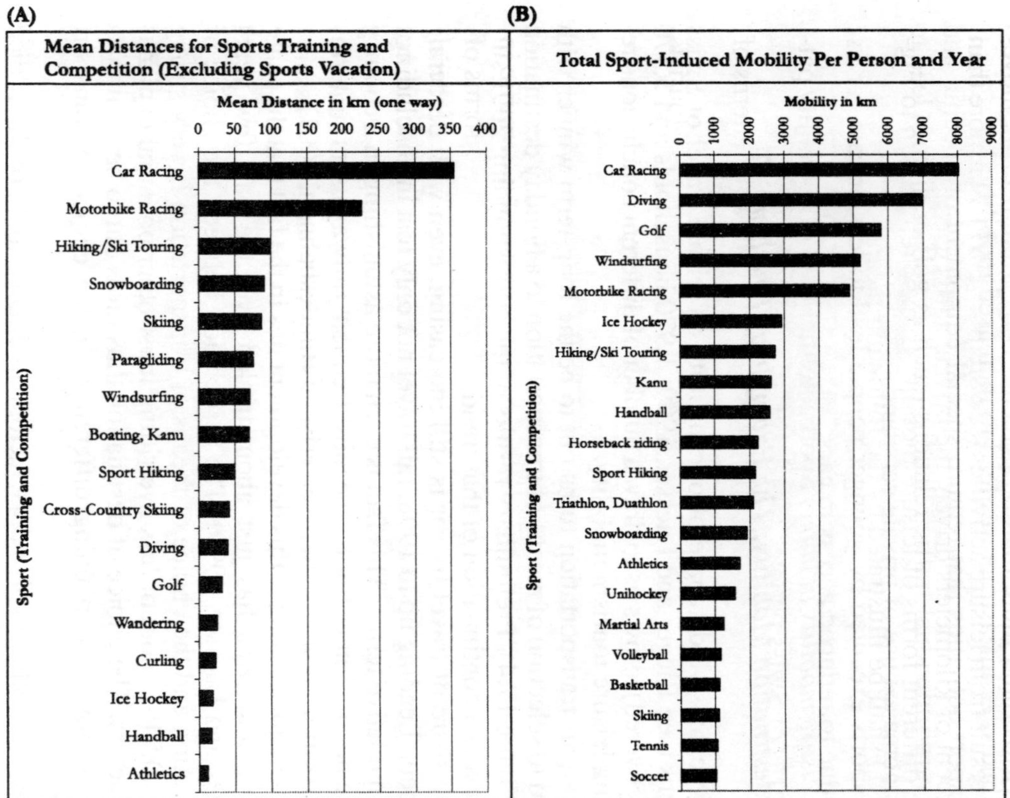

FIGURE 17.3. Quantity Structure of Sport-Induced Mobility (*Source:* Adapted from Stettler, 1997.)

From these data it can be hypothesized that

1. mobility is influenced by sport activities;
2. sport activities requiring special natural conditions (mountains, lakes) or infrastructures lead to increased mobility;
3. sport activities that require special equipment or specific and very individual traffic relations (such as golf or diving) lead to increased use of private cars; and
4. sports executed by younger people lead to less private car use due to reduced access to cars.

Interdestination Mobility: The Example of Tourism

The extensive database of our institute on leisure travel of Swiss citizens (see Bieger and Laesser, 1999; 1,970 households and 5,570 trips covered) allows us to draw a number of different conclusions regarding leisure tourism mobility.

First, air transportation turns out to be the long-term winner with regard to selection of means of transportation to a holiday destination (see Figure 17.4). Preliminary results of the corresponding 2001 survey reveal a continuation of that trend.

The share of travel by car is still increasing, even with declining numbers. Leading up to 1998, rail travel not only lost in absolute but also in relative terms. This fact is even more astonishing in a country whose population is among the most frequent railway users (in terms of utilization intensity; Schweizerische Bundesbahnen, 2001).

The major reason for this development lies in the fact that the share of *long-haul trips* has just about tripled over the past few years (Bieger and Laesser, 1999). The association between the choice of destination and the choice of means of transportation is very strong (Phi = 0.940), more or less overriding most other potential explanatory factors. The choice of destination thus turns out to be a summarizing factor for explaining differences in the choice of transport mode.

However, other explanatory factors are independent of the choice of destination (Bieger and Laesser, 1999).

Some *types of travel* clearly induce mobility (Phi = 0.644). When looking at the means of transportation to the (first) holiday destination, the share of car use (with regard to number of trips, not distance) is predominant among travel types such as "winter holiday in the

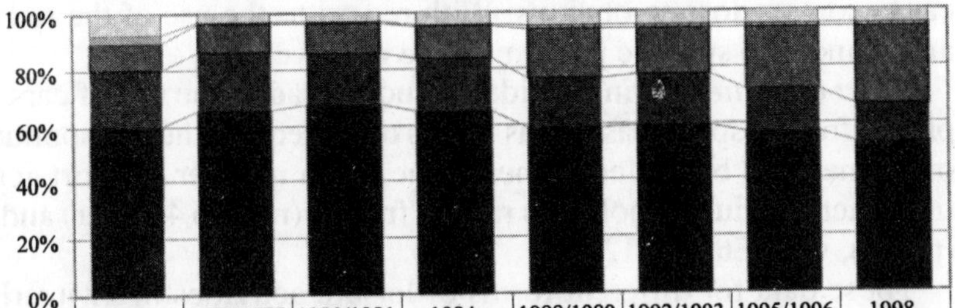

	1972 (%)	1976/1977 (%)	1980/1981 (%)	1984 (%)	1988/1989 (%)	1992/1993 (%)	1995/1996 (%)	1998 (%)
Bus	8	3	3	4	5	5	5	5
Boat/Ship	4	1	1	1	1	1	1	1
Plane	10	10	10	11	17	16	21	27
Railway	22	20	18	18	17	17	14	13
Car	66	65	66	63	57	57	54	51

FIGURE 17.4. Selection of Means of Transportation to Holiday Destinations. (*Source:* Data compiled from Bieger and Laesser, 1999.)

snow" (84 percent) and "holiday in the mountains" (81 percent). Planes, on the other hand, are a key means of transportation in the cases of "beach holiday" (44 percent), "city trip" (36 percent), and "sightseeing trip" (35 percent). The types of trip mentioned incorporate more than half of all trips, with the railway not having any predominant role.

Not surprisingly, the *duration of a trip* is another factor explaining the choice of transportation (Phi = 0.587). While the use of planes increases over the duration of the trip, the use of cars and trains decreases (Phi = 0.370).

The car turns out to be a mode of transportation for comparably larger travel groups. An average *size of travel group* from typical households averages 2.7 in the case of car use and 2.0 in the case of plane and train use, with Eta = 0.326. Budget reasons may be one of the potential determinants of this behavior.

The *age of traveler(s)* also seems to play a role in choosing the means of transportation (gender, on the other hand, is of no relevance). The highest share of car usage falls in the age groups < 15 and 26 to 45, with Phi = 0.310. This is yet another indication for the potential of a life-phase-based segmentation of travelers (Laesser, 2001; Bieger and Laesser, 2002). When traveling with children, the use of a car becomes close to obvious. With regard to the use of the railway and planes, no specific pattern can be observed.

Sport activities during holidays tend to lead to the use of cars and planes for transport reasons, as sports often require the transportation of (sometimes bulky) equipment. The mean number of sport activities practiced during holidays ranges from 3 (rail) to 4.7 (car) and 5.2 (plane), with Eta = 0.126.

These data for different forms of leisure activities in Switzerland provide evidence for the hypothesis that the type and form of leisure activity as well as specific context factors of the consumer have an important influence on mobility.

Intradestination Mobility: The Examples of Swiss Travelers' Mobility Patterns

The same database (Bieger and Laesser, 1999) also provides valuable insights for the use of means of transportation in a destination.

First, on an average trip Swiss travelers make use of about 1.4 different means of transportation. The private car is a key means of transportation during a stay in a destination (see Figure 17.5). Sixty-one percent of all travelers from Switzerland drive a vehicle while on a leisure trip, although some differentiations can be made (Bieger and Laesser, 1999).

Concerning the *type of trip* (Figure 17.6), examples of journeys inducing car mobility include "visit friends and relatives" (almost a third of all trips), "mountain vacation in" (not winter), and "vacation in the countryside." On the other hand it is not surprising that city trips and cruises induce the least car mobility of all. The association is significant but rather weak at Phi = 0.378.

The car also turns out to be a means of transportation for comparably larger travel groups within a destination. A *regular-sized travel group* averages 2.6 in the case of car use and 2.0 in cases in which other means of transportation are chosen, with Eta = 0.232. The earlier description of *mobility pattern by age* can also be observed on an intradestination level.

The *type of sport activities* is another reason for using cars. Sports which involve the transport of bulky items and sports involving the use of rather centrally located infrastructures tend to use car transportation most heavily. The determination is rather weak, however.

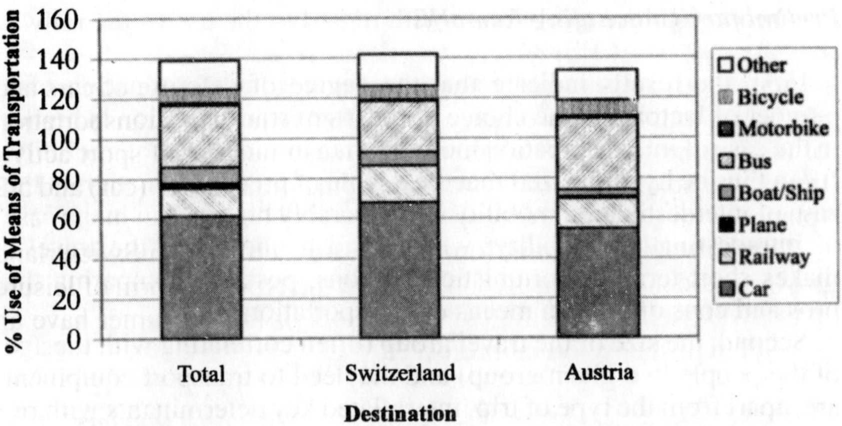

FIGURE 17.5. Use of Means of Transport in Destination (*Source:* Adapted from Bieger and Laesser, 1999).

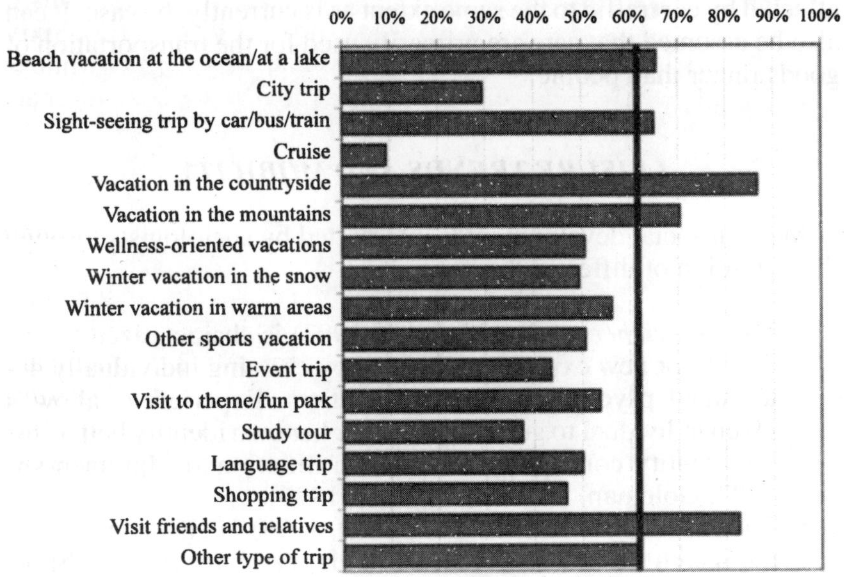

FIGURE 17.6. The Share of Swiss Travelers Using a Car While in a Destination (*Source:* Adapted from Bieger and Laesser, 1999.)

Preliminary Concluding Remarks

First, the results indicate that the degree of determination of a number of factors for the choice of means of transportation is higher in the case of interdestination mobility than intradestination mobility. It can thus be hypothesized that the degree of predetermination in the case of interdestination mobility is comparably higher than in the case of intradestination mobility; with regard to the latter, the traveler makes short-term, opportunistic decisions, possibly comparing the pros and cons of a given means of transportation.

Second, the size of the travel group (often correlating with the age of the people in a given group) and the need to transport equipment are, apart from the type of trip, interrelated key determinants with regard to the choice of means of transportation. For example, parents with children naturally travel with a comparably large number of sometimes bulky items.

With the Alps being a prominent destination for families (Laesser, 2001), and thus attracting comparably large travel groups with proportionately sized items to transport, the future will see these areas affected by car traffic to the same extent as is currently the case. It can also be assumed that cars are primarily used for the transportation of goods rather than people.

LEISURE TRENDS AND MOBILITY

Modern social development is interpreted by sociologists through the definition of different "societies."

- The *experience society* (Schulze, 1993) is characterized by the search for new experiences gained by crossing individually determined psychic or physical frontiers. Experiences allow a given individual to get to know his or her own identity better (for the identity concept please refer to Simon and Mummendey, 1997; Goleman, 1995; Baumeister, 1986).
- The *risk society* (Beck, 1986, 1989, 1999) is characterized by the search for new limits of risk. This search for risk can be interpreted as a search for experiences, aiming at getting to know oneself in new risk situations, allowing the strengthening of the individual identity.

- The *option society* (Poon, 1993; Gross, 1994) shows an ever-increasing choice of options in every dimension of individual life. For example, choices may include forms of life concepts, marriage, family structure, services, and goods. A growing number of people are keen on getting to know and taking advantage of the variety of options available, driven by increasing deregulation and individualization (which were regarded as the prominent values of the twentieth century). This leads to a reduction of the everyday significance of traditional norms and institutions.

These societal developments can be considered as megatrends from which specific consumer trends can be derived. Focusing on leisure activities, the following trends can be regarded as important (Bieger, 2000).

Multioptionalization

Consumers want to maximize their options and try to keep them open and accessible as long as possible. This leads to the need for having all possible sport equipment on hand (most often in the car) and having the flexibility to easily access all possible sport infrastructures (mostly by car).

Time Efficiency

The modern society is divided into (1) a group of well-educated employees having little time but enough income to spend and (2) a group with little work and income but plenty of time (Opaschowski, 1997). The average working time of employed people has increased, despite reduced legal working hours. As competition in the labor market is increasing, many people are either forced to work overtime or work multiple jobs to earn enough money. In addition, with the rise of female employment, the number of families with one person constantly at home is decreasing. Time constraints increase and many time-consuming obligations need to be fulfilled within free time, thus reducing leisure time. The modern citizen is stuck between scarcity of money or scarcity of time (Opaschowski, 1997).

Soft Individualism

Modern people have neither enough time for themselves nor for their friends and relatives. In times of multioptionality relatives become less important than friends (Opaschowski, 1997). People want to do something as an individual and at the same time be with their friends or a reference group (see Horx, 1996). Places of attraction where people can be together in homogenous groups and at the same time engage in individual activities are therefore becoming increasingly important.

Activity Instead of Relaxing

In the age of the experience society, any activity and experience is growing in importance. Passive relaxation is "out" and active experience is "in."

SUMMARY

The trends toward multioptionality, time efficiency, soft individualism, and activity lead to diversified and complex, time flexible and very individual mobility patterns. The average load of equipment that has to be transported is increasing. The concentration of activities on specific places will increase. It can even be hypothesized that the total amount of leisure mobility will further increase in the future. The need for flexible, convenient, and individual transport will add to the importance of the private car. These changes in leisure needs will also increase the amount and the share of private cars for interdestination mobility.

Leisure Needs and Modal Split

Different needs and preconditions lead to different preferences regarding the choice of means of transportation. In a contingency analysis, based on data from a survey of 700 people in Switzerland, the importance of different evoked criteria for the selection of transport means was evaluated. The actual decision behavior has been compared to the predisposition (individually estimated importance before taking a decision in a specific situation), thus revealing the alleged and effective demand structure at the same time. The study has shown a number of results (see Figure 17.7), described as follows:

1. *Traveling time* is the only criteria that allocates a high predispositional significance and a high degree of influence on situational decisions at the same time. It is thus a key decision factor, regardless of whether the majority of travel is related to leisure or business.
2. *Safety, flexibility,* and *convenience* (number of changes and connections) have a high predispositive relevance but are put aside in the actual situational decision. The question why tourists are not using trains more frequently can be answered by the following interpretation: People assume that public land transport for leisure purposes is safe, however it is neither flexible nor convenient (for example, with regard to transporting bulky items). As long as this assumption is not consistently disproved by personal experience, travelers stick to this expectation. Imprecisely and incompletely estimated travel costs, with regard to using cars for example (in most cases only marginal costs are estimated; Laesser, 1996), reinforce this effect.
3. *Relaxation/rest* and the *potential to dispose of time* are not evaluated highly before taking a trip but become more important once a mode of transport has been chosen. It can be hypothesized that *time efficiency* and the possibility to spend time productively are of major importance for the selection of transport methods. Safety and convenience seem to be important but have a reduced influence in the specific situation. This also leads to the conclusion that major differences exist between what people think is important for them and what in fact is of importance in a specific situation.

Traffic and Its Influence on Life Conditions and Leisure Behavior

The early stages of leisure research have already discussed the influence of traffic on living conditions and thereby on leisure activities (Krippendorf, 1984, 1986). The development of settlement structures in Switzerland indicate that good public transport attracts private households, especially singles and double-career couples without children.

Degree of influence on situational decision / **Predispositive relevance of quality criteria** (valuation before actual decision making)	**Relatively high**	**Relatively low**
Relatively high	I Traveling time	II Safety Number of changes Number of connections/ flexibility
Relatively low	III Relaxation/rest Productive use of time	IV Total costs Familiarity

FIGURE 17.7. The Significance of Predispositive Quality Criteria and Their Influence on Situational Decision Making (*Source:* Adapted from Bieger and Laesser, 2001.)

On the other hand, increasing car traffic leads to a reduced attractiveness and thus willingness to pay for private living. When evaluating living conditions, potential evasion of traffic noise and attractive public transport are both pull factors, i.e., attractive with regard to an alternative housing option (Laesser, 1996; Meyrat-Schlee, 1992). Moreover, three hedonic price analyses for the cities of Basel, Switzerland (Pommerehne, 1988), Zurich, Switzerland (Iten, 1990), and Helsinki, Finland (Vainino, 1995) showed that traffic noise significantly reduces housing rents.

Leisure activities as well as the derived mobility structure of people living in peripheral areas differ from people living in the town centers (Bieger and Laesser, 1999). Many people living in the peripheries own private houses with continually increasing comfort, confirming the tendency toward investments in living conditions at home. They therefore spend an increasing part of their leisure time at home (Heinze and Kill, 1997) and spend some of their active leisure time (exercise sports) in the neighborhood. The accompanying tendency to spend vacations at home and to undertake day trips results in an increase of leisure traffic. The existence of the following vicious circle can be hypothesized: People move to peripheral areas to get away from traffic externalities but then often rely on car-based mobility, especially due to the individual mobility patterns and decentralized origins. This leads to a further reduction in the attractiveness of the city centers and places close to important roads. If easily accessible, urban people more frequently rely on public transport. The average mobility is supposed to be smaller because a large variety of activities can be done nearby in the towns.

A study by Fuhrer (1993) used the example of the Swiss capital Bern to show that the following factors are influencing mobility:

- *Coziness:* Married people, for example, who feel at ease at home and who live in houses with gardens tend to show reduced mobility.
- *Traffic:* People who live beside a street with intense traffic tend to travel greater distances on the weekends.
- *Garden:* People who are able to shape their own gardens are more likely to stay at home.
- *Floor:* People living on the lower floors of apartment buildings are more likely to stay at home on free days.
- *Meeting people:* People who travel on free days most likely want to meet other people.
- *Car comfort:* The more comfortable and cozy an individual's car, the more likely the individual will be to travel by car and spend leisure time in the car.

It can therefore be hypothesized that (1) the trend toward better living conditions at home, (2) the higher share of car owners, and (3) the decentralization of homes will increase the need for leisure mobility.

Problem Areas and the Need for Solutions

Leisure time activities and the leisure industry must more and more rely on mobility. Because the time spent in cars or on trains further reduces already scarce leisure time, this development is counterproductive in a way. Mobility in the form of traffic externalities also reduces the quality of many leisure activities such as biking, walking, sight-seeing, etc. It can be hypothesized that this development will lead to segregation into two main markets:

1. A market for top leisure activities at top destinations for which individuals are ready to travel large distances.
2. Leisure time at home or in the immediate neighborhood. There might also be a market for leisure activities combined with transport, e.g., entertaining forms of train travel or entertainment in cars.

Conclusions to be drawn for the leisure industry at first sight might seem to be very simple.

- *Big (international) attractions* have to invest steadily to maintain their attractiveness and international competitiveness. International demand and willingness to pay for top attractions will provide the necessary financial power to do so, given the condition that no major regulatory disturbance with regard to mobility occurs (especially with regard to the pricing of mobility, an issue currently on the brink of political discussion).
- *Local attractions might experience a renaissance in demand,* as long as they can compete with regard to hygiene factors (e.g., minimal standards in comfort, safety, variety, etc.). Attractions in metropolitan or urban areas are more likely to be bound for success than ones in peripheral regions, as their basis for demand is larger and more specialized (which opens also the potential for niche products).
- *Mediocre leisure attractions at middle distance* will not necessarily lose market share in the short term but might lose their ability to generate willingness to pay and therefore suffer reduced income in the medium term. In the long run they will loose their investment power and—as a consequence—their attractiveness. Government, as a last resort, will then have to decide whether to subsidize these attractions, such as low-quality ski resorts in pre- or non-alpine regions or low-quality museums. They have to gain cost flexibility to serve demand and introduce cost savings at nonpeak times, as they will be struck by consumer concentration during best-suited times and places more than any other types of attractions.

REFERENCES

Baumeister, R.F. (1986). *Identity—Culture Change and the Struggle for Self.* Oxford/New York: Oxford University Press.

Beck, U. (1986). *Risikogesellschaft: Auf dem Weg in eine andere Moderne.* Frankfurt a/M: Suhrkamp.

Beck, U. (1989). *Risikogesellschaft—Die organisierte Unverantwortlichkeit.* St. Gallen: Universität Aulavorträge.

Beck, U. (1999). *Risk Society.* Cambridge, U.K.: Polity Press.

Bieger, T. (2000). *Dienstleistungsmanagement.* Bern/Stuttgart/Wien: Haupt.

Bieger, T. (2001). *Destinationsmanagement,* Fifth Edition. Müchen/Wien: Oldenbourg.

Bieger, T. and Laesser, C. (1999). *Reisemarkt Schweiz—Bericht.* St. Gallen: IDT.

Bieger, T. and Laesser, C. (2001). The role of the railway with regard to mode choice in medium range travel. *The Tourism Review,* 1/2, 33-39.

Bieger, T. and Laesser, C. (2002). Market segmentation on the basis of motivation factors. *Journal of Travel Research,* 41(1), 68-70.

Brög, W. and Erl, E. (1983). Application of a model of individual behavior (situational approach) to explain household activity patterns in urban areas and to forecast behavioral changes. In Carpenter, S. and Jones, P. (Eds.), *Recent Advances in Travel Demand Analysis.* Oxford: Oxford University Press.

European Conference of Ministers of Transport (1998). Round Tables: Infrastructure-Induced Mobility. No. 105. Paris and Washington, DC: Organisation for Economic Cooperation and Development.

European Conference of Ministers of Transport (2000). Round Tables: Transport and Leisure. No. 111. Paris and Washington, DC: Organisation for Economic Cooperation and Development.

Fuhrer, U. (Ed.) (1993). *Wohnen mit dem Auto—Ursachen und Gestaltung automobiler Freizeit.* Zürich: Chronos.

Goleman, D. (1995). *Emotional Intelligence.* New York: Bantam.

Gross, P. (1994). *Die Multioptionsgesellschaft.* Frankfurt a/M: Suhrkamp.

Hägerstrand, T. (1970). What about people in regional science. *Papers of the Regional Science Association,* 24, 7-21.

Heinze, G.W. and Kill, H.H. (1997). *Freizeit und Mobilität—Neue Lösungen im Freizeitverkehr.* Hannover: Akademie für Raumforschung und Landesplanung.

Hogrebe, P. and Strang, S. (1994). Typisierung von Verkehrsteilnehmern und Verkehrsteilnehmerinnen im Stadtverkehr am Beispiel der Stadt Köln. *Zeitschrift für Verkehrswissenschaft,* 1, 67-84.

Horx, M. (1996). *Megatrends für die späten neunziger Jahre.* Düsseldorf: ECON.

Inskeep, E. (1991). *Tourism Planning: An Integrated and Sustainable Development Approach.* New York: Van Nostrand D.

Iten, R. (1990). *Die mikroökonomische Bewertung von Veränderungen der Umweltqualität—dargestellt am Beispiel der Stadt Zürich.* Winterthur: Schellenberg.

Kaspar, C. (1996). *Die Tourismuslehre im Grundriss*. Bern: Haupt.

Krippendorf, J. (1984). *Die Ferienmenschen*. Zürich: Orell Füssli.

Krippendorf, J. (1986). *Alpsegen, Alptraum*. Bern: FIF.

Laesser, C. (1996). *Verkehrs- und Umweltproblematik in städtischen Gebieten*. Bern/Stuttgart/Wien: Haupt.

Laesser, C. (2001). Familientourismus in der Schweiz—Empirische Evidenz einer vielversprechenden Stossrichtung. In Bieger, T. and Laesser, C. (Eds.), *Jahrbuch der Schweizerischen Tourimsuswirtschaft*. St. Gallen: IDT, pp. 103-124.

Lawson, C.T. (2001). Leisure travel/activity decisions: Time and location differences. *Transportation Quarterly*, 55(3), 51-61.

Mentz, H.-J. (1984). *Analyse von verkehrsverhalten im Haushaltskontext*. Schriftenreihe des Instituts für Verkehrsplanung und Verkehrswegebau an der TU Berlin, Number 11. Berlin: Technische Universität.

Meyrat-Schlee, E. (1992). *Der mobile Stadtmensch und seine Umgebung—Hat die Siedlungsqualität Auswirkungen auf die Mobilitätsbedürfnisse der Menschen?* Bericht anlässlich der VLP-Tagung "Stadt und Mobilität" im Rahmen des NFP 25 "Stadt und Verkehr."

Müller, H.R., Flügel, M., Stettler, J., Eichenberger, U., and Willi, E. (1999). *Umweltverantwortliches Verkehrsmanagement in Ferienorten*. Wissenschaftlicher Schlussbericht D6 des NFP 41 "Verkehr und Umwelt." Bern/Brugg: Metron.

Opaschowski, H.W. (1997). *Deutschland 2010*. Hamburg: BAT.

Pommerehne, W.W. (1988). Measuring environmental benefits: A comparison of hedonic technique and contingent valuation. In Bös, D., Rose, M., and Seidl, C. (Eds.), *Welfare and Efficiency in Public Economics*. Berlin/Heidelberg/New York: Springer, pp. 363-400.

Poon, A. (1993). *Tourism: Technology and Competitive Strategies*. Wallingford, U.K.: CAB International.

Schulze, G. (1993). *Die Erlebnisgesellschaft*. Frankfurt/New York: Campus Verlag.

Schweizerische Bundesbahnen (2001). *Geschäftsbericht 2000*. Bern: Author.

Simon, B. and Mummendey, A. (1997). Selbst, Idetintät und Gruppe. In Mummendey, A. and Simon, B. (Eds.), *Identität und Verschiedenheit*, pp. 4-23. Bern/Göttingen: Huber.

Stettler, J. (1997). *Sport und Verkehr—Sportmotiviertes Verkehrsverhalten der Schweizer Bevölkerung*. Berner Studien zu Freizeit und Tourismus Number 36. Bern: FIF.

Vainino, M. (1995). *Traffic Noise and Air Pollution: Valuation of Externalities with Hedonic Price and Contingent Valuation Methods*. Helsinki: School of Economics.

Chapter 18

From "Predatory" to "Experience" Tourism: Estimating Tourist Fruition for a Greenway

Maria Carla Furlan
Sabrina Meneghello
Valeria Minghetti

INTRODUCTION

Tourism is by definition an experience product. New forms of tourism put "slow" and "soft" discovery of local environments and resources at the core of the tourist experience. However, current changes in tourism demand and the growth of a more aware and demanding consumer have started to shift the focus from "predatory" to "experience" tourism.

On the one hand, there is an increasing search for full immersion in nature and for new cultural motivations merging arts, living culture, local customs, gastronomy, etc. On the other hand, new holiday patterns combining traditional recreational activities (e.g., sun and beach) with new cultural experiences are emerging. Ecotourism, cycling tourism, rural tourism, and wine tourism are just some examples of new niche markets, which represent either an opportunity to diversify traditional supply and spread tourist flows over the territory or a specific tourism product with its own demand.

On the grounds of their development there is the belief that the exploitation of the environment stimulates the (tourism-related) usage of the territory and vice versa. Sustainable tourism contributes to the protection and safeguarding of rural areas. It is also important to consider the features and limited capacity of rural areas and to plan actions geared toward sustainability.

THE GREENWAY CONCEPT: MOBILITY AND TOURISM

A way to obtain this kind of tourist experience and to develop a nontraditional approach to tourism is the creation and the use of *greenways*. Greenways, vias verdes, voies lentes or douces, and green axes are some of the many terms used throughout Europe and the rest of the world to describe transport routes dedicated to light nonmotorized traffic. "Greenways can take on numerous different forms. There is no one simple definition of the concept, since it is intimately related to the history and culture [and to features] of the regions concerned" (European Greenway Association, 2000, p. 14).

The word also has a specific meaning in an ecological sense, related to the preservation of biodiversity. Greenways consist of any natural or landscaped course for pedestrian, bicycle, or horse passage that promote a healthier and more balanced way of life and transport, reduce the congestion and the pollution of cities, support rural development, active tourism, and local employment, encourage a more human and closer relationship between visitors and residents, and bring people closer to both their natural and cultural environment.

Greenways can take place (1) in urban and suburban areas for daily users; (2) in rural contexts, i.e., in areas with high environmental value both from a tourism and an ecological perspective; and (3) as part of a network at a regional, national, or international level.

From the tourism-planning point of view, the creation of greenways aims to spread visitor flows into less crowded areas and to increase the value of heritage, environmental goods, and cultural habits.

In many cases (European Greenway Association, 2000, p. 14) greenways are "former transport routes in a specific location, partly or completely decommissioned," e.g., disused railway lines, towpaths along rivers or canals, and great historic routes (pilgrimages). The trails can also connect to industrial heritage or nodes of the public transport systems.

Mobility along the journey becomes a tourist attraction in itself and an important component in the attractiveness of a rural destination, i.e., one of the major motivating factors for visitors. It is not simply a movement from one point to another but an alternative way of experiencing towns and the countryside.

It must be highlighted that in the case of a greenway the environmental preservation is aimed at the improvement of the territory and the creation of a tourism product, composed of tourism services and local resources. The tourist experience can be an *active* one. As another feature, greenways permit a tourist approach and so-called *people-to-people* tourism oriented toward relationships between local communities and visitors.

This chapter will describe the Lemene Greenway project in Italy, which can be easily adapted to other rural areas that share the same physical characteristics and features. Starting with a short description of the theoretical framework (the trade-off between environmental protection and exploitation, the current evolution of rural areas, the role of tourism as a development engine, the concept of greenway, etc.) and of the area where the project has been promoted, the procedure followed to estimate potential demand for a greenway and its economic impact will be discussed. Therefore, aside from precautionary ecological measures taken, the study gives a series of instructions about how to create a greenway. The focus is on cost and the expected return on investment.

For many reasons this study can be considered a model analysis for the creation of a tourist greenway, taking into account the importance of planning and organizing a network among tourist operators and rural communities in order to create an effective tourist product in accordance with visitor needs.

GREENWAYS: MAIN EXAMPLES IN EUROPE

In both Europe and North America we can find different examples of greenways. The trails are dedicated to slow (or light) means of transport, most frequently cyclists. In many cases the greenway networks are called cycling networks (see, e.g., EuroVelo). Depending on the features of the path, there can also be other users, including pedestrians, roller skaters, horse riders, etc. In some cases, as in Britain or in France, the main kind of mobility is by water (British Waterways) or along rivers.

One example of an important and well-organized greenway is the Prague-Vienna Greenway. It represents a good model of cooperation between nonprofit and commercial activities at an international level. Its objectives include

1. the protection of cultural and natural heritage;
2. the strengthening of communities and their cultural integrity;
3. the creation of conditions for economic prosperity based on the sustainable use of local resources;
4. public participation in planning and realization of projects to enhance quality of life and cooperation between local communities, civic initiative, and private and government organizations; and
5. the use of local conditions for developing sustainable tourism and creating tourist products.

These objectives are strongly related to social cohesion and development.

The Prague-Vienna trail links beautiful landscapes, parks, rivers, and a rich variety of cultural monuments and is arranged into different thematic routes (wine, castles, glass, etc.). A commercial tour operator deals with the organization and the supply of these products; U.S. citizens constitute the main target audience.

In Spain an important program exists to develop routes for nonmotorized transport (using decommissioned railway lines) called Vias Verdes. The program promotes the appreciation of the countryside and enhances the relationship between developed tourist destinations and rural villages. These Vias Verdes are characterized by the theme of the railways and the ancient activities carried out in the area (mines, etc.). An interesting example is the Via Verde in Catalonia (Ruta del Ferro, Carrilet), which links historical villages, natural parks near Barcelona, and the famous beaches of the Costa Brava. In Italy, there are some urban paths (in Milan, Ferrara, and Rome) and some tourist trails along the rivers in Northern Italy (Po River, Mincio River, Adige River).

It is difficult to count the consumers of this kind of product, because the greenways are open areas, and consequently it is impossible to control admittances; in addition, the data collected in some cases are nonhomogeneous. For example, in the Drava trails, there are about 140,000 users per year, in the Passau-Vienna about 150,000. Along the Austrian trail running alongside the Danube, there are about 3,500 daily visitors, i.e., 600,000 per season (April to October). It is estimated that about 250,000 travel packages per year are sold for a tour around Lake Constance.

THE LEMENE GREENWAY PROJECT

The Lemene Greenway project was carried out by Centro Internazionale di Studi e richerch sull' Economia Turistica (CISET) within the EU Interreg Programme for Italy-Slovenia. It aims at assessing opportunities and hindrances for the creation of a greenway near Venice and particularly along the Lemene River. The river flows in the lowlands and links historical places such as Portogruaro and Concordia Sagittaria, some crowded seaside destinations, and the Venetian lagoon; it also runs across rural areas of wide fields and marshlands.

The accommodation supply at the seaside destinations of this area reaches significant figures. About 100,000 beds are available in hotels, camping sites, and vacation homes. In the inland, tourism is less developed, and no more than 700 beds for tourists are available in the small towns of the area. As a consequence, the tourist flows show a huge difference. In the whole area there are 1 million tourist arrivals and 8.8 million overnight stays, only 1 percent of which occurs in the inland destinations.

The creation of a greenway can be considered an occasion of economic and social development for this area, in particular with regard to

1. the protection and creation of natural features in urban and rural areas,
2. the care for cultural heritage,
3. support for transportation solutions to increase the safety of pedestrians and cyclists, and
4. the possibility for the development of products and services for sustainable tourism, for society and the environment, and also for the agricultural sector.

The creation of a greenway also has a number of important effects on the local tourism system:

1. Differentiation and development of tourism supply (creation of new products)
2. Attraction and satisfaction of new segments of tourist demand (green tourism, bike tourism, etc.), in order to be more competitive in the tourism market
3. Diffusion of tourist flows from the most famous traditional yet overcrowded destinations to other lesser-known centers
4. Lengthening of the tourist season
5. Restyling of "old" tourism products (not only sun and beach or traditional art cities) and the linkages with other products (e.g., food)
6. Creation of conditions for economic prosperity based on the sustainable use of local resources leading to improved access to the countryside: greenways lead citizens, local governments, public and private organizations to work together to plan and improve their communities

The Lemene Greenway project must analyze the feasibility of the objectives summarized in this list by examining a number of aspects.

- Regarding *tourism demand,* it must be assessed whether a potential demand exists for this kind of tourist product, and whether there is an actual demand in the area of the Lemene River.
- The *characteristics of the region and actors* involved also play an important role. The feasibility of a greenway project depends, for example, on the importance of tourism for the local economy and the opportunity for creating environmentally friendly economic development for local communities, as well as on the presence of cultural and natural heritage. The need to restyle supporting tourism resources (beaches, etc.) and the required actions to convert decommissioned or currently used canals, rivers, towpaths, etc., into a greenway also determine the chances of success.
- The *greenway product itself* needs to be not only easily accessible but also carefully communicated and promoted. Supporting services and goods, sufficient resources and attractions, as well as a satisfactory yield on investment are additional success criteria.

In planning a greenway a number of factors have to be considered, which are illustrated in Table 18.1.

The region of the Lemene River supports the creation of a greenway for many reasons. First, the trail and the area near the river are quiet and scarcely visited, yet are characterized by heritage attractions and a striking landscape. The presence of a rural area with a low population density and the strong impact of agriculture on the economic system enforce the necessity of direct action in order to protect soil and biodiversity as well as the existing landscape variety. Creating a greenway provides various options for the protection of rare landscape elements endangered by conventional agricultural techniques.

TABLE 18.1. Planning a Greenway

Factor	Specification
Creation of a coordinated stakeholder group	Stakeholders can be both public (e.g., department of environment or transport, public transport associations) and private individuals or organizations (e.g., restaurants) and members of the national consumers association.
Participation	Companies and public bodies have to guarantee not only services but also specific activities (e.g., the creation of infrastructures for trails).
Financial support and fundraising	Not only from public funds but also from the sales of tourism products and services.
Analyze users	Pedestrians, cyclists, horse riders, etc., and how they will use the greenway.
Physical features	E.g., width, slope, presence of recreation areas, shade, length, and departure/arrival areas; some characteristics of trails can be useful for a specific target group only.
Understanding the aims of greenways	Reduction of pollution and traffic; leisure for local residents and tourists; care for local heritage.
Analyze the tourism product and its services	E.g., accommodations, restaurants, equipment, information, and communication. Sometimes greenways can be proposed by tour operators for groups, while other greenways can be accessed by independent travelers.
Verify relationships within the territory and community	Proximity to an urban center and other attractions in the area.

The area of the Lemene River has cultural and natural resources which encourage the rediscovery of the important relationship between river and community through slow transportation. The closeness to large tourism destinations with more developed service supplies (hotels, restaurants, etc.) and larger visitor numbers combined with strong local participation and support for sustainable economic activities in tourism, agriculture, and heritage further contribute to the success of the Lemene project. Present sustainable actions in the area are, for example, the creation of protected areas (Lemene-Reghena Park, proposals for a lagoon park, etc.) and the creation of biking itineraries for sustainable tourism (e.g., the literary park of the writer Ippolito Nievo and the Stalis mills).

The Lemene River region is also interested in the planning and realization of development projects enhancing the economy and the quality of life (e.g., EU Leader projects). Finally, the greenway is in line with the tourist promotion and plans of the Veneto region.

Estimating Demand for Lemene's Greenway

As it is very difficult to estimate or forecast the potential demand for a new kind of tourist product, it is also problematic to calculate the demand for green or rural tourism. However, according to our research it is possible to identify some indicators to measure the propensity for using greenways. Table 18.2 summarizes useful indicators to estimate the demand for ecotourism products such as a greenway.

In planning a greenway it is important that all stakeholders involved are aware of the potential demand patterns and the estimated use of this kind of infrastructure. The Lemene Greenway research attempted to answer the following questions: (1) Who will be the target market interested in this product? (2) How many visitors can use the trail? (3) Can the value or the economic impact of the greenway be estimated, not only from an agricultural point of view, but also from a tourist expenditure point of view?

Due to the specific location of the Lemene Greenway, a visitor overview will be described to measure the use of the greenway by three main target groups. For residents the greenway is a place of leisure and rest, or they use greenways on a daily basis to walk or cycle to leisure activity centers and to keep fit. Residents' children use greenways as play areas. Beach tourists come from neighboring sea-

TABLE 18.2. Demand Forecast for Ecotourism

Indicator	Specification
Consumption behavior	Number of visitors to selected and significant attractions (natural parks) or destinations Type of accommodation (hotel, camping, etc.)
Habits or attitudes regarding the environment	Waste reuse or reduction Energy saving Use of alternative means of transportation, etc.
Surveys	Travel motives and expectations Expensive method to explore consumers' interest in green or active tourism
Knowledge about different sending markets	Characterized by specific behavior or interests, e.g., German-speaking tourists tend to be more involved in the "environmentally oriented" tourist experience
Knowledge about specific targets or consumer groups	Segmentation Special interests
Memberships	Associations Syndicates Lobby groups, e.g., World Wildlife Fund

side resorts. For them greenways are an alternative way of spending their spare time. They are aware of the safety offered by these routes and the physical separation from the main tourism flows' road networks. Special interest tourists are national and international tourists attracted by special activities such as cycling, horseback riding, trekking, bird-watching, wine and food tasting, etc., in an attractive area.

A more thorough examination of these target groups will help to estimate the final amount of trips/excursions in the Lemene Greenway and the economic impact on the area. Each group will be analyzed by applying existing indicators such as the propensity to travel in a rural context or the use of "soft" means of transport.

Residents in the Surrounding Area

About 4,980,000 people can reach the Lemene Greenway in less than three hours. Results of previous surveys or statistics reveal that in this area (the Italian provinces of Veneto and Friuli Venezia Giulia) residents are more accustomed to doing their daily trips by bicycle than other Italian people: 42 percent of the inhabitants in the surrounding area use the bicycle at least on the weekend. According to previous surveys, 35 percent of residents spent their leisure time in a green area or engage in some type of sport activities. Combining this information allows us to calculate the probability that the inhabitants are interested in enjoying a greenway in their leisure time. The probability will be different according to length or difficulty of the trail. However, it is also possible to consider the alternative experiences or destinations which compete for potential visitors. In conclusion, we estimate that within one year these residents can make roughly 34,000 excursions in the Lemene Greenway.

The total expenditure of these day-trippers can thus be estimated to be approximately EUR 980,000 (average daily expenditure of EUR 29 per capita) including the costs of travel and local services.

Beach Tourists

By "beach tourists" we mean visitors spending their holiday in seaside destinations (Caorle and Bibione in particular) of the Venetian area (the total amount of arrivals is 2 million, and the overnights are about 10 million).

The analysis of this group's inclination to undertake excursions in the green, rural inland areas is based on existing information and data collected by conducting interviews. As a first step, the analysis considered the origin market of tourists and then applied the propensity to use the soft transportation means, such as the bicycle, to each segment. Data from the European Union (EU) (quoted in Maccarini, 2000) explain that German, Dutch, and Danish people are accustomed to using bikes both at home and in leisure time (45 percent), which indicates that this inclination may be even stronger during their holidays. This probability can thus be applied to German-speaking tourists in seaside destinations. A different probability will be ascribed to the other sending countries (e.g., Italian or French visitors). Further distinction can be made with regard to the kind of accommodation. According to opinion leaders and tourist operators, the results show that visitors who choose to camp have a higher propensity to prefer green experiences and inland short trips than do hotel tourists.

The holiday season also has an influence on the propensity to use a greenway. In May or June, tourists are more interested in exploring the surrounding area and enriching the standard product of "sun and beach." By combining these variables, an estimated 35,000 tourists per year are expected to make day trips to the Lemene Greenway.

Based on previous CISET studies (see, for example, Manente and Minghetti, 1996; Costa, Manente, and Minghetti, 1996) about tourist expenditure, the total economic impact is calculated to be roughly EUR 1,050,000 per year (EUR 30 per capita).

Special Interest Tourists or Specific Target Groups

Special interest tourists covers people traveling with the specific motivation of green or active tourism, often already organized in groups (bikers, bird-watchers, educational tourists). They should be attracted by the Lemene Greenway product itself. Although this is a small target market, it is significant from a marketing point of view, as special interest tourists can be easily reached through dedicated communication channels. In addition, people with special interests can work as opinion leaders.

Special interest groups usually consume the full tourism product, including accommodations, catering services, etc. This means that the economic impact can be relevant despite the limited number of tourists. By conducting interviews with niche tour operators and opinion leaders, and by comparing Lemene Greenway with other products, the total number of tourists attracted to the area is expected to be around 5,000, generating an economic impact of about EUR 40,000 (average daily expenditure of 80 Euro per capita).

CONCLUSION

The analysis of the Lemene Greenway provides a model to evaluate the success of a new tourist product in the market. It must also be kept in mind that the creation of this product should involve the stakeholders of the local area and stimulate the activities and the rejuvenation of the tourist supply. In addition, through the creation of the greenway the environment can also be put to better use and agricultural activities can be boosted. However, it is important to plan the product in an effective way, considering the different needs and features of various target markets, and to promote the sustainable use of rural territory.

BIBLIOGRAPHY

Associazione Italiana Greenways (AIG) (1999). Second European Conference on Greenways: A Way of Rediscovering and Improving the Landscape, Milan, October 22.

Becheri, E. (2001). *X Rapporto sul turismo in Italia.* Firenze, Italy: Mercury.

Costa, P., Manente, M., and Minghetti, V. (1996). *Tourism demand segmentation and consumption behavior: An economic impact.* Venice: CISET.

European Commission, Enterprise Directorate General, Tourism Unit (1999). Toward quality rural tourism. Integrated Quality Management (IQM) of rural tourist destinations. Brussels: Author.

European Greenway Association (2000). *The European Greenways Good Practice Guide.* Narnur, Belgium: Author.

Federazione Italiana Amici della Bicicletta (FIAB) (2000). XIII National Rally, Provincia di Torino, Italy, June 29-July 2.

Maccarini, A. (2000). L'Europa che pedala. *Qui Touring* 30(11): 60-71.

Manente, M. and Minghetti, V. (1996). *La spesa dei turisti nel Veneto.* Venice: International Center of Studies on the Tourist Economy (CISET).

Moore, R. L. and Shafer, C. S. (2001). Introduction to special issues trails and greenways: Opportunities for planners, managers and scholars. *Journal of Park and Recreation Administration* 19(3): 123-125.

SECTION V: INFORMATION TECHNOLOGIES IN LEISURE AND TOURISM

In early January 2003, the Austrian online tourism platform Tiscover reported record access numbers: during peak time 1,000 users per minute visited the site to obtain information about Austrian tourism products. This is just one more piece of evidence for the sweeping success of information technologies in leisure and tourism. E-tourism is more than a new buzzword—the electronic processing of business transactions creates added value in most areas of the tourism value chain.

Today, the tourism industry is one of the major users of Internet technology. Daniel Fesenmaier and Ulrike Gretzel go one step further and take a look into the future of leisure trends related to information technology and identify five major trends.

Despite the overwhelming worldwide acceptance of tourism on the Internet, e-tourism in Italy is still in its infancy. Magda Antonioli Corigliano and Rodolfo Baggio assess Italian tourism Web sites to outline possible reasons for the weak performance of Italian e-tourism.

Introducing information technologies into the tourism value chain means that an abundance of travel information becomes available to tourists. Benedict Dellaert and Gerald Häubl examine how the use of a relatively new e-tourism tool, electronic tourist recommendation agents, can improve the decision quality of tourists and simultaneously reduce search time. Karl Wöber, on the other hand, presents the successful marketing decision support system TourMIS, which satisfies the complex information needs of tourism suppliers due to growing market dynamics.

Chapter 19

Searching for Experience: Technology-Related Trends Shaping the Future of Tourism

Daniel R. Fesenmaier
Ulrike Gretzel

We overestimate the pace of progress near-term and underestimate progress long-term.

Bill Gates

INTRODUCTION

It is well accepted that the Internet has had a substantial impact on the consumer and will continue to shape business-customer relationships with the emergence of new technology infrastructures and applications. Today the tourism industry is one of the major users of Internet technology, with between 33 and 50 percent of all consumer-based Internet transactions being tourism related (Werthner and Klein, 1999). For the tourism industry the Web is simultaneously the biggest opportunity and the biggest challenge because changes are mainly driven by consumers who are hybrid in their tastes, spontaneous, and unpredictable (Poon, 1993; Schwartz, 1998). Looking to the future, of course, is a complex endeavor; however, a number of trends are indicative of the directions in which leisure might develop. In this chapter we will consider five important trends related to information technology which have the potential to significantly impact leisure behavior. These are as follows:

1. The continuing increase in speed and sophistication of information technology;
2. The continuing growth in the use and number of uses of information technology in tourism;
3. The changing forms of information technology as a medium for communication;
4. The emergence of a new consumer; and
5. The recognition of experience as the foundation for defining tourism products.

The following section will identify and briefly discuss each trend, focusing attention on its impact on leisure within the context of the tourism industry.

FIVE TRENDS

Many issues must be considered when relating the nature, role, and impact of information technology to developments in society (Barney, 2000; Jonscher, 1999). We believe the following five trends provide an important foundation for assessing and understanding the future of information technology for tourism from the consumer perspective.

The Continuing Speed and Sophistication of Information Technology

The personal computer (PC) has only recently celebrated its twentieth birthday. In a recent article in *PC Magazine,* the PC was described as one of the most profound inventions in the history of humankind (Miller, 2002). From its inception in 1981, the development of computer technology has been shown to follow Moore's Law—that chip density and therefore the speed of computers will double every eighteen months. Thus, computers and computer technology have grown from the very primitive precursors to today's high-performance machines. Over the years various competitors infused the market with a variety of innovations focused on expanding the power of the machine, increasing the ability of the system to address workplace needs, and encouraging society to think and dream about what might be when . . . (Miller, 2002).

As systems grew more sophisticated and powerful and arguably more humancentric, the power of the network was recognized and spurred even greater innovation. In 1990 the World Wide Web was born, along with a new generation of innovators seeking to build an information infrastructure that could enable individuals to collaborate from distant locations. The outcome was Mosaic and a decade of unparalleled innovation and "build out" in information infrastructure. This new orientation also led to the development of a variety of computer-enabled devices, such as mobile phones and personal digital assistants, which are now beginning to pervade human society (Norman, 1999).

A number of scholars have recently reflected on the progress of computer technology and have concluded that much remains to be accomplished before computers/information technologies can truly enable society to benefit from their power. In the *Unfinished Revolution,* Dertouzos (2001, p. 6) argues that "the real utility of computers, and the true value of the Information Revolution, still lie ahead." He suggests that over the past twenty years society has evolved to "fit" around computers and that the productivity gains from computer technology have been "more hype than reality." Supporting this argument, Norman (1999) suggests that the real benefits will be realized only when computer technology becomes more human centered, that is, when technology adapts to the needs and lifestyles of human beings. They argue that information appliances—computer systems which focus on specific tasks and are connected through the Internet or wireless technology—are the basis of a humancentric, and thus invisible, computer. It appears that the focus of emerging technology is on empowering the individual within the framework of the human experience rather than defining human behavior around the needs of computer designers.

The Continuing Growth in the Use and Different Forms of Uses of Information Technology in Tourism

The number of Internet users continues to grow worldwide, and as a result, the Internet's potential as a marketing medium has expanded greatly and continues to expand. Internet revenues also show a robust growth, from about $7.8 billion in 1997 to a projected $34 billion in 2002. The characteristics of the Internet have considerably changed over the past five years. The present Internet users have become older, are considerably less male, have relatively less education, are more likely to have families, are more likely to live in geographical regions corresponding to the general U.S. population distribution, and are more likely to represent a broader range of occupational categories than their predecessors. The average age of today's Internet user is approximately thirty-eight years as compared to thirty-four years in 1994. The largest group of today's Internet users is the baby boomer segment (thirty to forty-nine years). Some demographic and lifestyle characteristics of baby boomer Internet users conclude that they are in their prime professional and family formation years, are employed by large corporations, have Internet access from work, and that there are many women in this group (FIND/SVP, 1994-1997).

Women represent over 40 percent of today's Internet user population. Women tend to use the Internet both for personal and business uses. However, women score higher on personal usage and lower on business usage than men. Female Internet use is generally characterized by shorter online sessions, less weekly usage, online access from home, and extended use of e-mail, which surpassed men's use in early 1996. Women tend to be more interested than men in new interactive services such as movies on demand, interactive banking, health information, and educational programming. Surveys show that women are more task and goal oriented than men when it comes to using computers and going online. A close observation of today's Internet industry reveals that the Internet and the majority of online services were designed and nurtured by male-oriented content and technologies that do not respond to the basic needs of women (Clemente, 1998). It is very important to understand the needs and characteristics of the female market and to redesign Internet technology and content in an effort to effectively target female online customers.

Today's Internet users are among the most educated people in the United States. However, the proportion of Internet users having achieved at least a college degree has steadily declined. Internet users earn on average $51,900 per year, substantially more than the average American. Yet again, the average household income of Internet users has significantly declined, from $66,300 in 1994 to $51,900 in 1997, and is expected to continue to change until it reflects the income distribution of the general population. The presence of children in Internet user households has increased since 1994. In 1994, 30 percent of

Internet user households included children under the age of eighteen living at home. At the turn of the century, that number has increased to over 40 percent, underscoring the importance of the Internet to families for purposes of education and information (FIND/ SVP, 1994-1997).

Internet Uses

The three leading uses cited by all WWW users include information gathering, searching, and browsing. While male users are more likely to use the WWW for information gathering, work, and shopping, female users are more likely to use the WWW for searching, browsing, and education (Pitkow, 1997). According to the latest FIND/SVP study (1994-1997), the Internet is considered indispensable by 73 percent of users describing the impact of the Internet on their lives. An overwhelming majority (over 91 percent) use the Internet for personal reasons such as searching for news, product information, educational information, or entertainment. Business use was reported by 60 percent of all adult Internet users (21.7 million users) and includes applications such as file transfer, searching for business news, conducting business research, or shopping for business-related goods and services. Overall, 68 percent of users reported both personal and business uses of the Internet. Further, the FIND/SVP study (1994-1997) indicates a substantial increase in online use in terms of the average online session length, the number of hours spent online per week, and the number of Web sites visited regularly, registered with, and paid for by users. Currently about 40 percent of adult users report less than five hours per week of usage, while 33 percent report they are online for ten hours per week.

Online Commerce and Online Purchase Habits

The key to success for online business is to know the content customers are looking for when searching the Web. News leads the list of content desired by today's Internet users, as it has in previous years. Hobby-related and travel-related information rank second and third, highlighting the leisure aspect of Internet use. Other findings include the following:

- Interest in using categories such as news, travel, government/community issues, health/medicine, product information, personal investing, and food increases with age.
- Women are more likely than men to use travel, health/medicine, food, and parenting information.
- Higher-income users are more interested in travel, product information, sports, and investing.
- Lower-income users are more interested in hobbies, community issues, music, games, adult education, and parenting.

Online commerce (e-commerce) is a growing aspect of today's Internet industry. Web-based companies such as Amazon.com and eBay.com have created profitable businesses selling products and services to consumers on the Web. This trend of online retailing holds great potential and is becoming increasingly popular as technological developments, lower costs, and increasing ease of use create a cheaper and convenient option for shopping. The 1997 FIND/SVP survey indicated that during the past twelve months, 40 percent of adult Internet users had searched for personal product information online, 36 percent had clicked on advertisements at least once to learn more, and 27 percent had made online purchases, up from 19 percent reported in 1995. The most commonly cited reasons for not making an online purchase, reported by 40 percent, were the lack of need or interest and security/trust concerns. However, the trend for online commerce continues to grow, as 31 percent of all Internet users indicated they were very likely and an additional 34 percent were somewhat likely to search for product information online in the next twelve months.

Contrary to all previous studies and reports, the large majority of online purchasers used their credit cards when paying in the course of their online transaction. Only 18 percent of those surveyed indicated they placed their actual order over the telephone, and 19 percent said they used some other method to pay for their orders.

Travelers and Internet Use

The Internet and travel industry partnership has proved beneficial to both industries (Jupiter Communications, 1997; Gretzel, Yuan, and Fesenmaier, 2000; Hardie et al., 1997). Travelers' usage of the Internet has grown progressively from 1996 to 2001. The incidence of Internet use among American travelers has increased from 28 million Internet users in 1996 to 110 million in 2001 (Travel Industry Association of America [TIA], 1998, 2002). The Travel Industry Association of America Report on Technology and Travel for the year 2000 (TIA, 2001) reported that 89 percent of Internet users took at least one trip (for business or leisure) of 100 miles or more, one way, away from home during the year, and 44 percent of Internet users were frequent travelers. According to the 2001 National Travel Survey, 68 percent of current Internet users used the Internet to make travel plans (TIA, 2002). Travel plans include activities such as getting information on destinations or checking prices and schedules. This number was up from 27 percent of Internet users in 1997 and 10 percent in 1996. Among Americans who conducted travel planning over the Internet in 1997, 7 percent did all of their travel planning over the Internet, 16 percent did most of their travel planning over the Internet, and nearly one-third used the Internet half the time for collecting travel information. In 2001, one-third (33 percent) of American travelers who are online indicated they actually booked or made reservations online. The large majority of these travelers purchased airline tickets (80 percent), reserved a hotel room (62 percent), or rented a car (46 percent). In addition, many online travelers purchased a ticket for a cultural event (27 percent), sports event (16 percent), and/or an amusement park (14 percent).

Of the American adults who used the Internet for travel planning or making reservations in 1997, over 90 percent indicated they were extremely satisfied or satisfied with their most recent online experience (TIA, 1998). The most common reason cited for satisfaction with their travel-related Internet experience was that the Internet is a great information reference tool. Other popular reasons for satisfaction included convenience and ease of Internet use and good price offers. The most common reasons for dissatisfaction with their Internet experience were that the Internet did not provide the necessary information and prices were not as cheap compared to calling directly.

The Changing Forms of Information Technology As a Medium for Communication

Industry experts have increasingly questioned whether the Internet is different from other media and if it needs to be addressed in new ways using new strategies (Godin, 1999; Hoffman and Novak, 1995; Zeff and Aronson, 1999). Hoffman and Novak (1995, p. 7) describe the Internet as a form of communication that is characterized by an "interactive multimedia many-to-many communication model" in which interactivity can also be *with* the medium in addition to *through* the medium. Both consumers and firms can interact with the medium, provide content to the medium, communicate in one-to-one or one-to-many forms of communication, and have more direct control over the way they communicate than by using other media. When everyone can communicate richly with everyone else, not only the old communication models become obsolete but also communication channels that are based on them (Evans and Wurster, 1999).

In comparison to traditional media, the Internet combines and integrates the following functional properties: (1) information representation; (2) collaboration; (3) communication; (4) interactivity; and (5) transactions. As a consequence, Internet communication can be a much more holistic approach than traditional advertising. The Internet can simultaneously integrate informational, educational, entertainment, and sales aspects; this flexibility makes the Internet rich and appealing but also very complex and difficult to deal with. Using these capabilities may lead to deeper relationships with and greater personalization of goods and services. Travel and tourism fit especially well with interactive media because they are information-intensive and experience-based industries, and because current Web users are heavy users of travel and tourism products and services. Interactive media calls for interactive marketing, whose essence is to use "information *from* the customer rather than *about* the customer" (Day, 1998, p. 47). It differs from traditional marketing since it is based on a dialogue instead of a one-way communication, and it deals with individual consumers instead of mass markets (Parsons, Zeisser, and Waitman, 1998).

The Internet enables destination-marketing organizations to blend together publishing, real-time communication, broadcast, and narrowcast (Hoffman, Novak, and Chatterjee, 1995). It is a medium that attracts attention and creates a sense of community. It is a personal medium, an interactive medium, a niche, and a mass medium at the same time (Schwartz, 1998). In contrast to traditional media, the trade-off between richness and reach is not applicable to the Web. Evans and Wurster (1999) define richness as the quality of information (accuracy, bandwidth, currency, customization, interactivity, relevance, security). Reach refers to the number of people who participate in the sharing of that information. The trade-off between richness and reach leads to asymmetries of information. Thus, when destination-marketing organizations are able to distribute and exchange rich information without constraint "the channel choices for marketers, the inefficiencies of consumer search, the hierarchical structure of supply chains, the organizational pyramid, asymmetries of information, and the boundaries of the corporation itself will all be thrown into question" (Evans and Wurster, 1999, p. 37).

The Emergence of a New Consumer

The Internet changes how people communicate and exchange information. The resulting abundance of information and ease of communication have led to profound changes in consumer attitudes and behavior. What makes "new" consumers new is that they are empowered by the Internet, which provides them with easy and cheap access to various information sources and extended communities (Windham and Orton, 2000). New consumers are well informed, are used to having many choices, expect speed, and use technologies to overcome the physical constraints of bodies and borders. Lewis and Bridger (2000) describe the new consumer as being individualistic, involved, independent, and informed. The Internet is a highly personalized medium, and new consumers expect marketers to address and cater to their complex personal preferences. Consequently, new consumers are in control and have become important players in the process of creating and shaping brands.

New consumers are also very independent in making consumption decisions but, at the same time, like to share stories about their consumption experiences with members of different communities. Stories can convey emotional aspects of use experiences and product/service qualities that are generally hard to express in writing and, consequently, are rarely included in traditional product descriptions. Storytelling is an important means of creating and maintaining communities (Muniz and O'Guinn, 2000), and Internet technologies greatly facilitate this form of communication and community building. Importantly, the new scarcities of time and trust require new consumers to rely heavily on word of mouth and expert opinions of like-minded others (Muniz and O'Guinn, 2000).

A wealth of information creates a poverty of attention (Lewis and Bridger, 2000). New consumers try to cope with this problem by scanning information depending on personal relevance and have become very capable of ignoring nonrelevant advertising. They are, therefore, much more active in their information search than old consumers, who were largely passive information recipients. Attention is increasingly reserved for marketers who have asked for permission and have established a long-term relationship with the consumer (Godin, 1999). In return for their valuable attention, new consumers expect special benefits such as extremely personalized services. Attention peaks when new consumers reach a psychologically balanced state of mind, a so-called "flow" experience. Flow is a seamless, intrinsically enjoyable, self-reinforcing, and captivating experience (Feather, 2000). To capture the attention of new consumers requires more than traditional, static, and passive advertisements. New consumers expect personalized, emotional, and intriguing experiences through which they can learn about new products. In the world of the new consumer, the focus of advertising shifts from product attributes to consumption experiences.

Experience As the Foundation for Defining Tourism Products

It has long been recognized that travel is an experience and tourism is a key part of the "experience industry" (Pine and Gilmore, 1999). However, the role of experience in consumption (including pre-, during, and postpurchase) is only now being considered as one of the foundations for effective marketing. Recent efforts have shown that the experiential aspects of products and services provide the starting point for effecting marketing (O'Sullivan and Spangler, 1998; Pine and Gilmore, 1999; Schmitt, 1999). Experiences are personal events that engage the individual in a meaningful way. As shown in Figure 19.1, the core element of travel experiences is the travel activity, while the tourism industry plays the part of an experience facilitator; importantly, the social or personal setting in which activities occur contribute substantially to the nature of the experience. It is suggested that while the experiential aspects of travel are the foundation, the memories that are stored as a result of these experiences are key to at-

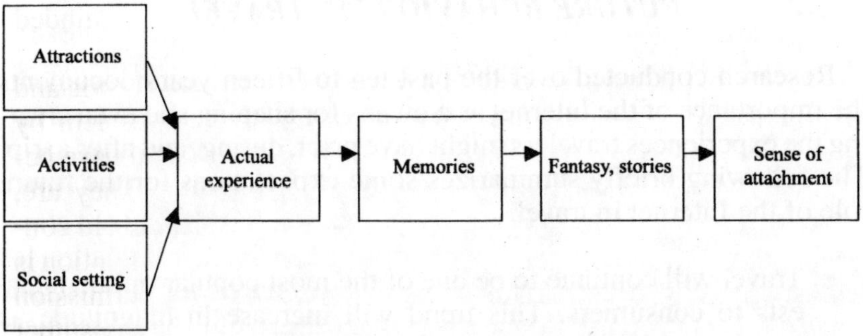

FIGURE 19.1. Sequence of Travel Experience

tracting new visitors as well as retaining current ones. Furthermore, it is suggested that stories—the mechanisms for communicating experiences through word of mouth or as "documentaries" of experiences (through articles, film, etc.)—provide the path through which the tourism industry can build and extend markets.

Schmitt (1999) and others have argued that the new consumer evaluates products more on their experiential aspects than based on objective features such as price, availability, etc., and that experiential marketing should focus on those experiential aspects which make the consumption of the product most compelling, i.e., the five senses. Effective experiential marketing is sensory and affective. It approaches consumption as a holistic experience and acknowledges that consumers can be either rational or emotional or both at the same time. While traditional marketing is based on consumer behavior, product features, benefits, and quantifiable market segments, experiential marketing is driven by an understanding of consumer experiences and the need for personalization. New consumers require advertising that is entertaining, stimulating, and at the same time informative. Brands are no longer seen as mere identifiers but become themselves sources of experiences by evoking sensory, affective, creative, and lifestyle-related associations (Schmitt, 1999). Thus, experiential marketing blurs the border between advertising, purchase, and use as it attempts to create a unique shopping experience and lets the new consumer anticipate what the consumption experience will be like.

FUTURE BEHAVIORS IN TRAVEL

Research conducted over the past ten to fifteen years documents the importance of the Internet as a means for shaping and even creating the experiences travelers might have prior, during, and after a trip. The following briefly summarizes some expectations for the future role of the Internet in travel.

- Travel will continue to be one of the most popular online interests to consumers. This trend will increase in magnitude as travel providers create more effective means with which to communicate the nature of their offerings.
- The Internet and alternate access devices are increasing the number of electronic connections between customers and the tourism industry. These new technologies will continue to provide an environment for creating relationships, allowing consumers to access information more efficiently, conducting transactions, and interacting electronically with businesses and suppliers.
- The changes in demographic profiles of Internet users over the past decade suggest that the evolving Internet and related systems will ultimately be adopted by the majority of the traveling public.
- The demands of travelers, in particular the purchase process(es) they use, will continue to evolve as consumers of travel products gain more experience and confidence in product purchasing over the Internet. Importantly, conversations among travelers (through travel clubs, virtual communities, etc.) will continue to grow and will be an important source for travel information.
- Experience-oriented Internet communications will grow in importance as humancentric computing and emotionally intelligent interfaces are offered on the Internet. These interfaces/systems will incorporate a variety of interpreted information, enabling potential visitors to gain extensive trial experiences prior to the actual trip.

The five trends identified set the stage for an interesting and challenging future for the travel and leisure industry. The incredibly rich informational environment, the availability of and access to an infinite number of experiential settings, and current changes in political systems worldwide empower the consumer in a variety of ways. The challenge for tourism and leisure organizations is to set stages for experience creation throughout their organizational structures and actively involve all employees in the design and marketing of experiences. Following from Naisbitt (1994), the "global paradox" for travel organizations lies in having to simultaneously compete not only at the local level for individual travelers but also at the national and international level. At the same time, the innovative power of the Internet provides stimulating input for new organizational strategies but also constrains the ability of current organizations to adjust to the new realities. Recent studies of the tourism industry support this finding, indicating that very few tourism destination-marketing organizations have been able to effectively integrate technology into their organizations and that new steps are needed to enable these organizations to more effectively market their destinations (Yuan and Fesenmaier, 2000; Yuan, Gretzel, and Fesenmaier, 2003). Finally, education and training come to the forefront as the demand for tourism and leisure professionals to embrace this new environment increases (Prokesch, 1997). The emergence of programs in Europe, Australia, and the United States that concentrate on Internet-related issues in tourism/leisure and provide interdisciplinary curricula is clear evidence for the beginning of this evolution.

REFERENCES

Barney, D. (2000). *Prometheus Wired: The Hope for Democracy in the Age of Network Technology*. Vancouver: UBC Press.

Clemente, P. (1998). *The State of the Net: The New Frontier*. New York: McGraw-Hill.

Day, G. S. (1998). Organizing for Interactivity. *Journal of Interactive Marketing*, 12(1): 47-53.

Dertouzos, M. (2001). *The Unfinished Revolution*. New York: HarperCollins Publishers.

Evans, P. and T. S. Wurster (1999). *Blown to Bits*. Boston, MA: Harvard Business School Press.

Feather, F. (2000). *FutureConsumer.Com*. Toronto, Canada: Warwick Publishing.

FIND/SVP (1994-1997). *American Internet User Surveys*. New York: FIND/SVP Inc.

Gates, B. (1999). *Business @ the Speed of Thought*. New York: Warner Books.

Godin, S. (1999). *Permission Marketing*. New York: Simon and Schuster.

Gretzel, U., Y. Yuan, and D. R. Fesenmaier (2000). White paper on Advertising and Information Technology in Tourism. National Laboratory for Tourism and eCommerce, University of Illinois, Champaign.

Hardie, M. E., W. M. Bluestein, J. McKnight, and K. Davis (1997). The Forrester Report: Entertainment and Technology Strategies [Online]. Forrester Research, Inc., Cambridge, Massachusetts, May 1, 1997. Available at <http://www.forrester.com>.

Hoffman, D. L. and T. P. Novak (1995). Marketing in Hypermedia Computer-Mediated Environments: Conceptual Foundations. Working Paper. Memphis, TN: Owen Graduate School of Management at Vanderbilt University.

Hoffman, D. L., T. P. Novak, and P. Chatterjee (1995). Commercial Scenarios for the Web: Opportunities and Challenges. Working Paper. Memphis, TN: Owen Graduate School of Management at Vanderbilt University.

Jonscher, C. (1999). *The Evolution of Wired Life: From the Alphabet to the Soul-Catcher Chip—How Information Technologies Change Our World.* New York: John Wiley and Sons, Inc.

Jupiter Communications (1997). *Travel and Interactive Technology: A Five Year Outlook.* Washington DC: Travel Industry Association of America.

Lewis, D. and D. Bridger (2000). *The Soul of the New Consumer.* London: Nicholas Brealey Publishing.

Miller, M. (2002). Living History: Retracing the Evolution of the PC and *PC Magazine. PC Magazine,* March 12, pp. 137-161.

Muniz, A. M. and T. C. O'Guinn (2000). Brand Community. *Journal of Consumer Research,* 27(4): 412-432.

Naisbitt, J. (1994). *Global Paradox.* New York: Avon.

Norman, D. A. (1999). *The Invisible Computer: Why Good Products Can Fail, the Personal Computer Is So Complex and Information Appliances Are the Solution.* Cambridge, MA: MIT Press.

O'Sullivan, E. J. and K. J. Spangler (1998). *Experience Marketing.* State College, PA: Venture Publishing.

Parsons, A., M. Zeisser, and R. Waitman (1998). Organizing Today for the Digital Marketing of Tomorrow. *Journal of Interactive Marketing,* 12(1): 31-46.

Pine B. J. and J. H. Gilmore (1999). *The Experience Economy.* Boston, MA: Harvard Business School Press.

Pitkow, J. (1997). The *WWW User Population: Emerging Trends.* Atlanta, GA: GVU Center, Georgia Institute of Technology.

Poon, A. (1993). *Tourism, Technology and Competitive Strategies.* Oxon, UK: CAB International.

Prokesch, S. E. (1997). Unleashing the Power of Learning: An Interview with British Petroleum's John Browne. *Harvard Business Review,* 75(5): 147-168.

Schmitt, B. H. (1999). *Experiential Marketing: How to Get Customers to Sense, Feel, Think, Act, and Relate to Your Company and Brands.* New York: Free Press.

Schwartz, E. I. (1998). *Webonomics: Nine Essential Principles for Growing Your Business on the World Wide Web.* New York: Broadway Books.

Travel Industry Association of America (1998). *Technology and Travel 1998: Executive Report.* Washington, DC: Travel Industry Association of America.

Travel Industry Association of America (2001). *Technology and Travel 2001: Executive Report.* Washington, DC: Travel Industry Association of America.

Travel Industry Association of America (2002). *Technology and Travel 2002: Executive Report.* Washington, DC: Travel Industry Association of America.

Werthner, H. and S. Klein (1999). *Information Technology and Tourism—A Challenging Relationship.* Wien, Austria: Springer Verlag.

Windham, L. and K. Orton (2000). *The Soul of the New Consumer.* New York: Allworth Press.

Yuan, Y. and D. R. Fesenmaier (2000). Preparing for the New Economy: The Use of the Internet and Intranet in American Convention and Visitor Bureaus. *Information Technology and Tourism,* 3(2): 71-86.

Yuan, Y., U. Gretzel, and D. R. Fesenmaier (2003). Managing Innovation: The Use of Internet Technology by American Convention and Visitors Bureaus. *Journal of Travel Research,* 41(3): 240-255.

Zeff, R. and B. Aronson (1999). *Advertising on the Internet,* Second Edition. New York: John Wiley and Sons, Inc.

Chapter 20

Italian Tourism on the Internet: New Business Models

Magda Antonioli Corigliano
Rodolfo Baggio

TOURISM ONLINE

The tourism sector, more than many others, is going through a series of major transformations, mainly due to the globalization process and the changed conditions of increasingly dynamic international competition. New origins and destinations of tourist flows, increasing use of new technologies, and growing diversification in the supply of tourism products are just a few examples. These elements involve all the steps of tourism production, but the introduction of new technologies in communication and information management is particularly relevant.

An effective e-commerce strategy is considered a key element in achieving a competitive advantage in the market today. The integration of the Internet with traditional distribution channels allows for satisfaction of customers' information needs in a highly competitive way and acquisition of new clients.

In any case, the introduction of e-commerce in tourism is guided by demand, and any possible development in this field depends on consumers' attitudes. On one hand, they require travel packages, including transportation, overnight stays, and other services. On the other hand, the so-called "do-it-yourself" customers are looking for the highest personalization and/or the most convenient price. The latter, in particular, promotes the creation of specialized portals which allow price comparisons and, at the same time, the offer of extra services for travelers.

The Evolution of Business Models

The European tourism market is characterized by new emerging actors who take advantage of the technologies introduced by the Internet. The Internet has produced several changes in the tourism industry; the main impact has been on the interrelation between service providers and traditional intermediaries (Antonioli and Baggio, 2002).

The tendency to *disintermediation* is so strong that it seems to generate conflicts among the actors of the supply chain. For this reason some intermediaries showed themselves quite hostile toward the e-commerce initiatives of hotels, airline companies, and tour operators.

Today, the most common strategy views e-commerce as complementary to traditional channels and thus applies integrative and not cannibalizing price policies. The electronic channel is seen as a way to reach higher revenues and better integration among different dealers.

Another kind of relationship deeply modified by the spread of e-commerce is the collaboration between different companies. The increasing awareness of the potentialities and the advantages connected with online commerce is the base of a progressive evolution from individual initiatives to cooperative strategies. This choice can be found, usually, in vertical markets, in which a high complexity requires strong cooperation among actors.

The relations between travel agencies and their suppliers have also been deeply modified by the spread of specific e-procurement initiatives. They tend to create economies of scale by exploiting optimization and higher efficiency in the value chain by means of online supplying systems.

The feasible advantages introduced by the Internet are even more evident in the business-to-consumer relationship, mainly within small and medium-sized enterprise segments. For end users the real advantages lie in improved price transparency, faster reservation procedures, and increased discount availability. Moreover, online commerce eases the creation of marketing databases by collecting large amounts of data on clients, allowing better segmentation of the market and the ability to customize the supply according to different targets.

Companies willing to implement an e-business system in the tourism sector might have to face some objective difficulties (European Information Technology Observatory [EITO], 2001), mostly related to required investments, possible conflicts with distribution channels, and a shortage in technical skills needed to implement timely interactive products.

Despite these worries, the digital travel segment, already one of the most important of the virtual world, is likely to be increasingly accessed by cybernauts. If we calculate* Web site distribution on the basis of subject or typology, tourism accounts for about 10 percent of sites all over the world (Figure 20.1).

Considering that areas such as entertainment and recreation are actually closely connected with tourism products, tourism appears by far to be the most active area of the Web. Interactive and multimedia possibilities of the Web match fairly well the requirements of presentation and promotion of places and tourist destinations.

According to analysts (eMarketer, 2001), this steady and remarkable growth will not only concern the number of users, but also the

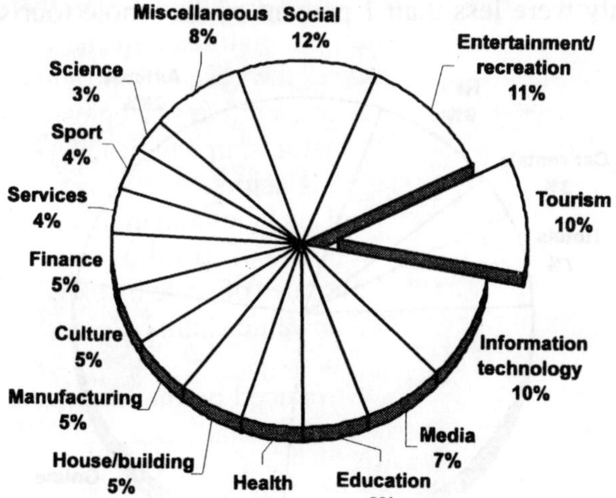

FIGURE 20.1. Internet Site Distribution

*Calculations were performed on the basis of Yahoo! (www.yahoo.com) classification and listings in the first months of 2001.

volume of commercial transactions. In the year 2000 the total revenues in Europe were about EUR 3 million. In 2002 the market reached EUR 7.6 billion, and growth to EUR 10.3 billion is estimated for 2003 (Marcussen, 2003).

The leading sectors are air ticketing, the actual forerunner of the phenomenon, accommodations, and all-inclusive packages offered by tour operators and travel agencies (Figure 20.2).

This popularity can be seen in preferences of European buyers, who put published goods (books and CDs) at first place, followed by information technology (IT) products (hardware and software), financial products, and tourist packages (Figure 20.3).

Purchasers are very demanding; before reserving a personal journey, more than 75 percent of them search the Internet looking for timetables, flights, discounts, and inclusive tours. These preferences are also confirmed by the future purchasing intentions declared by Italian Web surfers (Figure 20.4).

Regardless of favorable circumstances and extraordinary development forecasts, the market for Italian online tourism is far behind the rest of the world. In 2002 (WTO, 2003; Marcussen, 2003) electronic sales in Italy were less than 1 percent of the whole tourism market

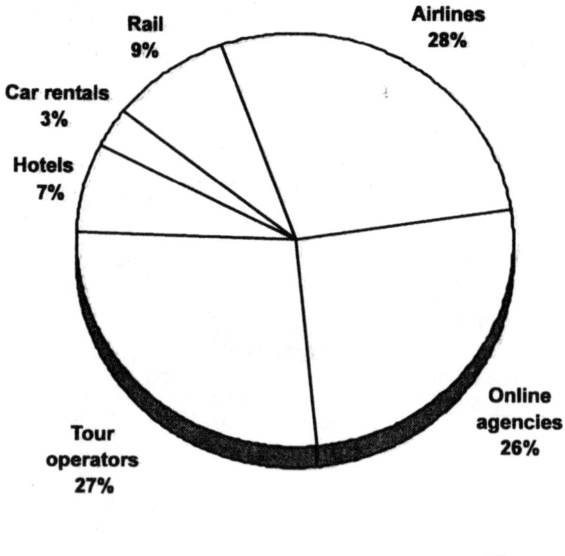

FIGURE 20.2. European Online Tourism Market Distribution (*Source:* Adapted from PhoCusWright, 2001.)

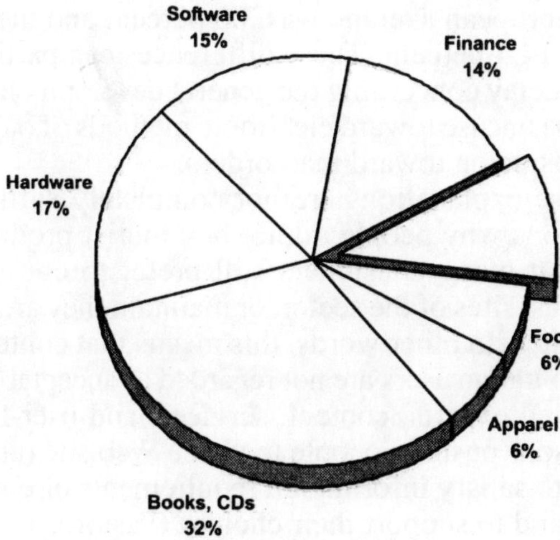

FIGURE 20.3. Products Purchased Online (*Source:* Summary from different sources, mainly Between, 2000; eMarketer, 2001.)

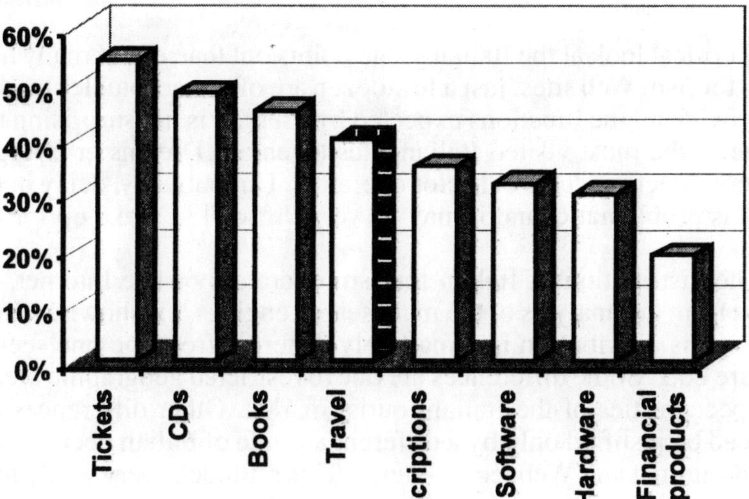

FIGURE 20.4. Purchase Intentions of Italian Online Customers (*Source:* Adapted from Between, 2000.)

size, while the European average was 3.6 percent and the American average reached 14.4 percent. These differences can partially be explained with the delay concerning the general development of e-commerce in Italy, the unease toward electronic methods of payment, and the traditional suspicion toward mail orders.

However, these explanations are not completely sufficient. Surveys on the reasons why people do not buy tourist products via the Internet show that many consumers still prefer to consult with an agency, do not trust sites of the sector, or maintain they are not able to find good Web sites. In other words, this means that content and services proposed to Italian users are not regarded as acceptable. According to analysts and experts, content, services, and user-friendliness are the main reasons pushing people to visit a Web site (at least relating to tourism), to satisfy information requirements or queries about the destination, and to support their choices (Pastore, 1999; Knowledge Systems and Research Institute [KSRI], 2001).

ITALIAN TOURISM ON THE WEB

A critical look at the Italian scene points out that, out of many hundred tourism Web sites, just a few dozen are of an acceptable standard or provide all the functions expected by users. It is not surprising that some of the most visited Italian sites (such as eDreams or eViaggi) are not direct products of sector operators. Undoubtedly, delay in this field is problematic, and it may be very difficult to make up for lost time.

The distribution of Italian tourism operators on the Internet, derived from the analysis of the main search engines,* is shown in Table 20.1. This distribution is remarkably different from the one seen in Figure 20.2. Some differences are due to restricted geographic area or the peculiarities of the Italian tourist market. Other differences can instead be justified only by a different attitude of Italian operators toward Internet and Web technologies. This attitude is very likely to be of deep distrust, especially among intermediaries, and travel agencies in particular, if the proportion of their online presence is so low.

*Yahoo.it (www.yahoo.it), Altavista.it (www.altavista.it), Virgilio (www.virgilio.it), and Arianna (www.arianna.it); the survey was performed in June and July 2001.

TABLE 20.1. Distribution of Italian Tourism Web Sites

Type	Percent (%)
Tourist information	37.0
Hotels and accommodations	35.5
Restaurants	14.2
Tour operators	4.3
Travel agencies	3.7
Public sector, associations, etc.	2.3
Transportation rentals	1.6
Vectors/transportation	1.4

Online Contents and Services

An investigation of Italian tour operators' and travel agencies' presence on the Web was conducted. A sample group of 175 Italian tourism Web sites was examined* in order to value the quantity and quality of their contents and services. Of these, sixty belonged to the tour operators and travel agencies segment, the remaining to the other sectors (hotels, public organizations, other accommodations). The sample was checked against a list containing the most important types of information and services generally offered on a Web site. The results are presented in Figures 20.5 and 20.6. The percentage values refer to the number of Web sites in the sample showing the presence of that particular item.

The results of the survey cannot really raise enthusiasm. Fascinating graphic effects are often paired with scanty information about offered packages and destinations. Paradoxically, the Internet, with all its multimedia potential and the huge possibility to store materials, is often much underexploited compared to the traditional and expensive paper catalogs. Interactive functions, such as the opportunity to arrange customized itineraries or to have real-time quotations and confirmations, are still very rare.

Direct buying and "easy reservation" systems are almost absent or are badly designed. On top of that, the company mission is often unclear. In many cases the user cannot understand clearly why he or she

*The survey was conducted during June and July 2001.

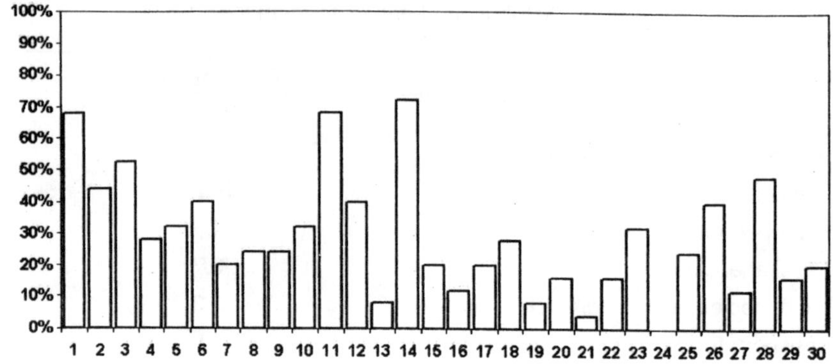

1 - Company full presentation
2 - Short descriptions
3 - Extended descriptions
4 - Multimedia descriptions
5 - Basic info on localization
6 - Extended info on localization
7 - Driving directions and maps
8 - Link to external sites on the area
9 - Articles on the area
10 - Info on events and similar topics
11 - Commercial info
12 - Info/prices updates
13 - Web-only special offers
14 - Basic interactivity (e-mail)
15 - Form for info/catalogs/brochures
16 - Newsletter/on-request updates
17 - Customizations
18 - Interactive simulators
19 - Games/prizes/contests
20 - Online purchase
21 - E-tickets
22 - Online reservations with offline purchase
23 - Secure transactions/full instructions
24 - Online customer support
25 - Partners/resellers/local offices directory
26 - Business to business
27 - Online merchandising purchase
28 - Downloadable software
29 - Downloadable documentation
30 - Internal search engines

FIGURE 20.5. Italian Tour Operators' Web Sites Contents Map

should choose that specific operator. Little is done to win the customer's trust, and indications about the consumer's rights and duties are fragmentary and incomplete.

We can group the items used in the survey into the following four areas:

- *customer relationship* (CUST.REL): contents which make relationships with clients and visitors easier and stronger;
- *e-commerce* (ECOMM): commercial and e-business functions;
- *informational contents* (INFO): information and documentation contents; and
- *interactive services* (SERV): general interactive functions and services.

A comparison including tour organizers, travel agencies, and the general Italian online tourism sector can be summed up as shown in Figure 20.7.

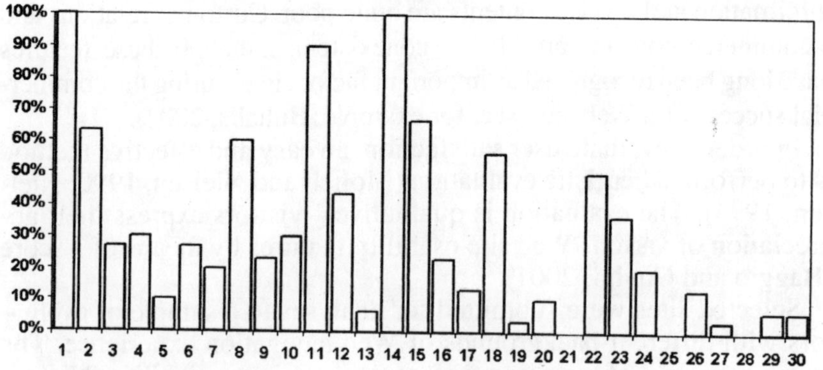

1 - Company full presentation
2 - Short descriptions
3 - Extended descriptions
4 - Multimedia descriptions
6 - Basic info on localization
6 - Extended info on localization
7 - Driving directions and maps
8 - Link to external sites on the area
9 - Articles on the area
10 - Info on events and similar topics
11 - Commercial info
12 - Info/prices updates
13 - Web-only special offers
14 - Basic interactivity (e-mail)
15 - Form for info/catalogs/brochures
16 - Newsletter/on-request updates
17 - Customizations
18 - Interactive simulators
19 - Games/prizes/contests
20 - Online purchase
21 - E-tickets
22 - Online reservations with offline purchase
23 - Secure transactions/full instructions
24 - Online customer support
25 - Partners/resellers/local offices directory
26 - Business to business
27 - Online merchandising purchase
28 - Downloadable software
29 - Downloadable documentation
30 - Internal search engines

FIGURE 20.6. Italian Travel Agencies' Web Sites Contents Map

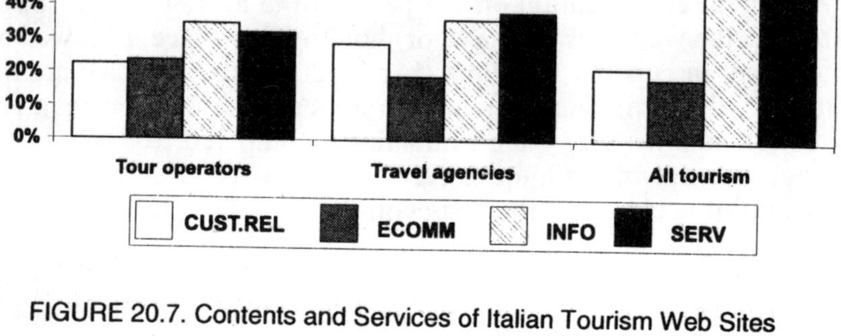

FIGURE 20.7. Contents and Services of Italian Tourism Web Sites

Information and service contents are quite poor. Customer relations and e-commerce contents are almost nonexistent, although these features have long been recognized as important factors in ensuring the commercial success of a Web site (see, for example, Buhalis, 2002).

In order to evaluate user satisfaction, an easy and effective method is to perform a heuristic evaluation (Molich and Nielsen, 1990; Nielsen, 1994). The evaluation is qualitative—visitors express their appreciation of various Web site usability features by means of a score (Baggio and Covini, 2001).

Selected sites were submitted for analyses to a sample of evaluators with different backgrounds of Web navigation experience. The group consisted of ten persons to grant sufficient reliability (Nielsen and Landauer, 1993). Evaluators were asked to award a score from 1 (minimum) to 10 (maximum) to a series of fifty items grouped in the following categories:

- *First impact:* general feeling during a first scan, before actually visiting the site
- *Design and graphics:* quality of graphical elements (pictures, symbols, photographs, etc.), balance between text and images
- *Information contents:* thoroughness of information, clarity of language
- *Interactivity and services:* number and quality of the interactive services, tested user-friendliness of the functions
- *Structure and navigation:* rationality of Web site navigation and structure
- *Technical management:* updating of contents, response times, errors or missing links

A general classification on the basis of the average score shows public sector Web sites (Pub.Sector) holding first place, followed by hotels and, in general, suppliers (Figure 20.8). In last place are the commercial intermediaries (tour operators and travel agencies). For the intermediaries sector the evaluations, compared to the industry average, are shown in Figure 20.9.

Overall it is clear that the fast evolution of information and communication technologies (ICT) has not been followed so far by a resolute change in the production and distribution of tourist products. Obviously, the reasons cannot be reduced only to oversimplified state-

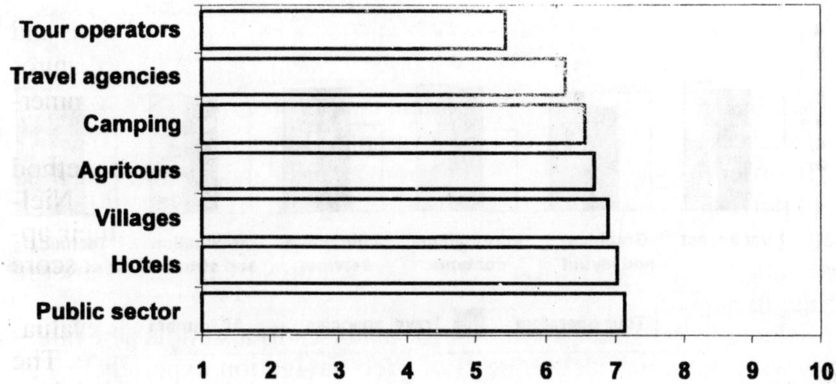

FIGURE 20.8. Italian Tourism Web Site Evaluations

ments about the cultural level or the extent of ICT and equipment diffusion. One of the major causes can be found in concerns about possible conflicts with traditional distribution channels. With its presence on the Web a tour operator will try not to disturb agencies, which are its main income source. In addition, the feared effects of disintermediation put a restraint on the development of online products, including all the services (mainly sale services) users would like to have.

FUTURE MODELS OF BEING ON THE WEB

Many new technologies are appearing in the fast-paced world of ICT. Among these, two seem very promising and very appropriate for the tourism industry: *mobile commerce* (m-commerce) and *recommendation systems*.

A recommendation system (see, for example, Ricci et al., 2002) provides the user with advanced functionalities to choose his or her own destination and to personalize travel by combining several elementary items (hotels, transportation, additional locations to visit, services, and activities). Artificial intelligence techniques make it easier for the user to peruse an information repository and allow ranking of the items included in a recommendation. The system is also

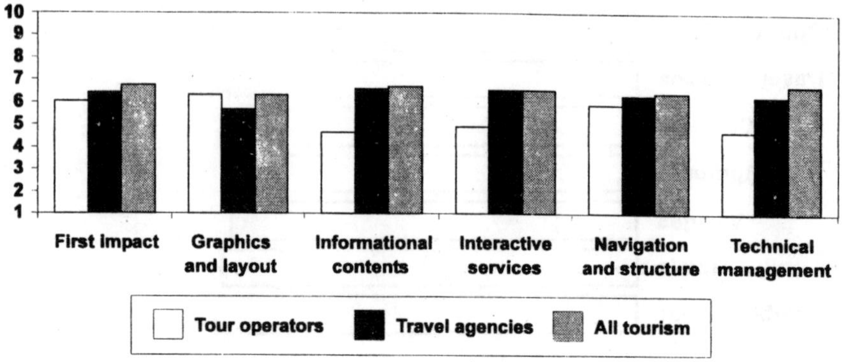

FIGURE 20.9. Tour Operator and Travel Agency Web Site Evaluations

able to suggest alternative solutions by taking into account expressed priorities.

Wireless technologies are increasingly diffusing. Europe, and Italy in particular, is the most penetrated area in the world. All the forecasts (EITO, 2001) expect an even stronger increase for the next three to five years. In addition, the advent of broadband wireless technologies (general packet radio service [GPRS] and universal mobile telecommunications system [UMTS]) can improve the user's attitude toward the commercial side of the business.

In this scenario, ticketing and travel products are the most favored candidates for good acceptance on the market (see, e.g., Goldman Sachs, 2000). Suppliers and travel service providers will be compelled to offer consumers specialized content and services over mobile devices. The benefits for tourists are obvious, as are the difficulties to implement high-value-added systems. Innovative services, well-organized contents, and rational structures will again be the main factors to guarantee good returns from these kinds of implementation.

Italian travel service providers will have to completely change their attitude toward new information and communication technologies. Even so, the original collaborative spirit of the Web could offer a solution to this dilemma. The value chain of a service organization, the majority of tourism companies, consists of a series of processes integrating activities directly addressed to the customer. A successful product requires perfect coordination of all these processes. This is made possible (Rayport and Sviokla, 1995) by a smooth flow of information, in which the consumer is not only the final addressee but also plays an active role. Furthermore, for many tourism products, processes are carried out by different actors, usually different firms, of different sizes, organizational structures, and policies.

Until the present day value chains of different actors remained well separated and had only traditional contact points generated within distribution chains. On the Web a significant change is needed, and the *value net* can be a winning concept. A value net (Bovet and Martha, 2000) is a dynamic, high performance network of customer and supplier partnerships and information flows supported by digital communications. Such virtual organizations are essential in the fragmented tourism industry characterized mostly by small or medium-size companies with limited resources and a great tendency toward outsourcing. Interaction among the members with the support of ICT leads to a reduction of transaction costs and can assure greater efficiency, even greater than that of a large traditional organization (Laesser and Jäger, 2001).

However ICT, and the Internet in particular, does not have merely structural importance, but also acts as a driver and facilitator. Compared to traditional means, the Web has all the features of a winning channel. It integrates, in a unified environment, many necessary and useful functions: information, collaboration, communication, interactivity, and transactions (Gretzel, Yuan, and Fesenmaier, 2000).

The tourism product has a sort of genetic relationship with Internet technologies and shares with them the critical success factors (Weber and Roehl, 1999). Tour operators and travel agencies are in direct contact with customers for the sale and distribution of products. Their success is strictly bound to their ability to exploit the chain processes and to use proper technologies. If they fail the user looks for other sources.

We witness on one side a disintermediation process, with clients directly applying to service providers (accommodation structures, transportation businesses, etc.). On the other side, where the quantity and quality of the supply does not allow for an easy choice, the rising of new intermediaries, capable of understanding requirements and offering products, whose appeal is in information and technological ability is needed.

If tour operators and travel agencies are reluctant (and, at the present, they definitely are) to offer their products on the Web, mostly because they want to avoid competition with the sale and distribution structures of the "real" world, then a possible solution would be to create a virtual representation of the physical *value net*. A possible model includes the creation of a "place" (site, portal) by mutual consent of a mixed group of actors. It would offer rich information contents and services, provide quality and updating of material, and help the visitor the entire way through the purchase. The customer would not be left halfway through the operations and be sent somewhere else. No confusing passages would hinder the visitor or push him or her to abandon the Web site.

Merging the functions of tour operators and travel agencies into a single component of the chain means the chain becomes shorter and value is generated for the client, reducing costs but still preserving vital mediation functions between primary suppliers and end users (see Figure 20.10). The combination of efforts helps to increase available financial and human resources, enriching contents and services, an essential condition for them to be well accepted by cybernauts. This kind of collaboration also allows for the creation of common services (business to business) which facilitate relationships and information exchange among partners. In the end this process reduces global transaction costs and consequently the final costs of the product. This grants a good competitive advantage.

CONCLUSION

Even if the demography of the Italian Internet tourism is in general agreement with that of the rest of the world, the e-commerce penetration is at a much lower level than in other countries. The survey performed on the Italian tourist Web sites showed that tour operators and

FIGURE 20.10. New Intermediation in Tourism Distribution Chain

travel agents have a lower than average amount of content and services, mainly in the customer relationship and e-commerce areas. Even the results of the qualitative evaluations confirm that Italian tourism intermediaries perform poorly.

The surveys confirm the fact that one of the main reasons for poor commercial performance of the Italian tourist sites is the relatively low quality of implementations. This low quality, however, poses a great risk of disintermediation for the whole sector. In the event of not finding helpful Web sites offered by traditional intermediaries, the user is more tempted to turn to the main providers to fulfill his or her needs.

The disintermediation effects and the fear of disturbing the traditional distribution channels are the main motivations that hold back the development of online products able to offer the content and services users would like to have.

Present forecasts for technology developments in the near future show two main areas in which many efforts are concentrated: m-commerce and tourism recommendation systems. In both cases the requirement of high-quality and highly usable implementations is of paramount importance in obtaining good economic performance.

Future Web site implementations could exploit the original collaborative spirit of the Web by adopting a new business model in which different operators, without sacrificing their uniqueness, can share skills and experiences to provide a high-quality proposal. Such a *value net,* with a strong focus on the end user, can be of great significance for both operators and customers. It would be able to provide a content-rich site, efficient business-to-customer services, effective business-to-business tools for participants, and an economic means of reducing the time to market for all the products, while the shortening of the distribution chain can reduce costs to the customers. Finally, having the opportunity to reach a critical mass of investment will make it possible to thwart objections to the rising costs of high-quality commercial Web site implementations.

REFERENCES

Antonioli Corigliano, Magda and Rodolfo Baggio (Eds.) (2002). *Internet and Turismo*. Milano: EGEA.

Baggio, Rodolfo and Andrea Covini (2001). *Il paradosso del ragno*. Milano: Franco Angeli.

Between (2000). Weekly Observatory of the Web—Special e-Commerce #7, October 2000, Milan. Available at <www.between.it>.

Bovet, David and Joseph Martha (2000). *Value Nets: Breaking the Supply Chain to Unlock Hidden Profits*. New York: Wiley and Sons.

Buhalis, D. (2002). *eTourism: Information Technology for Strategic Tourism Management.* London: Pearson (Financial Times/Prentice Hall).

eMarketer (2001). *The eTravel Report.* New York: eMarketer.

European Information Technology Observatory (2001). *European Information Technology Observatory 2001.* Frankfurt, Germany: Author.

Goldman Sachs (2000). *Internet: Consumer e-commerce—Europe.* London: Goldman Sachs.

Gretzel, Ulrike, Yu-Lan Yuan, and Daniel R. Fesenmaier (2000). Preparing for the New Economy, Advertising Strategies and Change in Destination Marketing Organizations. *Journal of Travel Research,* 39, 146-153.

Knowledge Systems and Research Institute (2001). Online User Panel: Web Site Design, April 2001. Available at <http://www.ksrinc.com/research/pdfs/webdesign_WEB.pdf>.

Laesser, Christian and Silvio Jäger (2001). Tourism in the New Economy. In Keller, Peter and Thomas Bieger (Eds.), *Tourism Growth and Global Competition,* Proceedings of AIEST 51st Congress 2001. St. Gallen, Switzerland: AIEST, pp. 39-84.

Marcussen, C.H. (2003). Trends in European Internet Distribution of Travel and Tourism Services. Available at <http://www.crt.dk/uk/staff/chm/trends.htm>.

Molich, Rolf, and Jakob Nielsen (1990). Improving a human-computer dialogue. *Communications of the ACM,* 33(3) (March), 338-348.

Nielsen, Jakob (1994). Heuristic evaluation. In Nielsen, Jakob and Robert L. Mack (Eds.), *Usability Inspection Methods.* New York: John Wiley and Sons, pp. 25-62.

Nielsen, Jakob and Thomas K. Landauer (1993). A mathematical model of the finding of usability problems. In *Proceedings of the SIGCHI Conference on Human Factors in Computing Systems,* Amsterdam, The Netherlands. New York: ACM Press, pp. 206-213.

Pastore, Michael (1999). Reasons Visitors Return to Sites. Available at <http://www.cyberatlas.com/big_picture/traffic_patterns/article/0,,5931_152091,00.html>.

PhoCusWright (2001). *The European Online Travel Marketplace, 2000-2002.* Sherman, CT: Author.

Rayport, Jeffrey F. and John J. Sviokla (1995). Exploiting the Virtual Value Chain, *Harvard Business Review,* 73(6), 75-85.

Ricci, Francesco, Dennis Blaas, Nader Mirzadeh, Adriano Venturini, and Hannes Werthner (2002). Intelligent Query Management for Travel Products Selection. ENTER 2002 Conference, Innsbruck, January 22-25.

Weber, Karin and Wesley S. Roehl (1999). Profiling People Searching for and Purchasing Travel Products on the World Wide Web. *Journal of Travel Research,* 37, 291-298.

World Tourism Organization (2003). *WTO World Tourism Barometer,* 1(1) (June). Available at <http://www.world-tourism.org/market_research/WTOBarom03_1.pdf>.

Chapter 21

Electronic Travel Recommendation Agents and Tourist Choice

Gerald Häubl
Benedict G. C. Dellaert

INTRODUCTION

The growing use of electronic communication channels such as the Internet, on-location information kiosks, and mobile telephones is increasing the information density with which tourists are faced. In the future this density is likely to increase even further, as more and more intermediaries (such as travel agents and tour operators), local tourist organizations, destinations, and transportation and accommodation firms are expanding their online presence (see, e.g., Sigala et al., 2000). Additional trends such as marketing strategies that focus on customer relationships and total experience management also generate increasingly intense tourism information environments and require more frequent information exchanges between firms and individual tourists (Minghetti, Moretti, and Micelli, 2000).

For tourists, having easy access to these large amounts of travel information is both a blessing and a curse. It is a blessing in the sense that more information may allow them to select travel options which better match their personal preferences than they would otherwise. However, the curse of having access to vast amounts of information is that tourists are likely to be unable to adequately process all this information due to limits to their cognitive capacity and will become

The authors would like to thank the Tilburg University Faculty of Economics and Business Administration for support of the data collection reported in this paper. These data were collected through the CentER*data*-panel.

frustrated at using the different information sources such as the Internet (e.g., Pan and Fesenmaier, 2000).

One promising way to overcome these limitations are individual-level decision support systems and recommendation agents which assist tourists in making better decisions (Ansari, Essegaier, and Kohli, 2000). To date, relatively little is known about how such systems affect tourist decision processes. Although indications exist that recommendation agents may indeed improve individuals' choice outcomes in online shopping decisions (Häubl and Trifts, 2000) many open questions remain about how different types of agents, operating in different market contexts, affect decision quality and effort.

This study analyzes whether, and if so how, tourists may benefit from electronic agents that assist them in choosing between large numbers of travel alternatives.

THEORY

The notion that human decision makers have limited resources for information processing—whether those limits are in memory, attention, motivation, or elsewhere—has deep roots in psychology and management science (Payne, Bettman, and Johnson, 1993; Simon, 1955). These limitations can affect tourists' choices considerably, even in digital environments in which tourists are not constrained by the availability of travel information, because human cognitive capacity still limits the processing of this information.

Although humans tend to do quite well at selecting the criteria that should be used in making a decision, computers are particularly useful for methodically searching through a problem space in order to compile and retain large amounts of information. As a consequence, electronic travel recommendation agents have the potential to be of significant value to tourists. An electronic recommendation agent may (like a real-world travel agent) ask a tourist a set of questions in an attempt to understand his or her preferences and then do the work of searching through the available travel options to find the most appropriate alternative travel options to recommend. For example, the Web site <www.activebuyersguide.com> allows tourists to get personal recommendations on, for example, visiting national parks in the United States. Thus, the potential exists for an electronic recommendation agent to assist tourists in their decision making by reducing their efforts as well as improving the outcome of their decisions.

This study analyzes the impact of the availability of a particular type of recommendation agent on tourist choice. We study recommendation agents that ask tourists about their preferences in terms of travel features and then use this preference information to rate each travel option in terms of its attractiveness for the individual. In doing so, the agent is able to provide personalized recommendations from a large number of possible travel options. The question addressed is as follows: How does the availability and configuration of this type of electronic agent influence the *quality* and *efficiency* of the tourist choice process? We study the impact that the use of a recommendation agent has on how close a tourist's choices are to his or her preferences given the set of available products (choice quality) and on how much effort is required to arrive at the travel decisions (choice efficiency).

RESEARCH METHOD

A controlled experiment was conducted to examine the effects of recommendation agents on these aspects of tourist decision making in an online environment. The main task for participants consisted of looking for and booking a holiday home for a short weekend break in a nearby tourist region. In total 500 travel options were available. All options were fictitious but representative of the holiday home category. The following seven attributes varied across the alternatives: privacy, landscaping in the park, sauna nearby, swimming pool quality, independent general quality rating for the park, sports facilities, and price. All attributes were varied in terms of their attractiveness using four different levels.

Data during the experiment were collected using an ongoing consumer panel in the Netherlands. All members of the panel had access to home computers. Respondents for this study were screened as having an interest in short weekend breaks. Based on these selection criteria and the elimination of some incomplete responses, a total of 405 responses were obtained. Approximately one-quarter of this group (a randomly drawn subset) responded to an experimental task without a recommendation agent. The remaining respondents interacted with a recommendation agent in making their decisions. After connecting to the survey Web site respondents were informed that they would be pilot testing a new online travel-shopping environment.

Participants started by providing preference ratings in response to a sequence of eight conjoint profiles describing different holiday home options. In the conjoint profiles only two out of the four possible levels were used, to reduce the size of the task for the respondents. More specifically, the experimental design for the conjoint analysis was an eight-profile fraction of a 2^7 full factorial design in which all attribute levels were varied independently (Louviere, 1988). Respondents' ratings were given on an eleven-point preference response scale ranging from 0 (very unattractive) to 10 (very attractive). From these responses the electronic recommendation agent calculated individual utility scores for each respondent and for all 500 options in the market. The utility V_{it} per individual per travel option can be expressed as follows:

$$V_{it} = \alpha_i + \beta_i X_t + \varepsilon_{it} \qquad (21.1)$$

where, α_i is individual i's average utility across all travel options, β_i is a vector of coefficients relating the different attribute levels to the individual's utility, and X_t is a vector of attribute levels for travel option t. These scores were then used to provide a personalized recommendation list to each respondent in the second part of the experiment.

In this second part, respondents were able to use the recommended list to request detailed information about particular travel options and to book their most preferred holiday home. This booking as well as their search behavior was registered in a database. Subjects in the condition in which no recommendation agent was present were taken to a randomly ordered list of all holiday home options and could search and make a booking from this list.

MEASURES

Decision quality was measured with a metric anchoring the utility of the respondent's chosen alternative to two reference values. The maximum value reference point was the utility of the optimal alternative that each respondent could have chosen based on his or her own previous preference responses ($V_{i.optimal}$). The individual's expected utility of a randomly drawn alternative from the total list of travel options, also based on the tourist's previous preference responses ($V_{i.random}$), was used as minimum value. These reference points were then related to the utility of the actual chosen alternative ($V_{i.chosen}$) to obtain the following standardized individual level measure of decision quality (Q_i):

$$Q_i = \frac{V_{i.chosen} - V_{i.random}}{V_{i.optimal} - V_{i.random}} \tag{21.2}$$

Decision effort was measured with three variables: (1) the total time spent by the individual in making a decision (T_i); (2) the total number of alternatives viewed by the individual in making a decision (N_i); and (3) based on the first two measures, the average consideration time (t_i) per alternative calculated by dividing T_i by N_i.

FINDINGS

On average, respondents evaluated the different holiday home options positively in the conjoint analysis stage of the experiment (average score was 5.55 out of 10, with a standard deviation [SD] of 1.31). The directions of the attribute coefficient values obtained in the model were as expected, with more attractive levels receiving higher utility scores.

Out of the total number of 405 respondents, 352 responses were used after screening for outliers and missing values. Of these respondents, 288 were faced with the recommendation list that was generated based on the preference responses in the first stage, and sixty-four respondents were faced with a randomly ordered list of holiday homes. All respondents could access all 500 available holiday homes in the market if they so wished.

Table 21.1 summarizes the results for the decision quality measure and the three effort measures, comparing the observations in which a recommendation agent was present to those in which no recommendations were given. Independent samples t-tests were used to test the significance of the differences observed between the two conditions for each of the measures. The assumption of equal variances between

TABLE 21.1. Comparison of Quality and Effort in Decisions With and Without Electronic Recommendation Agent

Recommendation agent	Decision quality	Total time*	Number viewed	Average time per option*
Present				
mean	0.70	363.66	7.87	75.74
SD	0.49	357.83	10.80	65.19
N	305	311	335	307
Absent				
mean	0.42	504.84	12.54	59.17
SD	0.44	569.87	23.31	38.38
N	64	64	70	64

*Time in seconds

the two conditions was rejected and tests were run accordingly. In two out of four cases (decision quality and consideration time per alternative) the difference between the recommendation agent condition and the no recommendation agent condition was significant at the 0.05 confidence level. In the other two cases (total time and number of alternatives viewed) the difference was significant at the 0.10 confidence level.

Jointly, these results indicate that the recommendation agent allowed tourists to engage in fewer searches, while improving the quality of their travel decisions. Tourists who were able to use a recommendation agent were significantly more likely to choose a holiday home option that was close to their stated preference. The difference in the decision quality measure *Q* was significant at the 0.00 significance level (t-test value of 6.87). With regard to effort we observed that tourists who had access to a recommendation agent spent less time searching (363.66 versus 504.84 seconds, t-test value of 1.93, significance level of 0.06) and looked at fewer travel options (7.87 versus 12.54 alternatives searched, t-test value of 1.73, significance level of 0.09) than did those who were not assisted. Interestingly, tourists spent more time per alternative when the recommendation agent was present (75.74 versus 54.19 seconds, t-test value of 2.75, significance level of 0.01).

DISCUSSION AND CONCLUSION

The results of the experiment and analysis have shown that electronic travel recommendation agents can allow tourists to make better decisions with less effort. However, despite these two beneficial trends, it was also observed that tourists spent more time per alternative when choosing from a list of recommendations. This finding may be explained in part because respondents studied only a smaller number of alternatives in the recommendation agent condition and therefore the learning time required to acquaint oneself with the alternative presentation format was divided over fewer alternatives. An additional explanation of the finding may be the trade-off that difficulty increased when recommendation agents presented tourists with multiple more or less equally attractive alternatives. For example, Shugan (1980) has argued that choices between two alternatives that are closer together in terms of utility are harder to make than choices between alternatives that differ strongly in utility. Trade-off difficulty may further be increased if two alternatives offer competing relative benefits (e.g., one holiday home could be simple but inexpensive and quiet, while another home may be more expensive but luxurious and of high quality). If this hypothesis holds true, then the type of electronic agents tested in this study may be more helpful in reducing tourist search duration than they are in facilitating the choices that tourists make between competing alternatives. In other words, tourists need to look at fewer alternatives but may find it harder to make a decision between them.

In this context it is also important to note that the recommendation agent available to tourists in this study was fully cooperative and was carefully designed to effectively screen the marketplace on behalf of the consumer based on preference information provided by the consumer. Real-world recommendation agents may not be as altruistic or as complete in their design. For example, they may not cover all available travel options, but instead represent only the options of one tour operator or hotel chain. This research takes the view that firms supporting tourists in making decisions which provide each tourist with the highest utility will be the firms that are most successful in the long run. Therefore, future research that further investigates which type of electronic agent may be most beneficial to tourists in different market contexts is expected to be most relevant both from the firm's and the individual tourist's perspective.

REFERENCES

Ansari, Asim, Skander Essegaier, and Rajeev Kohli (2000). Internet recommendation systems. *Journal of Marketing Research* 37(August): 363-375.

Häubl, Gerald and Valerie Trifts (2000). Consumer decision making in online shopping environments: The effects of interactive decision aids. *Marketing Science* 19(1): 4-21.

Louviere, Jordan J. (1988). *Analyzing Decision Making: Metric Conjoint Analysis, Quantitative Applications in the Social Sciences.* Beverly Hills, CA: Sage Research Productions.

Minghetti, Valeria, Andrea Moretti, and Stefano Micelli (2000). Intelligent museum as value creator on the tourism market: Toward a new business model. In Fesenmaier, Daniel R., Stefan Klein, and Dimitrios Buhalis (Eds.), *Information and Communication Technologies in Tourism 2000* (pp. 114-125). Vienna: Springer-Verlag.

Pan, Bing and Daniel R. Fesenmaier (2000). A typology of tourism related web sites: Its theoretical background and implications. In Fesenmaier, Daniel R., Stefan Klein, and Dimitrios Buhalis (Eds.), *Information and Communication Technologies in Tourism 2000* (pp. 381-396). Vienna: Springer-Verlag.

Payne, John W., James R. Bettman, and Eric J. Johnson (1993). *The Adaptive Decision Maker.* New York: Cambridge University Press.

Shugan, Steven M. (1980). The cost of thinking. *Journal of Consumer Research* 7: 99-111.

Sigala, Marianna, David Airey, Peter Jones, and Andrew Lockwood (2000). The diffusion and application of multimedia technologies in the tourism and hospitality industries. In Fesenmaier, Daniel R., Stefan Klein, and Dimitrios Buhalis (Eds.), *Information and Communication Technologies in Tourism 2000* (pp. 397-407). Vienna: Springer-Verlag.

Simon, Herbert A. (1955). A behavioral model of rational choice. *Quarterly Journal of Economics* 69(February): 99-118.

Chapter 22

The Assessment of Tourism and Leisure Trends by Means of Online Management Information Systems

Karl Wöber

INTRODUCTION

Due to the vital role of tourism in many European countries and regions, a number of programs concerning tourism promotion have been implemented. Tourism societies, associations, bodies under public law, and privately organized tourism institutions have been established in order to strengthen tourism destinations. The general aim is to increase the added value of a region. The major tasks of these institutions are

1. to provide consumers with information on the destination;
2. to coordinate and execute sales-promoting measures;
3. to provide tourism advertising;
4. to support sales and distribution; and
5. to coordinate and execute market research projects.

For most of these tasks, except the coordination and execution of market research projects, the tourism-promoting institutions provide efficient methods. The actual effect of the last item mentioned has been overlooked in the past due to inefficient instruments relating to the transmission and utilization of declarative and procedural knowledge. Now with the development of cheaper hardware and software, many tourism organizations are reconsidering their promotion policy in this field.

In almost all industries, marketing information systems are being developed in order to support investment decisions and marketing planning (Wierenga and van Bruggen, 2000). The tourism industry also developed decision support systems and the following are the most important applications:

1. systems supporting marketing decisions in national tourism organizations (Mazanec, 1986; Rita, 1993)
2. travel counseling systems (e.g., Hruschka and Mazanec, 1990)
3. systems supporting regional planning regarding the optimal selection of locations in which to invest (Calantone and di Benedetto, 1991)
4. systems providing tourism portfolio analyses (Mazanec, 1994, 1998; Wöber, 1998)
5. simulation tools for forecasting tourist travel behavior in certain tourism regions (van Middelkoop, 2001)

In 1982 the Austrian Society of Applied Research in Tourism (ASART) started a project aimed at the development of a marketing information system for the national tourism organization in Austria (Austrian National Tourist Office). The first version of the tourism marketing information system (TourMIS) consisted of a database installed on a mainframe system at the Scientific Computer Center in Vienna and was used in conjunction with an optimization program developed with the advertising budget of the Austrian National Tourist Office (Mazanec, 1986). Although the programs were adapted in 1991 in favor of personal computer (PC) software, and hence became accessible to a greater number of people (mainly employees of tourism organizations in the federal provinces), areawide information supply for top managers in the tourism industry did not begin until 1999 when the Internet version (www.tourmis.wu-wien.ac.at) was introduced.

DEVELOPMENT OF TOURMIS

The major aim of TourMIS is to provide an optimal information supply and decision support system for the tourism industry. The first step is to provide online tourism survey data, as well as evaluation programs to transform data into precious management information. The TourMIS system is comprised of the following three modules:

1. a database containing tourism market research data (declarative knowledge);
2. a number of program modules (method base, procedural knowledge) converting market research data by means of acknowledged methods/models into valuable management information; and
3. various administrative programs which help to maintain the database and control the information behavior of users.

The Internet supports the transport and presentation of animated and unanimated pictures, sound and video recordings, as well as text and numerical data and is expandable. A high-performance SQL-database and a general user interface for TourMIS based on hypertext and Perl permits the development of interactive applications. The program modules contained in the method base are developed according to the specific requirements of tourism managers. The Internet offers a number of advantages compared to the old PC solution. Because changes in the database have immediate worldwide effect, the speed of information transmissions can be reduced to the availability of the information source. For example, TourMIS makes the monthly projections of *Statistik Austria* (Statistics Austria) available within the shortest time to all regional managers of the Austrian National Tourist Office, regardless of whether they are in New York, Sydney, Tokyo, or Madrid. Anyone provided with Internet access and user passwords for TourMIS may access data and information, execute calculations or simulations, send or receive data—without tiresome postal procedures, danger of loss or delays, and high costs. All these advantages have led to a significant expansion in the number of users.

TourMIS has strict access control and used to be accessible only to certain users. In TourMIS users need to register, however registration and access to the vast majority of data sources are available free of charge. In this respect the application does differ from other traditional Internet offers and cannot be compared to previously discussed Intranet options. Unlike an Intranet, which supports internal information management systems, TourMIS is not owned by a certain organization but is open to all authorized tourism organizations, societies, tourism consultants, companies, tourism training centers, lobby groups, etc., in Austria and abroad. A consortium of the most important initiators of market research projects in Austria (Austrian National Tourist Office, nine provincial tourism organizations, Hotel and Restaurant Associations of the Federal Chamber of Commerce, Federal Ministry for Economic Affairs and Labor) cover the maintenance cost and thus guarantee the continuous updating of the comprehensive database. Since 2000 this initiative has provided the Austrian tourism industry with free access to the complete database and all functions (with some exceptions) of TourMIS. The necessary hardware resources are situated at the Institute for Tourism and Leisure Studies, Vienna University of Economics and Business Administration, where a major part of the necessary maintenance work is executed.

In the beginning TourMIS contained data that were strongly influenced by the internal interests of its commissioner, the Austrian National Tourist Office. In this respect international tourism statistics, empirical tourism studies, and economic indicators for the most important sending markets for the Austrian tourism industry have been collected in TourMIS. The PC version, developed in the early 1990s, contained more than 10,000 time series. The periodicity of information was generally based on annual data, while the most significant time series have also been recorded for shorter periods.

Over the years the database has continually expanded. Due to the increasing importance of overseas markets additional information has been required. Unequal needs of provincial tourism organizations lead to additional statistics regarding the federal provinces, and Vienna, being both a city and a federal province, requires special data treatment. Furthermore, data on Austrian and international city tourism have been added. The most important available data sources of TourMIS are indicated in Table 22.1. In addition to the basic information search functions, the method base has also been continually upgraded. The system more and more meets the requirements of an efficient decision-support tool. The following section presents an example of the information services offered by TourMIS.

THE AUSTRIAN GUEST SURVEY IN TOURMIS

Since 1988 and alternating every three years, a comprehensive visitor survey in Austria has been executed. The Austrian Guest Survey (AGS) is one of the most important sources of information in tourism

TABLE 22.1. Data Sources in TourMIS

Source	Feature	Evaluation	Period	Update	Data format
Statistik Austria	Bed nights, arrivals, capacity (suppliers and beds)	50 countries of origin (markets), 13 types of accommodation—for Austria and her 9 provinces	since 1960	monthly	secondary data in time series format
Austrian Guest Survey	250 variables including intention to revisit, guest satisfaction, type of travel, means of transport, duration of stay, travel motive, expenses, selection of accommodation, activities, net income of the household, profession, education, etc.	16 countries of origin (markets)—for Austria and her 9 provinces	since 1991	each third year	primary data
ETC (European Travel Commission)	bed nights, arrivals, capacities (beds)	21 countries of origin (markets)—for 33 destinations (countries) in Europe	since 1990	annually	secondary data in time series format
ECT (European Cities' Tourism)	bed nights, arrivals, capacities (beds)	21 countries of origin (markets)—for 80 European cities	since 1983	annually	secondary data in time series format
Number of visitations in Austrian attractions (Austrian National Tourist Office)	number of visitations for 240 Austrian attractions	federal provinces of Austria	since 1998	annually	secondary data in time series format
Austrian Hotel and Restaurant Panel	60 variables including net product, fixed and working assets equity and debt capital, cash flow, profitability figures, etc.	location, size, category, and type of business	since 1982	annually	primary data

market research. It provides vital information on guest profiles, customer satisfaction, information and booking behavior, type of travel, destination, means of transport, accommodations, activities, expenditure, and other current topics.

Because the Austrian Guest Survey is a primary study it presents some features which complicate the information diffusion in TourMIS. Causes for these additional difficulties are (1) the scope of the study; (2) the demand of data analysis; and (3) special features resulting from the sampling technique.

The AGS has more than 200 features, which are partially modified for each survey, and offers more than one million, solely descriptive, investigation possibilities per survey. Traditional forms of information dissemination (development of market research reports, press releases, etc.) can cover only a very small part of the overall evaluation potential. These constitute important questions asked by managers that frequently remain unanswered, although theoretically the answers already exist.

In the AGS, there are 10,000 interviews per survey, all of the features being available in disaggregated quantitative form. Information processing, however, requires the application of methods of analysis ranging from determining the simple mean to complicated statistical procedures (i.e., data mining). Necessary methodological knowledge has to be obtained from expensive statistics experts. Therefore, many questions raised by managers remain unanswered, due to the lack of statistical know-how of the managers and/or the lack of financial strength of the industry, despite the availability of data.

Contrary to a census, as found in official statistics, partial surveys do not integrate all elements of the whole picture into the study. The major aim in statistics is to draw from a limited number of elements reliable conclusions regarding the entire group of elements. The previously mentioned evaluation procedures take more effort and interpretation depends on the features of the sample (size and selection of the sample).

To know whether a study result may be regarded as reliable also requires some statistical knowledge. On the other hand, statisticians frequently possess insufficient technical knowledge to evaluate the fault tolerance for certain problems in the tourism industry.

Thus, information processing by means of electronic media becomes very interesting for primary surveys. The challenge is to combine expert know-how from two different fields, statistics and tourism. The aim is to create an arena for practitioners, allowing them access to all possible evaluations concerning a data item, without considering the necessary procedures of analysis (Figure 22.1). TourMIS offers help in the selection of simple, descriptive evaluation methods. Depending on the level of measurement of the features selected by the user, the appropriate evaluation method is applied. In addition, the user may select only a certain part of the overall data set for evaluation (i.e., data of a certain province or market). In order to prevent interpretation errors due to the unreliability of results, those values based on a small sample are indicated only after informing the user about the problem.

The evaluation takes place in real time (Figure 22.2). TourMIS provides the facilities to evaluate more than one survey, offering both longitudinal and cross-sectional analyses. The first application informs the tourism manager about changes in the guest behavior over a specific period of time. Query support is provided by offering only vari-

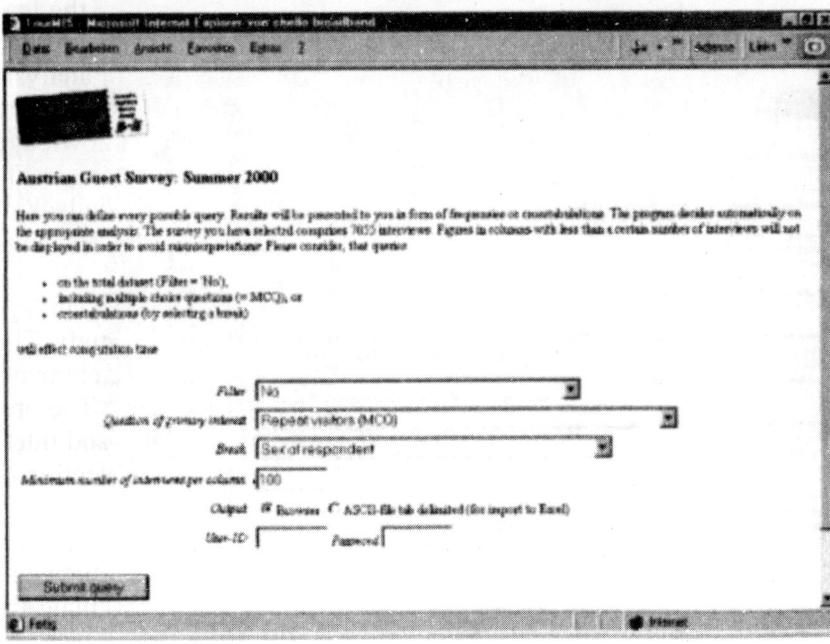

FIGURE 22.1. Query—Austrian Guest Survey

ables surveyed that were unmodified over the overall selected period of time (standard questionnaire program). The latter application increases the sample size (for four surveys more than 45,000 interviews) which makes answers to detailed questions possible (assuming a particular time invariance, of course). This function permits, for example, reliable results on the share of side expenses of Italian guests in the federal province of Salzburg during the winter season.

ANALYSIS OF USER BEHAVIOR OF TOURMIS

The success of a marketing information system can be measured directly by the economic or personal success of its users or indirectly by the frequency of usage. Several authors have shown that the frequency of usage is determined by the perceived usefulness (textual component) and the ease of use (technical component) (Davis, 1989).

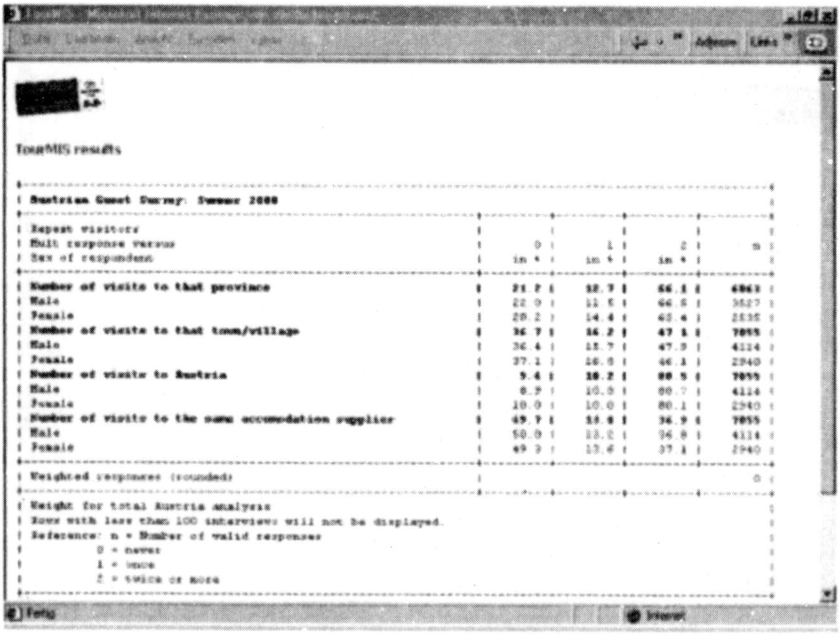

FIGURE 22.2. Query Result—Austrian Guest Survey

The acceptance of TourMIS can be determined by means of constantly updated statistics available online. Contrary to the general practice of measuring the number of hits to a particular Web site, these statistics calculate on the basis of virtually answered queries. Results of the TourMIS statistics are therefore not influenced by Web site characteristics but do represent the genuine user acceptance. The comprehensive protocol system also permits the analysis of queries broken down into various user groups, information sources, and the type of query (i.e., textual options for the compilation of tables and reports, data queries, etc.).

The community of TourMIS users has developed continually. In 1998 there were only fifty registered users at the Austrian National Tourist Office and at the end of 2001 more than 1,000 TourMIS users were registered. The distribution of user groups indicates that TourMIS is favored not only by tourism managers (45.6 percent), but also by employees, students, and pupils (53.4 percent of all queries) of education and research institutions. The distribution of various user groups is presented in Table 22.2.

The right column of Table 22.2 shows the average number of queries per user in 2001 and thus indicates the frequency of use for a specific TourMIS user group. The employees of provincial tourism organizations use TourMIS most (ninety-two queries per user) due to the comprehensive data material available on the federal provinces. The largest user group—students—shows a relatively low number due to temporal interest (for a seminar paper or a diploma thesis they need access to data material only once).

Overall about 34,600 queries were processed in 2001, signifying an increase of 35.5 percent in comparison to the pervious year. Table 22.3 presents the significance of the various data sources for information supply.

About half of all queries are made regarding the official Austrian tourism statistics. The industry appears to be very interested in the development of the major markets of origin and accommodation types in the federal provinces (fifty queries per day). Regarding the official statistics for Austria, most queries are made in connection with information concerning the current year (20.3 percent of all queries). The international data sources ECT and ETC represented 18.9 percent and 17.7 percent, respectively, and lie directly behind the official statistics. The significant increase of queries regarding these

TABLE 22.2. Origins of TourMIS Users

User groups	Users in 2001 (%)	Queries 2000	Queries 2001	Queries 2001 (%)	Queries per user
National tourism organizations	11.3	4,844	4,957	14.4	44
Branch offices of national tourism organizations	5.7	3,541	2,970	8.6	52
Provincial tourism organizations	4.5	3,072	4,132	12.0	92
City tourism organizations	6.1	1,125	1,488	4.3	24
Regional tourism organizations	2.8	78	204	0.6	7
Accommodation suppliers	4.9	392	679	2.0	14
Restaurants	1.9	177	348	1.0	18
Tour operators	1.9	180	304	0.9	16
Travel agencies	1.8	24	327	0.9	18
Common carriers	0.4	193	67	0.2	17
Culture, sport, and leisure suppliers	1.0	90	197	0.6	20
Other tourism suppliers	2.3	161	442	1.3	19
Universities and universities of applied sciences	9.0	1,850	4,790	13.9	53
Other educational institutions	2.2	105	220	0.6	10
Students	20.4	3,027	5,429	15.7	27
Management or tax consultants	6.9	644	2,669	7.7	39
Public institution, pressure group	2.9	625	1,110	3.2	38
Other organizations/businesses	8.6	4,938	3,064	8.9	36
Private persons	5.4	426	1,141	3.3	21

two international data sources as well as the tendency toward English queries indicate a growing international interest in TourMIS.

CONCLUSION

Generally tourism managers benefit from access to the Internet in two ways: the Internet provides the opportunity to communicate and serves as a platform for new distribution channels. This chapter does

TABLE 22.3. Usage of TourMIS Sources

Sources	2000	Percent (%)	2001	Per- cent (%)	2000- 2001 % increase
Statistik Austria monthly data	6,510	29.5	6,919	20.3	6.3
ECT	4,568	20.7	6,449	18.9	41.2
ETC	342	1.6	6,049	17.7	1,668.7
Statistik Austria seasonal data	3,120	14.1	5,105	15.0	63.6
Statistik Austria annual data	3,398	15.4	4,495	13.2	32.3
Austrian Guest Survey	2,185	9.9	2,240	6.6	2.5
Austrian Hotel and Restaurant Panel	1,938	8.8	2,094	6.1	8.0
Number of visitors*			784	2.3	

*New in 2001.

not deal with new distribution channels and new booking systems in the tourism industry. This undoubtedly important topic has been discussed in a number of publications and symposia (Sheldon, 1997; Werthner and Klein, 1999).

The major reason for the poor application of process methods in tourism management is the insufficient education levels of practitioners and inadequacy of problem solving in user tools, expensive related issues, and complicated programs for the processing of current data. The development of simple, affordable (shareware) programs is the first step into a new era of dialogue between research and practice. Within a short time there will be high-performance computer languages available—which are now being developed by major international software producers specifically for Internet applications—for internal diagnosis, forecasts, and simulations.

Technological progress will also offer benefits for the electronic transmission of tourism market research data. Interdisciplinary research projects will be challenged with tourism research, research in statistics, and commercial information technology. For example, a number of problems remain to be solved in order to be able to jointly use ecoscopic and demoscopic tourism data within a marketing information system. These combination options require a constant standardization of information sources as well as new approaches toward the methodological processing of data gained from various studies.

The sudden explosion of data and the growing need for information challenge basic research as far as data-reduction and decision-support methods are regarded. Thus existing concepts for qualitative forecasts and market reaction models and their calibration options in a marketing information system have to be reconsidered. In this respect projects considered to be promising are aimed at a systematic and regular compilation of experiences regarding various technical subjects (i.e., short-term development of singular markets of origin). It is their aim to provide an improved evaluation of future market developments and eventually to integrate the findings into the strategic planning of national and regional tourism organizations and businesses.

The trend toward globalization in research, in which the Internet plays a vital role, also refers to tourism research. To those critics who labeled the Internet uncontrolled, complicated, and too playful, supporters pointed out that one day smart and profitable applications would be found. That is where we stand now. The new fields of responsibility that regional and national tourism managers are confronted with today not only indicate shortcomings in education but also promise new options to acquire status for the next generations of management.

REFERENCES

Calantone, R.J. and C.A. di Benedetto (1991). Knowledge acquisition modeling in tourism. *Annals of Tourism Research* 18(2): 202-212.

Davis, F.D. (1989). Perceived usefulness, perceived ease of use, and user acceptance of information technology. *MIS Quarterly* 13: 318-340.

Hruschka, H. and J.A. Mazanec (1990). Computer-assisted travel counseling. *Annals of Tourism Research* 7(2): 208-227.

Mazanec, J.A. (1986). A decision support system for optimizing advertising policy of a national tourist office: Model outline and case study. *International Journal of Research in Marketing* 3: 63-77.

Mazanec, J.A. (1994). International tourism marketing—Adapting the growth share matrix. In Montana, J. (Ed.), *Marketing in Europe, Case Studies* (pp. 184-203). London: Sage Publications.

Mazanec, J.A. (1998). International tourism marketing: A multi-factor portfolio model. In Hartvig-Larsen, H. (Ed.), *Cases in Marketing* (pp. 115-141), London: Sage Publications.

Rita, P. (1993). A knowledge-based system for promotion budget allocation by national tourism organizations. Doctoral thesis, University of Wales, College of Cardiff.

Sheldon, P. (1997). *Tourism Information Technology.* Wallingford, U.K.: CABI.

van Middelkoop, M. (2001). Merlin: A decision support system for outdoor leisure planning: Development and test of a rule-based microsimulation model for the evaluation of alternative scenarios and planning options. Doctoral thesis, Technical University Eindhoven, Netherlands.

Werthner, H. and S. Klein (1999). *Information Technology and Tourism—A Challenging Relationship.* Wien-New York: Springer.

Wierenga, B. and G. van Bruggen (2000). *Marketing Management Support Systems. Principles, Tools and Implementation.* Boston: Kluwer.

Wöber, K.W. (1998). TourMIS: An adaptive distributed marketing information system for strategic decision support in national, regional, or city tourist offices. *Pacific Tourism Review* 2(3/4): 273-286.

Index

2020 Vision report, 123

ABS. *See* Australian Bureau of Statistics
Acceleration, defined, 83
Accepting midlifers, New Zealand, 56, 60
Accounting, global, 10
Active family values, New Zealand, 56, 59, 60
Activity
  aging and participation, 24-25
  costs, 25
  growth results, 29-32
  leisure, 69, 70-71
  participation survey, 26-29
  youth. *See* Youth leisure
Age of Enlightenment, 84
Aging
  activity participation, 26-29
  framework, 22-24
  impact on leisure and tourism, 19, 21-22, 32-33
  interdestination mobility and, 259-260
  intradestination mobility and, 260-261
  leisure futures, 29-32
  total activity participation, 24-25
  world population, 4
AGS (Austrian Guest Survey), 328, 330-332
AIO (attitudes, interests, and opinions), 54
Airlines
  interdestination mobility, 258-260
  low-cost carriers, 177-178
  market identification, 107
Alpine regions
  AMAS 2000 research project, 202-207
  health tourism, 199, 202-207
  medicine, 202, 203
  slow tourism. *See* Alpine regions and slow tourism
  tourists. *See* Leisure mobility
Alpine regions and slow tourism
  Heinzenberg hut, 179
  impact of environment, 95
  mobility patterns, 172
  overview, 93-95, 102
  principles of slow tourism, 100-102
  slow food, slow cities, 97-99
  society and work, 96-97
  Swiss. *See* Switzerland
  theme parks, 229
  trends, 95-96
Altitude study (AMAS 2000), 202-207
AMAS 2000 (Austrian Moderate Altitude Study), 202-207
America. *See* United States
Anthill, stomping of, 1, 6
Antileisure, 136
Ap, John, 121, 123
Architecture, slow tourism principle, 100
Arianna, 306
Artificial experience worlds, 230
Arts tourism
  Australia, 140-141
  defined, 138-139
ASART (Austrian Society of Applied Research in Tourism), 326
Asia
  collectivism, 125-127, 129, 131-132
  face, 127, 129, 131-132

Asia *(continued)*
  future leisure market, 121, 123-125
  future of leisure, 133
  hierarchy of needs, 127-130
  implications for leisure service provisions, 131-133
  leisure concept, 129-131
  personal values, 125
  societal values, 125
  wellness resorts, 190
Aspen, Colorado, winter destination, 175, 218
Atmosphere, theme parks, 231-232
Attention poverty, 294
Attitudes, interests, and opinions (AIO), 54
Attractions, theme park, 233
Australia
  the arts, 140-141
  cultural participation, 141-145
  cultural tourism, 138-140, 145-148
  leisure and tourism, 135-138
  leisure paradigm, 135, 149
  sporting events study, 239-250
  Tourism Commission, 248-249
  wellness resorts, 190
  youth leisure case study, 43-44, 48
Australian Bureau of Statistics (ABS)
  cultural participation survey, 142, 143-144
  cultural tourism survey, 140, 145-146
Austria
  greenways, 274-275
  interconcept distance, 77-78
  Klöstereich, 179
  role in alpine medicine, 202
  short trips, 177
  Statistik Austria, 327
  Tiscover, 283
  TourMIS. *See* TourMIS
  wellness hotels, 188
Austrian Guest Survey (AGS), 328, 330-332
Austrian Moderate Altitude Study (AMAS) 2000, 202-207
Austrian Society of Applied Research in Tourism (ASART), 326
Auto travel
  in galactic cities, 15
  impact of population density, 3
  impact of traffic, 254, 256, 265-267
  interdestination mobility, 258-260
  intradestination mobility, 260-261
  leisure behavior and. *See* Leisure mobility at home
Autobahn roadhouse, 179-180
Ayurveda, 186

Baby boomer generation
  Internet use, 288
  leisure futures, 29-32
  lifestyles, 217
  meaning of, 212
Backhaus, Klaus, 96
Bad Kissingen spa town, 191-192
Baggio, Rodolfo, 283, 301
Bahamas, event leveraging, 238
Baldwin, Cheryl K., 19, 35
Bandwidth, free, 11
Bangladesh natural disasters, 14
Barefoot parks, German, 179
Barker, R., 232
Beach tourists and greenways, 278-279, 280-281
Beauty shop services, 174
Behavior setting, 232
Belongingness, Asian, 126
Benchmarking, 196
Bennett, T., 141
Best of the Alps, 175
Bieger, Thomas, 172, 253
Big business, New Zealand, 58
Biotopes, 97
"Blue Blood Estates" versus "Public Assistance," 212
Body as a branding tool, 176-180
Bodymania, 175
Bond, M., 127
Bondage, steel case of, 85-86

Boredom
  Australian youth leisure case study, 43-44
  South Africa youth leisure case study, 39
  youth leisure time, 47
Bowen, John, 154
Brands
  body as branding tool, 176-180
  experiential marketing and, 295
  lifestyle, 211
  Veblenian sense of, 211
Breathing spaces, 97
Bridger, D., 293
Brightbill, C. K., 135
Brown, Graham, 172, 237
Bruckner, P., 83-84
Bureau of Tourism Research (BTR) survey, 145-148
Burnout syndrome, 94

Caldwell, Linda L., 19, 35
Canadian Council on Social Development, 35-36, 46
Canadian Policy Research Networks, Inc., 35-36, 46
Capital resource, time, 37
Capitalism
  forecasting supply and demand, 105, 108-109
  revisionist economists and, 107
Case studies
  Australia, 43-44, 48
  Chile, 44-45, 48
  South Africa, 38-39, 48, 49
  spacing and timing, 75-79
  Sweden, 45, 47
  Togo, 39-42, 48, 49
Casual leisure, 138
CDC (Centers for Disease Control and Prevention) survey, 26-29
Center, defined, 137
Center-out-there, 137
Centers for Disease Control and Prevention (CDC) survey, 26-29
Centro Internazionale di Studi e richerch sull' Economia Turistica (CISET), 275, 281
CHAID (chi-squared automatic interaction detector), 164, 165-166
Chalip, L., 238
Chile youth leisure case study, 44-45, 48
China. *See* People's Republic of China
Chi-squared automatic interaction detector (CHAID), 164, 165-166
Chôros, 71
Christianity religious trends, 13
Chronotopes, 97
Ciarlante, D., 128, 130, 132
CISET (Centro Internazionale di Studi e richerch sull' Economia Turistica), 275, 281
Cities
  galactic, 15
  slow, 67, 98
Civic competence hypothesis, 36, 48
Claritas, 107
Climate, impact on leisure behavior, 14
Clock, Long Now, 97
Clustering procedure, New Zealand Generation X lifestyle study, 58
Coevolved customers, 10
Cohen, E., 136-137
Collectivism, 125-127, 129, 131-132
Colorado
  Aspen winter destination, 175, 218
  property prices, 217-218
  ski industry. *See* Colorado ski industry
Colorado ski industry, 222
  employee groups, 214-217
  guest groups, 220-222
  leisure-lifestyle segmentation, 211-212

Colorado ski industry *(continued)*
  management implications, 222-223
  research directions, 223
  resident groups, 217-220
  service quality, 209-211, 214
  study methodology, 213
Committed types, 160, 161
Commodification of leisure, 112-113
Commodity fetishism, 112
Communication through information technology, 55, 291-293
Community attachment, Togo, 42
Company wellness, 97
Computers. *See also* Internet
  globalization and, 9
  impact on New Zealand, 55
  management. *See* TourMIS
Condemned to Happiness: Modernity's Curse, 83-84
Conflict and capitalism, 108
Confucianism, 124, 125, 130
Conservative quiet lifers, New Zealand, 56, 60
Conspicuous consumption, 112
Consumption
  experiential marketing and, 294-295
  New Zealand Generation X lifestyle study, 59
  population and increase in, 14
  tourism, 139
Containment, 109
Cooperative competition, 196
Corigliano, Magda Antonioli, 283, 301
Cosmetics, 177
Cosmological innocence, loss of, 80
Costa Rican niche markets, 118
Costs
  activities, 25
  Colorado vacation properties, 217-218
  low-cost airlines, 177-178
  natural disaster, 14
  opportunity, 111
  vacation, 89
Cruise liners, market saturation, 110
Cruises, 178-179
Csikzentmihalyi, M., 129
Cultural tourism
  arts and hobbies, 139
  Australia, 138-140, 145-148
  defined, 121
  mobility and, 253, 254
Cultures
  conflicts, 108
  impact on investments, 118
  market identification for future supply and demand, 107
  time perception, 77-78
Customers, coevolved, 10
Customization, 1, 16-17
  globalization. *See* Globalization
  living arrangements, 1-6
  mass, 10, 15-16
  postcapitalist economies, 7-9
  travel patterns, 15
  work, 6-7
  world population, 1-6
Cycling networks, 273

Dancing and human development, 47
Data, networked, knowledge-based, 10
Day spas, 178
DCM (dynamic cash movement), 79
Death, premature, 185, 186
Deceleration, 177-178
Decision support systems, 326
Defamilied nations, 4
Definitions for wellness, 196
Dellaert, Benedict G. C., 283, 317
Demand. *See* Supply and demand
Demographic change, defined, 24
Demographics
  aging trend. *See* Aging
  conclusion, 32-33
  equation, 22-25
  overview, 21-22
  supply and demand projections, 106
  survey results, 26-29
Denmark, interconcept distance, 77-78
Depression generation, 217

Dertouzos, M., 287
Destination management, 175
Destination management organization (DMO), 237
Destination skiers, 221-222
Developing nations, population growth, 2
DFM (dynamic financial management) radar chart, 79
Die Zeit slogan "Discover what is relevant," 180
Diet. *See* Foods
Digital money, 11
DINK households, 94, 212
Disease, impact of population density, 3
Disintermediation, 302, 313
Distributed cores, 9
Diversionary mode, 137
DMO (destination management organization), 237
DNA (dynamic net assets), 79
DNC (dynamic net contribution), working capital, 79
Dobson-Patterson, R., 43
Documentaries as marketing tools, 295
Douces, 272
Downshifting, 116-117
Drava trails, 274
Dubois, Bernard, 154
Dunn, Halbert, 96, 183
Dynamic cash movement (DCM), 79
Dynamic financial management (DFM) radar chart, 79
Dynamic net assets (DNA), 79
Dynamic net contribution (DNC), working capital, 79

E-commerce, 289-290, 302
E-freaks, 155-157
E-procurement initiatives, 302
E-tourism, 283. *See also* Information technology
E-world, 69
Eberling, Matthias, 97
Echo Boom, 29-32
Ecological psychology approach, 232
Ecological systems theory (EST), 36-37, 46, 48-49
Ecology, industrial, 10
Economy
- conflicts, 108
- experience. *See* Experience economy
- impact of greenways, 281
- "just in time," 83, 98
- knowledge, 8
- networked, 9-11
- New Zealand, 54-55
- postcapitalist, 7-9
- slow tourism and, 101-102
- tourism statistics, 93

Ecotourism, demand forecast, 279
Educated liberals, New Zealand, 56, 59-60
Education. *See also* School
- Asian values, 130-131
- factory approach to, 6
- impact on leisure behavior, 5
- Internet use and, 288-289
- skill-based leisure, 118
- wellness, 197
- women and, 5-6

Efficiency
- production, 10, 74, 86-87
- time, 263, 265, 266

Eigenzeit, 98-99
Electronic travel recommendation agents
- background, 317-318
- research of impact on tourism, 319-324
- theory for use of, 318-319

Elements of leisure, 135-136
Employees
- Colorado resort community, 214-217
- migrant, 216-217
- service quality and, 210

Employment. *See* Work
Energy banks, 178

England. *See* Great Britain
Enterprise, theme park, 229
Entrepreneurs in Colorado ski resort communities, 219-220
Environment
  greenways, 272, 273
  impact of population density, 3
  impact on tourism, 95
  overuse of, 110
  pollution and leisure mobility behavior, 254
  resource-based outdoor recreation, 110
  slow tourism and, 101-102
  weather and climate, 13-14
Equations
  behavioral and demographic information, 22-24
  demographic change, 24-25
  leisure futures, 29
Ernst and Young company, 96-97
Escuela Superior de Administración y Dirección de Empresas (ESADE), 154-155
ESPA (European Spa Association), 192, 193
EST (ecological systems theory), 36-37, 46, 48-49
Ethnic tourism, 139
Europe. *See also* specific country
  business models, 304-306
  early health tourism, 188, 190
  greenways, 273-275. *See also* Lemene Greenway project
  health care trends, 182-183
  history, 181
  leisure time and working time, 69
  men-only wellness center, 177
  migrant employees, 216
  tourism trends, 94
  wellness resorts, 190, 195-197
European Spa Association (ESPA), 192, 193
Evans, P., 292-293
Event leveraging, 238
Event packages, Australian, 246
Exercise
  activity growth, 29-32
  activity participation by age, 26-29
  Far Eastern relaxation, 84
Existential mode, 137
Exosystem, 36, 46
Experience
  defined, 230-231
  defining tourism products, 294-295
  economy. *See* Experience economy
  flow, 294
  leisure, 173
  society, 227, 262
  tourism, 271
  youth. *See* Experience, youth
Experience economy
  development of, 8-9, 227-228
  experience setting, 228-230
  trends, 94
Experience, youth
  Australia, 43-44
  Chile, 44-45
  human development and, 46-48
  South Africa, 39
  Togo, 40-42
Experiential mode, 137
Experimental mode, 137
Exploitative markets and investment, 112
Extinction of animals and plants, 14
Extroverts, success-driven, 55-56, 60

Face, 127, 129, 131-132
Factory approach to public education, 6
Familiarization tours, 246
Family
  Asian, 126-127, 131
  impact of modernity on structure, 4
  values, New Zealand, 56, 59, 60
Fast leisure, 89
Fast-food restaurants, effect of, 74
Feeling types of individuals, 75-77
Females. *See* Women
Feminization of society, 176, 177

Fesenmaier, Daniel R., 283, 285
Field theory, 232
Financial management, spacing and timing, 78-79
FIND/SVP study, 289, 290
Finland, interconcept distance, 78
Fitness and wellness, 185
Fitzgerald, H., 124, 132
Flex manufacturing, 10
Flow
 the arts and, 140-141
 defined, 129-130
 experience, 294
Foods
 health, 98. *See also* Wellness
 New Zealand Generation X, 62
 Relax Restaurants, 178
 Slow Food, 67, 74, 98
Foot, David K., 19, 21
Framework of behavioral and demographic information, 22-24
France
 leisure styles comparison, 151-152, 169
 leisure styles described, 155-164
 leisure styles survey, 152-153
 leisure trends, 167-168
 lifestyles segmentation criterion, 153-155
 variations of leisure styles, 164-167
Free bandwidth, 11
Free time, importance of, 47
Frequency of activity participation by age, 26, 28-29
Fuhrer, U., 267
Furlan, Maria Carla, 172, 271
"Furs and Station Wagons" versus "Shotguns and Pickups," 212
Future
 Asian leisure market, 121, 123-125, 133
 health care, 182-183
 impact of demography on leisure futures, 26-29
 Internet and travel, 296-297
Future *(continued)*
 Italian Web models, 311-314
 leisure. *See* Leisure futures
 sporting events, 249-250
 supply and demand, 105-109
 youth leisure, 45-46

Galactic city, 15
Galbraith, J. K., 110
Gambling
 investment in, 111
 soaring rates of, 110
 United States, 106, 110
Gates, Bill, 285
Generalists, 5-6
Generation X
 demographic, 19, 53-54. *See also* Demographics
 meaning of, 212
German Travel Analysis 1999, 188
Germany
 Autobahn roadhouse, 179-180
 barefoot parks, 179
 Berlin dormitories, 178
 Die Zeit slogan "Discover what is relevant," 180
 German Travel Analysis 1999, 188
 health tourism, 201
 history of spas, 191-195
 leisure styles comparison, 151-152, 169
 leisure styles described, 155-164
 leisure styles survey, 152-153
 leisure trends, 167-168
 lifestyles segmentation criterion, 153-155
 personal hygiene, 177
 short trips, 177
 slow tourism, 98-99
 time experiments, 97
 variations of leisure styles, 164-167
 wellness hotels, 188
Getz, Donald, 172, 237
Giddens, Anthony, 176

Gilmore, J. H., 227, 234
Global paradox, 297
Global warming, 14
Globalization
  health culture, 186
  impact on commerce, 11-12
  networked economies, 9-11
  politics and power, 12-13
  trends, 67
  wellness programs, 196
Gnoth, Juergen, 19, 53
Godbey, Geoffrey, 1, 136, 140
Golden weeks, 3-4
Golf courses, limited resources, 106
Great Britain
  leisure styles comparison, 151-152, 169
  leisure styles described, 155-164
  leisure styles survey, 152-153
  leisure trends, 167-168
  lifestyles segmentation criterion, 153-155
  London energy banks, 178
  sporting events study, 239-250
  variations of leisure styles, 164-167
Greek space and time terms, 71-73
Green, B. C., 238
Green axes, 272
Greenways, 271, 281-282
  background, 272-273
  defined, 272
  economic and social development, 275
  effects on local tourism, 276
  European, 273-275
  Lemene Greenway project, 273, 275-282
  planning, 277
  Prague-Vienna Greenway, 273-274
Greie, Sven, 171, 199
Gretzel, Ulrike, 283, 285
Group conformity, Asian, 126
Grown experience worlds, 230
Gruner, Kai, 96
Guest groups, Colorado ski resorts, 220-222
Hairdressers as holistic beauty providers, 174
Han Chinese culture, 124
Happiness in extremes, 174
Häubl, Gerald, 283, 317
Hawthorne, Nathaniel, 93
Health. *See also* Wellness
  defined, 183, 185, 186, 199
  future of health care, 182-183
  policy recommendations, 197
  tourism, 200-202
Hedonists, 155, 156
Heintel, Peter, 97-98
Here-point, 72
Heritage tourism, 138
Hervé, Edmond, 102
Hierarchy of needs, 127-130
High-level wellness, 184, 185, 187
Hillis, Daniel, 97
Hirons, M., 142-143
Historic tourism, 138
Hitchcock, D., 124
Hoffman, D. L., 292
Holidays. *See also* Vacations
  Chinese "golden weeks," 3-4
  customized, 12
  packages, 88
  wellness, 201
Homogenization of leisure styles in Europe, 164-167, 169
Hong Kong educational values, 130-131
Hospitals, 190
Host-community residents, 210, 217-220
Hotels
  market identification, 107
  Slowtels, 101
  timeless, Swiss, 99-100
  wellness, 96, 188, 190
  wellness trend, 171
Housing
  impact of traffic on condition, 254, 265-267
  revolution, 1-6
Hudson, Simon, 172, 237

Hughes, H. L., 138
Huizinga, J., 140
Human capital, 37
Human development hypothesis, 35, 46-47
Humancentric computer, 287
Humpeler, Egon, 171, 199
Huntington, S., 12
Hwang, K. H., 127
Hybrid markets, 174-175
Hypotheses
 civic competence, 36, 48
 ecological systems theory, 36-37, 46, 48-49
 human development, 35, 46-47
 inadequacy, 36, 48
 insufficiency, 36, 48

ICD (interconcept distance), 77-78
ICT (information and communication technologies), 310-311, 313
Illness/wellness continuum, 184, 185
Immediately, defined, 83
Immigrants, culture of, 2
Inadequacy hypothesis, 36, 48
Individualism, soft, 264
Industrial ecology, 10
Industrialism changes, 5-6
Infinity concept, 71
Information and communication technologies (ICT), 310-311, 313
Information technology, 296-297. *See also* Internet; World Wide Web
 communication, 291-293
 growth of use in tourism, 287-291
 leisure behavior trends, 285-295
 overview, 283
 speed and sophistication, 286-287
Innovation buzzword, 83
Institution of leisure time, 85-88
Insufficiency hypothesis, 36, 48
Insurance laws, 191-192, 194
Interconcept distance (ICD), 77-78
Intercultural leisure behavior
 Asia. *See* Asia
 overview, 121
Interdestination mobility
 model, 254
 overview, 253
 tourism example, 256, 258-260
Intermediation, 314
Internet. *See also* Information technology; World Wide Web
 communications, 55, 291-293
 e-commerce, 289-290
 future role in travel, 296-297
 growth of use, 287-289
 Italy. *See* Italy, tourism on the Internet
 management. *See* Online management information systems
 management tools. *See* TourMIS
 new consumer, 293-294
 recommendation agents. *See* Electronic travel recommendation agents
 traditional media versus, 292
 use by travelers, 290-291
 uses of, 289
Intradestination mobility
 model, 254
 overview, 253
 Swiss travelers' mobility patterns, 256, 260-261
Intuitive types of individuals, 75-77
Investment. *See also* Supply and demand
 bias, 111, 114-115
 economic power and, 115
 production of divided markets, 111-112
 return on, 111, 114
 system changes for viable returns on, 117-119
Islam religious trends, 13
Italy
 business models, 302-306
 greenways, 274

Italy *(continued)*
- interconcept distance, 77-78
- Internet. *See* Italy, tourism on the Internet
- leisure styles comparison, 151-152, 169
- leisure styles described, 155-164
- leisure styles survey, 152-153
- leisure trends, 167-168
- Lemene Greenway project, 273, 275-282
- lifestyles segmentation criterion, 153-155
- Slow Cities, 98
- Slow Food movement, 98
- Time Offices, 97
- variations of leisure styles, 164-167

Italy, tourism on the Internet, 314-315
- business models, 302-306
- distribution of Web sites, 306, 307
- future Web models, 311-314
- online contents and services, 307-311
- overview, 301
- purchase intentions, 304, 305
- tour operators' Web sites, 306, 308
- travel agencies' Web sites, 307, 309
- Web site evaluations, 310-311, 312

Japan
- five-day workweek, 131
- karoshi, 94
- lifetime employment, 7

"Just in time" economy, 83, 98

K-means on SPSS, 58
Kairos, 72
Kanuk, L., 128-129
Karoshi, 94
Kaspar, C., 201
Kelly, John R., 67, 105, 140
Kelly, K., 9-11
Kiwi attitude, New Zealand, 58-59
Knowledge-based, networked data, 10
Knowledge economy, 8
Knowledge society, 184-185
Kotler, Philip, 154
Koutakis, 47
Kronos, 72
Kurt, Matthias, 99

Laesser, Christian, 172, 253
Lake Constance greenway, 275
Lambin, Jean Jacques, 154
Landscape, defined, 73
Language, English as unifying language, 12
Larson, R., 37
Lawson, Rob, 19, 53
Lech altitude study, 205-206
Lee, Y., 129

Leisure
- elements, 135-136
- types, 138-140

Leisure activities
- study of, 70-71
- time budget, 69

Leisure futures
- activity growth, 29-32
- activity participation, 26-29
- space and time, 71

Leisure mobility
- categories, 253
- at home. *See* Leisure mobility at home
- impact of activities, 256-262
- modal split, 264-265, 266
- model, 253-255
- problems and solutions, 267-268
- trends, 262-264

Leisure mobility at home
- model, 254
- overview, 253
- sports activities example, 256-258

Leisure styles
- committed types, 160, 161
- e-freaks, 155-157

Leisure styles *(continued)*
hedonists, 155, 156
passive types, 162-164
routine types, 160, 162
social freaks, 158-159
well-established types, 161-162, 163
workaholics, 157-158
Leisure time, 85-88
Lemene Greenway project
background, 273, 275-278
beach tourists, 278-279, 280-281
estimating demand, 278-279
local residents, 279-280
special interest tourists, 281
Lewin, K., 231-232
Lewis, D., 293
Lewis, P., 15
Liberals, educated, New Zealand, 56, 59-60
Life Balance program, 97
Life course, impact of modernity, 4
Life cycles, 106, 110
Life expectancy increases, 4
Lifestyle brands, 211
Lifestyles
defined, 211-212
enclaves, 107
European segmentation criterion, 153-155
segmentation, 211-212
wellness, 184
Living arrangements, 1-6, 254, 265-267
Living conditions, impact of traffic, 254, 265-267
Lobo, Francis, 45-46, 121, 135
Local skiers, 220-221
London energy banks, 178
Long Now clock, 97
Lüneburger Heide, 229

Macrolevel, 36-37, 46
Mahoney, J. L., 45, 47
Makens, James, 154
Manpower Inc., largest United States employer, 6-7
Manufacturing, 10, 74, 86-87
Market
identification, 107
investment and divided markets, 111-112, 114
segmentation, 209-212
Marketing
capital investment and, 110
experiential, 294-295
information systems, 326
services marketing triangle, 209
transnational marketing community, 175
wellness programs, 196
Marx, 112
Maslow, A., 127-130
Mass customization, 10, 15-16
Mass markets and investment, 112, 115
Mass transit, impact of population density, 3
Materialism scale, 57
Matos, Rafael, 67, 93
Mazanec, Joseph, 154
McDonaldization, 12
M-commerce, 311
Meaning of life question, 179-180
Media
impact on leisure time, 115, 119
Internet. *See* Internet
sporting events coverage, 246, 247
Medicine, customized, 15-16
Meditation, 186
Megaperspectives, supply and demand, 109-113
Megatrends Asia, 124
Men, changing roles of, 5-6
Meneghello, Sabrina, 172, 271
Merwin, W. S., 1, 16
Mesolevel, 36, 46, 108
Metabolic syndrome, 204
Mexican migrant employees, 216
Microsystem, 36, 46
Midlifers, New Zealand, 56, 60
Migrants, 216-217

Migration, 2
Miller, Graham, 172, 237
Minghetti, Valeria, 172, 271
Mobile commerce, 311
Mobility. *See also* Leisure mobility
 impact of, 74
 patterns, 172
 trends, 69-70, 262-264
Models
 business, 302-306
 leisure mobility, 253-255
Modern Age
 personal time formation, 84
 time measurement, 86
Modern systems theory (MST), 74-75
Modes, 136-137
Moles, Abraham, 72
Molicki, Manfred, 98
Møller, V., 39
Money, digital, 11. *See also* Costs
Monochronicity, 73
Moore's Law, 286
Morello, Gabriele, 67, 69
Morse, J., 238
Mosaic, 287
MST (modern systems theory), 74-75
Müller, Hansruedi, 102
Multicivilizational politics and power, 12-13
Multioptionalization, 263
Multipolar politics and power, 12-13
Multipresence, 73
Music and human development, 47
Myerscough, J., 138-139

Nahrstedt, Wolfgang, 171, 181
Naisbitt, John, 124, 297
National Culture/Leisure Industry Statistical Framework, 135, 142, 149
Natural disaster costs, 14
Needs, hierarchy of, 127-130
Nervous system and altitude adaptation, 204-205
Netherlands
 interconcept distance, 78
 recommendation agent experiment, 319-320
Networked economies, 9-11
Nevada Long Now clock, 97
New consumer, 293-294, 295
New Zealand Generation X lifestyle study
 background, 54-56
 discussion, 63-64
 function, 19, 53-54
 lifestyle segments, 55-56
 methodology, 56-58
 results, 58-63
NGO (nongovernmental organization), 49
Niche markets, 118-119, 271
NIMBY (not in my backyard), 222
Nongovernmental organization (NGO), 49
Norman, D. A., 287
North America
 greenways, 273
 sporting events study, 239-250
 wellness resorts, 190
Novak, T. P., 292

OECD (Organisation for Economic Co-Operation and Development), 21
Olson, E., 45-46
Online management information systems
 applications, 326
 background, 325
 benefits of use, 334-335
 poor application of, 335
 problems, 335-336
 TourMIS. *See* TourMIS
Online purchase habits, 289-290
Opportunity costs, 111
Option society, 263

Organisation for Economic Co-Operation and Development (OECD), 21
Orientation modes, 136-137
Overwork trends, 94
Ozone depletion, 14

Pampering, 177-178
Passau-Vienna, 274
Passive relaxation, 264
Passive types, 162-164
Patterson, I., 43
PC (personal computer), 286
Pegg, S., 43
People's Republic of China
  five-day workweek, 131
  national holiday "golden weeks," 3-4
People-to-people tourism, 273
Perception, theme parks, 231
Perdue, Richard, 172, 209
Personal computer (PC), 286
Personal time, formation of, 84-85
Petrini, Carlo, 98
Philippe, Patek, 173
Pine, J., 227, 234
Plastic surgery, 177
Play, 135-136, 140
Pleasure seekers, New Zealand, 61, 62-64
Policy initiatives and youth leisure, 35-36
Politics, 12-13, 117
Pollution, 254
Polychronicity, 73
Popular culture, 139
Population
  aging, 4
  changing roles of women and men, 5-6
  growth projections, 2
  impact of density, 2-4
  political control, 13
  revolution, 1-6
  rising consumption, 14
Portugal
  leisure styles comparison, 151-152, 169
  leisure styles described, 155-164
  leisure styles survey, 152-153
  leisure trends, 167-168
  lifestyles segmentation criterion, 153-155
  variations of leisure styles, 164-167
Positioning of health programs, 196
Post hoc test (SNK test), 246, 248
Postcapitalist economy, 7-9
Poverty and women, 5-6
Poverty of attention, 294
Powder flu, 214, 216
Pragmatic strugglers, New Zealand, 56, 60
Prague-Vienna Greenway, 273-274
Predatory tourism, 271
Premature death, 185, 186
PRIZM categories, 212
Product life cycles, 83
Production of products, 10, 74, 86-87
Professionalization, wellness, 197
Provincia Autonoma di Trento, 78
Psychography, 154, 169
"Public Assistance" versus "Blue Blood Estates," 212

Qualities, cultural tourism, 139-140
Quality management, wellness, 186, 188, 189, 196
Quality, service, 209-211, 214

Rail travel, 258, 265
Rasender Stillstand, 72
Reach, defined, 292-293
Reciprocity, Asian, 126
Recommendation agents. *See* Electronic travel recommendation agents
Recommendation systems, 311-312
Recreational mode, 137

Recreations Trends and Markets, 106
Redneck, 212
Reisinger, Y., 139
Reiter, Andreas, 171, 173
Relax Restaurants, 178. *See also* Foods
Relaxation, passive, 264
Religion trends, 13, 62
Religious conflict, 108
Relocation patterns, impact of traffic, 254, 265-267
Request character, 231
Research
  recommendation agents, 319-324
  sporting events impact, 246, 248
Reservations on the Internet, 307
Residents in resort communities, 210, 217-220
Resource limitations, 106
Revolution
  conclusion, 16-17
  environment, 13-14
  globalization. *See* Globalization
  living arrangements, 1-6
  postcapitalist economies, 7-9
  urban areas, 15
  work, 6-7
  world population, 1-6
Richins's materialism scale, 57
Richness, defined, 292-293
Risk society, 262
Roberts, K., 135-136
Rohmer, Elizabeth, 72
Routine types, 160, 162
Rovira, Alex, 154

Satellite office, 7
Saturation
  cruise liners, 110
  goods and services, 114-115
Scheurer, Roland, 171, 227
Schiffman, L., 128-129
Schmitt, B. H., 295
Schober, R., 231
Schobersberger, Wolfgang, 171, 199
School. *See also* Education
  benefits for youth, 37
  customized, 16
  skill-based leisure, 118
Schulze, G., 227
Schütte, Hellmut, 124, 128, 130, 132
Search engines, 306
Segmentation
  lifestyle, 154, 211-212
  market, 209, 210-212
  research directions, 223
Self-actualization, 128
Self-esteem, Asian, 126
Self-image enhancement, 139
Self-protection, 109
Sensation types of individuals, 75-77
September 11, 2001
  impact on cruise lines, 110, 178-179
  impact on leisure markets, 115
  meaning of life question and, 179
Serious leisure, 138, 139
Service opportunities for youth, 48-49
Service quality
  importance in tourism industry, 209-211
  ski bums, 214
Services marketing triangle, 209
Shopping in Australia, 145-146, 147
Short trips, 177-178
"Shotguns and Pickups" versus "Furs and Station Wagons," 212
Shugan, Steven M., 323
Sicilian tourism study, 76-77
Singapore, status and conspicuous consumption, 128-129
Ski bums, 214-216
Ski industry. *See* Colorado ski industry
Skiers, Colorado ski resorts, 220-222
Slobbies, 96-97
Slow Cities, 67, 98
Slow Food movement, 67, 74, 98
Slow leisure, 90-91
Slow tourism principles, 100-102. *See also* Alpine regions and slow tourism

Slowness
leisure time institution, 85-88
overview, 83-84
personal time formation, 84-85
trends, 67
vacation time, 90-91
Slowtels, 101
SlowUp Days, 99
Smith, V., 139
Snaith, Bill, 79
SNK test (post hoc test), 246, 248
Snow package, 95
Social
conflict, 108
freaks, 158-159
identity formation, 87
insurance laws, 191-192, 194
strivers, 56, 61
Society
experience, 227, 262
option, 263
risk, 262
Sociocultural aspect of slow tourism, 101-102
Socioeconomics, youth social and leisure activities, 44
Soft individualism, 264
Software, K-means on SPSS, 58
South Africa
interconcept distance, 77-78
youth leisure case study, 38-39, 48, 49
Space
Greek terms, 71, 72
overdose, 74
temporal typologies and, 75-77
time and, 71-73
Space 1
described, 71-72
research, 73
Sicilian tourism study, 77
Space 2
described, 72
research, 73
Sicilian tourism study, 77
Spacing
financial management, 78-79
overview, 73-75, 79-80
temporal typologies and, 75-77
Spain
leisure styles comparison, 151-152, 169
leisure styles described, 155-164
leisure styles survey, 152-153
leisure trends, 167-168
lifestyles segmentation criterion, 153-155
variations of leisure styles, 164-167
Vias verdes, 272, 274
Spas
day spas, 178
history, 182, 191-195
Spatial relationship, 229
Spatiotemporal perspective of behavior, 71
Special interest tourists and greenways, 281
Specialization
defined, 87
trends, 67
Speed
culture of, 74
negative effects, 67
vacation time, 89
Spiritual trips, 179
Sporting events
destination goals, 237
event leveraging, 238
future research, 249-250
mobility and, 253, 254, 256-258, 260
study discussion, 248-249
study limitations, 249-250
study method, 238-239
study objectives, 238
study results, 239-248, 249
Sports and human development, 46. *See also* Exercise
Staging, theme parks, 232-234, 235
Stakeholders, slow tourism, 100-101

Standardization of work and leisure, 6-7
Stanford Research International, 107
Stattin, H., 45, 47
Status, Asian, 126, 128-129
Stebbins, R. A., 139
Steel case of bondage, 85-86
Stettler, J., 256
Storey, J., 139
Stories as marketing tools, 295
Strohhofer, Toni, 179-180
Styles, 107. *See also* Cultures
Success-driven extroverts, New Zealand, 55-56, 60
Suicide, impact of population density, 3
Supply and demand
  alternatives, 116-119
  future of leisure, 105-109, 114-116
  investment bias, 111, 114
  megaperspectives, 109-113
  overview, 105
Supply side study, 70
Sureda, Joan, 121, 151
Surveys
  Australian cultural participation, 142-145
  Australian cultural tourism, 138-140, 145-148
  impact of demography on leisure futures, 26-29
  New Zealand Generation X lifestyle study, 57
  TourMIS, 328-332
Sustainable tourism, 90-91
Sweden youth leisure case study, 45, 47
Switzerland
  DINK households, 94
  leisure mobility. *See* Leisure mobility
  slow tourism, 99-100
  tourism economic impact, 93-94
  traditional materials in modern architecture, 100
  wellness products, 96
  wellness tourism market, 188
Symbols and capitalism, 108-109
Sympathicotonia, 204-205
Tai chi, 186
Target groups, 191, 196, 281
Taxes
  demand for lowering of, 111
  resort community, 217
  social welfare funding, 219
Tay, S., 130
Taylor, Fredrick, 6
Techies, 218-219
Technographics, 212
Technology
  adaptive, 9-10
  impact on New Zealand, 55
  work revolution, 6-7
Telecommuting, 7
Tele-conditioned, 63-64
Temporal typologies, 75-77
Temporalizing perspective, 85
Terrorism
  cruise lines and, 110
  globalization and, 11-12
  impact on leisure markets, 115
Theme parks, 234-235
  atmosphere, 231-232
  background, 228-229
  experience settings, 230-234
  experiences, 227-228
  motives, 230
  staging, 232-234, 235
  traditional tourist destinations versus, 229-230
Thinking types of individuals, 75-77
Time
  capital resource, 37
  cultural perceptions, 77-78
  ecology, 97
  efficiency, 263, 265, 266
  Greek term, 72-73
  impact on travel, 265, 266
  leisure time as an institution, 85-88
  modern age transformation, 86
  offices, 97
  space and, 71-73
  vacation time. *See* Vacations
Time 1, 72-73
Time 2, 72-73

Time use, youth
  Australia, 43
  Chile, 44-45
  human development and, 46-48
  South Africa, 38-39
  Togo, 40
Timescape, defined, 73
Timing
  cultural differences, 77-78
  financial management, 78-79
  overview, 73-75, 79-80
Tiscover, 283
Todd, Sarah, 19, 53
Togo youth leisure case study, 39-42, 48, 49
Tour operators
  Internet and business success, 313
  value net, 314
  Web sites, 306-308, 312
Tourism
  described, 136
  types, 138-140
Tourism marketing information system. *See* TourMIS
TourMIS (tourism marketing information system), 283
  Austrian guest survey, 328, 330-332
  data sources, 328, 329
  development, 326-328
  functions, 327-328
  history, 326
  user behavior analysis, 332-334, 335
Traditional values, New Zealand, 60
Traffic and leisure behavior, 254, 265-267
Trails. *See* Greenways
Train travel, 258, 265
Transnational marketing community, 175
Travel agency. *See also* Electronic travel recommendation agents
  impact of the Internet, 302
  information technology and, 312-313
  Internet and business success, 313
  Italian preferences of, 306
  Italian Web sites, 307, 309
  value net, 314
Travel Industry Association of America Report on Technology and Travel, 291
Travis, John W., 184
Trends
  assessment by computer. *See* Online management information systems
  European leisure patterns, 167-168
  experiences economy, 94
  globalization, 67
  information technology, 285-295
  mobility, 69-70, 262-264
  slow tourism, 95-96
  specialization, 67
  wellness, 90-91, 96
Trentino tourism, 78
Trust fund babies, 217-218
Tsang, E., 132
T-tests, 248, 321, 322
Turner, V., 137

Unemployment trends, 69
UNEP/UNESCO, 64
UNESCO, 142
Unfinished Revolution, 287
United Kingdom. *See* Great Britain
United Nations Environment Program/United Nations Scientific and Cultural Organization (UNEP/UNESCO), 64
United States
  Claritas, 107
  Colorado. *See* Colorado
  gambling, 106, 110
  impact of policy on investment, 115
  Internet use, 288-289
  Internet use by travelers, 290-291
  Manpower Inc., largest employer, 6-7
  Nevada Long Now clock, 97
  personal values, 125
  plastic surgery, 177

United States *(continued)*
  private leisure activities, 114
  social welfare funding, 219
  societal values, 125
  wellness concept, 188
  wellness resorts, 190
Upscale markets and investment, 111-112, 114
Urban Healing Center in Antwerpen, 177
Urbanization, 2-4, 15
Urry, J., 136, 139
U.S. National Health Institute Survey, 26-29

Vacations. *See also* Holidays
  consumer behavior study, 70
  costs, 89
  home real estate, 219
  scarcity of time, 88-89
  slowness, 90-91
  time of, 88-89
  wellness, 186, 187
Vail Ski Resort, 215
Valls, Josep-Francesc, 121, 151
Value and Lifestyles Segmentation (VALS), 154-155
Value net, 313, 314
Van Crevald, Martin, 11
Veblen, 112
Veblenian sense of brands, 211
Verma, S., 37
Vias verdes, 272, 274
Vineyards, Sicilian, 76-77
Virgilio, 306
Visitors, theme park, 234
Voies lentes, 272
Volkering, M., 141
Volunteering
  Chile youth leisure time, 44-45
  human development and, 47

Walker, Jane, 79
Wars and globalization, 11-12
Waterscapes and parks, 178
Weather, impact on leisure behavior, 14
Web sites
  activebuyersguide, 318
  Altavista.it, 306
  Arianna, 306
  German slow travel, 98
  Italian tour operators, 307, 308
  Italian tourism, 306, 307, 309
  Italian travel agencies, 307, 309
  Long Now, 97
  Slow Food, 98
  SlowUp Days, 99
  Swiss slow tourism, 99
  TourMIS, 326
  Virgilio, 306
  Yahoo!, 303, 306
Wegner, L., 38, 39
Welfare, impact of population density, 3
Well-established types, 161-162, 163
Wellness, 176
  centers, 171
  corporate, 176
  defined, 176, 199-200
  European concept, 181-182
  facilities, 96, 188, 190
  feminization and, 176, 177
  health culture globalization, 186
  high-level, 185, 187
  knowledge society and, 184-185
  Life Balance program, 97
  men-only center, 177
  overview, 183-184
  quality management, 186, 188, 189, 196
  recommendations, 195-197
  tourism, 186, 187, 200-202
  trend, 90-91, 96
Welltain holiday, 206-207
WHO. *See* World Health Organization
WHO (World Health Organization), 183, 185, 186, 199
Williams, R., 139
Wireless technology, 312
WLRA (World Leisure and Recreation Association), 35-36

Wöber, Karl, 283, 325
Woehler, Karlheinz, 67, 83
Wöhler, Kh., 229
Women
  changes in leisure activities, 113
  changing roles, 5-6
  Internet use, 288
  New Zealand working women, 59
  poverty and, 5-6
Wong, E., 130-131
WOOF (well-off older folks), 212
Work
  five-day workweek, 131
  leisure time and working time, 69
  revolution, 6-7
Workaholics, 157-158
Working capital DNC, 79
Working Group for Children and Youth, 35
World Health Organization (WHO), 183, 185, 186, 199
World Leisure and Recreation Association (WLRA), 35-36
World Tourism Organization (WTO)
  2020 Vision report, 123
  evolution of economy, 94
  travel statistics, 93
World Wide Web (WWW). *See also* Information technology; Internet; Web sites
  history, 287
  Italy. *See* Italy, tourism on the Internet
WTO. *See* World Tourism Organization
Wurster, T. S., 292-293
WWW. *See* World Wide Web
www.activebuyersguide.com, 318
www.altavista.it, 306

Yahoo!, 303, 306
Yankelovitch, 154
Yellowstone National Park entrepreneurs, 219
Yoga, 186
Young pleasure seekers, New Zealand, 61, 62-64
The Youth Centre Project, 38
Youth leisure, 35-38, 49
  case studies, 38-45
  EST concept, 36-37, 46, 48-49
  future of, 45-46
  human development and, 46-48
  learning through recreation hypotheses, 35-36, 46
  service opportunities, 48-49
Yuppie, 212

Zeisel, J., 232
Zumthor, Peter, 100